Waiting for Spring 6

Anashin

Waiting
for Spring
vol.6

Presented by
Anashin

CONTENTS

WAITING FOR SPRING
Harumatsu Bokura

Character & Story

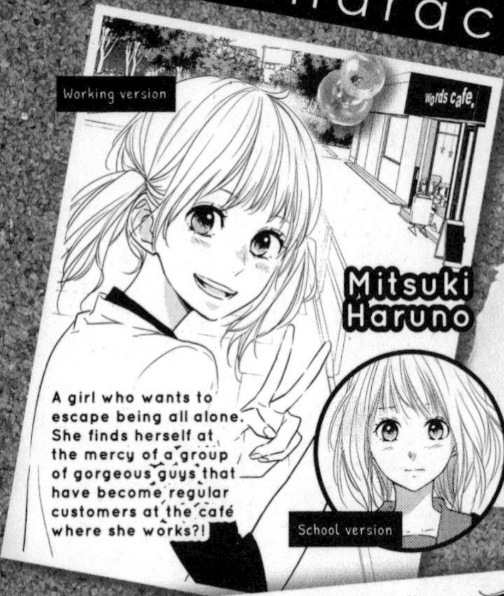

Working version

School version

Mitsuki Haruno

A girl who wants to escape being all alone. She finds herself at the mercy of a group of gorgeous guys that have become regular customers at the café where she works?!

To be like her role model Aya-chan, Mitsuki is determined to make some real friends in high school. One day, the school celebrities—the Elite Four Hotties of the basketball team—appear at the café where she works! Before she knows it, Mitsuki gets caught up in their silly hijinks, but as she gets to know the four of them, she manages to make new friends, and begins to crush hard on her classmate Towa. When she goes to a practice game, she is reunited with Aya-chan and is stunned to learn that her childhood best friend was actually a boy! What's more, he really wants to date her! When the first summer break rolls around, Towa realizes how he feels about Mitsuki, but as soon as the new term begins, Aya-chan declares war with a joint practice session?! Meanwhile, Mitsuki has decided to work hard as a school festival committee member.

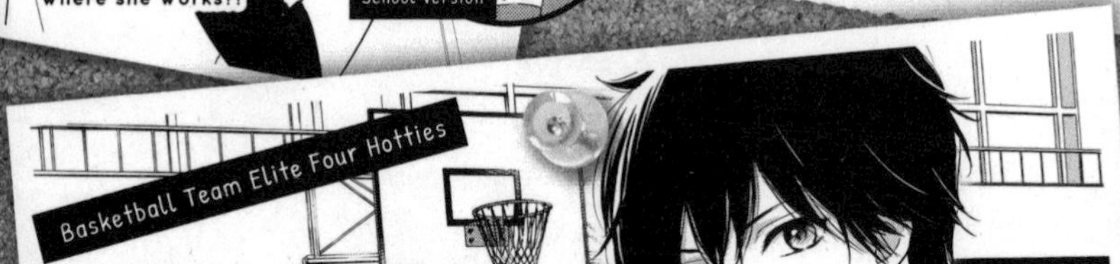

Basketball Team Elite Four Hotties

Towa Asakura

Mitsuki's classmate. He's quiet and a bit spacey, but he's always there to help her.

Rui Miyamoto

A first-year in high school. His innocent smile is adorable, but it hides a wicked heart?!

Kyōsuke Wakamiya

A second-year in high school. Mysterious and always cool-headed, he's like a big brother to everyone.

Ryūji Tada

A second-year. Comes off as a bad boy but is rather naïve. He's crushing on the Boss's daughter, Nanase-san.

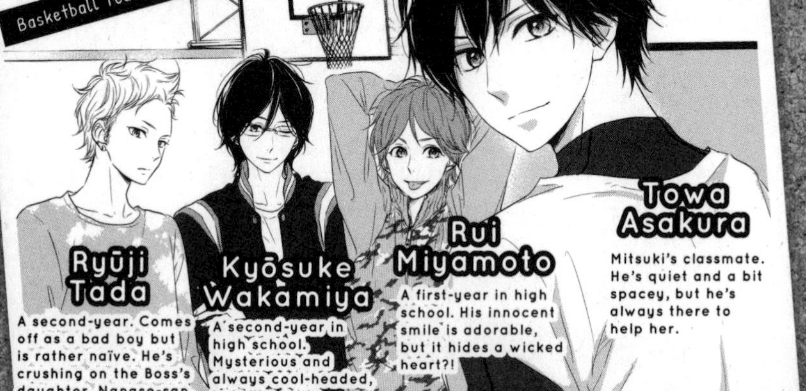

Aya-chan

Mitsuki's best friend from elementary school. When they finally meet again, she discovers he was a boy!

Reina Yamada

Mitsuki's first friend from her class. She has somewhat eccentric tastes?!

Maki-chan

A first-year on the girls' basketball team who gets along with Mitsuki. Apparently she has a crush on Towa?!

Nana-san

The Boss's daughter. Straightforward and resolute, she is a reliable, big-sister type.

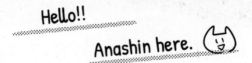

Thank you so much for picking up Volume 6!!

To me, it feels like it's been no
time at all since Volume 5 came out. ;

But it's actually been five
months. I'm always so grateful
to all of you who wait patiently
for the release dates.

Thank
you!

And most of all, Mitsuki is on the cover this time!
Perhaps some of you have been looking forward to that, too...maybe?! (ha ha)
Sorry to keep you waiting!

She's the one who waited most impatiently.

I'm happy for you. I'm so happy for you, Mitsuki. ♫

Wow!

I'm a
cover
girl!!

Cover
girl!

It's very
important
to her.

Shh!

I preferred
the men's
covers.

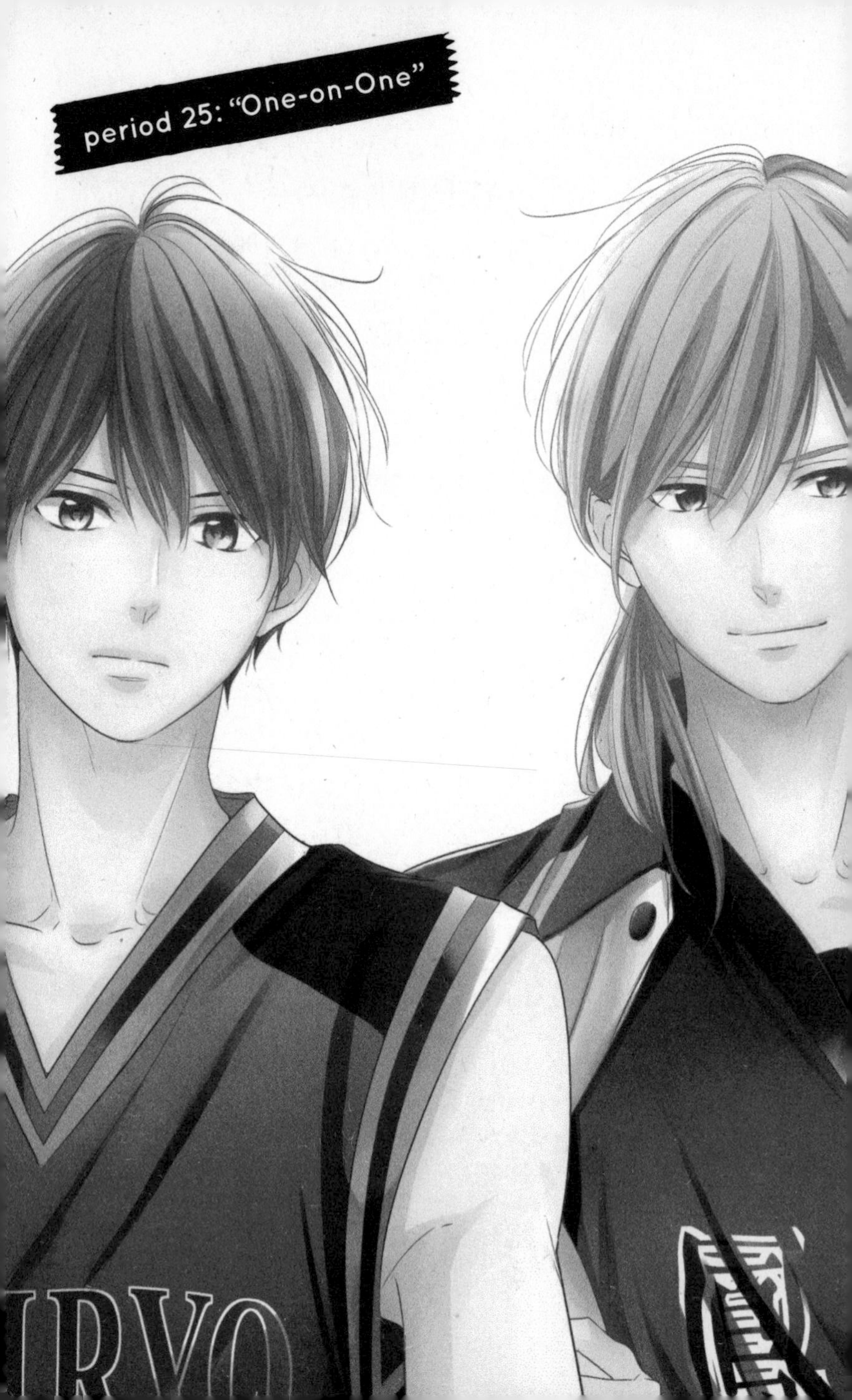
period 25: “One-on-One”

As a matter of fact, this is a rough draft I did for the cover of Volume 1.

Mitsuki was actually going to be on it, too.
Oh, the memories.

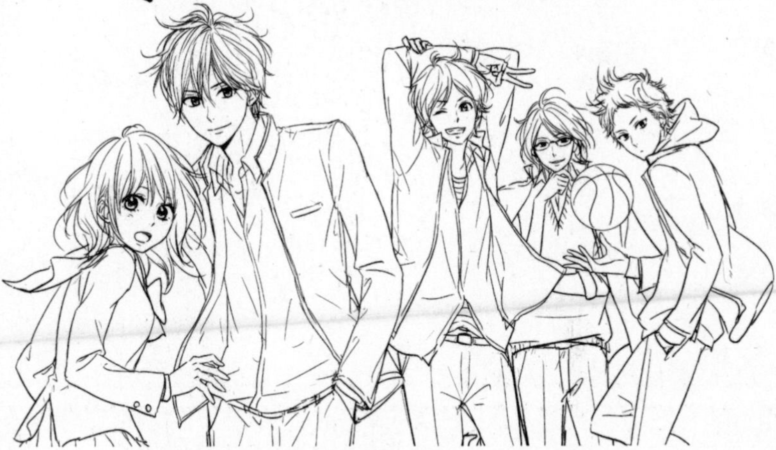

Two years after this draft was rejected, Mitsuki-chan finally made it onto the cover.

Still, since it's my first cover with a girl on it all by herself, I was oddly nervous about it.
I still get anxious when I draw covers for the graphic novels or for Dessert Magazine, and my heart always pounds out of my chest, but this time there was a new, added layer of pressure.
But now I managed to get all six characters on the covers, so I'm just a little relieved.

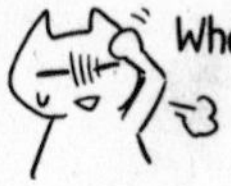

Whew.

School Festival
A Play
Café
AND SO...
TAK
YES!
...IT'S DECIDED. WE'LL BE DOING A CAFÉ FOR THE SCHOOL FESTIVAL!
THIS IS A GOOD START FOR MY TERM AS FESTIVAL COMMITTEE MEMBER!
GOOD
Actually knows something about cafés.

Now what in the world will I do for the cover of Volume 7?!
Even I can't imagine it yet. What?! Could it possibly be Reina-chan?! (ha ha)
I hope you all have fun predicting what it will be.

What?!
Guy-on-guy, of course.
It should be a two-shot!!

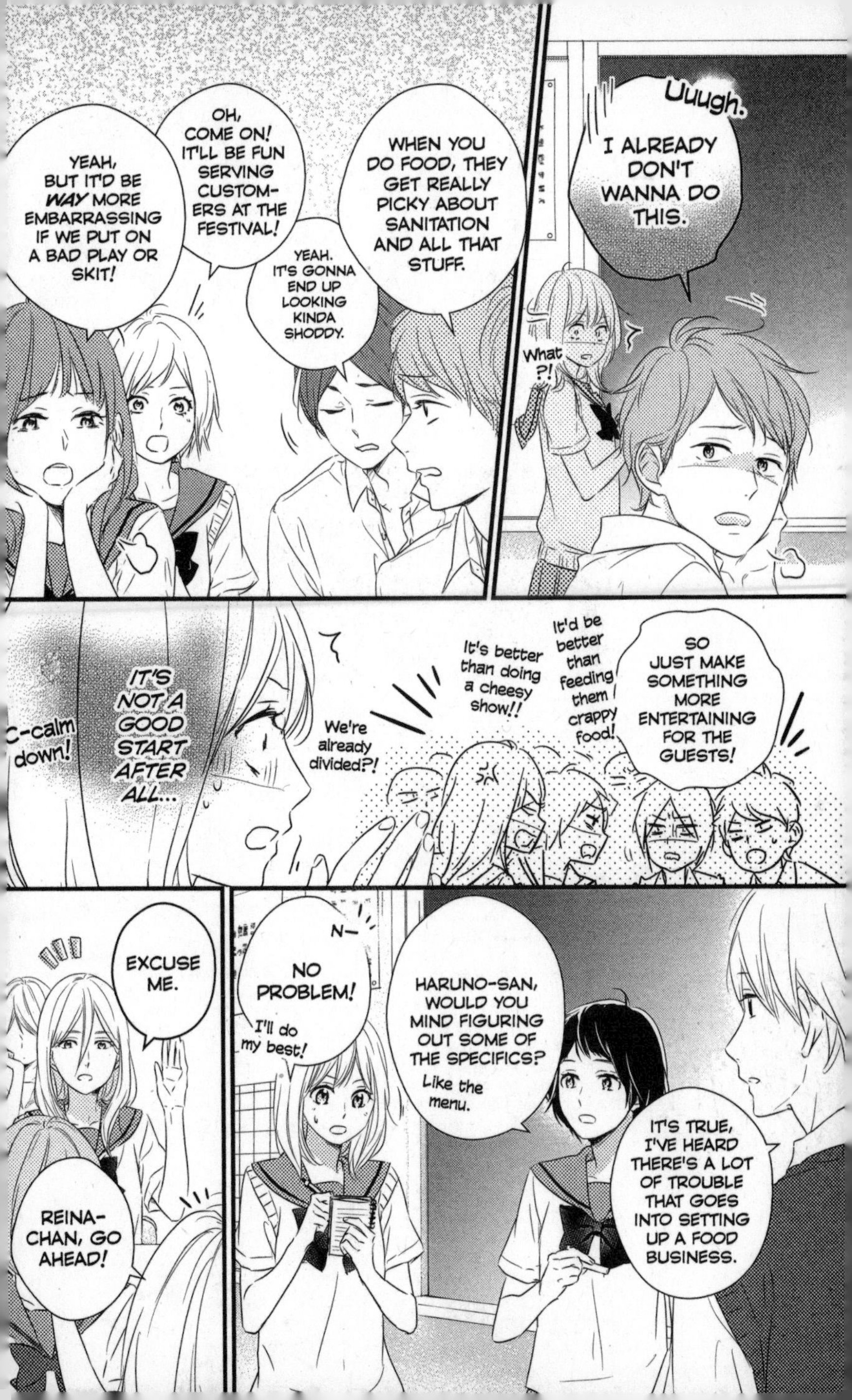
Uuugh.
I ALREADY DON'T WANNA DO THIS.
What?!
WHEN YOU DO FOOD, THEY GET REALLY PICKY ABOUT SANITATION AND ALL THAT STUFF.
YEAH. IT'S GONNA END UP LOOKING KINDA SHODDY.
OH, COME ON! IT'LL BE FUN SERVING CUSTOM-ERS AT THE FESTIVAL!
YEAH, BUT IT'D BE *WAY* MORE EMBARRASSING IF WE PUT ON A BAD PLAY OR SKIT!
SO JUST MAKE SOMETHING MORE ENTERTAINING FOR THE GUESTS!
It'd be better than feeding them crappy food!
It's better than doing a cheesy show!!
We're already divided?!
IT'S NOT A GOOD START AFTER ALL...
C-calm down!
HARUNO-SAN, WOULD YOU MIND FIGURING OUT SOME OF THE SPECIFICS?
Like the menu.
IT'S TRUE, I'VE HEARD THERE'S A LOT OF TROUBLE THAT GOES INTO SETTING UP A FOOD BUSINESS.
N— NO PROBLEM!
I'll do my best!
EXCUSE ME.
REINA-CHAN, GO AHEAD!

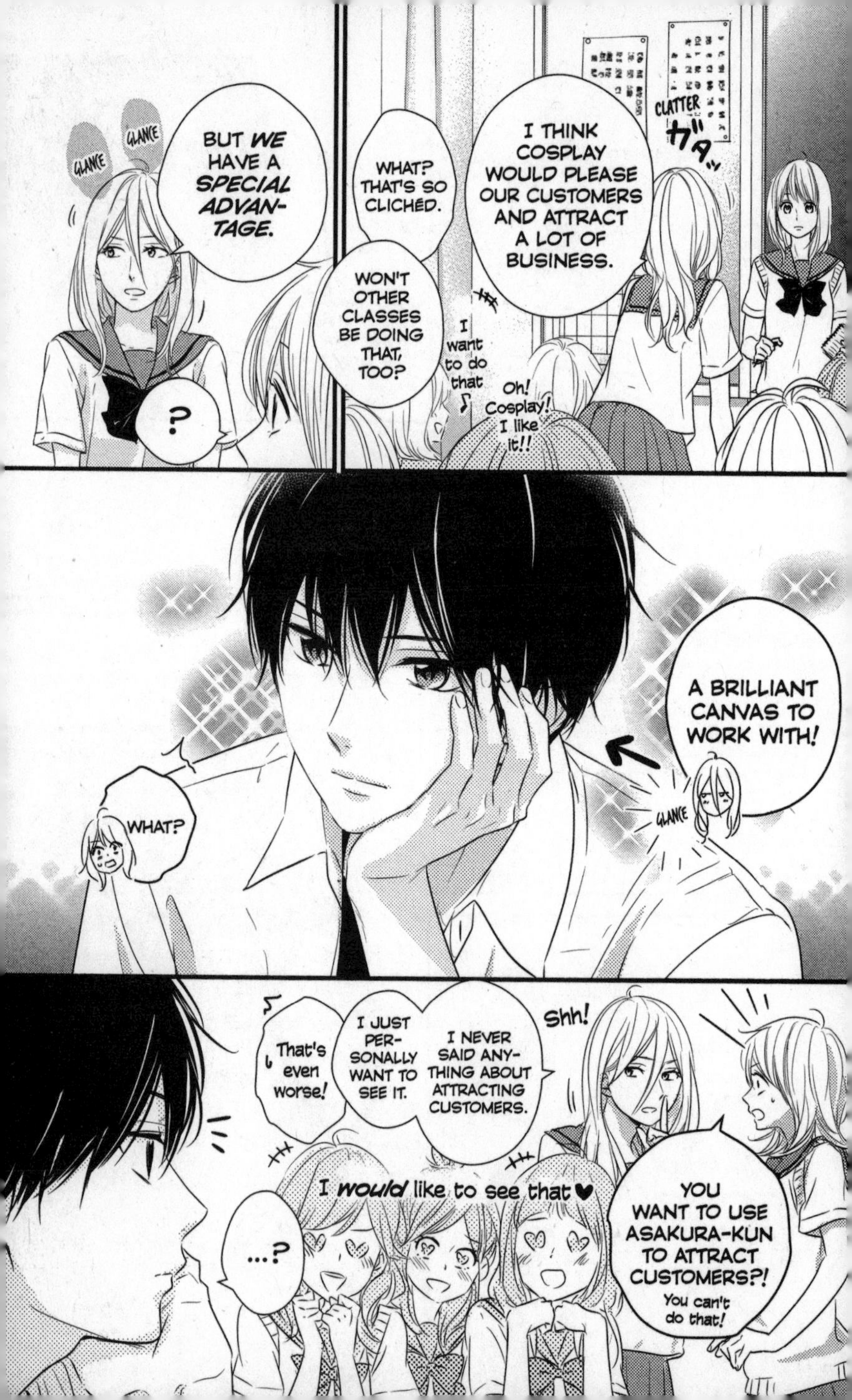
CLATTER
ガタッ
I THINK COSPLAY WOULD PLEASE OUR CUSTOMERS AND ATTRACT A LOT OF BUSINESS.
WHAT? THAT'S SO CLICHED.
I want to do that ♪
Oh! Cosplay! I like it!!
WON'T OTHER CLASSES BE DOING THAT, TOO?
GLANCE
GLANCE
BUT *WE* HAVE A *SPECIAL ADVANTAGE.*
?
A BRILLIANT CANVAS TO WORK WITH!
GLANCE
WHAT?
YOU WANT TO USE ASAKURA-KUN TO ATTRACT CUSTOMERS?!
You can't do that!
Shh!
I NEVER SAID ANYTHING ABOUT ATTRACTING CUSTOMERS.
I JUST PERSONALLY WANT TO SEE IT.
That's even worse!
I *would* like to see that ♥
...?

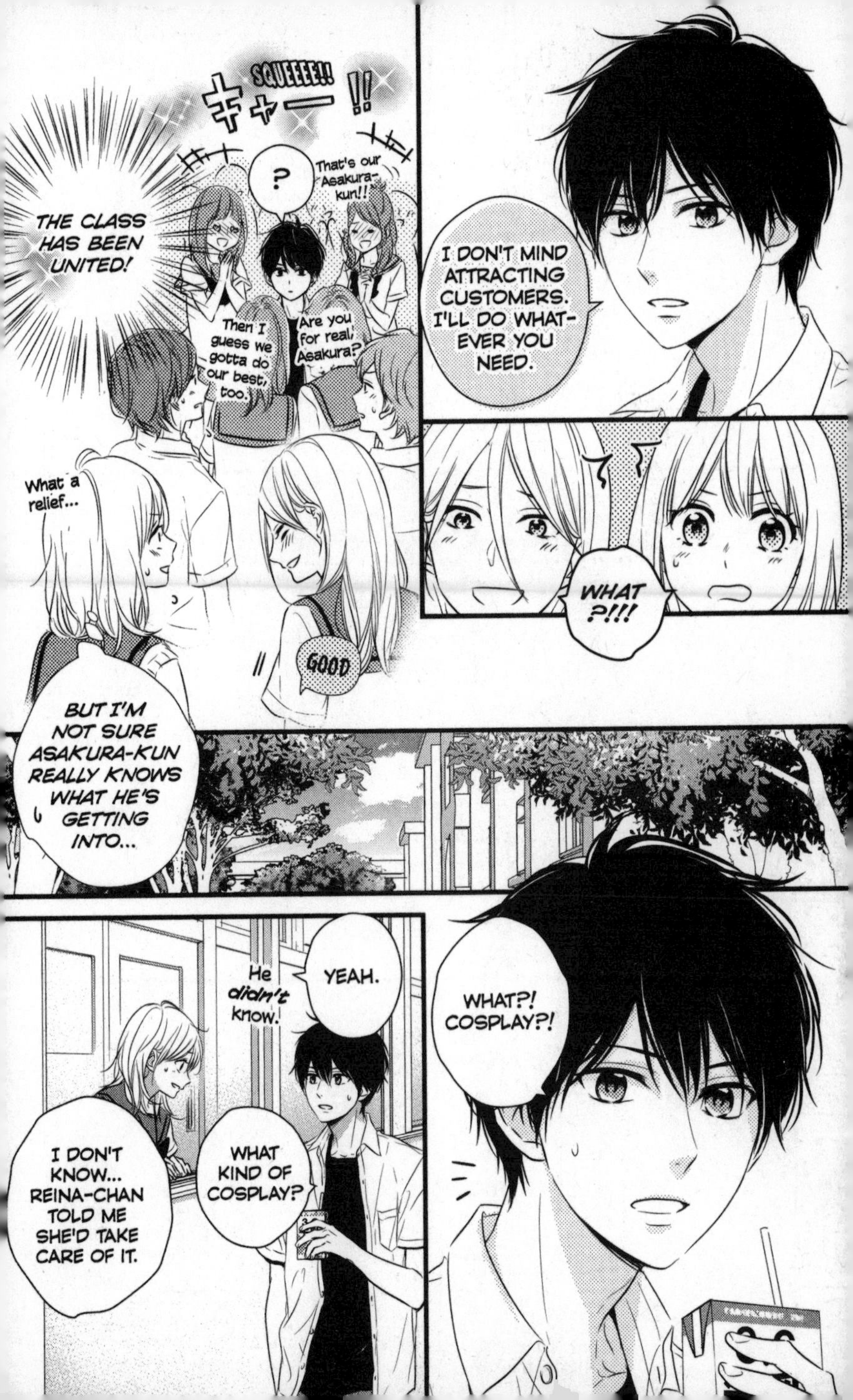
I DON'T MIND ATTRACTING CUSTOMERS. I'LL DO WHATEVER YOU NEED.
WHAT ?!!!
SQUEEEEE!!
キャー!!
?
That's our Asakura-kun!!
THE CLASS HAS BEEN UNITED!
Are you for real, Asakura?
Then I guess we gotta do our best, too.
What a relief...
GOOD
BUT I'M NOT SURE ASAKURA-KUN REALLY KNOWS WHAT HE'S GETTING INTO...
WHAT?! COSPLAY?!
YEAH.
He didn't know.
WHAT KIND OF COSPLAY?
I DON'T KNOW... REINA-CHAN TOLD ME SHE'D TAKE CARE OF IT.

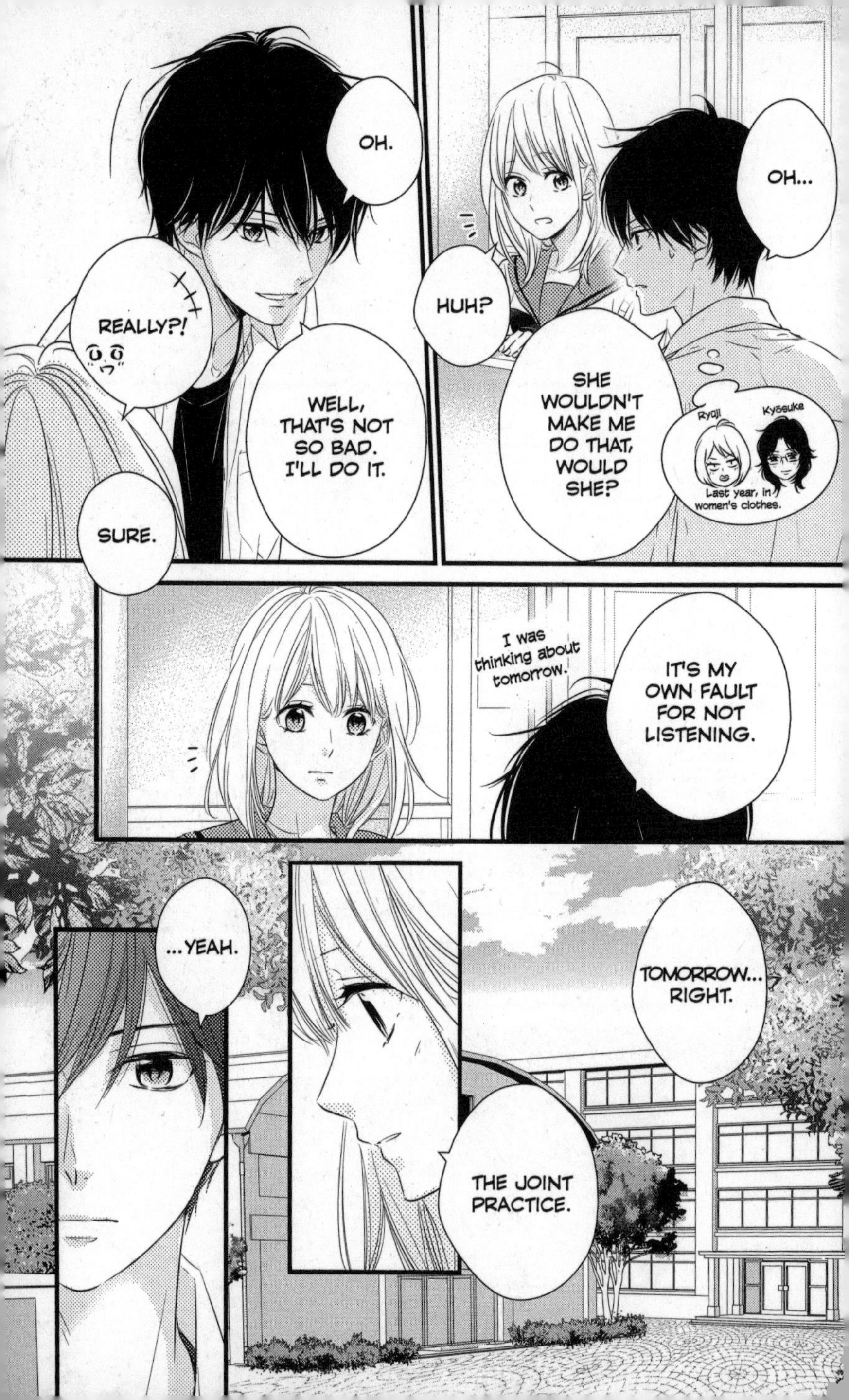
OH...
HUH?
SHE WOULDN'T MAKE ME DO THAT, WOULD SHE?
Ryuji
Kyosuke
Last year, in women's clothes.
OH.
REALLY?!
WELL, THAT'S NOT SO BAD. I'LL DO IT.
SURE.
IT'S MY OWN FAULT FOR NOT LISTENING.
I was thinking about tomorrow.
TOMORROW... RIGHT.
THE JOINT PRACTICE.
...YEAH.

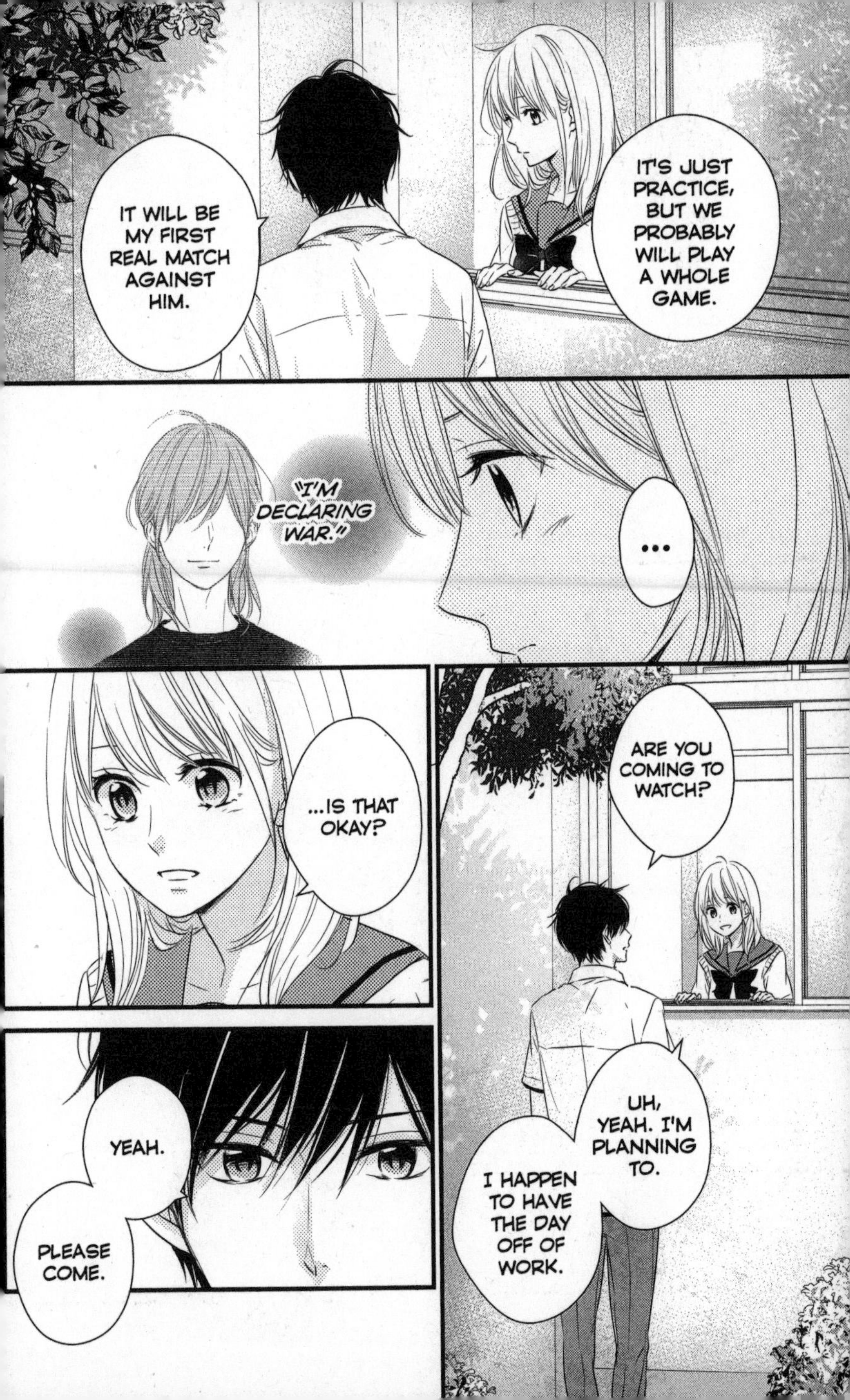
IT'S JUST PRACTICE, BUT WE PROBABLY WILL PLAY A WHOLE GAME.
IT WILL BE MY FIRST REAL MATCH AGAINST HIM.
...
"I'M DECLARING WAR."
ARE YOU COMING TO WATCH?
UH, YEAH. I'M PLANNING TO.
I HAPPEN TO HAVE THE DAY OFF OF WORK.
...IS THAT OKAY?
YEAH.
PLEASE COME.

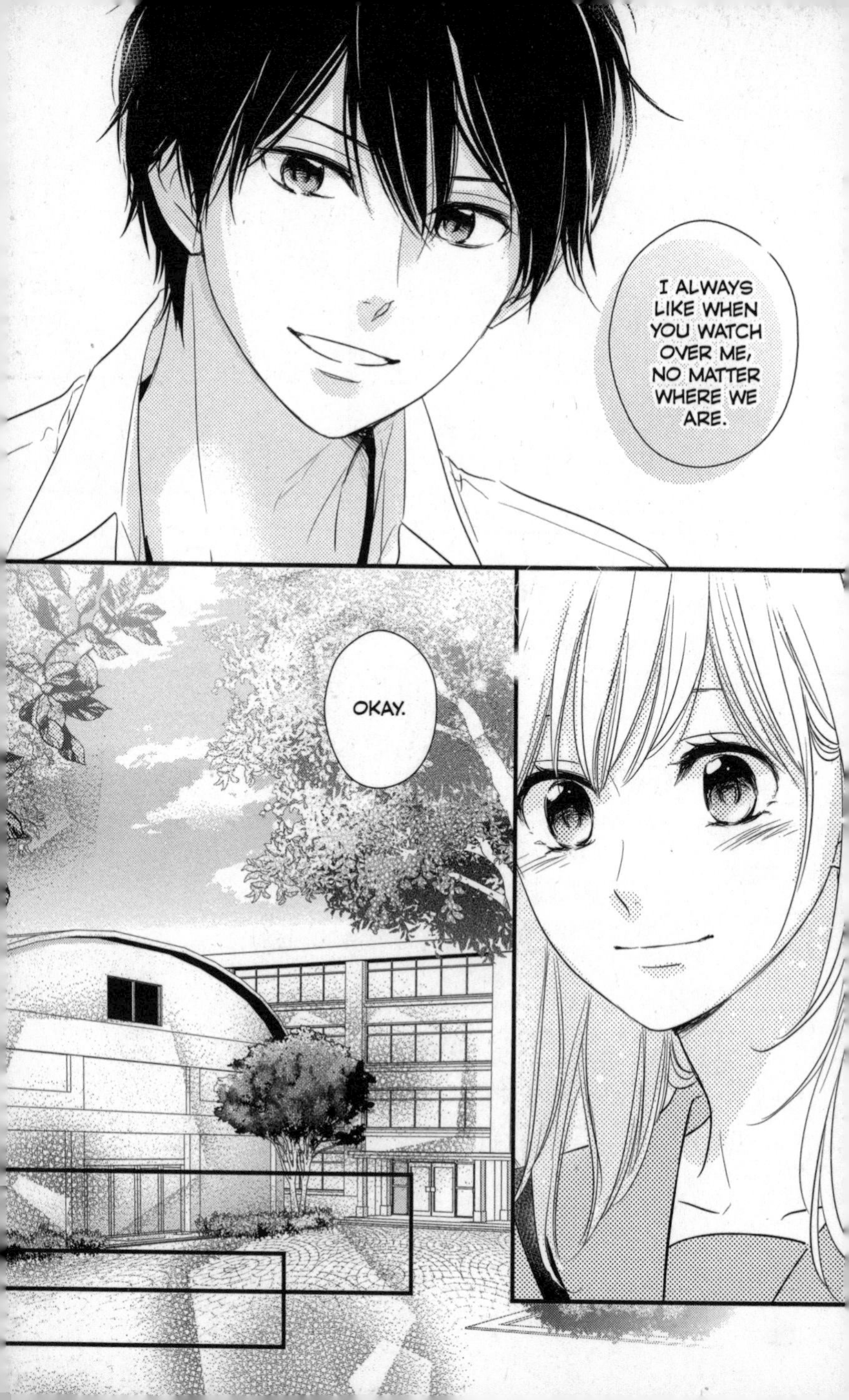
I ALWAYS LIKE WHEN YOU WATCH OVER ME, NO MATTER WHERE WE ARE.
OKAY.

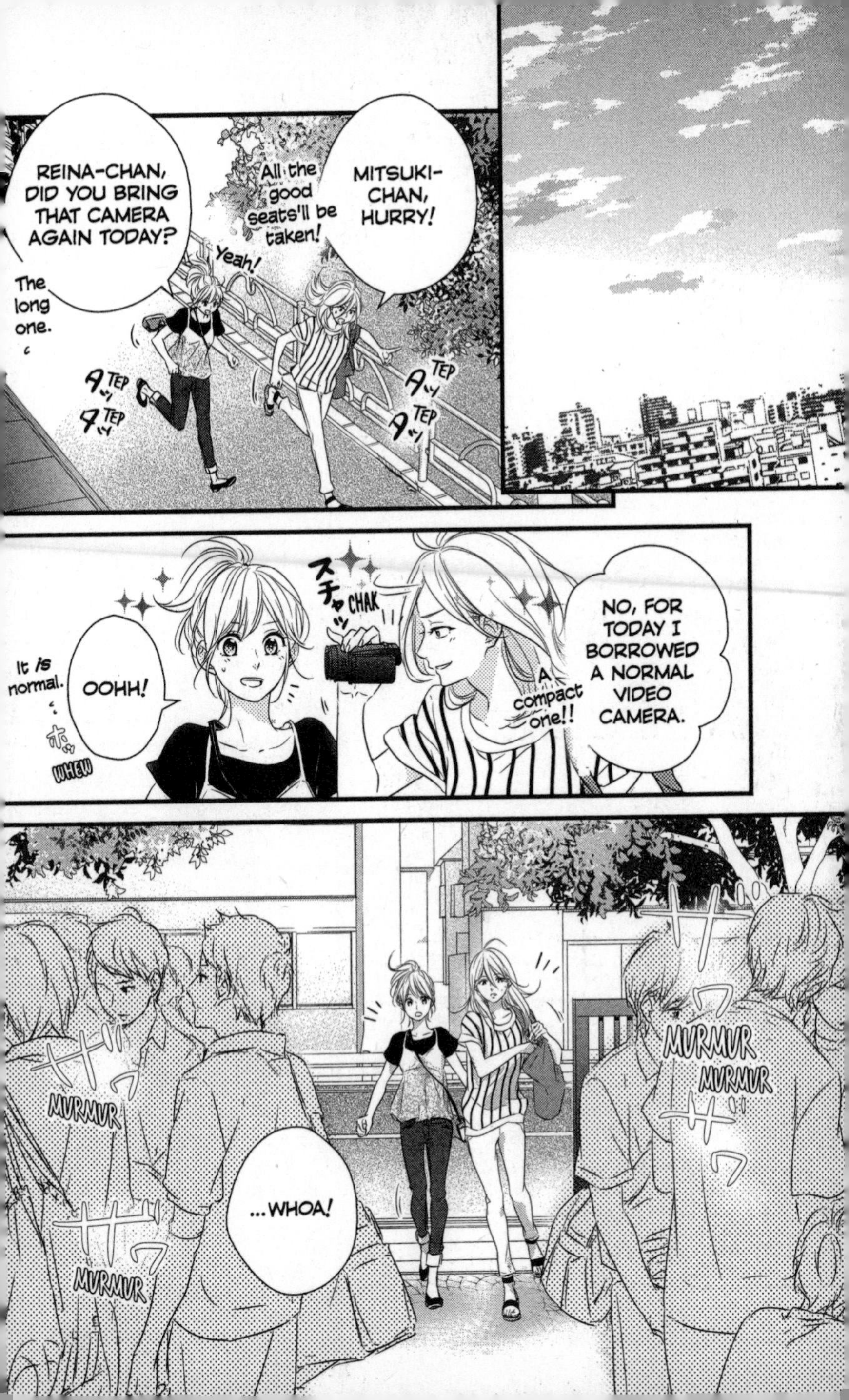
MITSUKI-CHAN, HURRY!
All the good seats'll be taken!
Yeah!
REINA-CHAN, DID YOU BRING THAT CAMERA AGAIN TODAY?
The long one.
TEP
TEP
TEP
TEP
NO, FOR TODAY I BORROWED A NORMAL VIDEO CAMERA.
A compact one!!
CHAK
OOHH!
It is normal.
WHEW
MURMUR
MURMUR
...WHOA!
MURMUR
MURMUR

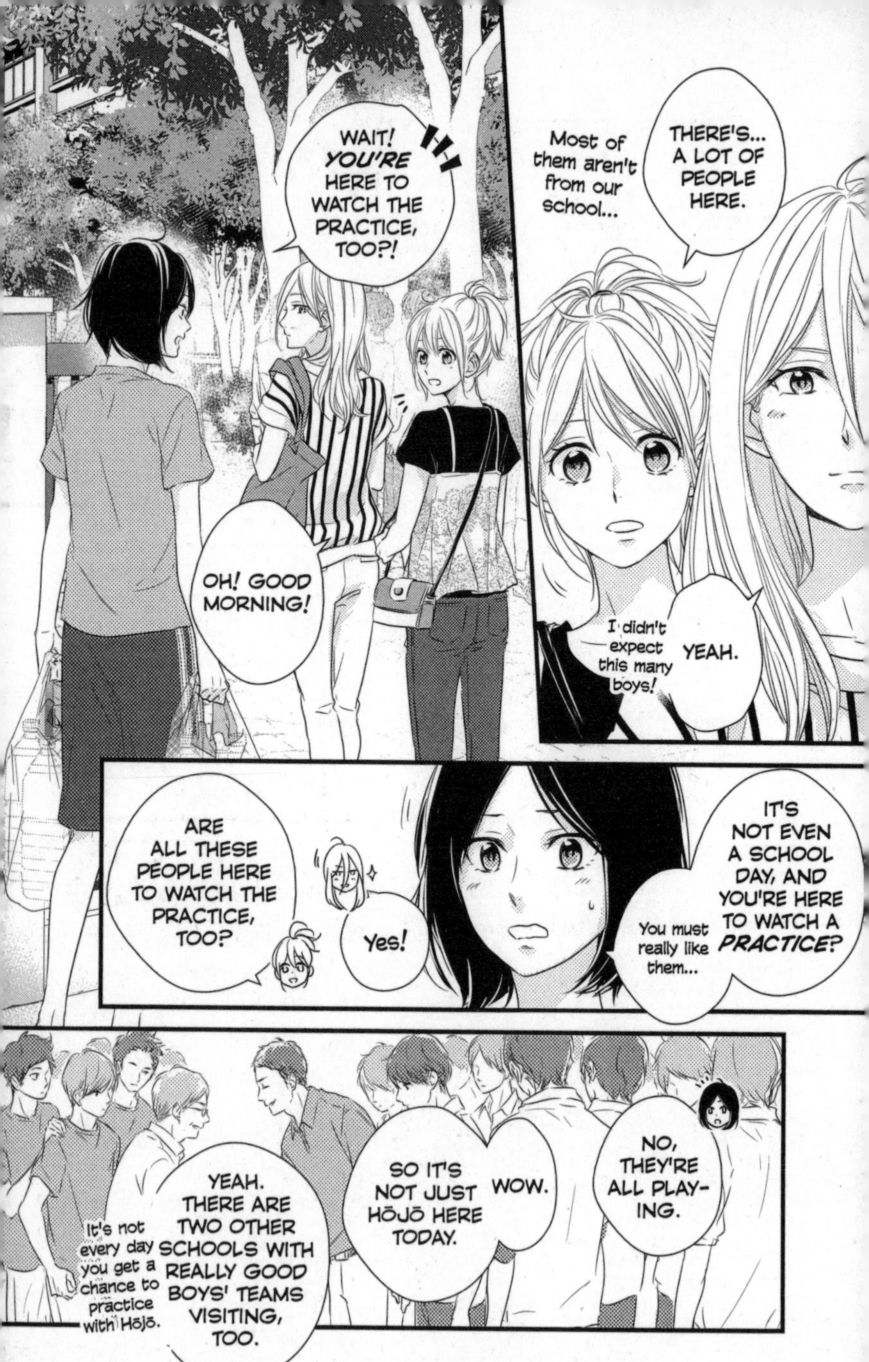
THERE'S... A LOT OF PEOPLE HERE.
Most of them aren't from our school...
YEAH.
I didn't expect this many boys!
WAIT! *YOU'RE* HERE TO WATCH THE PRACTICE, TOO?!
OH! GOOD MORNING!
IT'S NOT EVEN A SCHOOL DAY, AND YOU'RE HERE TO WATCH A *PRACTICE*?
You must really like them...
Yes!
ARE ALL THESE PEOPLE HERE TO WATCH THE PRACTICE, TOO?
NO, THEY'RE ALL PLAY-ING.
WOW.
SO IT'S NOT JUST HŌJŌ HERE TODAY.
YEAH. THERE ARE TWO OTHER SCHOOLS WITH REALLY GOOD BOYS' TEAMS VISITING, TOO.
It's not every day you get a chance to practice with Hōjō.

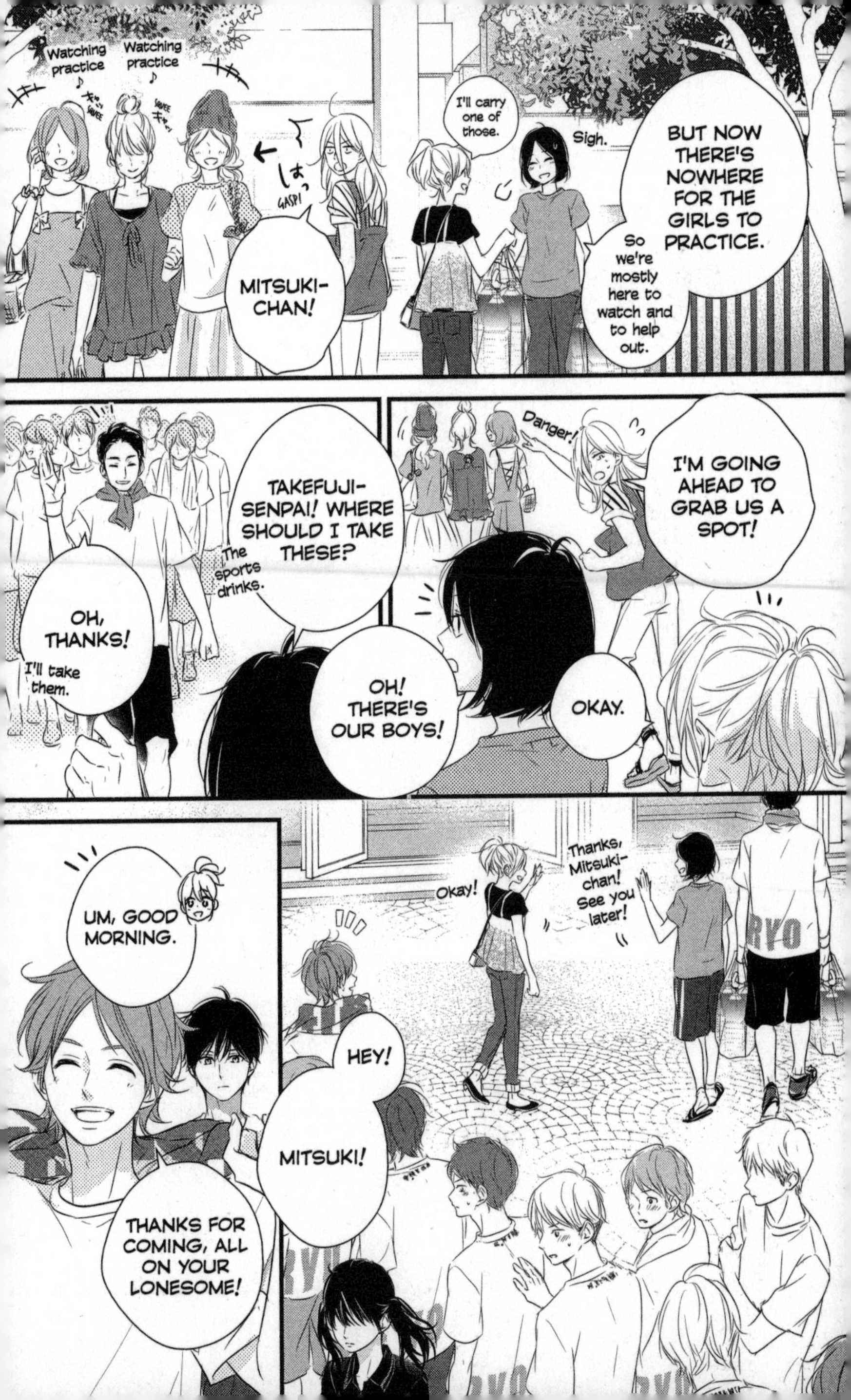
BUT NOW THERE'S NOWHERE FOR THE GIRLS TO PRACTICE.
So we're mostly here to watch and to help out.
Sigh.
I'll carry one of those.
MITSUKI-CHAN!
GASP!
Watching practice ♪
Watching practice ♪
SQUEE
SQUEE
I'M GOING AHEAD TO GRAB US A SPOT!
Danger!
OKAY.
OH! THERE'S OUR BOYS!
TAKEFUJI-SENPAI! WHERE SHOULD I TAKE THESE?
The sports drinks.
OH, THANKS!
I'll take them.
Thanks, Mitsuki-chan! See you later!
Okay!
HEY!
MITSUKI!
UM, GOOD MORNING.
THANKS FOR COMING, ALL ON YOUR LONESOME!

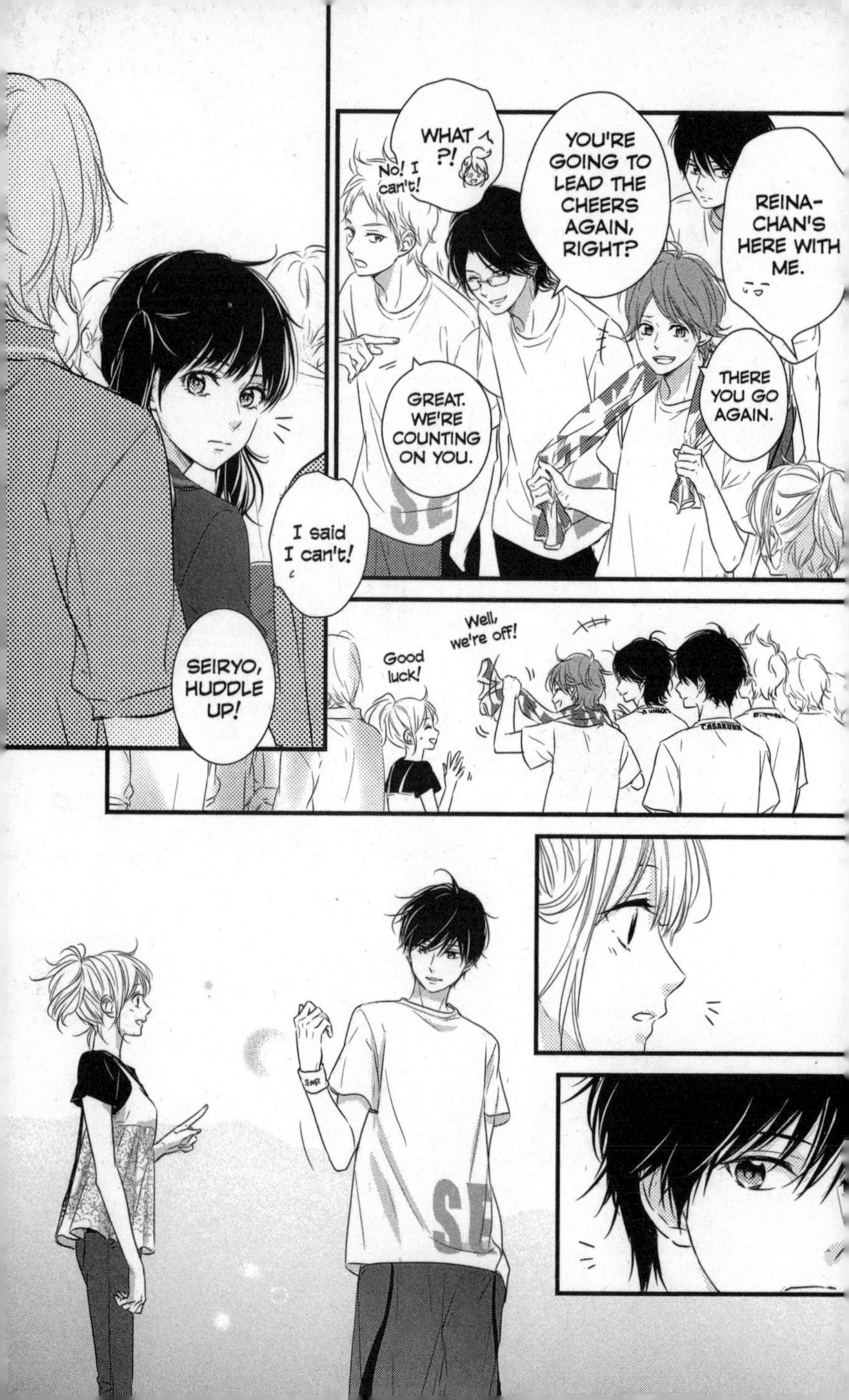
REINA-CHAN'S HERE WITH ME.
YOU'RE GOING TO LEAD THE CHEERS AGAIN, RIGHT?
WHAT ?!
No! I can't!
THERE YOU GO AGAIN.
GREAT. WE'RE COUNTING ON YOU.
I said I can't!
SEIRYO, HUDDLE UP!
Well, we're off!
Good luck!

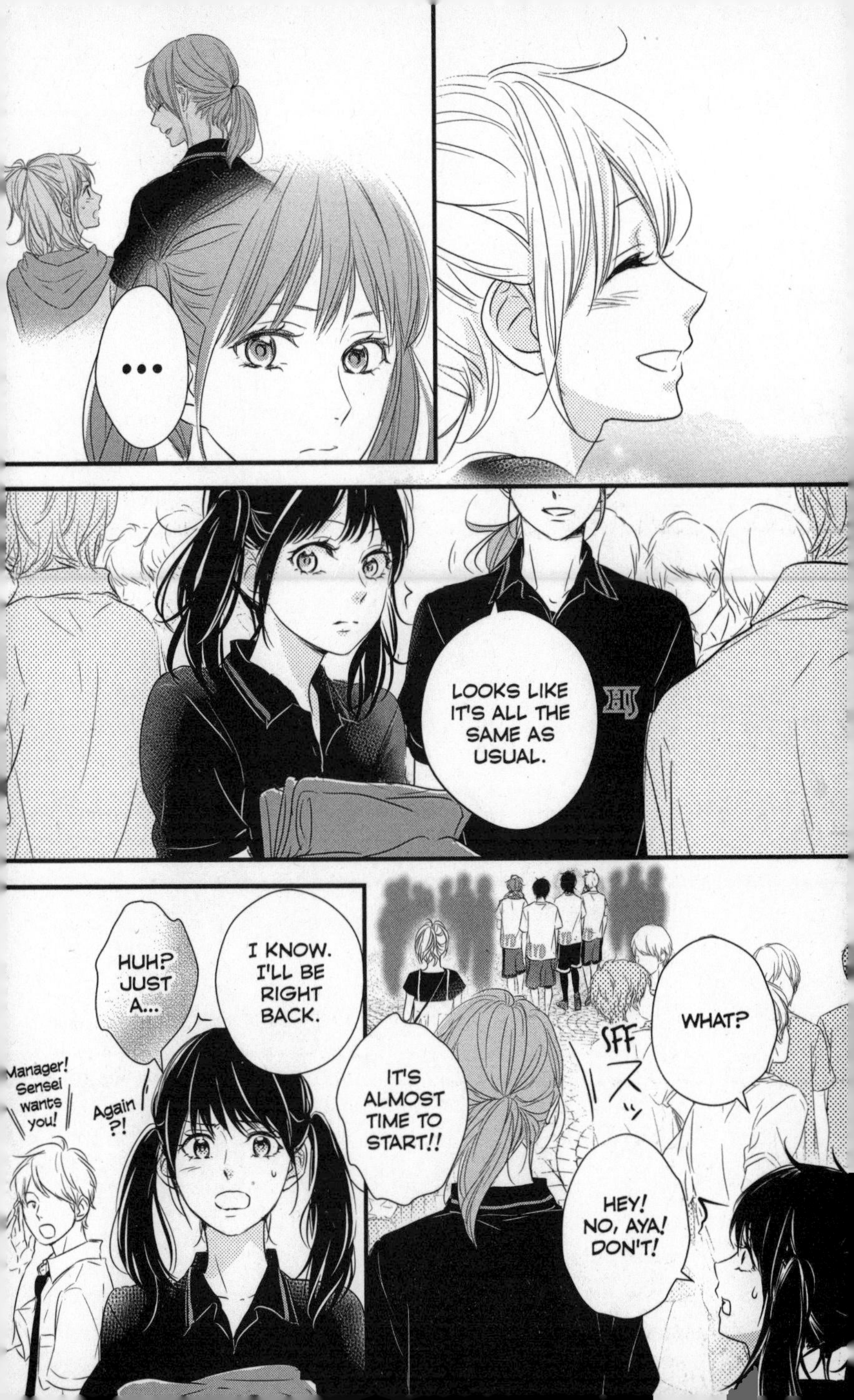
...
LOOKS LIKE IT'S ALL THE SAME AS USUAL.
WHAT?
SFF スッ
HEY! NO, AYA! DON'T!
IT'S ALMOST TIME TO START!!
I KNOW. I'LL BE RIGHT BACK.
HUH? JUST A...
Again?!
Manager! Sensei wants you!

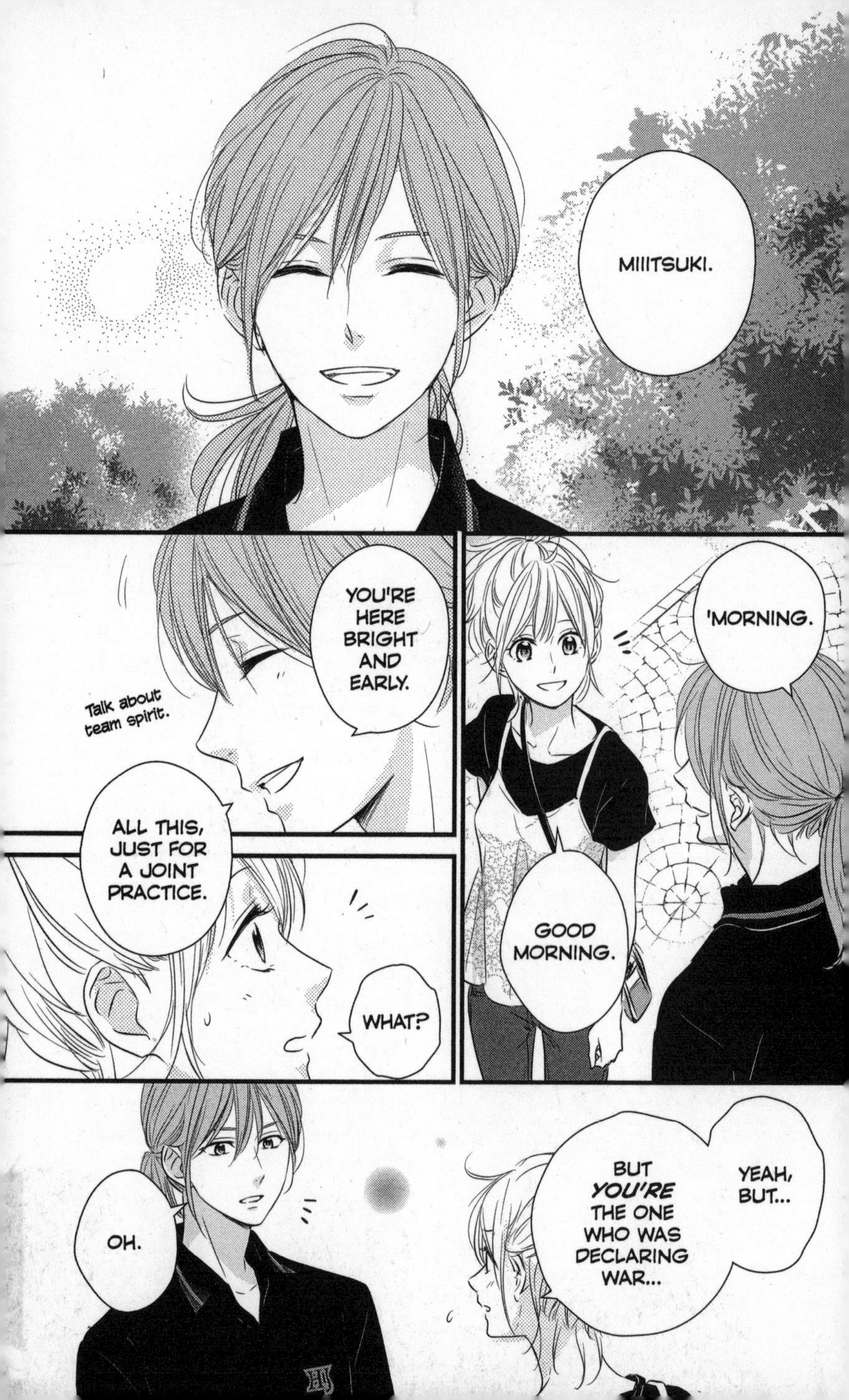
MIIITSUKI.
'MORNING.
GOOD MORNING.
YOU'RE HERE BRIGHT AND EARLY.
Talk about team spirit.
ALL THIS, JUST FOR A JOINT PRACTICE.
WHAT?
YEAH, BUT...
BUT *YOU'RE* THE ONE WHO WAS DECLARING WAR...
OH.

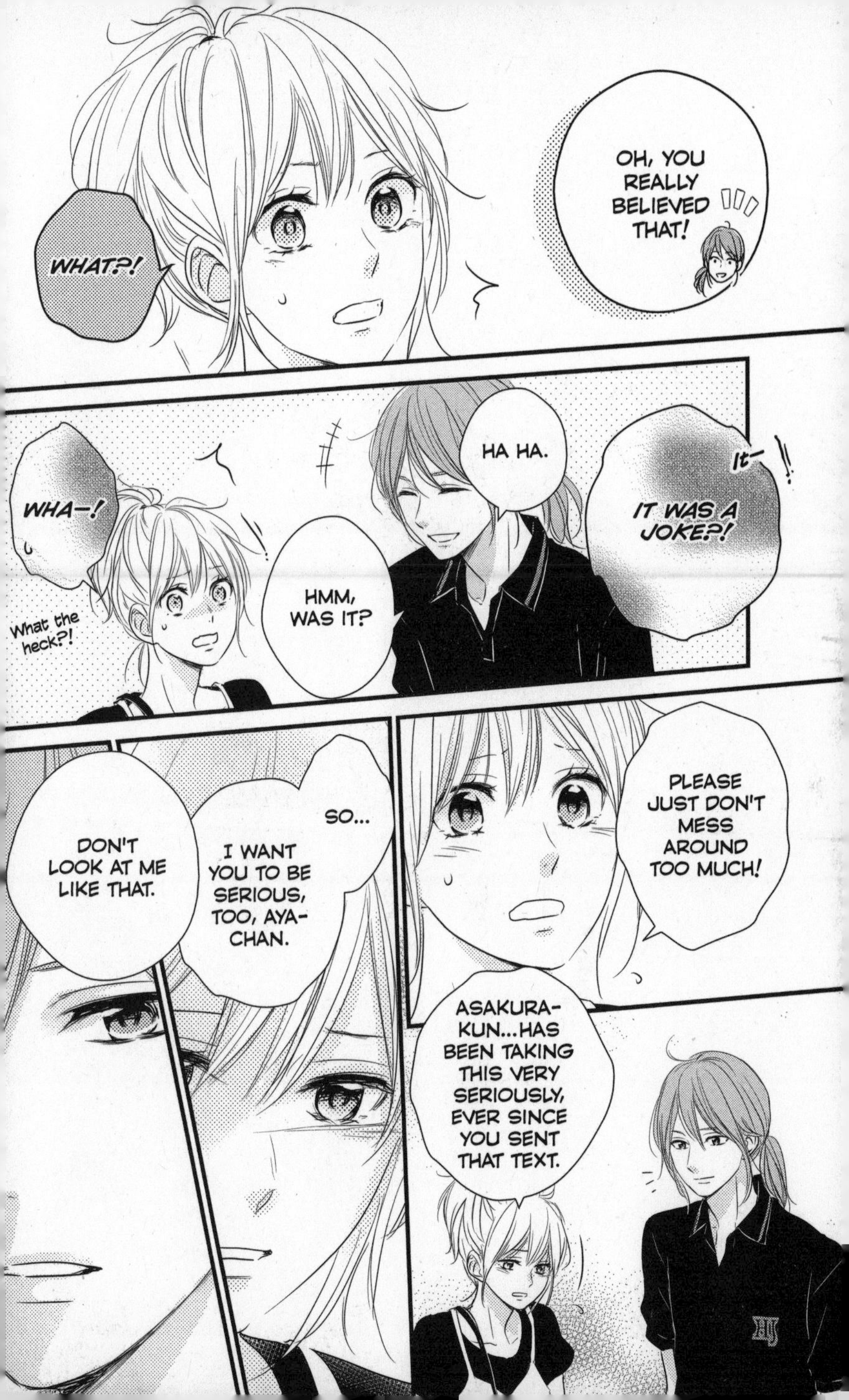
OH, YOU REALLY BELIEVED THAT!
WHAT?!
It— IT WAS A JOKE?!
HA HA.
HMM, WAS IT?
WHA—!
What the heck?!
PLEASE JUST DON'T MESS AROUND TOO MUCH!
ASAKURA-KUN...HAS BEEN TAKING THIS VERY SERIOUSLY, EVER SINCE YOU SENT THAT TEXT.
SO... I WANT YOU TO BE SERIOUS, TOO, AYA-CHAN.
DON'T LOOK AT ME LIKE THAT.

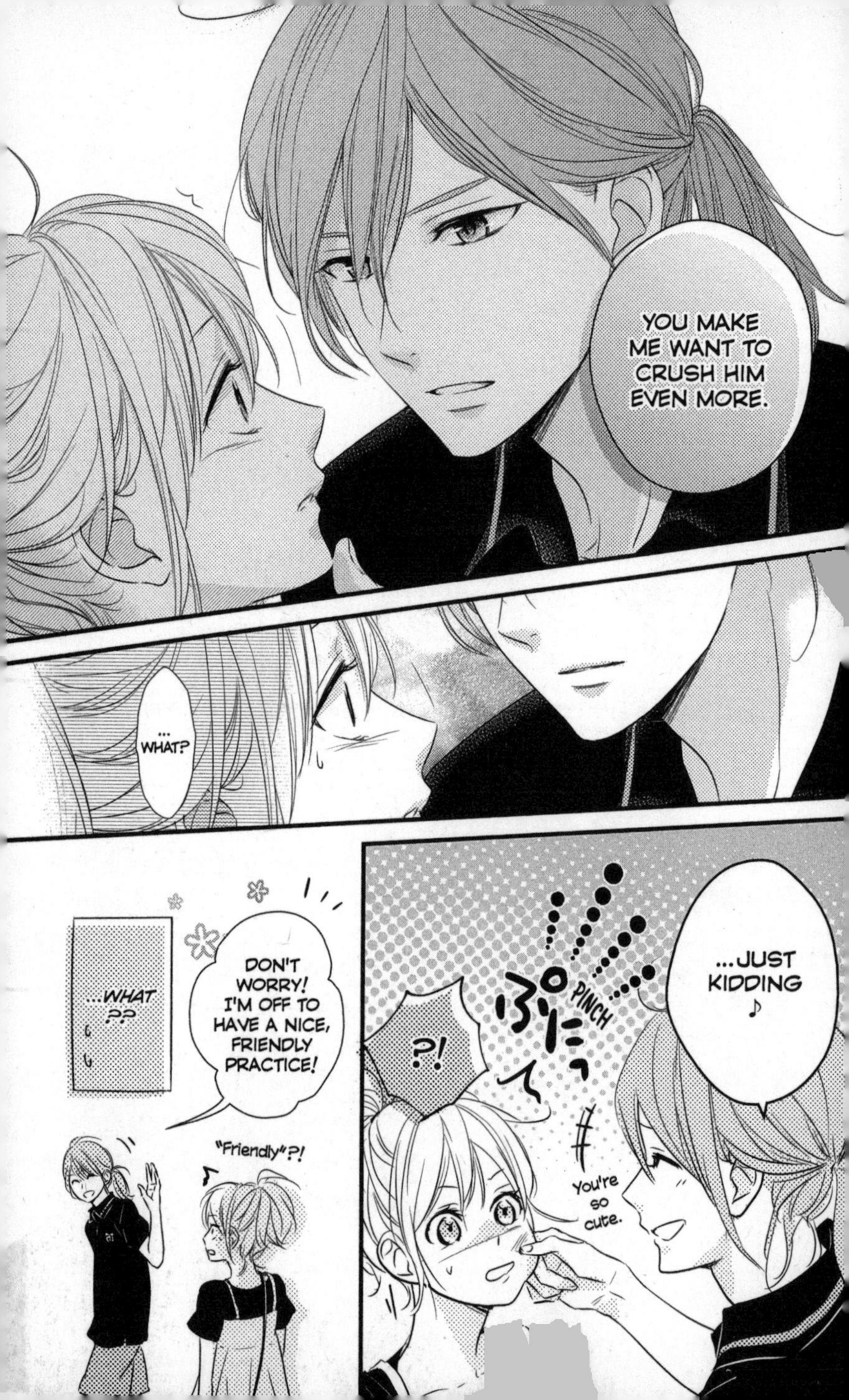
YOU MAKE ME WANT TO CRUSH HIM EVEN MORE.
...WHAT?
...JUST KIDDING ♪
PINCH
?!
You're so cute.
DON'T WORRY! I'M OFF TO HAVE A NICE, FRIENDLY PRACTICE!
...WHAT ??
"Friendly"?!

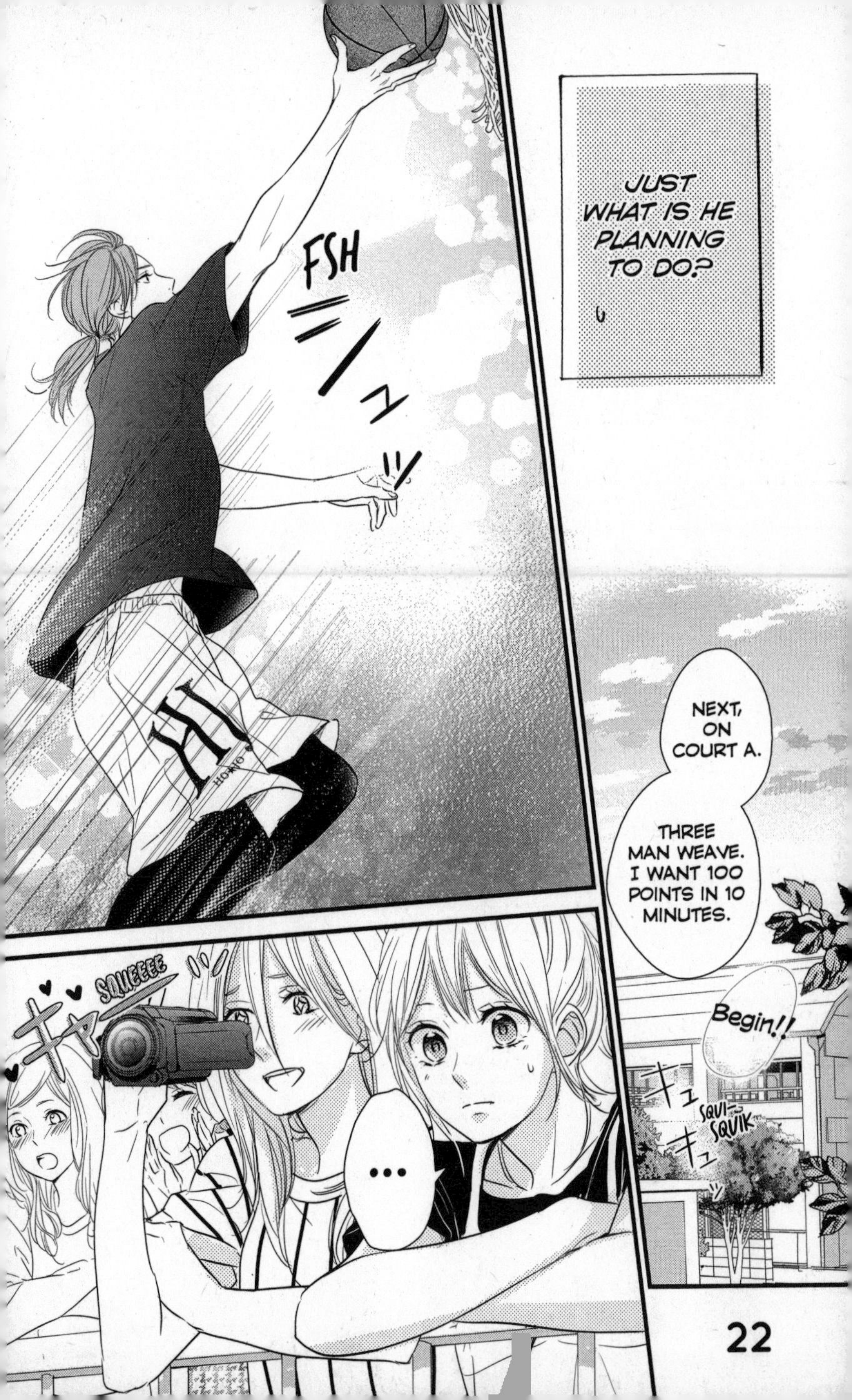
JUST WHAT IS HE PLANNING TO DO?
NEXT, ON COURT A.
THREE MAN WEAVE. I WANT 100 POINTS IN 10 MINUTES.
Begin!!
SQUI-SQUIK
FSH
SQUEEEE
...

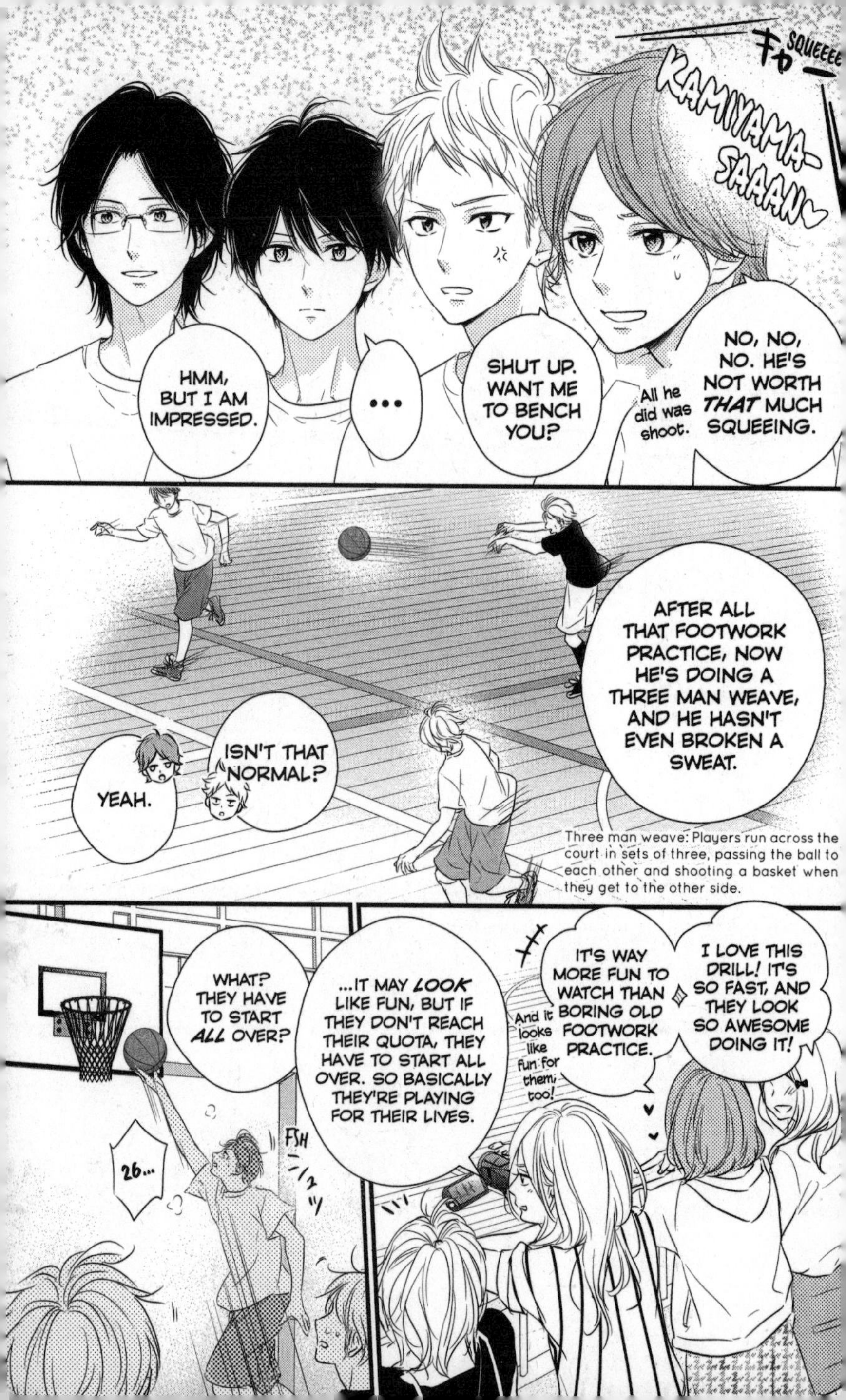
SQUEEEE
KAMIYAMA-SAAAAN♥
NO, NO, NO. HE'S NOT WORTH *THAT* MUCH SQUEEING.
All he did was shoot.
SHUT UP. WANT ME TO BENCH YOU?
...
HMM, BUT I AM IMPRESSED.
AFTER ALL THAT FOOTWORK PRACTICE, NOW HE'S DOING A THREE MAN WEAVE, AND HE HASN'T EVEN BROKEN A SWEAT.
ISN'T THAT NORMAL?
YEAH.
Three man weave: Players run across the court in sets of three, passing the ball to each other and shooting a basket when they get to the other side.
I LOVE THIS DRILL! IT'S SO FAST, AND THEY LOOK SO AWESOME DOING IT!
IT'S WAY MORE FUN TO WATCH THAN BORING OLD FOOTWORK PRACTICE.
And it looks like fun for them, too!
...IT MAY *LOOK* LIKE FUN, BUT IF THEY DON'T REACH THEIR QUOTA, THEY HAVE TO START ALL OVER. SO BASICALLY THEY'RE PLAYING FOR THEIR LIVES.
WHAT? THEY HAVE TO START *ALL* OVER?
FSH
26...

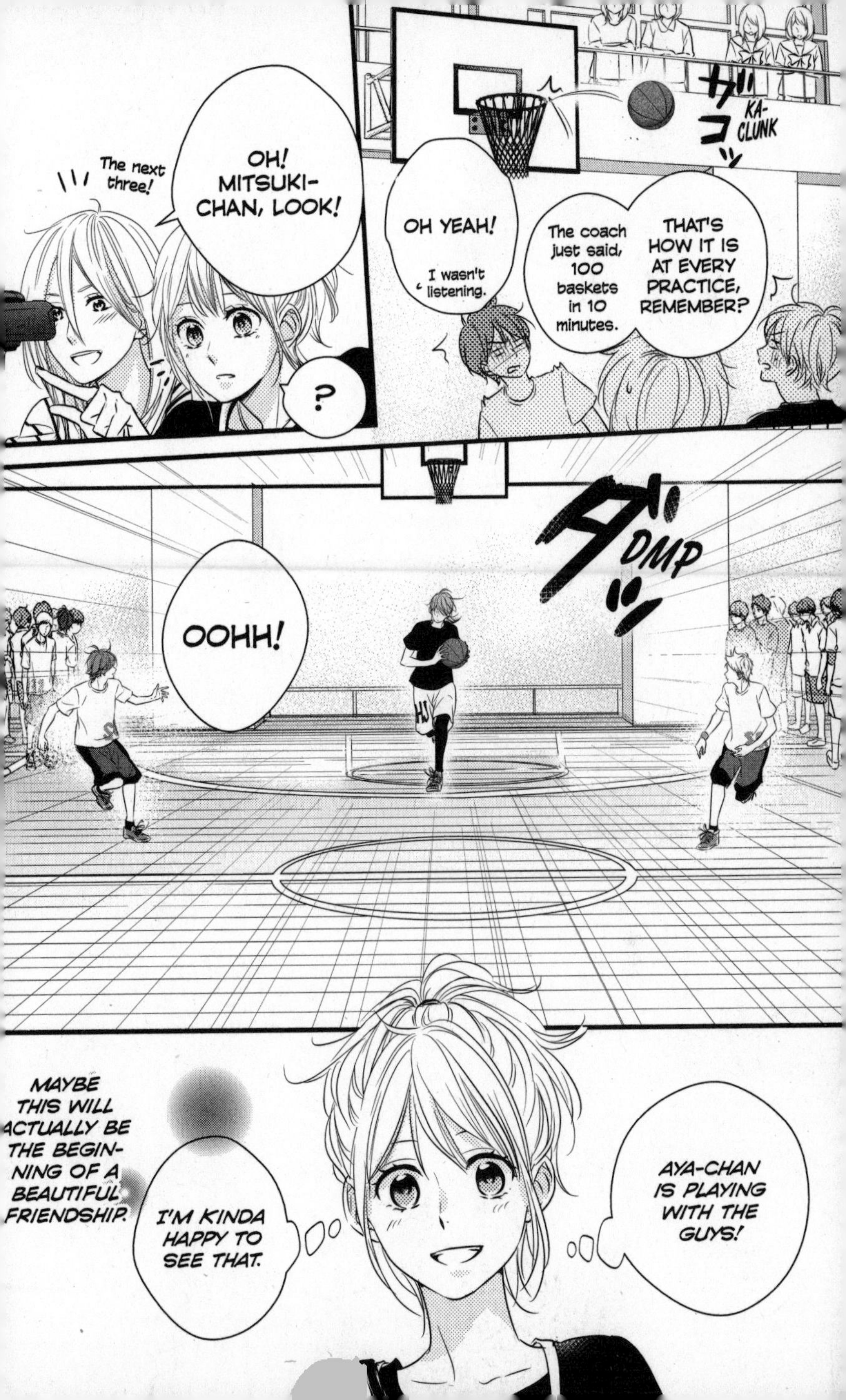
KA-CLUNK
THAT'S HOW IT IS AT EVERY PRACTICE, REMEMBER?
The coach just said, 100 baskets in 10 minutes.
OH YEAH!
I wasn't listening.
OH! MITSUKI-CHAN, LOOK!
The next three!
?
DMP
OOHH!
AYA-CHAN IS PLAYING WITH THE GUYS!
I'M KINDA HAPPY TO SEE THAT.
MAYBE THIS WILL ACTUALLY BE THE BEGINNING OF A BEAUTIFUL FRIENDSHIP.

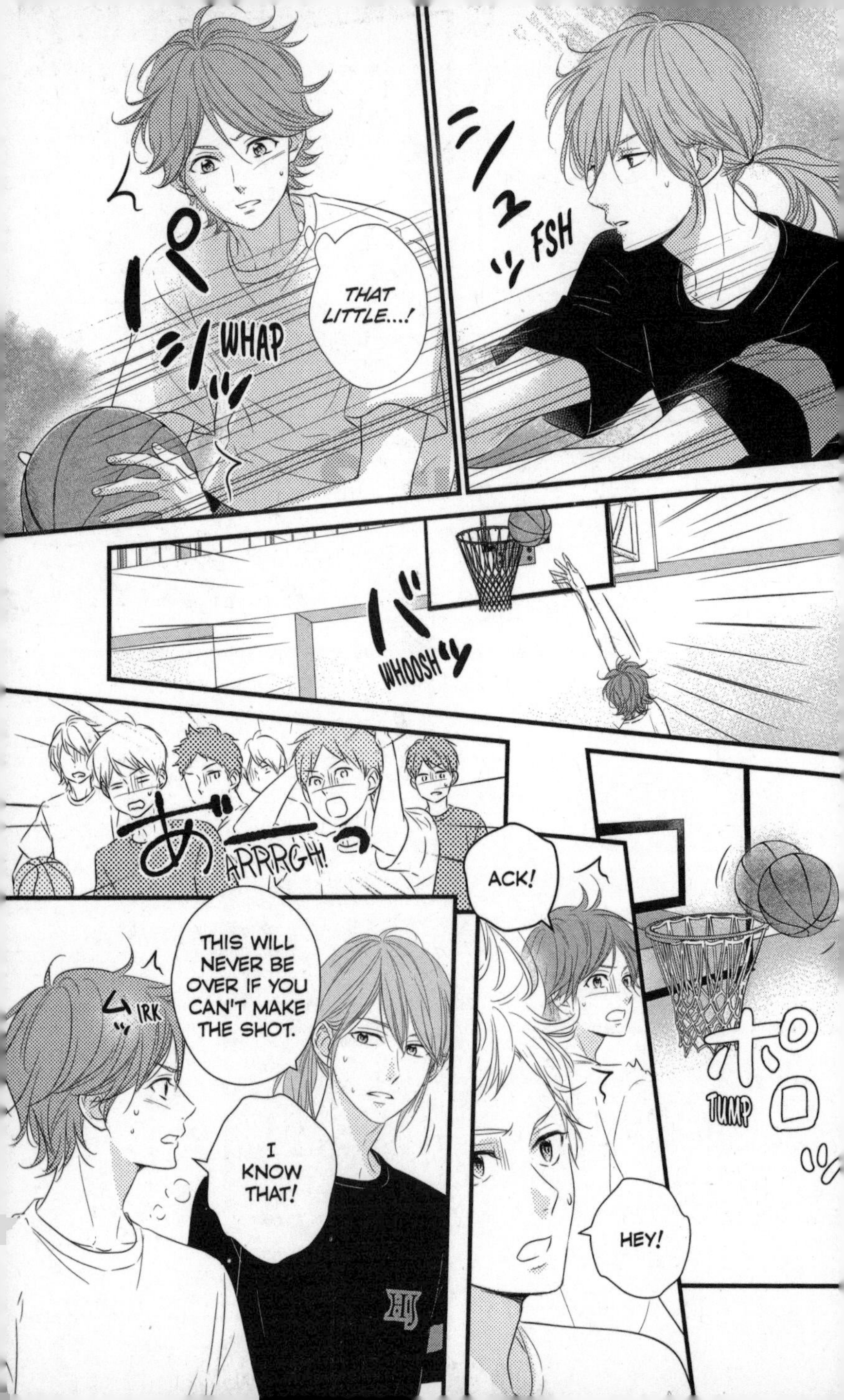
FSH
THAT LITTLE...!
WHAP
WHOOSH
ACK!
TUMP
HEY!
ARRRGH!
IRK
THIS WILL NEVER BE OVER IF YOU CAN'T MAKE THE SHOT.
I KNOW THAT!

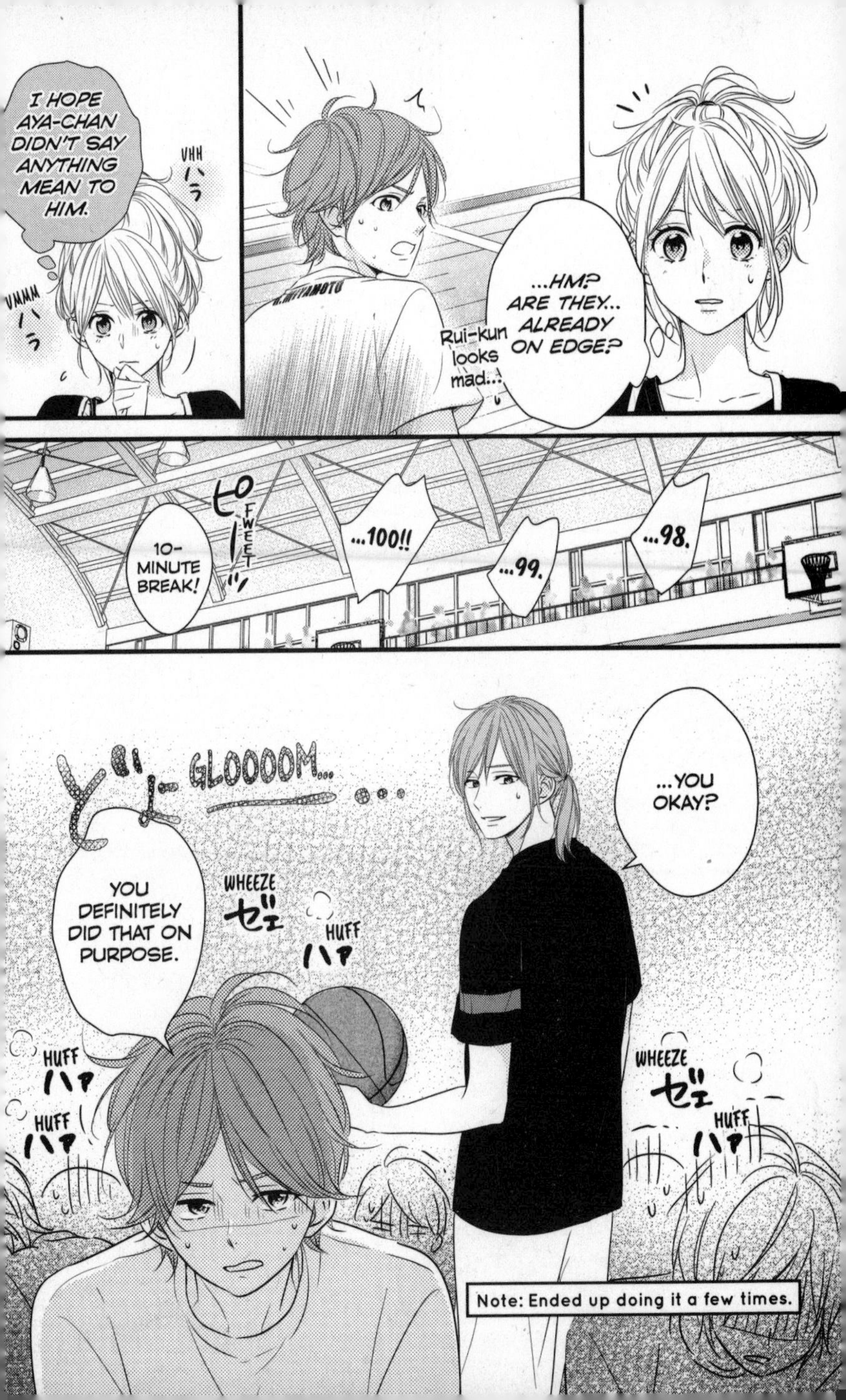
...HM? ARE THEY... ALREADY ON EDGE?
Rui-kun looks mad...
I HOPE AYA-CHAN DIDN'T SAY ANYTHING MEAN TO HIM.
UHH ハラ
UMMM ハラ
...98.
...99.
...100!!
FWEET ピーッ
10-MINUTE BREAK!
...YOU OKAY?
GLOOOOM...
YOU DEFINITELY DID THAT ON PURPOSE.
WHEEZE ゼェ
HUFF ハァ
HUFF ハァ
HUFF ハァ
WHEEZE ゼェ
HUFF ハァ
Note: Ended up doing it a few times.

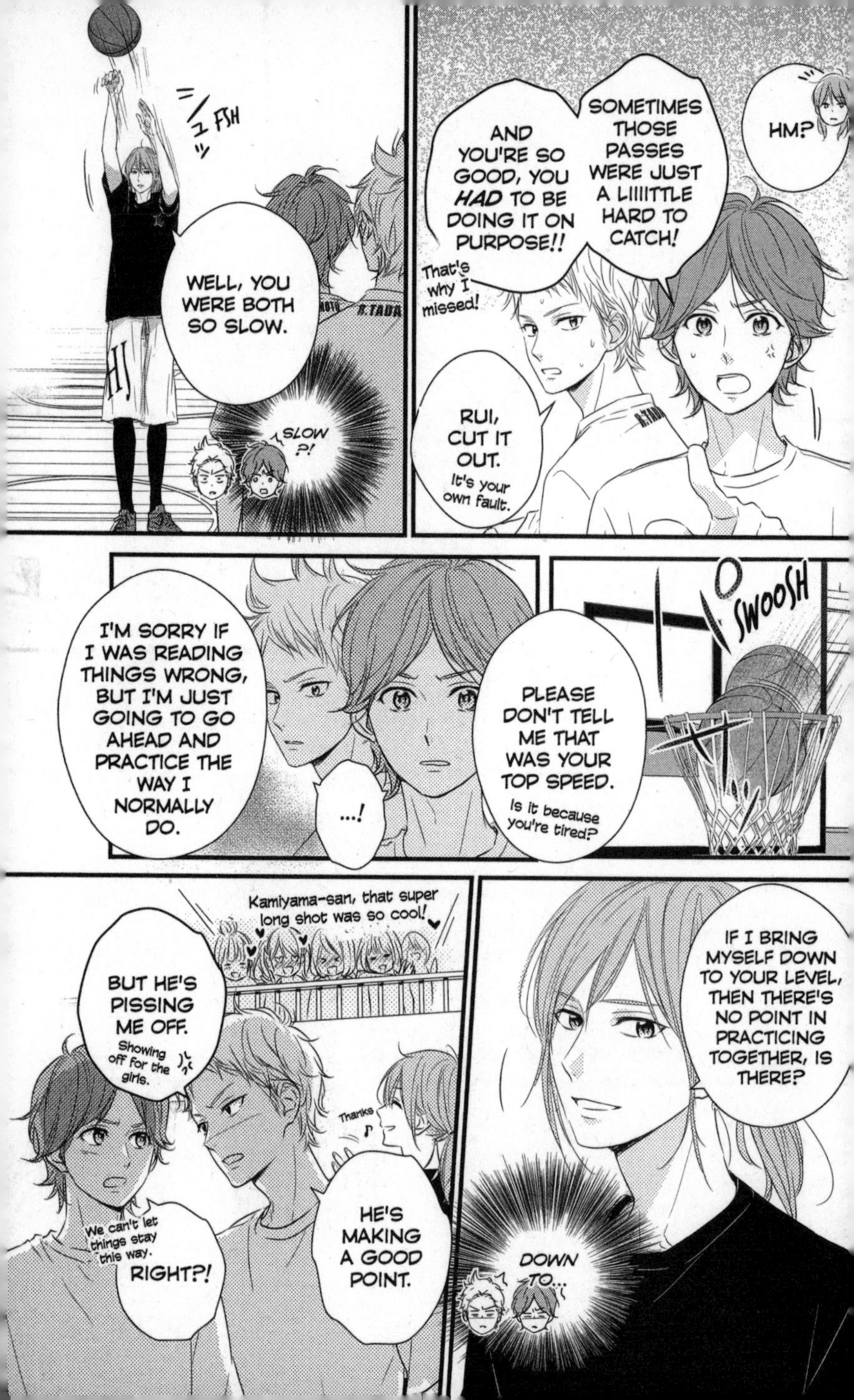
HM?
SOMETIMES THOSE PASSES WERE JUST A LIIIITTLE HARD TO CATCH!
AND YOU'RE SO GOOD, YOU *HAD* TO BE DOING IT ON PURPOSE!!
That's why I missed!
RUI, CUT IT OUT.
It's your own fault.
FSH
WELL, YOU WERE BOTH SO SLOW.
SLOW ?!
SWOOSH
PLEASE DON'T TELL ME THAT WAS YOUR TOP SPEED.
Is it because you're tired?
I'M SORRY IF I WAS READING THINGS WRONG, BUT I'M JUST GOING TO GO AHEAD AND PRACTICE THE WAY I NORMALLY DO.
...!
IF I BRING MYSELF DOWN TO YOUR LEVEL, THEN THERE'S NO POINT IN PRACTICING TOGETHER, IS THERE?
DOWN TO...
Kamiyama-san, that super long shot was so cool!
BUT HE'S PISSING ME OFF.
Showing off for the girls.
Thanks ♪
HE'S MAKING A GOOD POINT.
We can't let things stay this way.
RIGHT?!

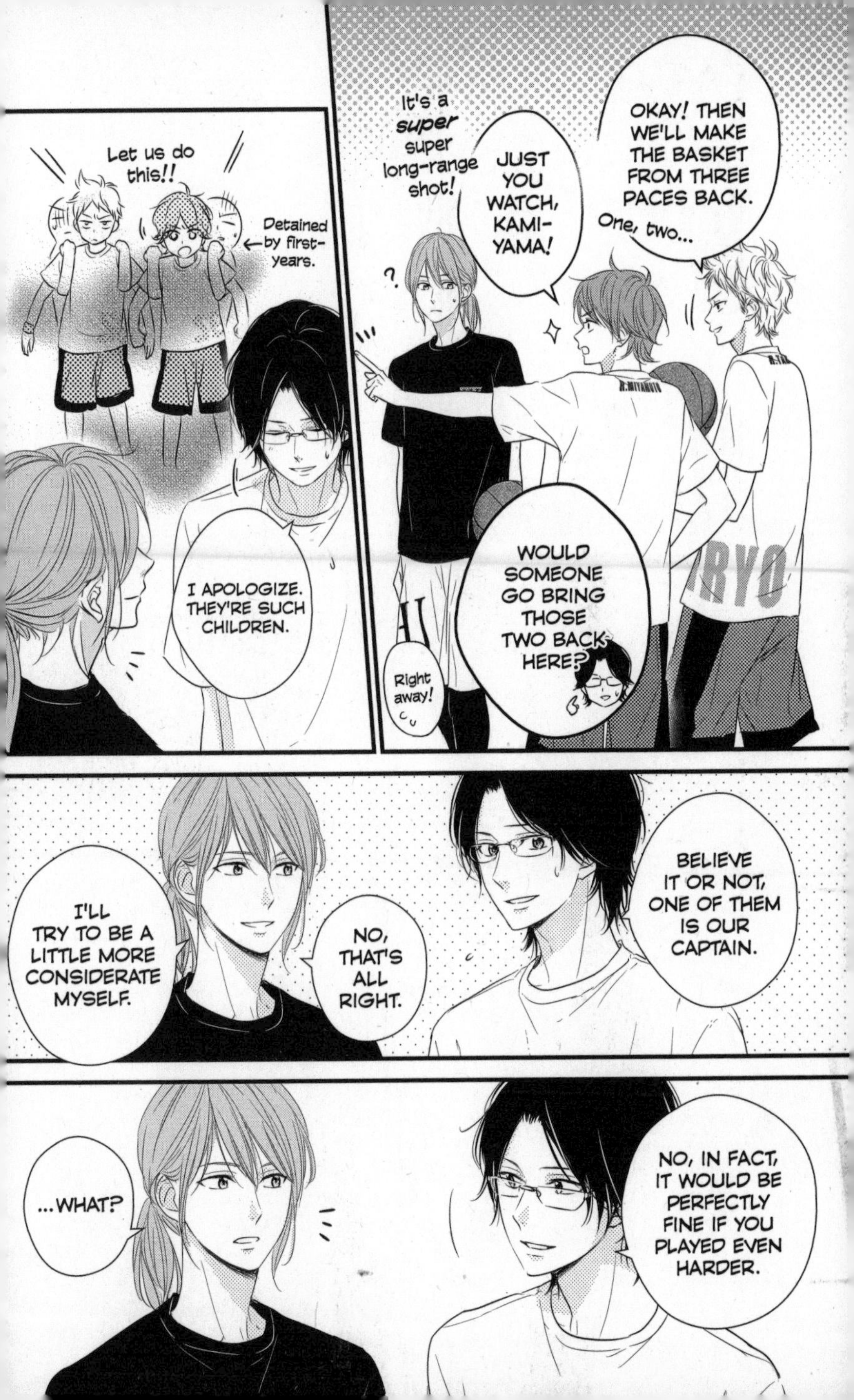

OKAY! THEN WE'LL MAKE THE BASKET FROM THREE PACES BACK.
One, two...
JUST YOU WATCH, KAMI-YAMA!
It's a *super* super long-range shot!
WOULD SOMEONE GO BRING THOSE TWO BACK HERE?
Right away!
Let us do this!!
Detained by first-years.
I APOLOGIZE. THEY'RE SUCH CHILDREN.
BELIEVE IT OR NOT, ONE OF THEM IS OUR CAPTAIN.
NO, THAT'S ALL RIGHT.
I'LL TRY TO BE A LITTLE MORE CONSIDERATE MYSELF.
NO, IN FACT, IT WOULD BE PERFECTLY FINE IF YOU PLAYED EVEN HARDER.
...WHAT?

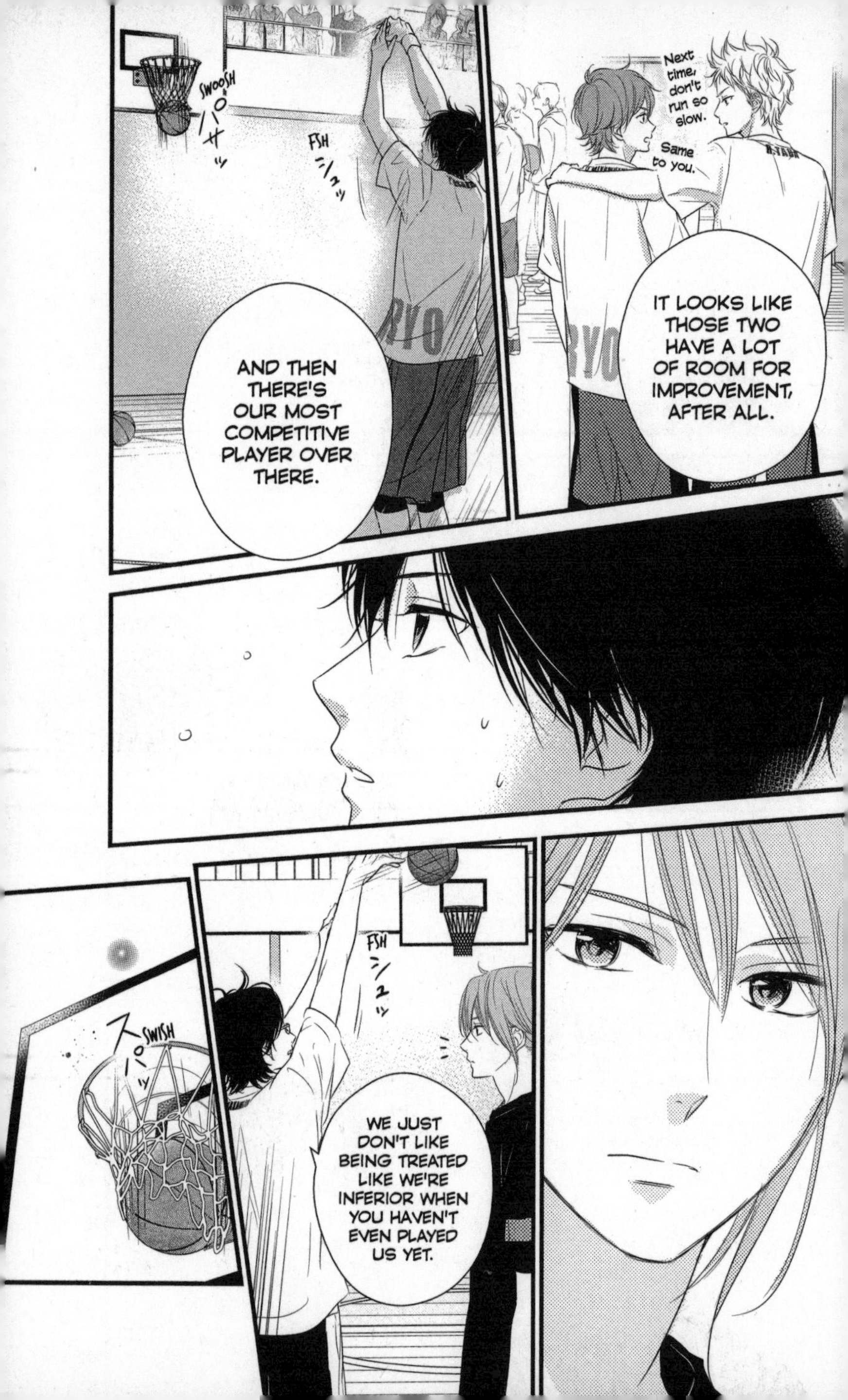
Next time, don't run so slow.
Same to you.
IT LOOKS LIKE THOSE TWO HAVE A LOT OF ROOM FOR IMPROVEMENT, AFTER ALL.
SWOOSH
パサッ
FSH
シュッ
AND THEN THERE'S OUR MOST COMPETITIVE PLAYER OVER THERE.
FSH
シュッ
WE JUST DON'T LIKE BEING TREATED LIKE WE'RE INFERIOR WHEN YOU HAVEN'T EVEN PLAYED US YET.
SWISH
スパッ

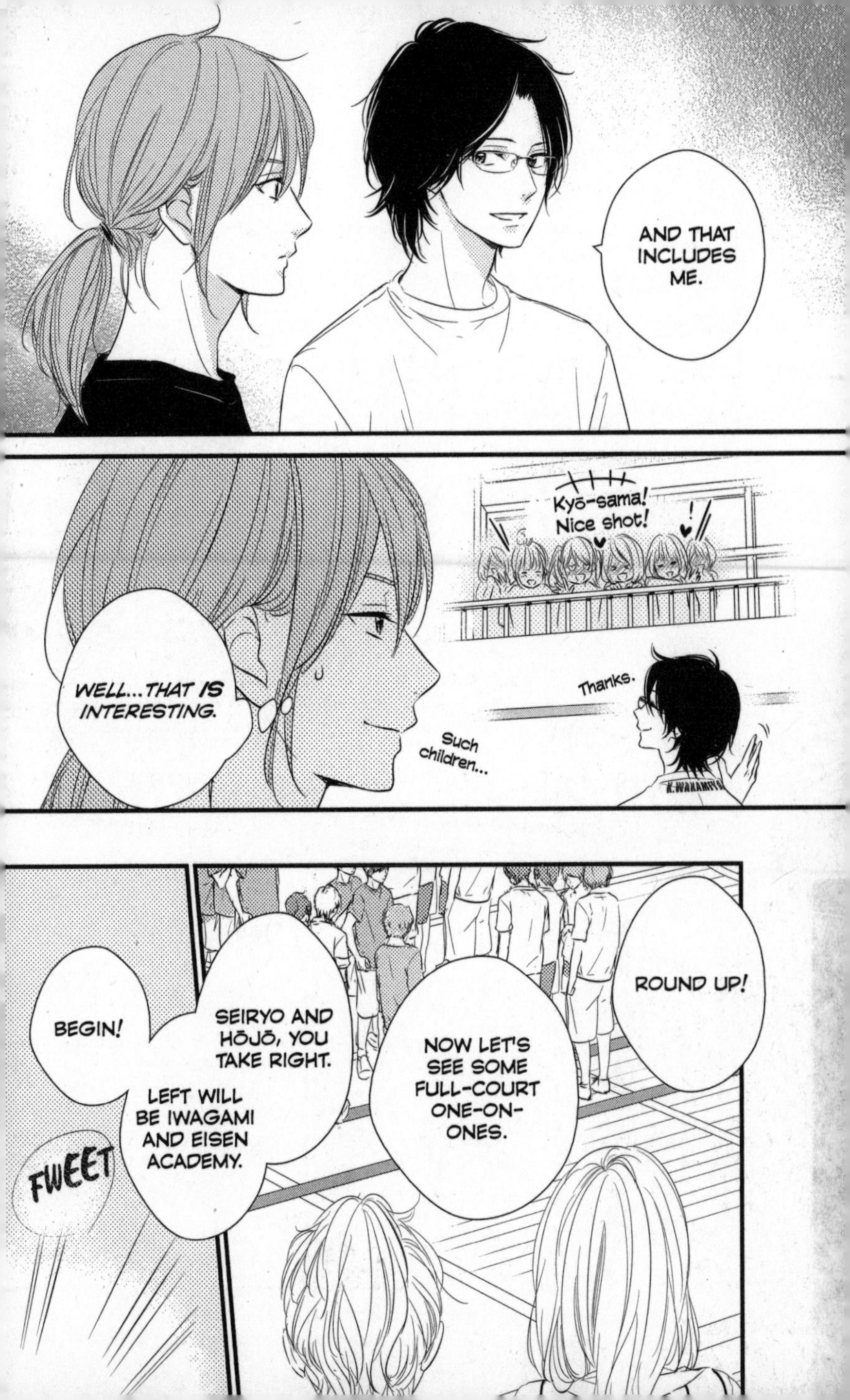
AND THAT INCLUDES ME.
Kyō-sama! Nice shot!
Thanks.
Such children...
WELL...THAT IS INTERESTING.
ROUND UP!
NOW LET'S SEE SOME FULL-COURT ONE-ON-ONES.
SEIRYO AND HŌJŌ, YOU TAKE RIGHT.
LEFT WILL BE IWAGAMI AND EISEN ACADEMY.
BEGIN!
FWEET

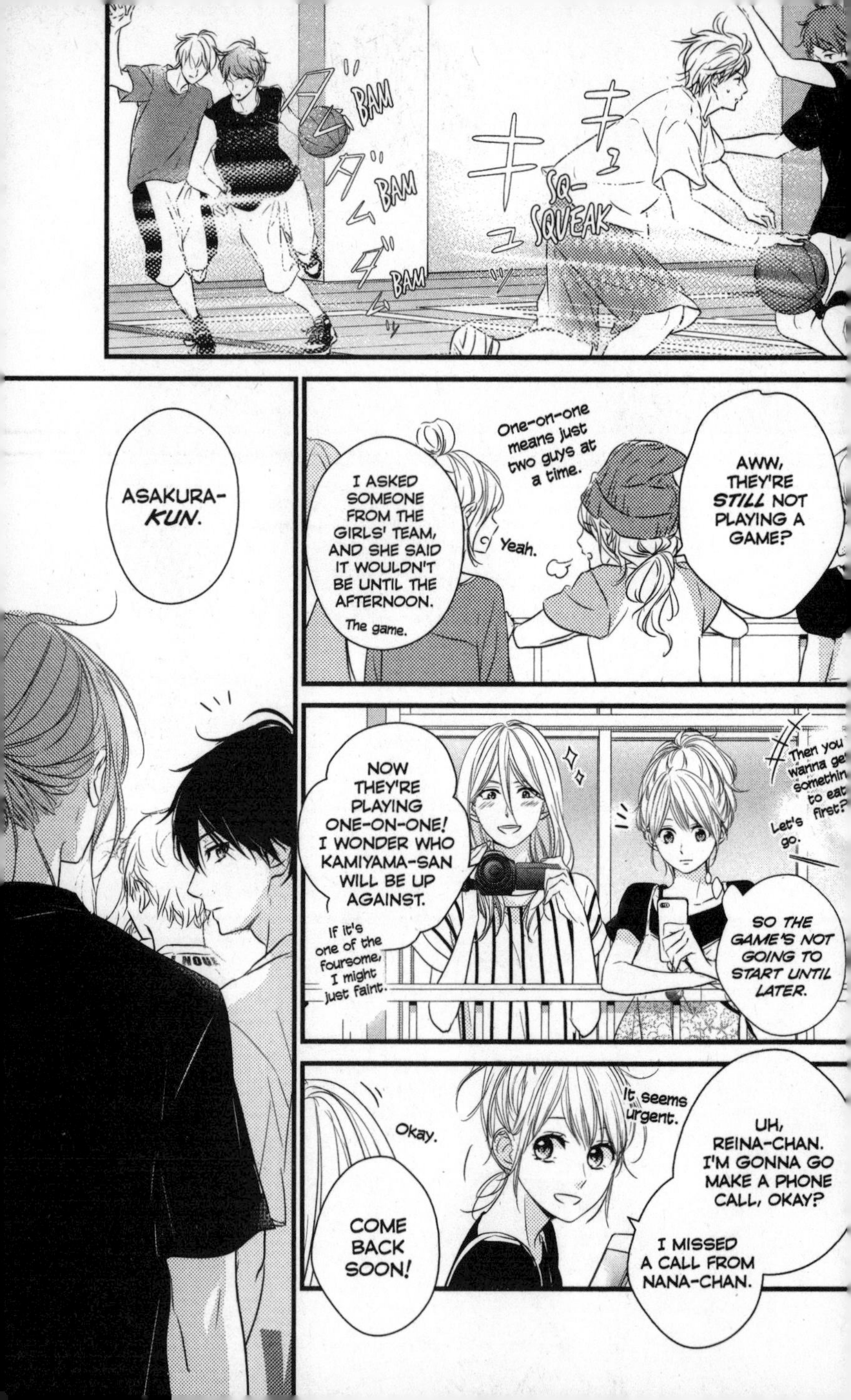
SQ-SQUEAK
BAM
BAM
BAM
AWW, THEY'RE *STILL* NOT PLAYING A GAME?
One-on-one means just two guys at a time.
Yeah.
I ASKED SOMEONE FROM THE GIRLS' TEAM, AND SHE SAID IT WOULDN'T BE UNTIL THE AFTERNOON.
The game.
Then you wanna ge somethin to eat first?
Let's go.
SO THE *GAME'S* NOT GOING TO START UNTIL LATER.
NOW THEY'RE PLAYING ONE-ON-ONE! I WONDER WHO KAMIYAMA-SAN WILL BE UP AGAINST.
If it's one of the foursome, I might just faint.
UH, REINA-CHAN. I'M GONNA GO MAKE A PHONE CALL, OKAY?
I MISSED A CALL FROM NANA-CHAN.
It seems urgent.
Okay.
COME BACK SOON!
ASAKURA-*KUN*.

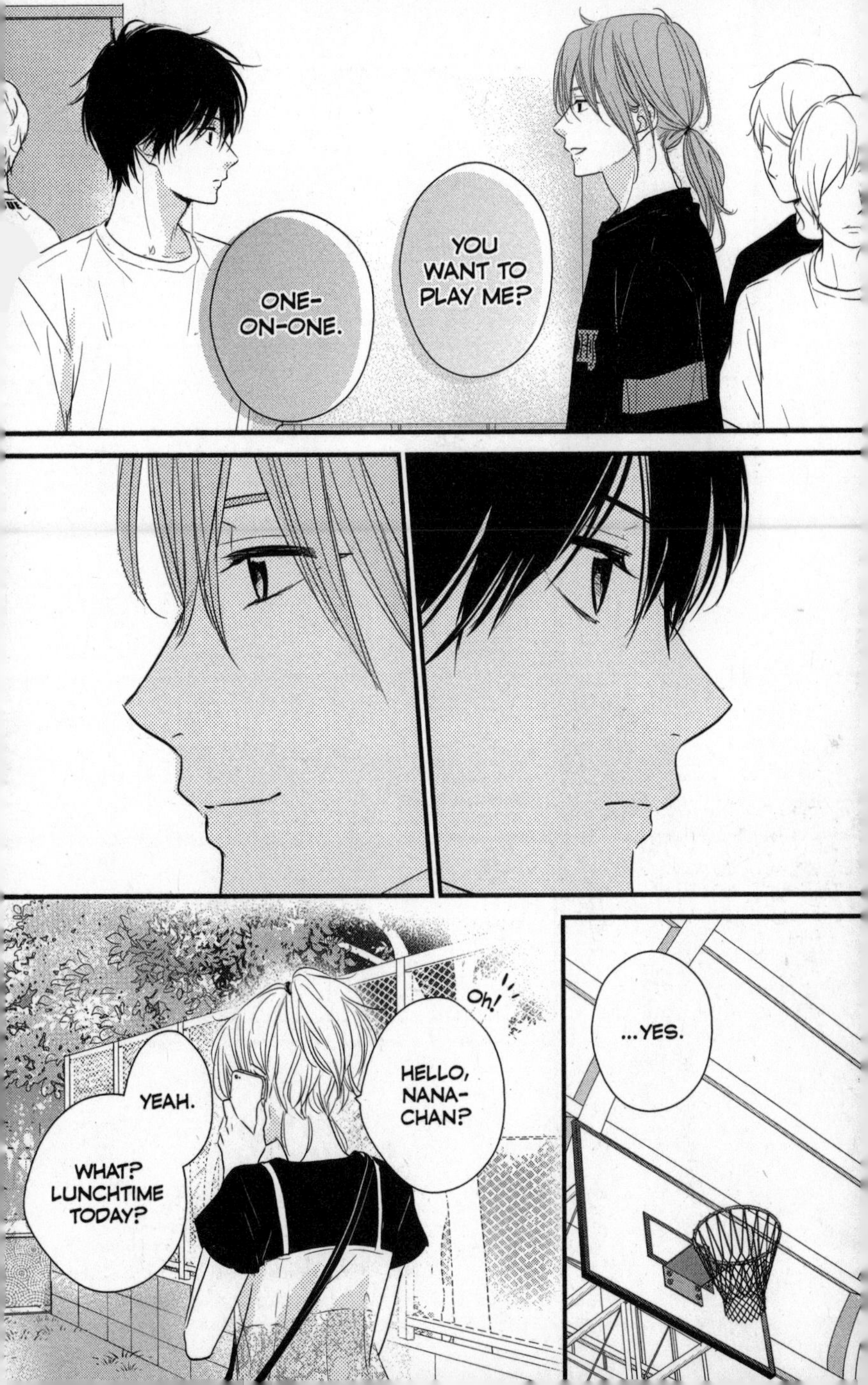
YOU WANT TO PLAY ME?
ONE-ON-ONE.
...YES.
Oh!
HELLO, NANA-CHAN?
YEAH.
WHAT? LUNCHTIME TODAY?

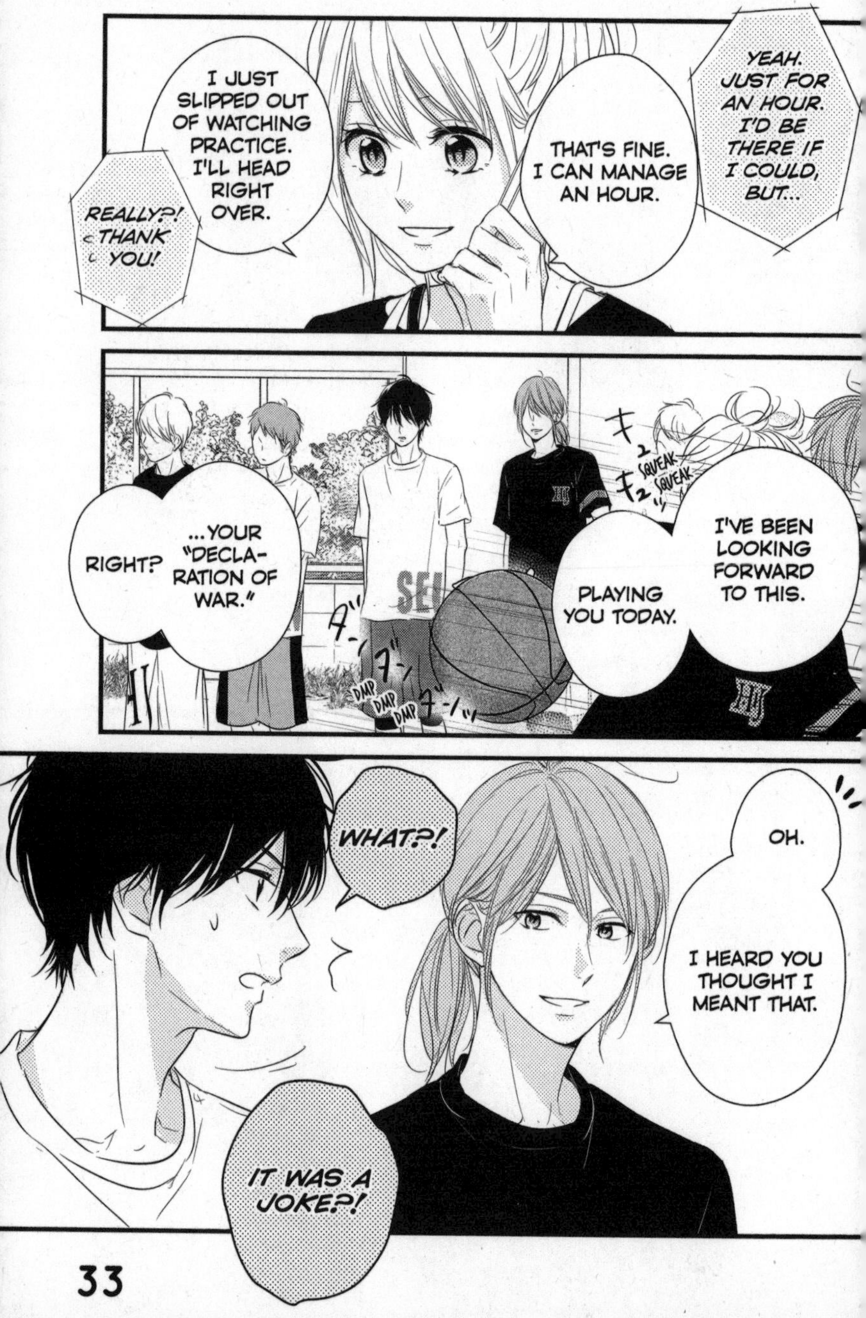
YEAH. JUST FOR AN HOUR. I'D BE THERE IF I COULD, BUT...
THAT'S FINE. I CAN MANAGE AN HOUR.
I JUST SLIPPED OUT OF WATCHING PRACTICE. I'LL HEAD RIGHT OVER.
REALLY?! THANK YOU!
SQUEAK SQUEAK
I'VE BEEN LOOKING FORWARD TO THIS.
PLAYING YOU TODAY.
...YOUR "DECLARATION OF WAR."
RIGHT?
DMP DMP DMP
OH.
I HEARD YOU THOUGHT I MEANT THAT.
WHAT?!
IT WAS A JOKE?!

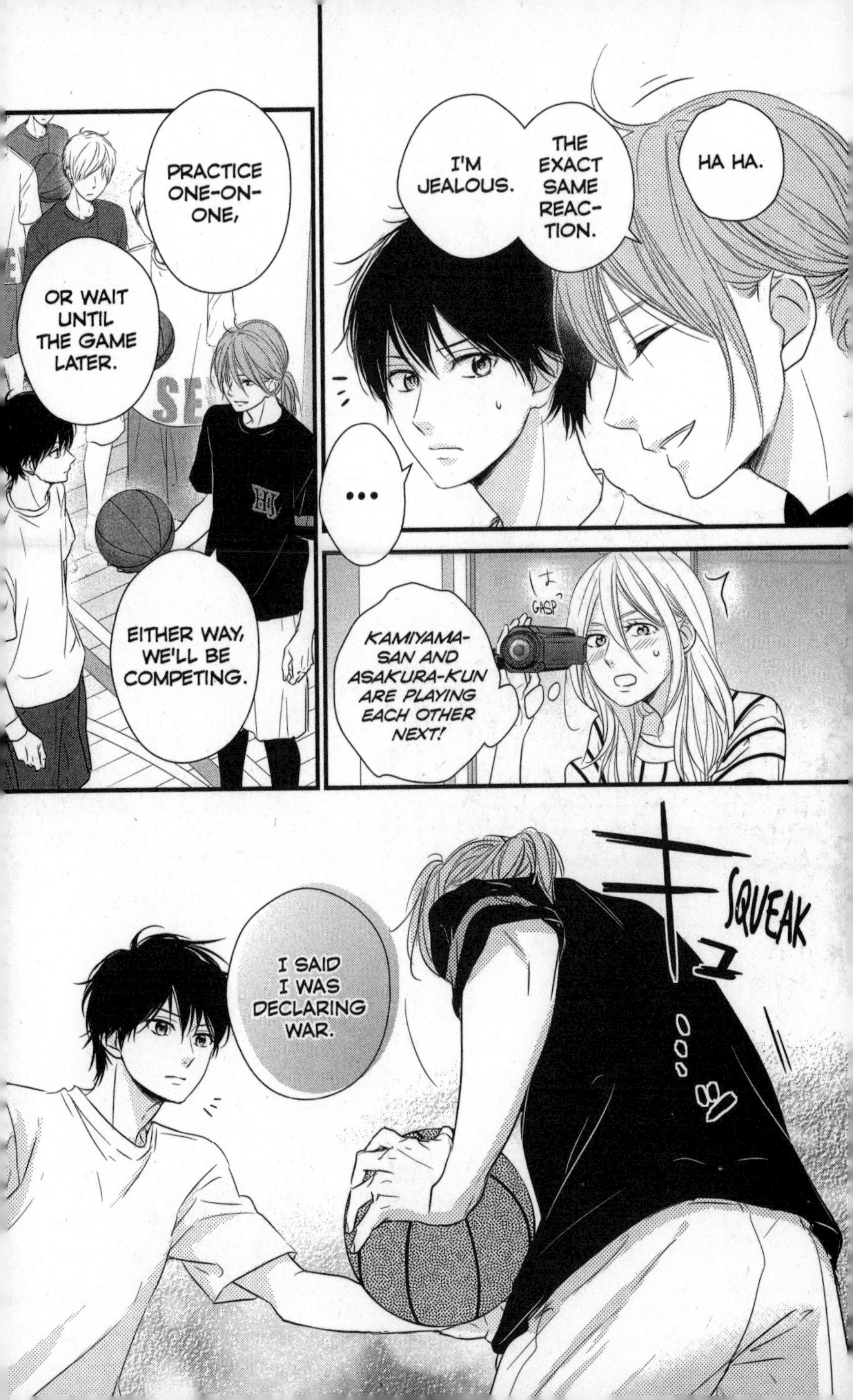
HA HA.
THE EXACT SAME REACTION.
I'M JEALOUS.
...
GASP
KAMIYAMA-SAN AND ASAKURA-KUN ARE PLAYING EACH OTHER NEXT!
PRACTICE ONE-ON-ONE,
OR WAIT UNTIL THE GAME LATER.
EITHER WAY, WE'LL BE COMPETING.
SQUEAK
I SAID I WAS DECLARING WAR.

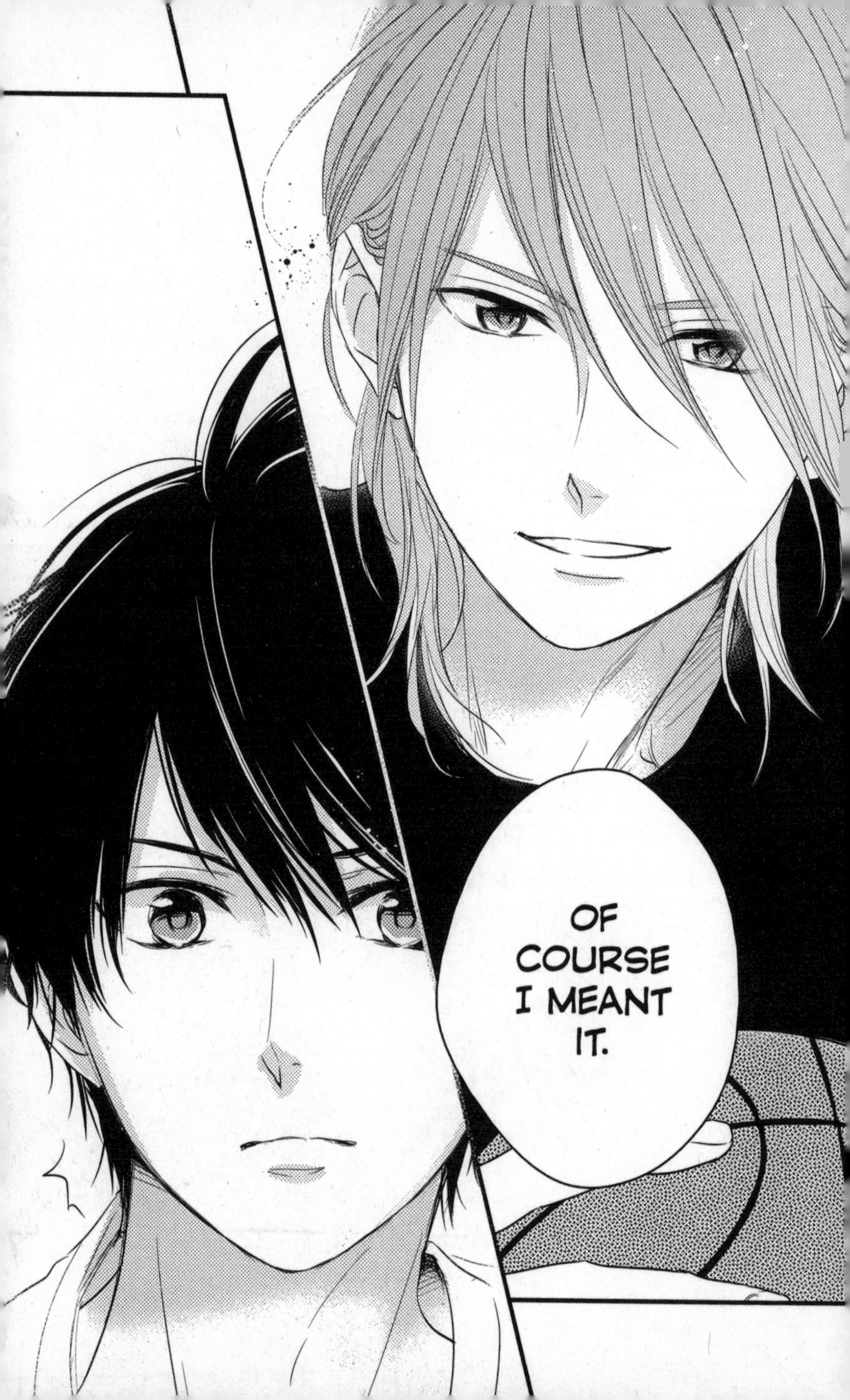
OF COURSE I MEANT IT.

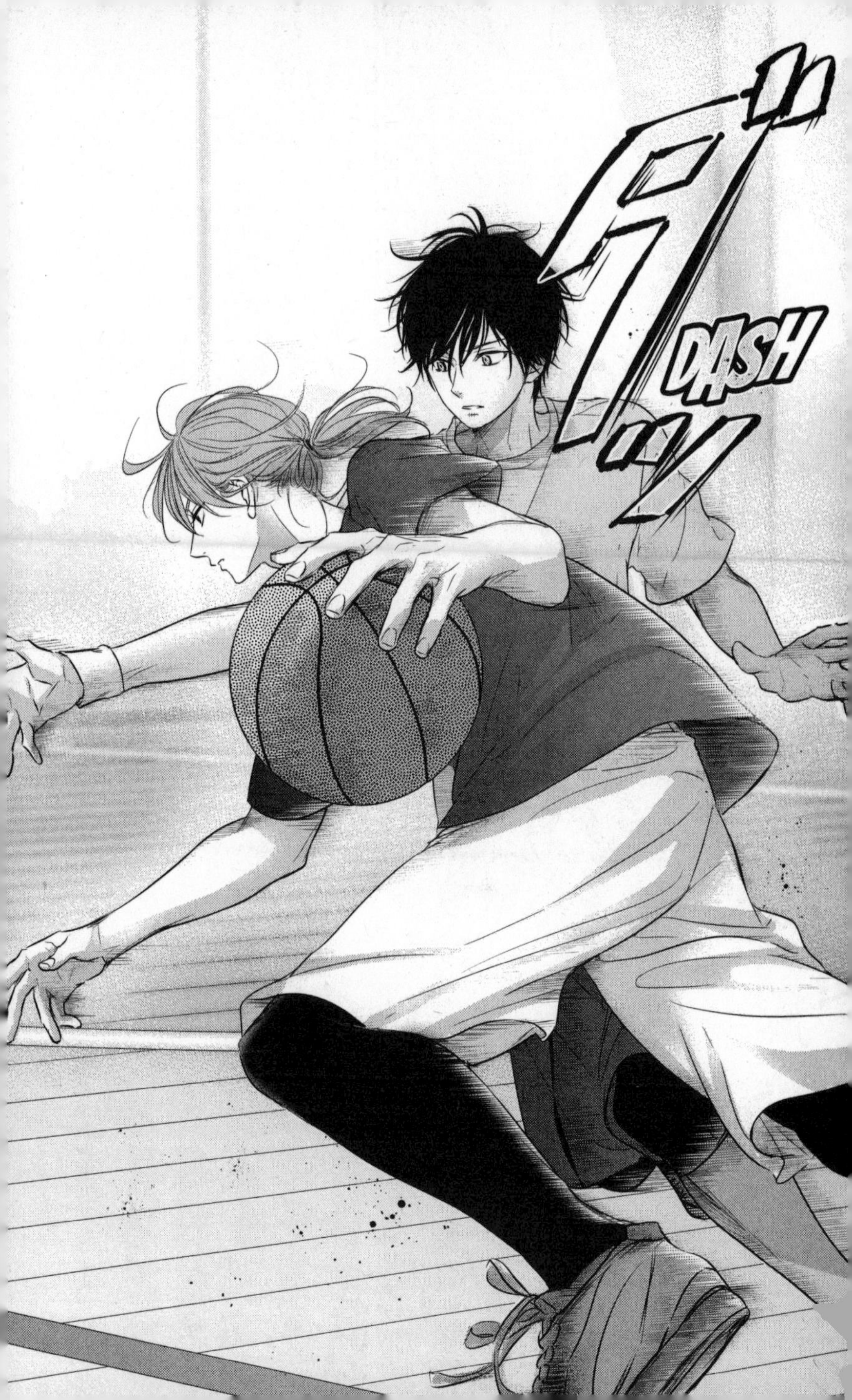
DASH

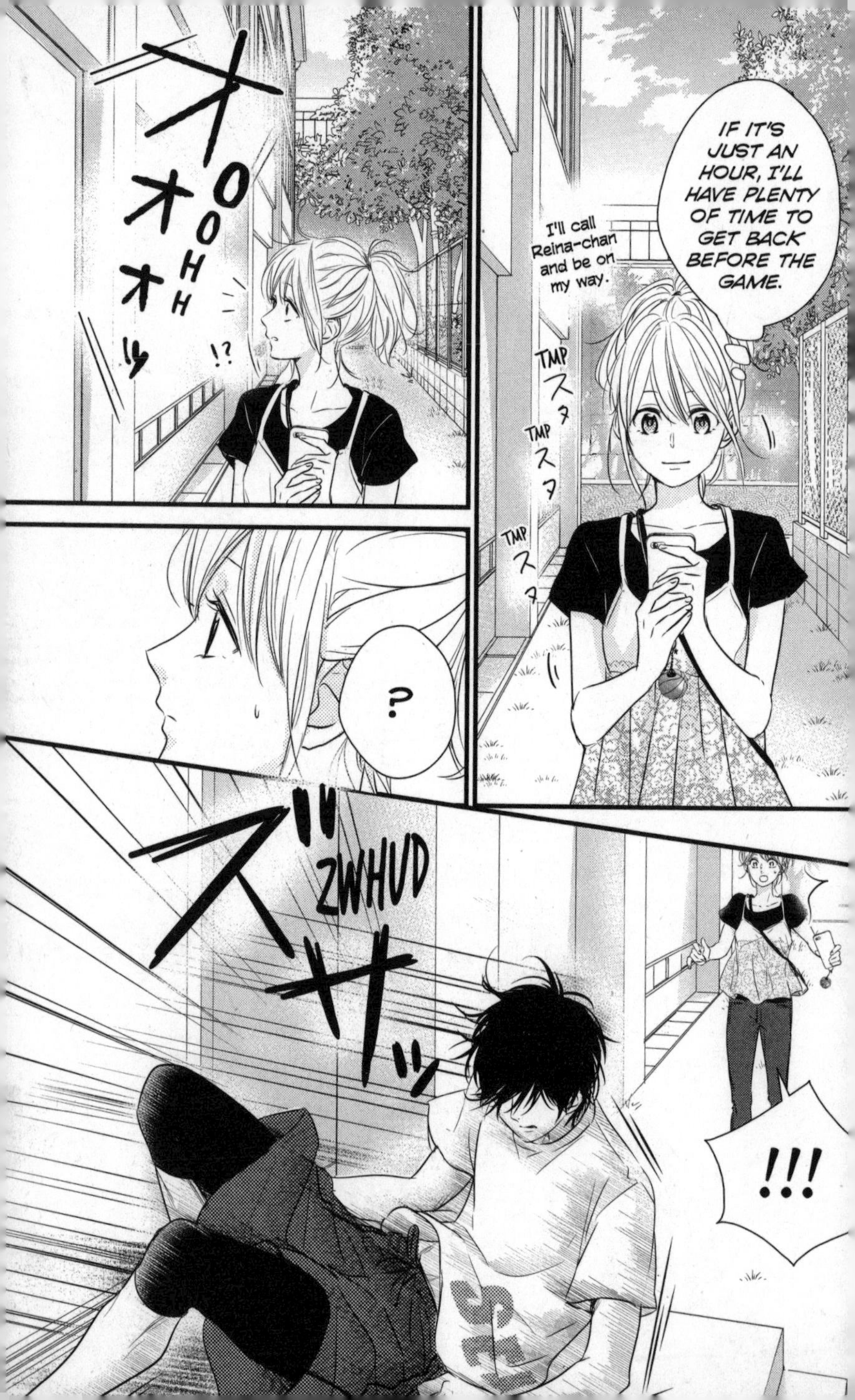
IF IT'S JUST AN HOUR, I'LL HAVE PLENTY OF TIME TO GET BACK BEFORE THE GAME.
I'll call Reina-chan and be on my way.
TMP スタ
TMP スタ
TMP スタ
オオオオッ
OOOHH
!?
?
ズザッ
ZWHUD
!!!

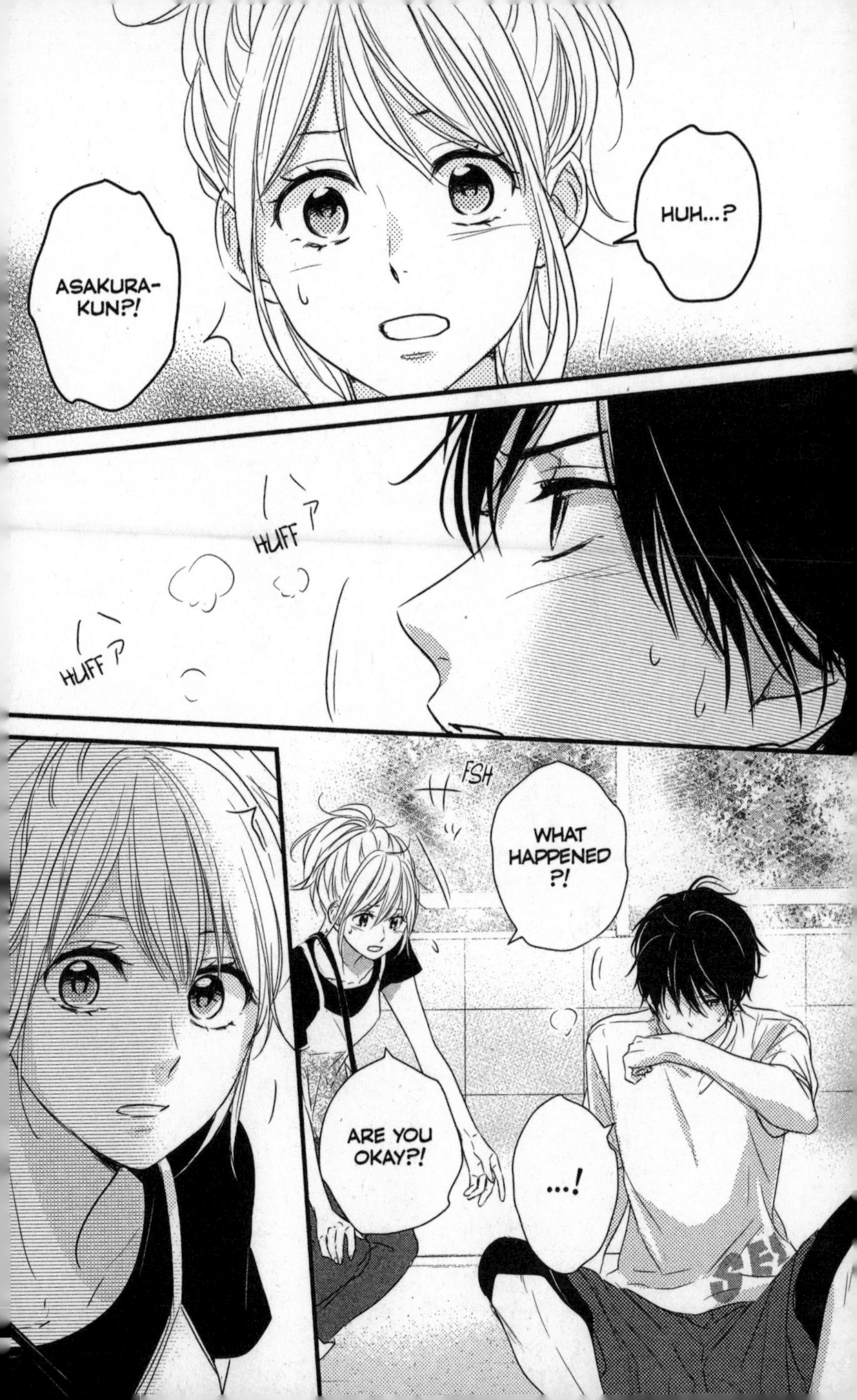
HUH...?
ASAKURA-KUN?!
HUFF
HUFF
FSH
WHAT HAPPENED ?!
ARE YOU OKAY?!
...!

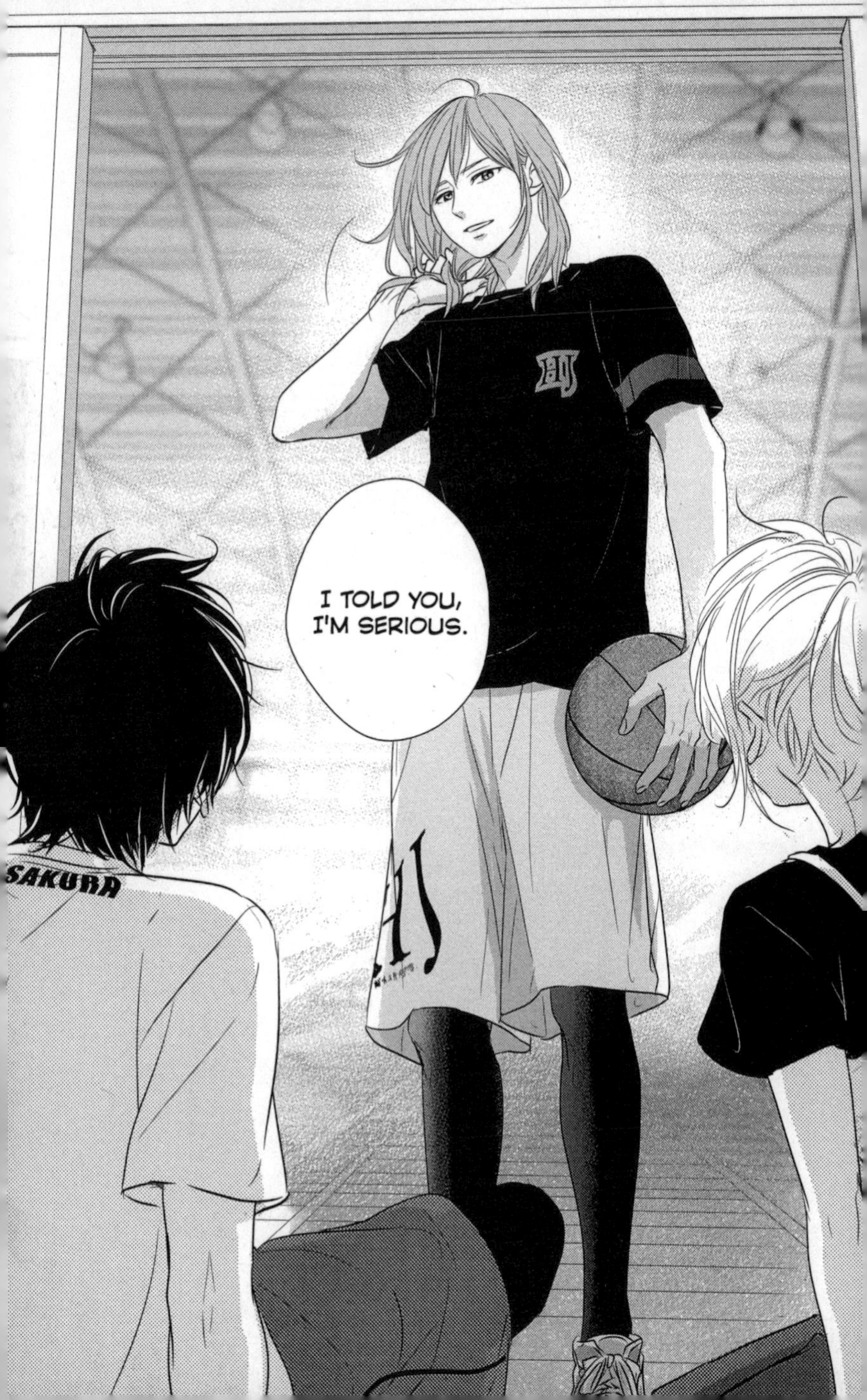
I TOLD YOU, I'M SERIOUS.
SAKURA

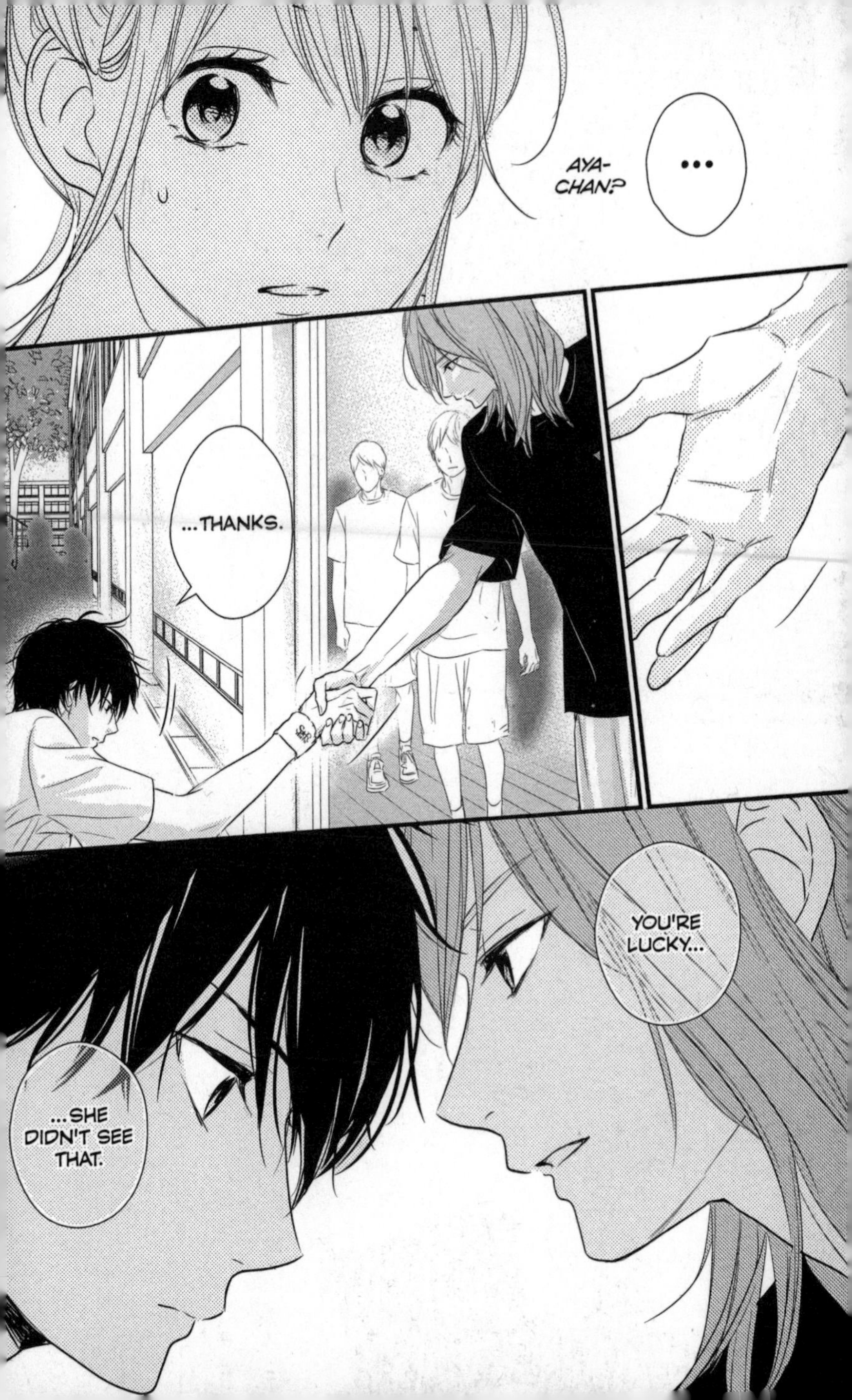
...
AYA-CHAN?
...THANKS.
YOU'RE LUCKY...
...SHE DIDN'T SEE THAT.

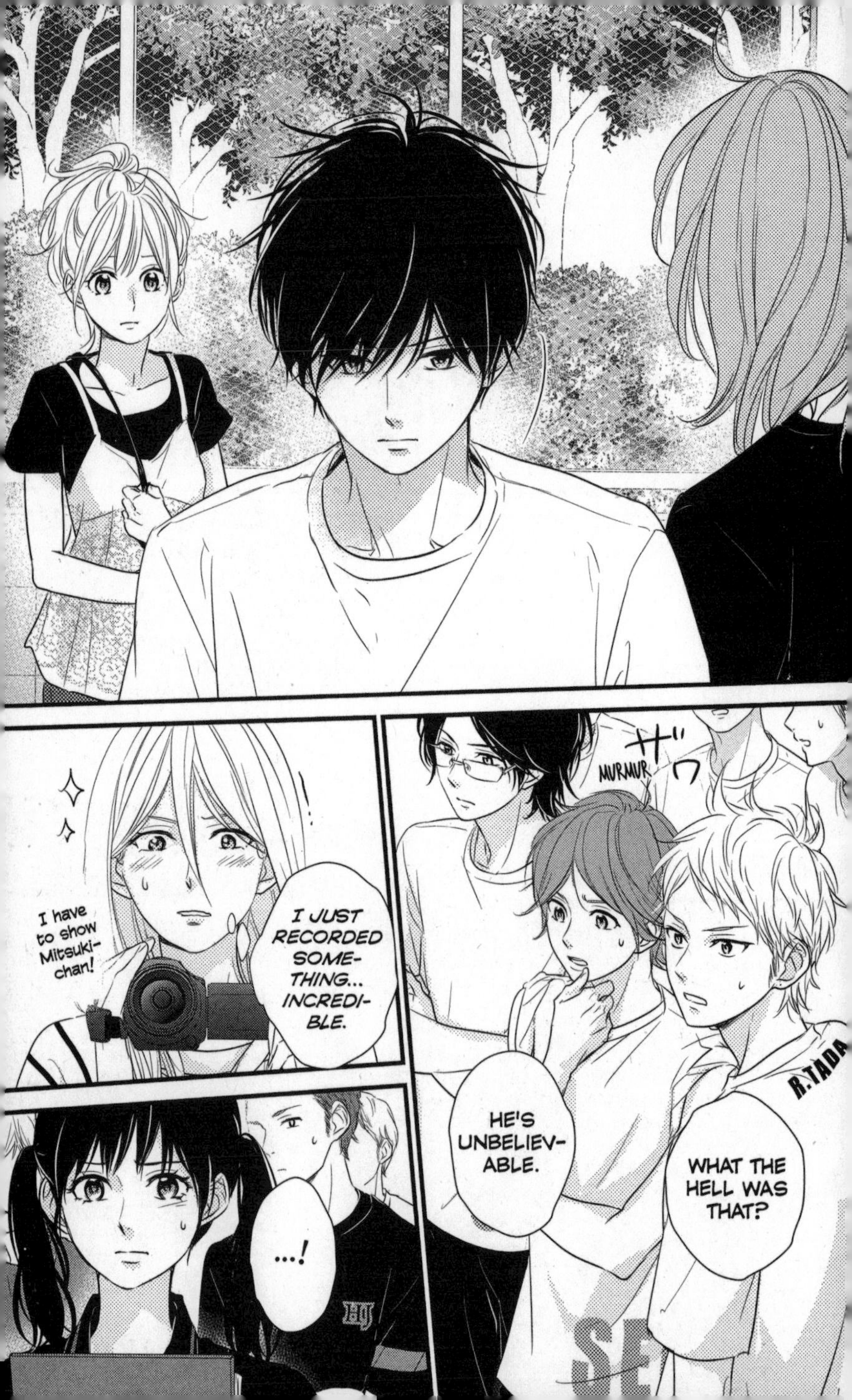
ザワ
MURMUR
WHAT THE HELL WAS THAT?
HE'S UNBELIEVABLE.
R.TADA
I JUST RECORDED SOMETHING... INCREDIBLE.
I have to show Mitsuki-chan!
...!

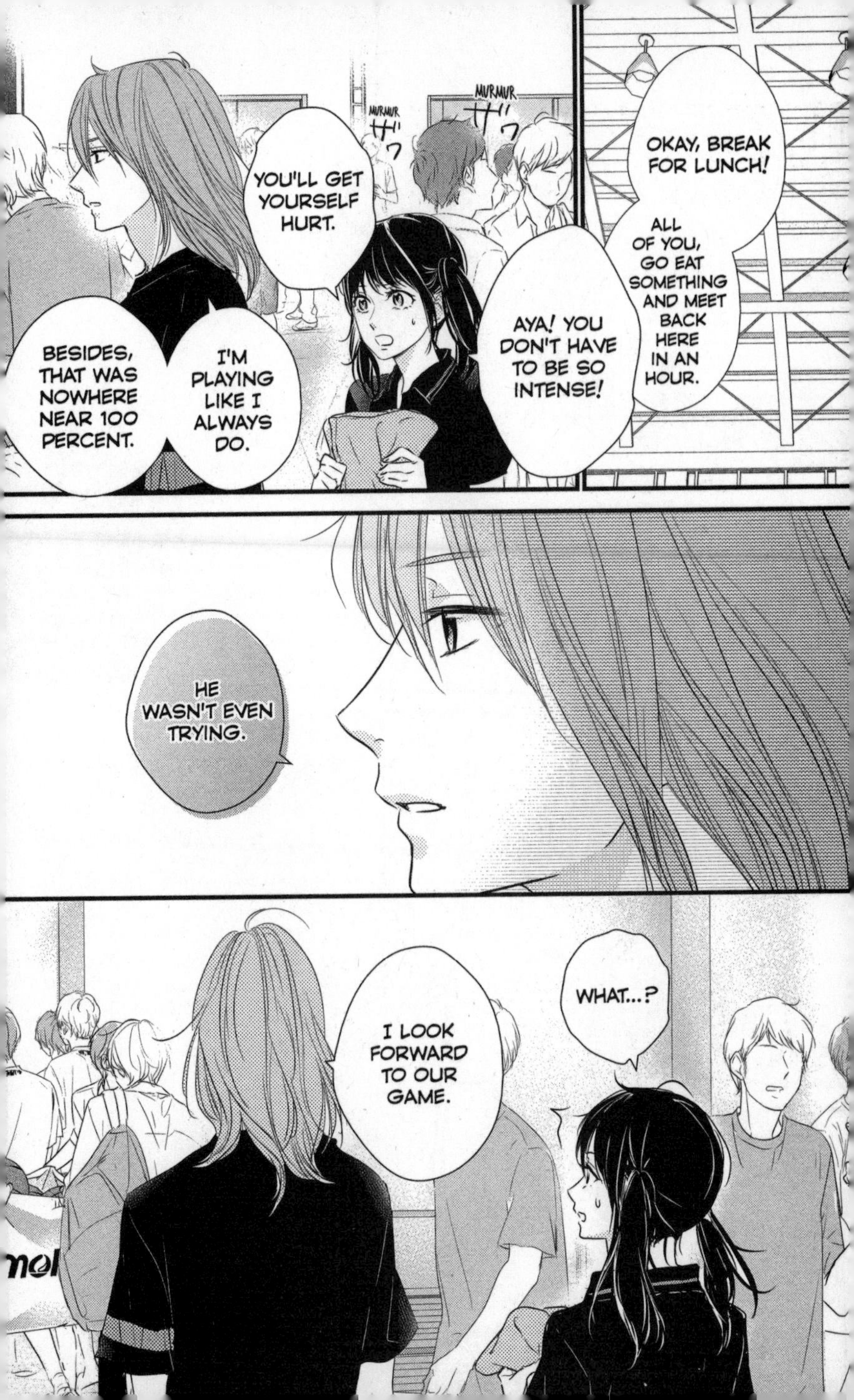
OKAY, BREAK FOR LUNCH!
ALL OF YOU, GO EAT SOMETHING AND MEET BACK HERE IN AN HOUR.
AYA! YOU DON'T HAVE TO BE SO INTENSE!
MURMUR ザワ
MURMUR ザワ
YOU'LL GET YOURSELF HURT.
I'M PLAYING LIKE I ALWAYS DO.
BESIDES, THAT WAS NOWHERE NEAR 100 PERCENT.
HE WASN'T EVEN TRYING.
I LOOK FORWARD TO OUR GAME.
WHAT...?

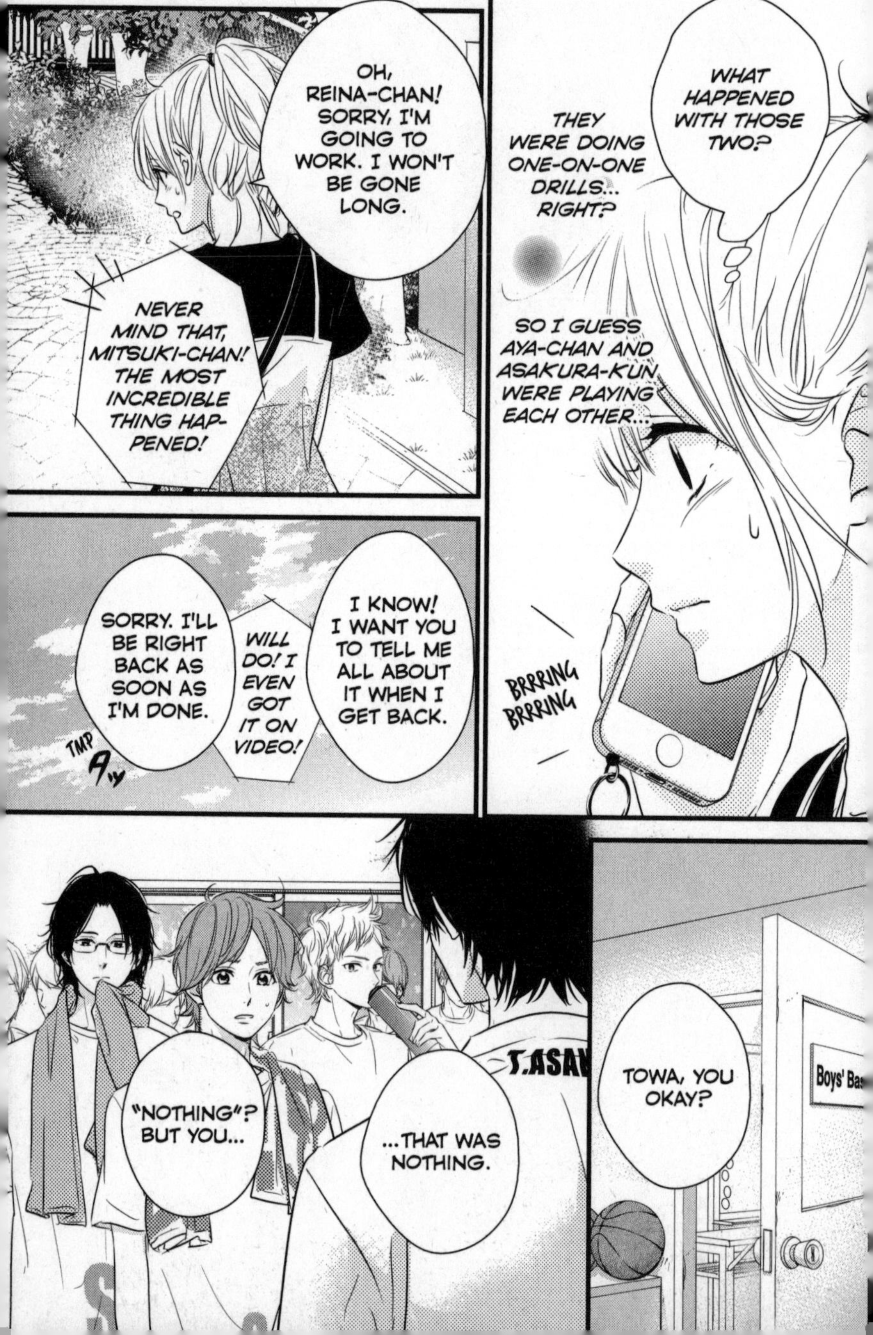
WHAT HAPPENED WITH THOSE TWO?
THEY WERE DOING ONE-ON-ONE DRILLS... RIGHT?
SO I GUESS AYA-CHAN AND ASAKURA-KUN WERE PLAYING EACH OTHER...
BRRRING BRRRING
OH, REINA-CHAN! SORRY, I'M GOING TO WORK. I WON'T BE GONE LONG.
NEVER MIND THAT, MITSUKI-CHAN! THE MOST INCREDIBLE THING HAP-PENED!
I KNOW! I WANT YOU TO TELL ME ALL ABOUT IT WHEN I GET BACK.
WILL DO! I EVEN GOT IT ON VIDEO!
SORRY. I'LL BE RIGHT BACK AS SOON AS I'M DONE.
TMP
TOWA, YOU OKAY?
...THAT WAS NOTHING.
"NOTHING"? BUT YOU...

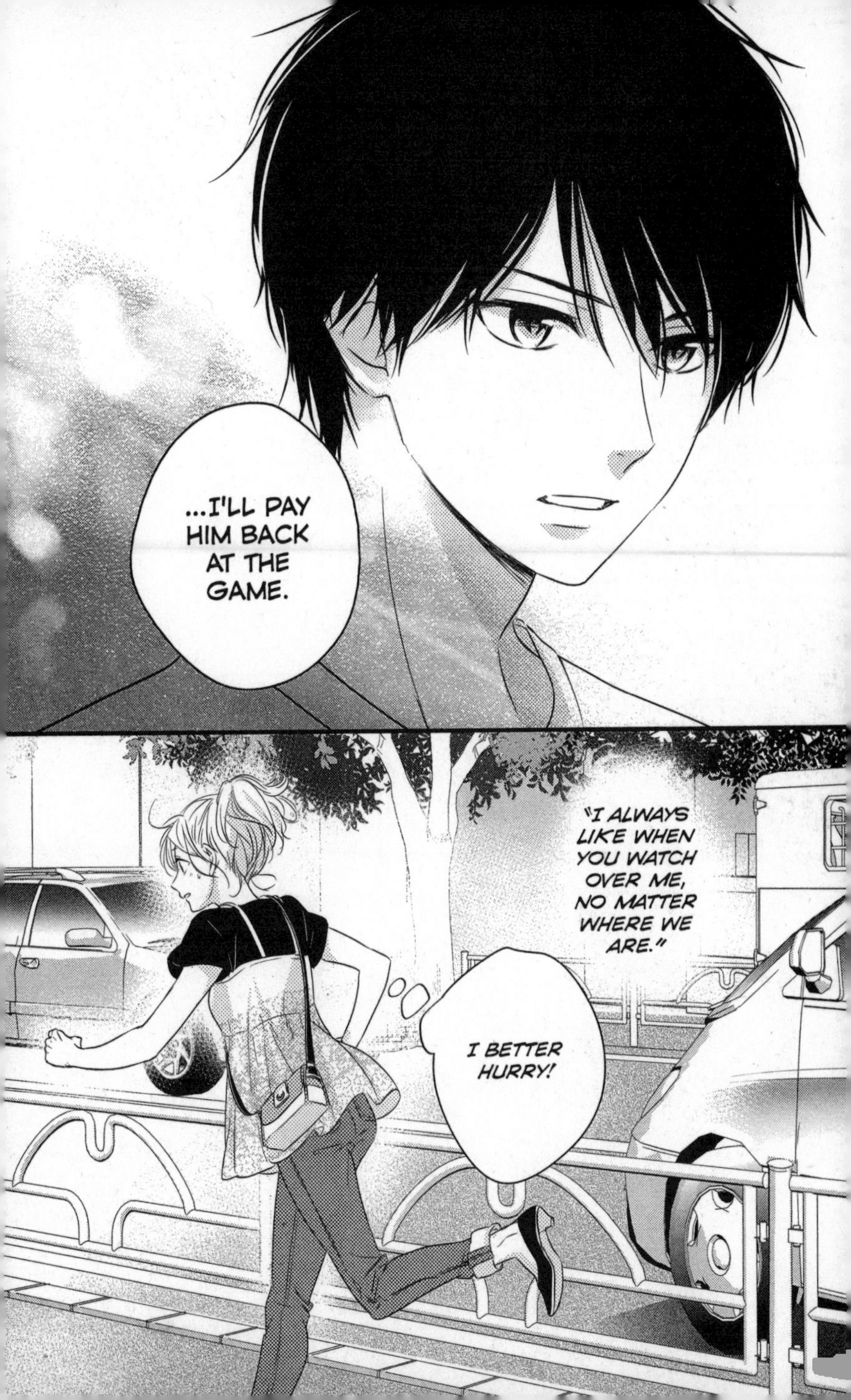
...I'LL PAY HIM BACK AT THE GAME.
"I ALWAYS LIKE WHEN YOU WATCH OVER ME, NO MATTER WHERE WE ARE."
I BETTER HURRY!

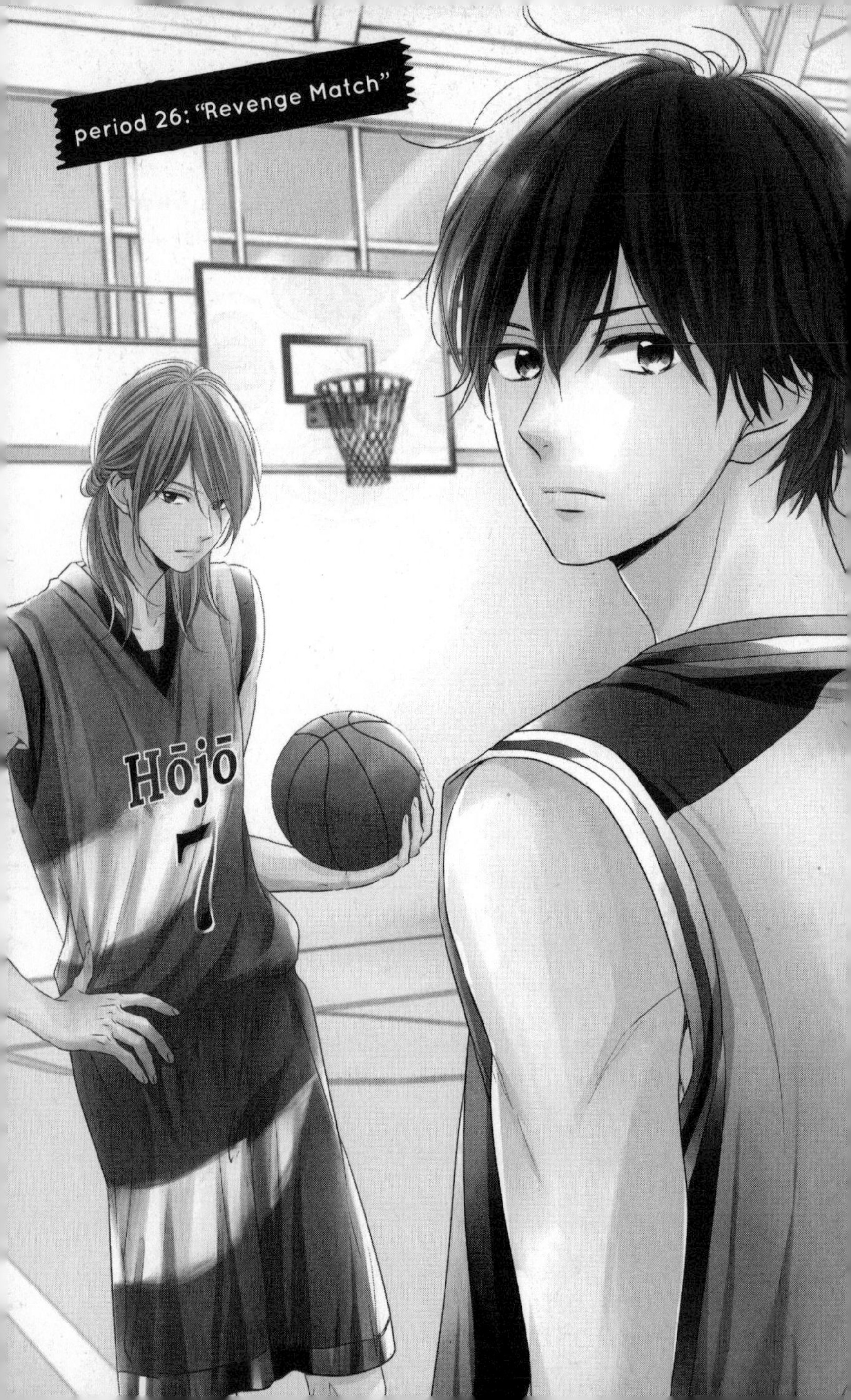
period 26: "Revenge Match"
Hōjō
7

~ About this volume's bonus manga ~

When Volume 5 came out, we had a *Waiting for Spring* character popularity vote on Twitter, and now, for the end of this volume, I've written a bonus manga starring the winner.

And so, the number one most popular character was this guy! Towa!

↓

Congratulations!!

The cover of Dessert October Issue

Incidentally, second was Aya-chan, third: Rui, fourth: Kyōsuke, fifth: Mitsuki, sixth: Ryūji...etc.
And those were the results.

So we added a mini-manga about Towa to the end of this volume.
Please enjoy it.
(The most difficult character. Ha ha)

Thank you so much to everyone who voted! ♢♢

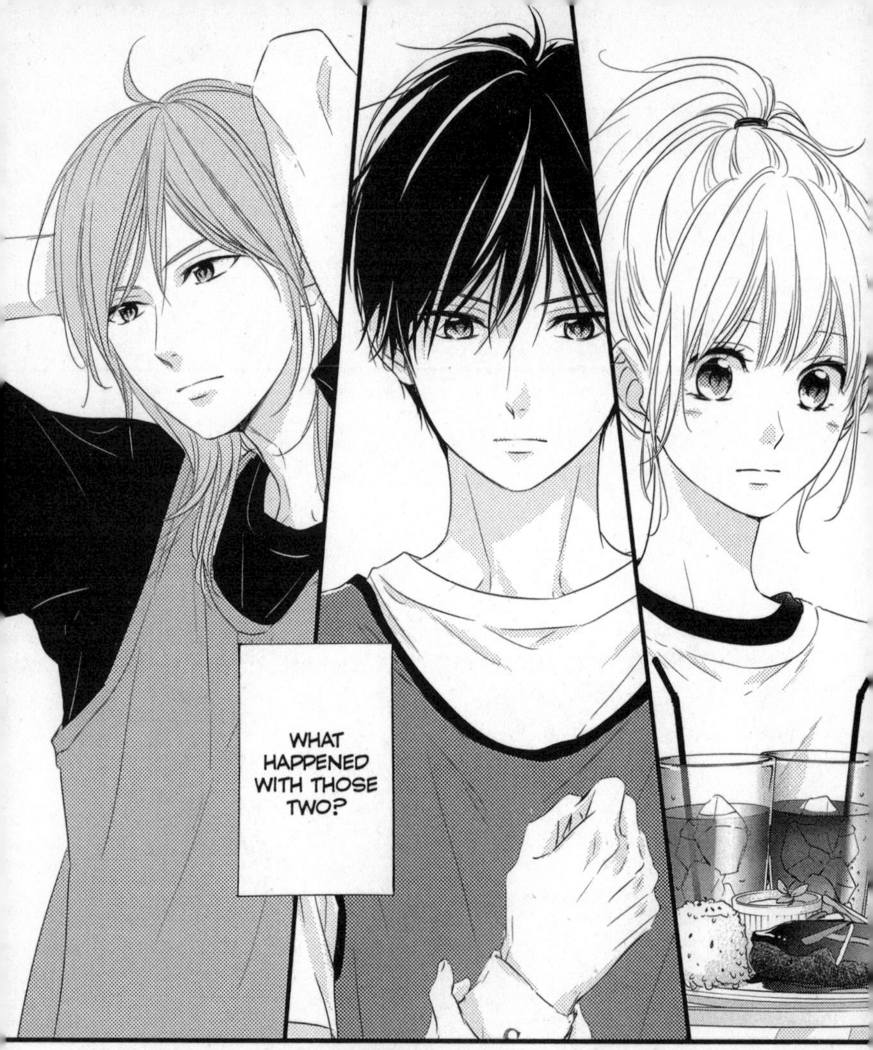
WHAT HAPPENED WITH THOSE TWO?

What do you think of the voting results? It was pretty much what you expected...or was it? I've often been asked who my favorite *Waiting for Spring* character is, and after having this popularity vote, I have decided on a definite winner.

It was this guy →

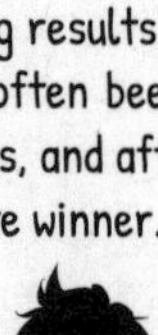

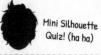

Mini Silhouette Quiz! (ha ha)

The answer is on the next summary space (p.86)

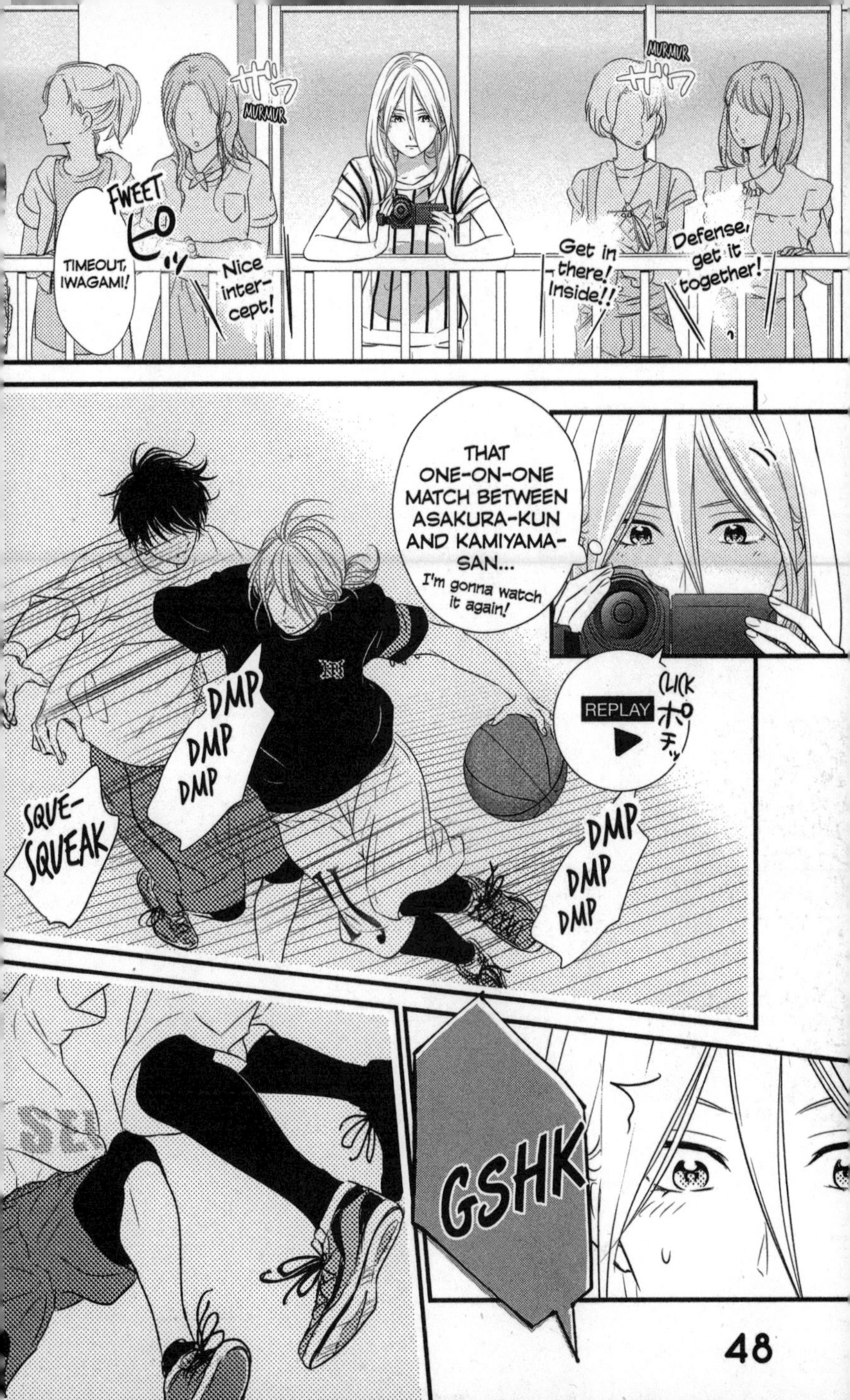

Defense, get it together!
MURMUR
ザワ
Get in there! Inside!!
ザワ
MURMUR
Nice intercept!
FWEET
ピッ
TIMEOUT, IWAGAMI!
THAT ONE-ON-ONE MATCH BETWEEN ASAKURA-KUN AND KAMIYAMA-SAN...
I'm gonna watch it again!
CLICK
ポチッ
REPLAY
DMP DMP DMP
DMP DMP DMP
SQUE-SQUEAK
GSHK

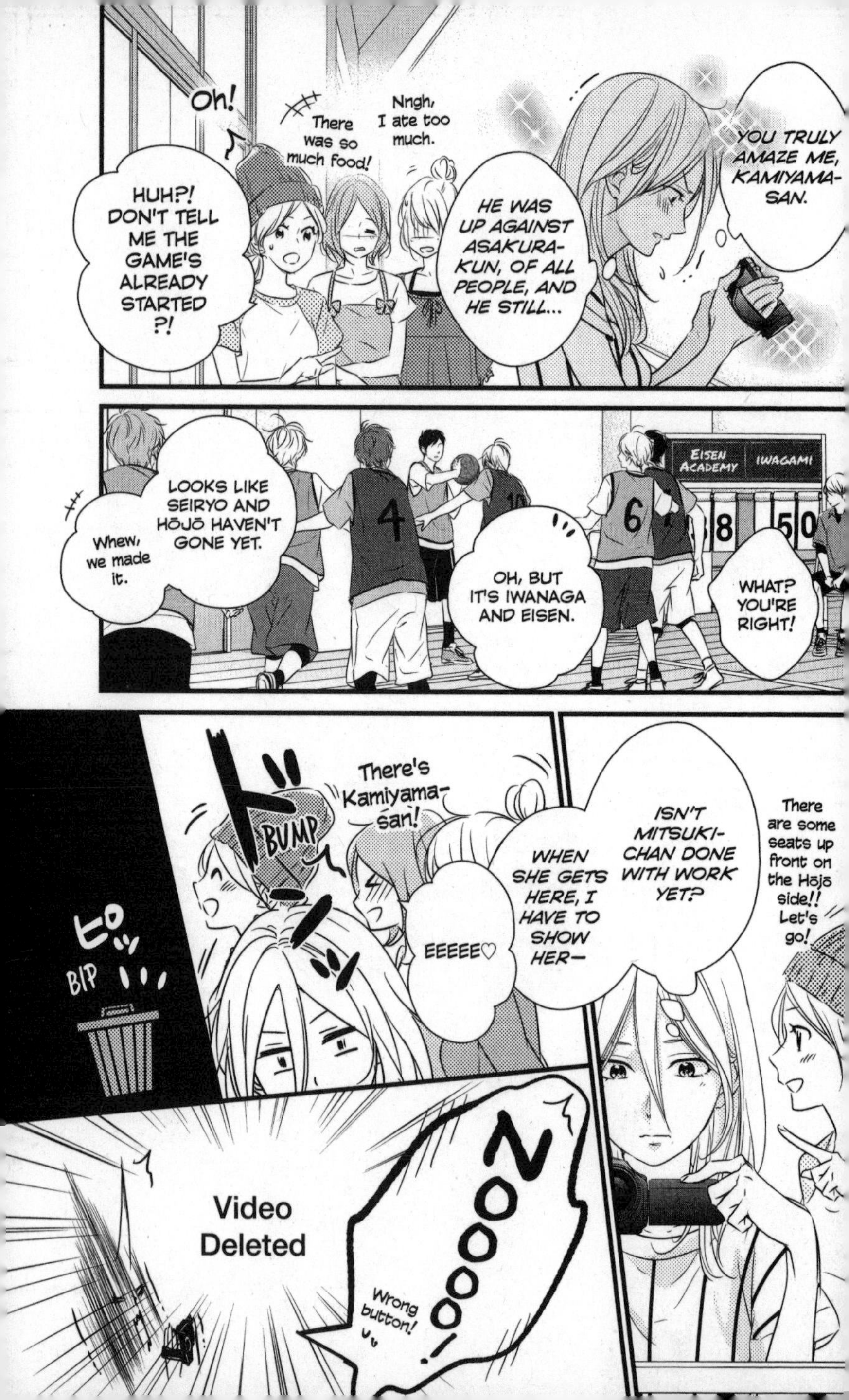
YOU TRULY AMAZE ME, KAMIYAMA-SAN.
HE WAS UP AGAINST ASAKURA-KUN, OF ALL PEOPLE, AND HE STILL...
Nngh, I ate too much.
There was so much food!
Oh!
HUH?! DON'T TELL ME THE GAME'S ALREADY STARTED?!
EISEN ACADEMY
IWAGAMI
WHAT? YOU'RE RIGHT!
OH, BUT IT'S IWANAGA AND EISEN.
LOOKS LIKE SEIRYO AND HŌJŌ HAVEN'T GONE YET.
Whew, we made it.
There are some seats up front on the Hōjō side!! Let's go!
ISN'T MITSUKI-CHAN DONE WITH WORK YET?
WHEN SHE GETS HERE, I HAVE TO SHOW HER—
EEEEE♡
There's Kamiyama-san!
BUMP
ピッ
BIP
NOOOOO!
Wrong button!
Video Deleted

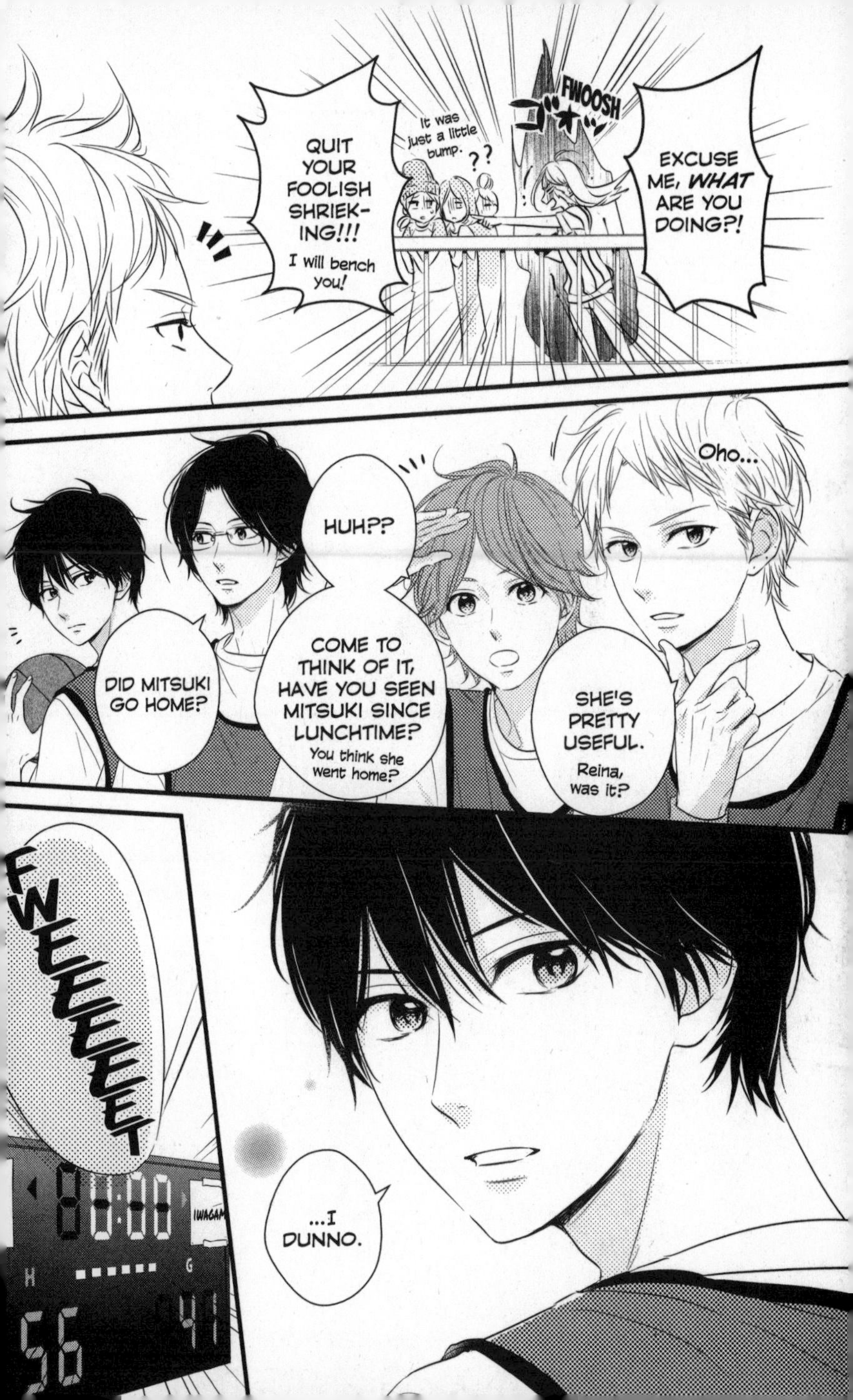
EXCUSE ME, *WHAT* ARE YOU DOING?!
FWOOSH
It was just a little bump.
??
QUIT YOUR FOOLISH SHRIEK-ING!!!
I will bench you!
Oho...
SHE'S PRETTY USEFUL.
Reina, was it?
HUH??
COME TO THINK OF IT, HAVE YOU SEEN MITSUKI SINCE LUNCHTIME?
You think she went home?
DID MITSUKI GO HOME?
...I DUNNO.
FWEEEEEET
IWAGAM
56
41

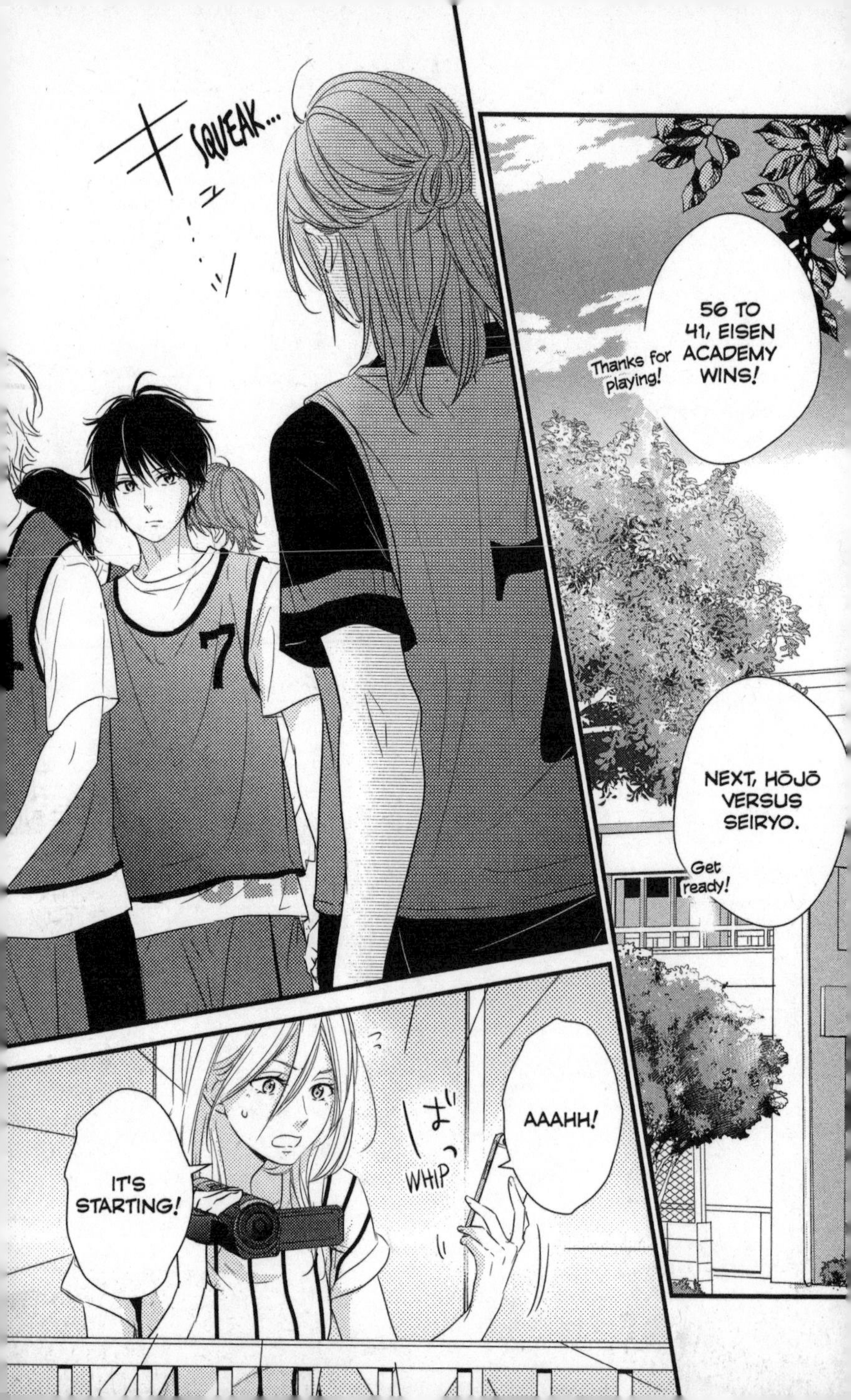
56 TO 41, EISEN ACADEMY WINS!
Thanks for playing!
NEXT, HŌJŌ VERSUS SEIRYO.
Get ready!
SQUEAK...
AAAHH!
WHIP
IT'S STARTING!

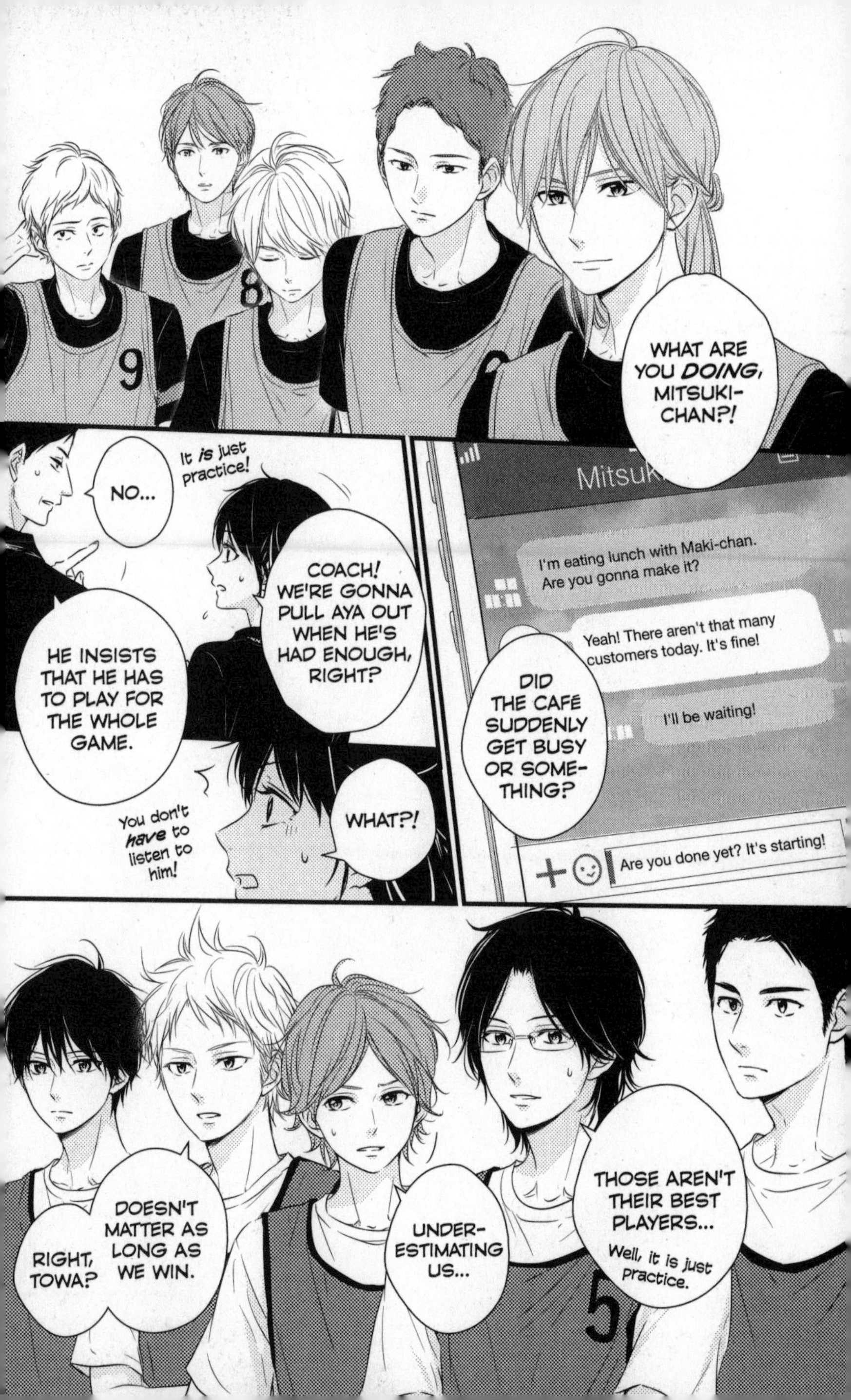
WHAT ARE YOU DOING, MITSUKI-CHAN?!
I'm eating lunch with Maki-chan. Are you gonna make it?
Yeah! There aren't that many customers today. It's fine!
I'll be waiting!
Are you done yet? It's starting!
DID THE CAFE SUDDENLY GET BUSY OR SOMETHING?
COACH! WE'RE GONNA PULL AYA OUT WHEN HE'S HAD ENOUGH, RIGHT?
It is just practice!
NO...
HE INSISTS THAT HE HAS TO PLAY FOR THE WHOLE GAME.
WHAT?!
You don't have to listen to him!
THOSE AREN'T THEIR BEST PLAYERS...
Well, it is just practice.
UNDER-ESTIMATING US...
DOESN'T MATTER AS LONG AS WE WIN.
RIGHT, TOWA?

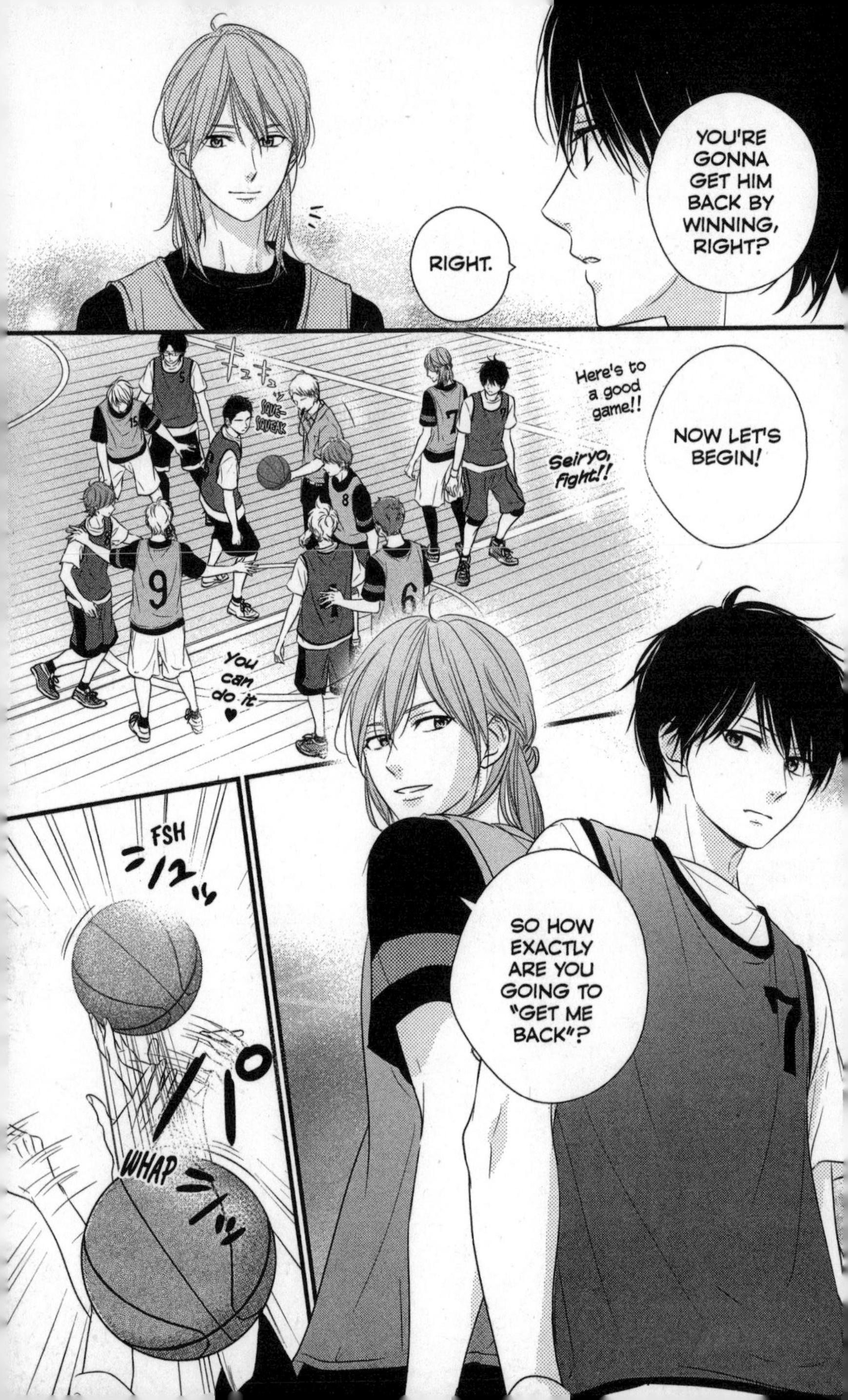
YOU'RE GONNA GET HIM BACK BY WINNING, RIGHT?
RIGHT.
NOW LET'S BEGIN!
Here's to a good game!!
Seiryo, fight!!
SQUE-SQUEAK
You can do it ♥
SO HOW EXACTLY ARE YOU GOING TO "GET ME BACK"?
FSH
WHAP

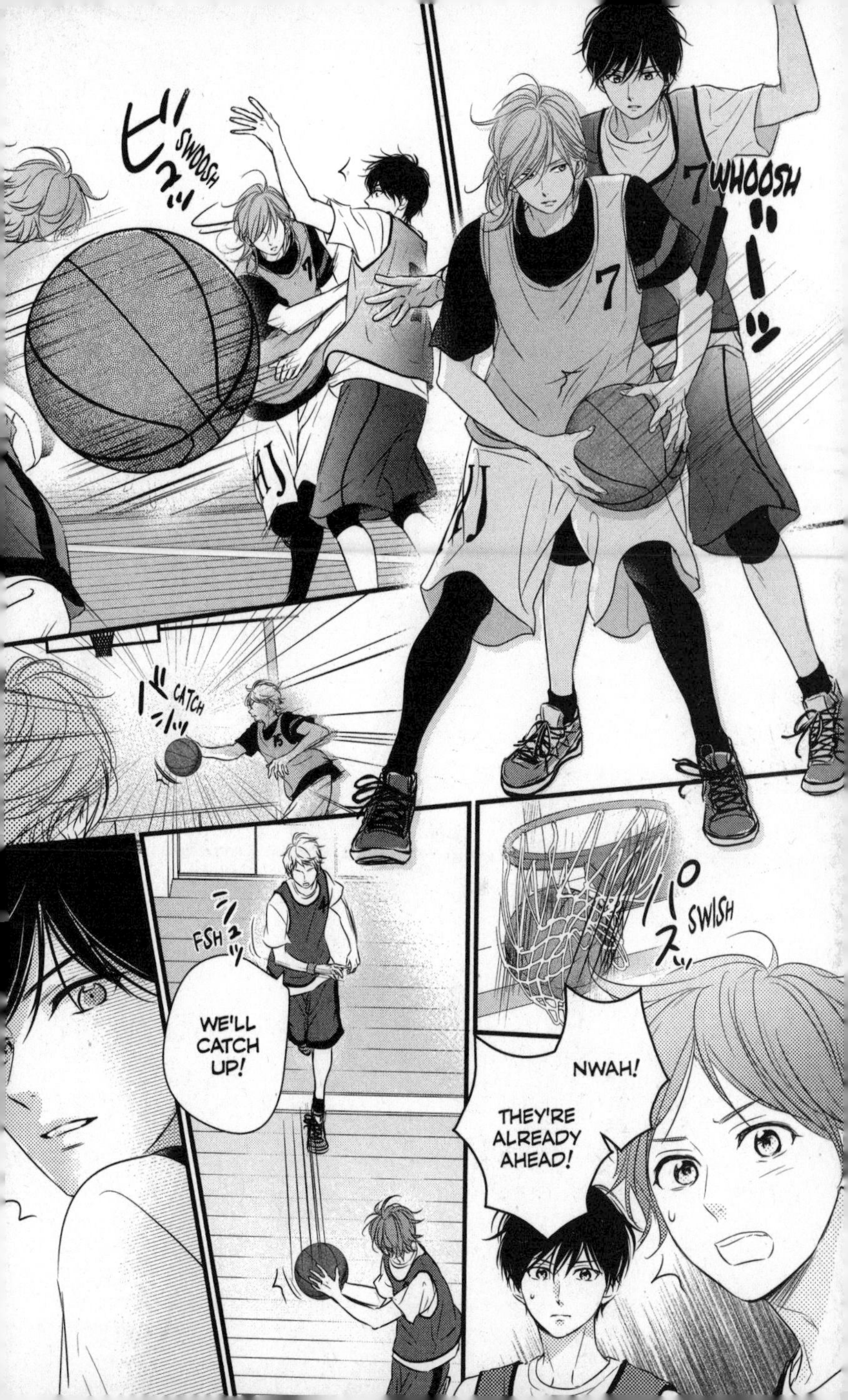
WHOOSH
SWOOSH
CATCH
SWISH
NWAH!
THEY'RE ALREADY AHEAD!
FSH
WE'LL CATCH UP!

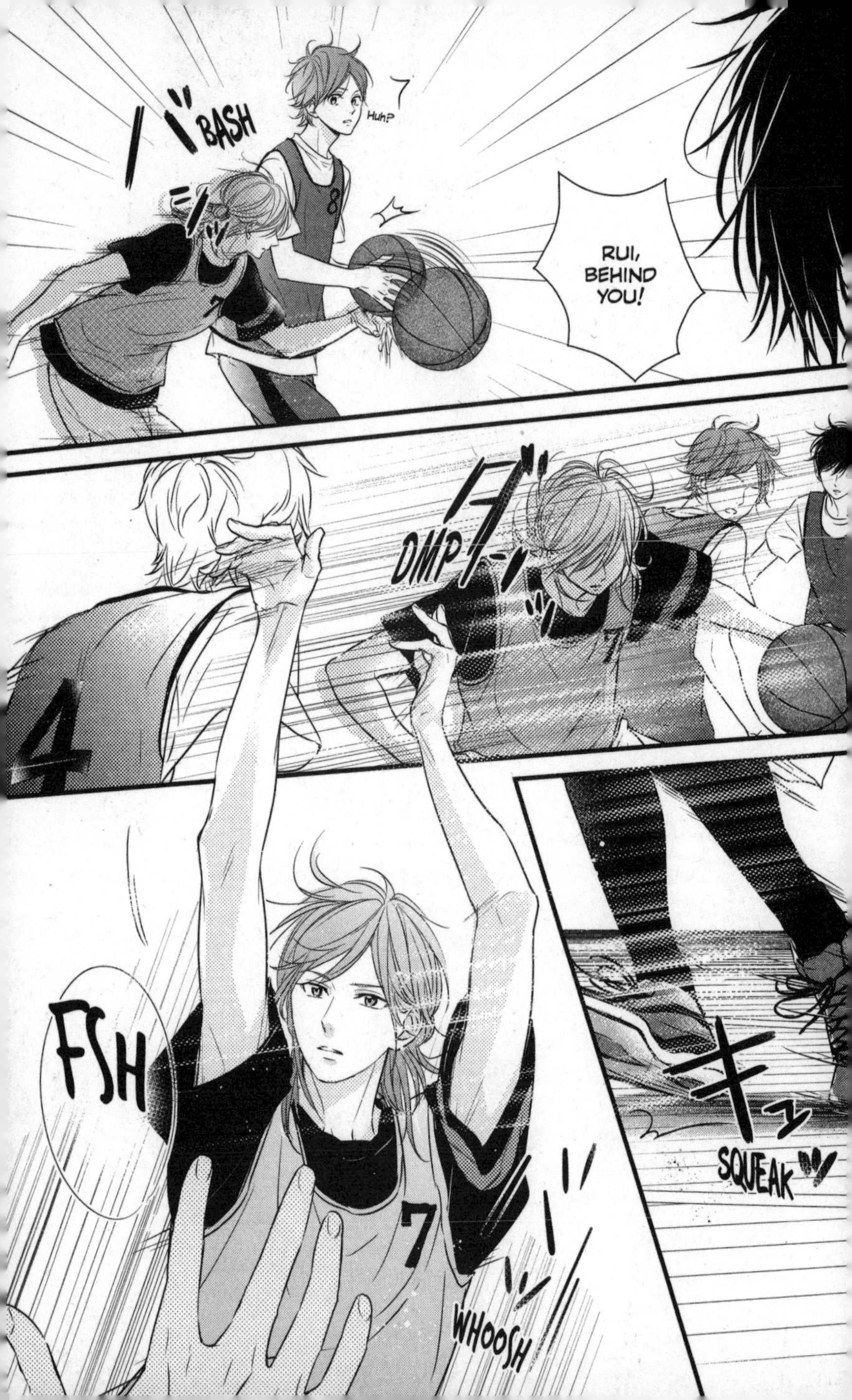
RUI, BEHIND YOU!
Huh?
BASH
DMP
SQUEAK
FSH
WHOOSH

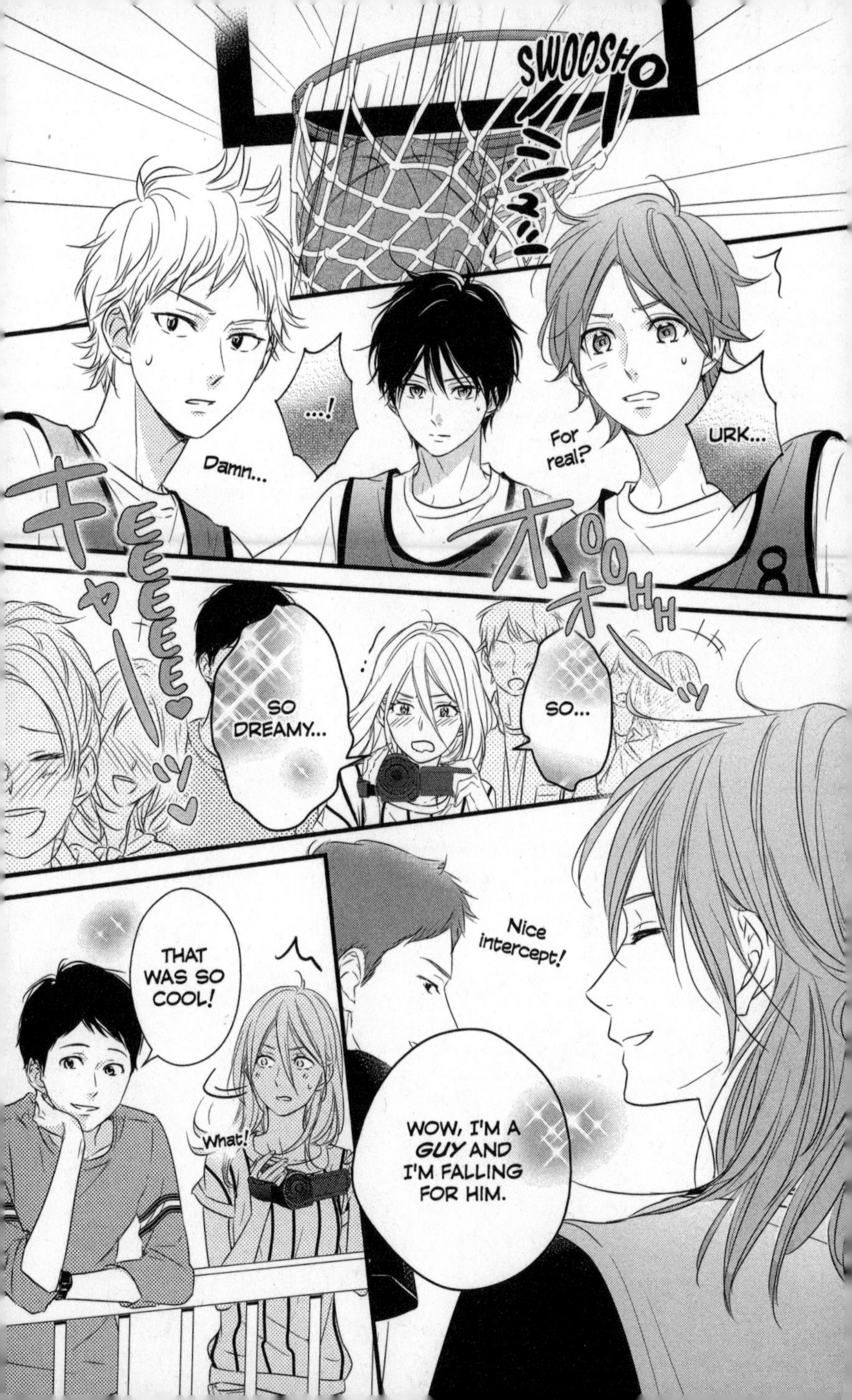
SWOOSH
URK...
For real?
...!
Damn...
OOHH
EEEEEE
SO...
SO DREAMY...
Nice intercept!
WOW, I'M A *GUY* AND I'M FALLING FOR HIM.
THAT WAS SO COOL!
What!

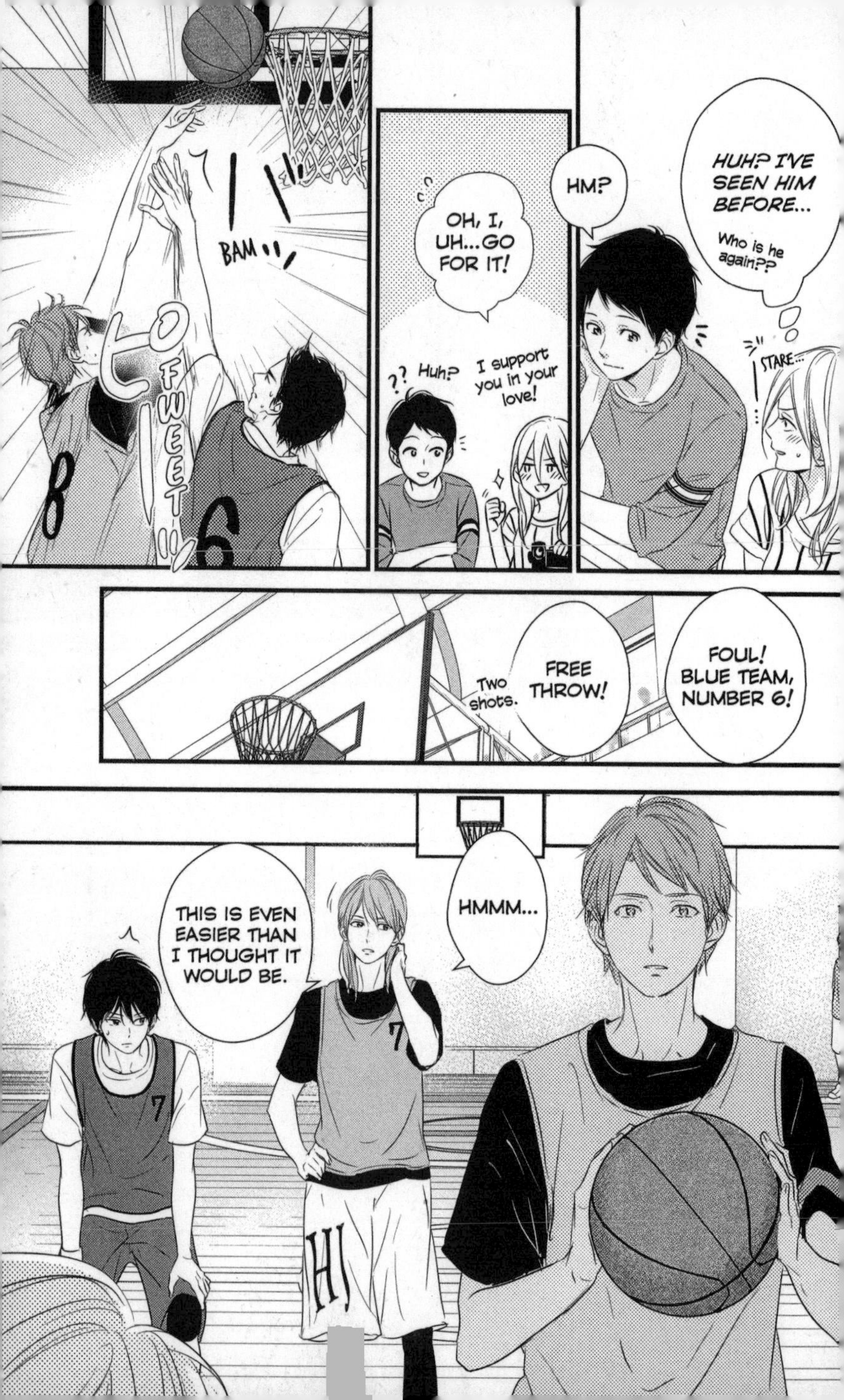
HUH? I'VE SEEN HIM BEFORE...
Who is he again??
HM?
STARE...
OH, I, UH...GO FOR IT!
I support you in your love!
Huh?
BAM
FWEET
FOUL! BLUE TEAM, NUMBER 6!
FREE THROW!
Two shots.
HMMM...
THIS IS EVEN EASIER THAN I THOUGHT IT WOULD BE.

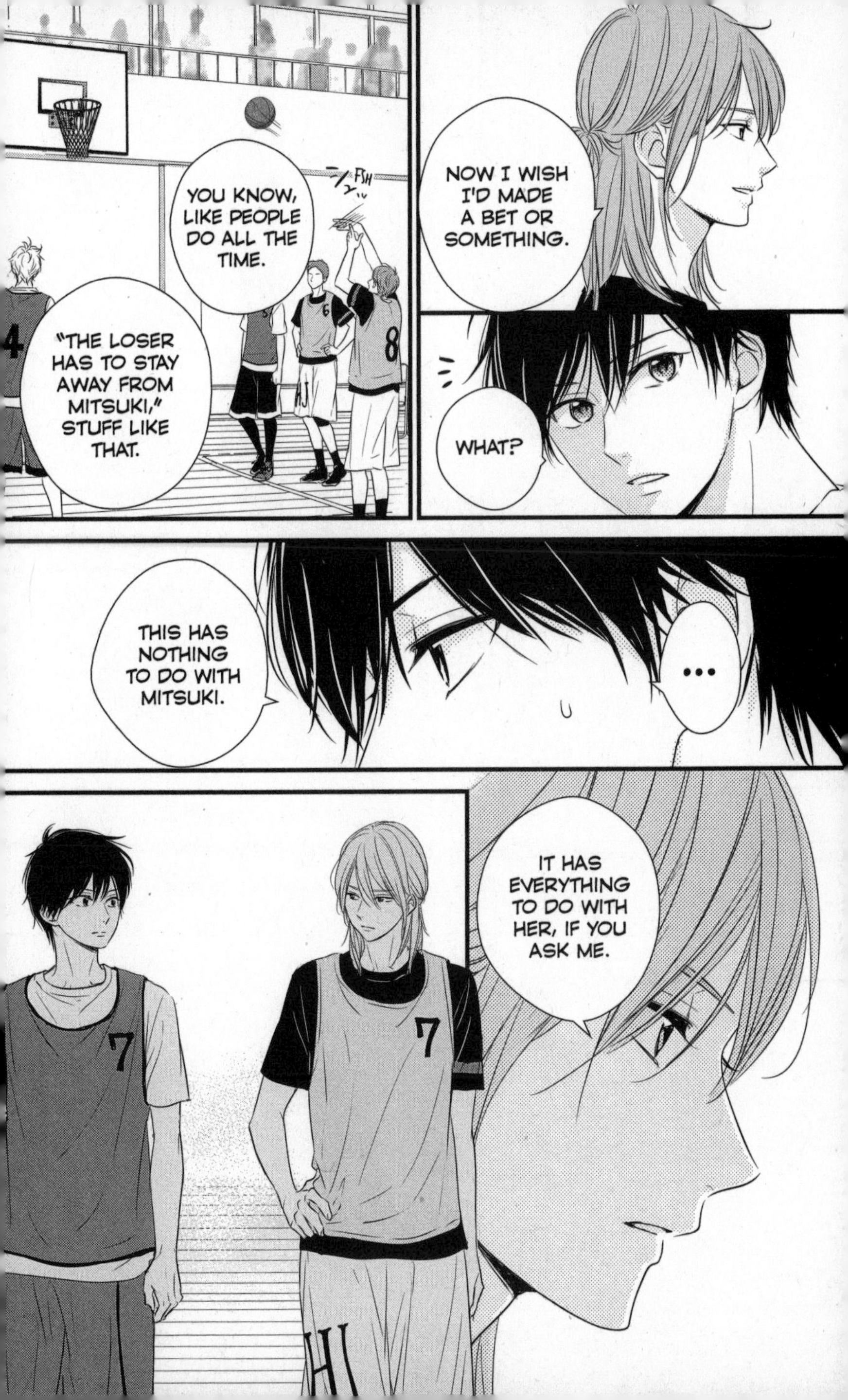
NOW I WISH I'D MADE A BET OR SOMETHING.
WHAT?
FSH
YOU KNOW, LIKE PEOPLE DO ALL THE TIME.
"THE LOSER HAS TO STAY AWAY FROM MITSUKI," STUFF LIKE THAT.
...
THIS HAS NOTHING TO DO WITH MITSUKI.
IT HAS EVERYTHING TO DO WITH HER, IF YOU ASK ME.

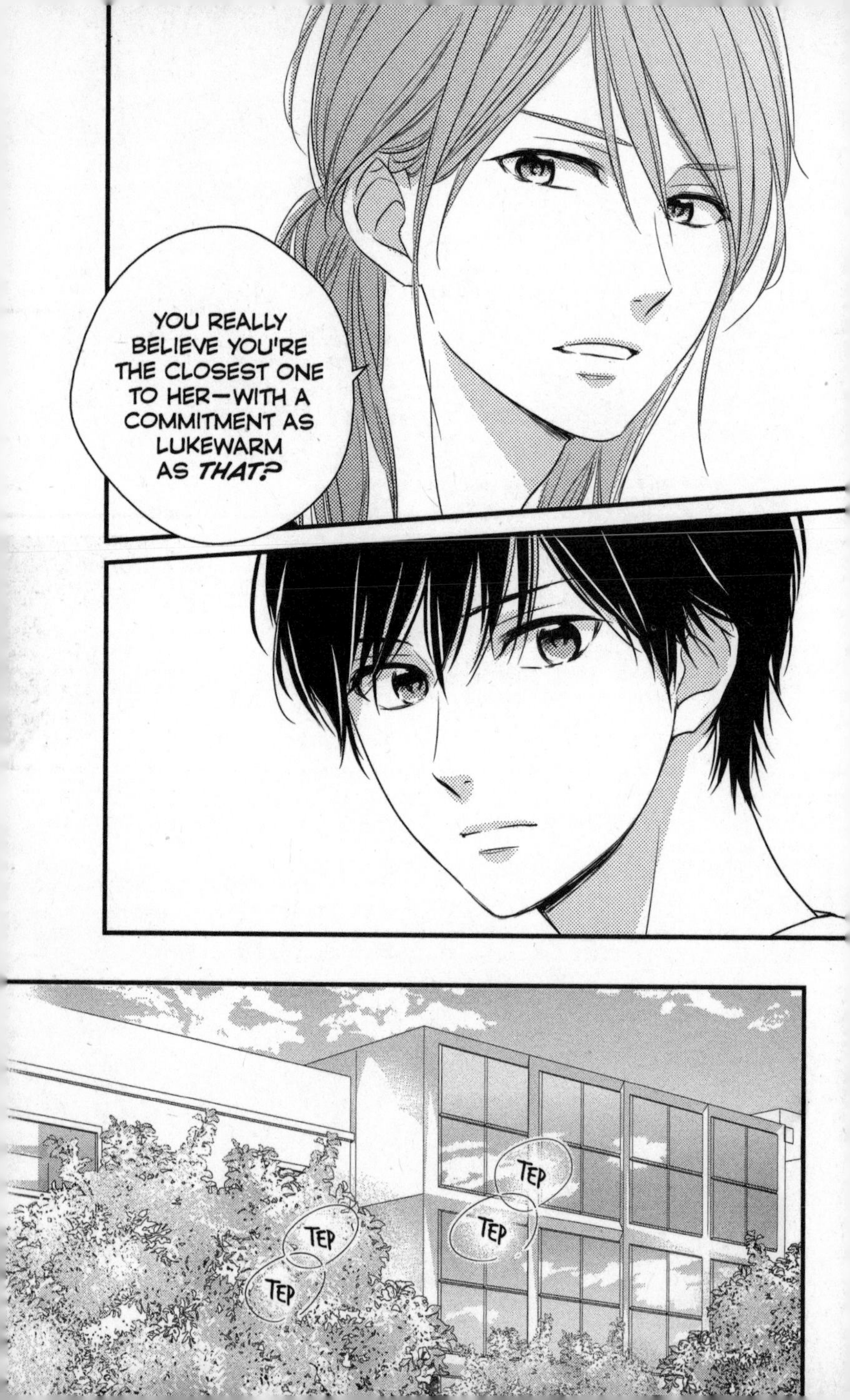
YOU REALLY BELIEVE YOU'RE THE CLOSEST ONE TO HER—WITH A COMMITMENT AS LUKEWARM AS *THAT?*
TEP
TEP
TEP
TEP

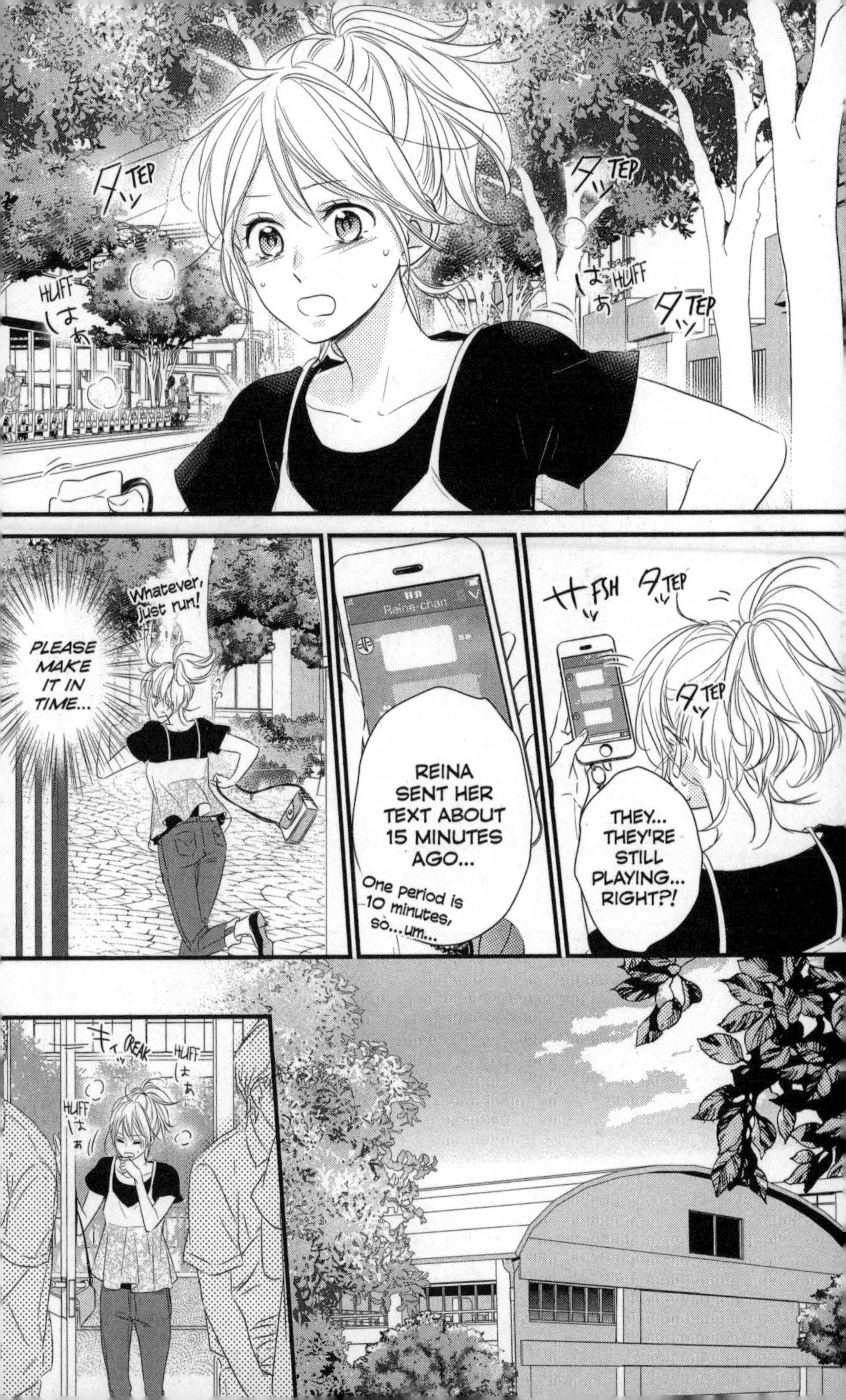
タッ TEP
はぁ HUFF
タッ TEP
タッ TEP
HUFF はぁ
サッ FSH
タッ TEP
タッ TEP
THEY... THEY'RE STILL PLAYING... RIGHT?!
Reina-chan
REINA SENT HER TEXT ABOUT 15 MINUTES AGO...
One period is 10 minutes, so...um...
Whatever, just run!
PLEASE MAKE IT IN TIME...
キィ CREAK
HUFF はぁ
HUFF はぁ

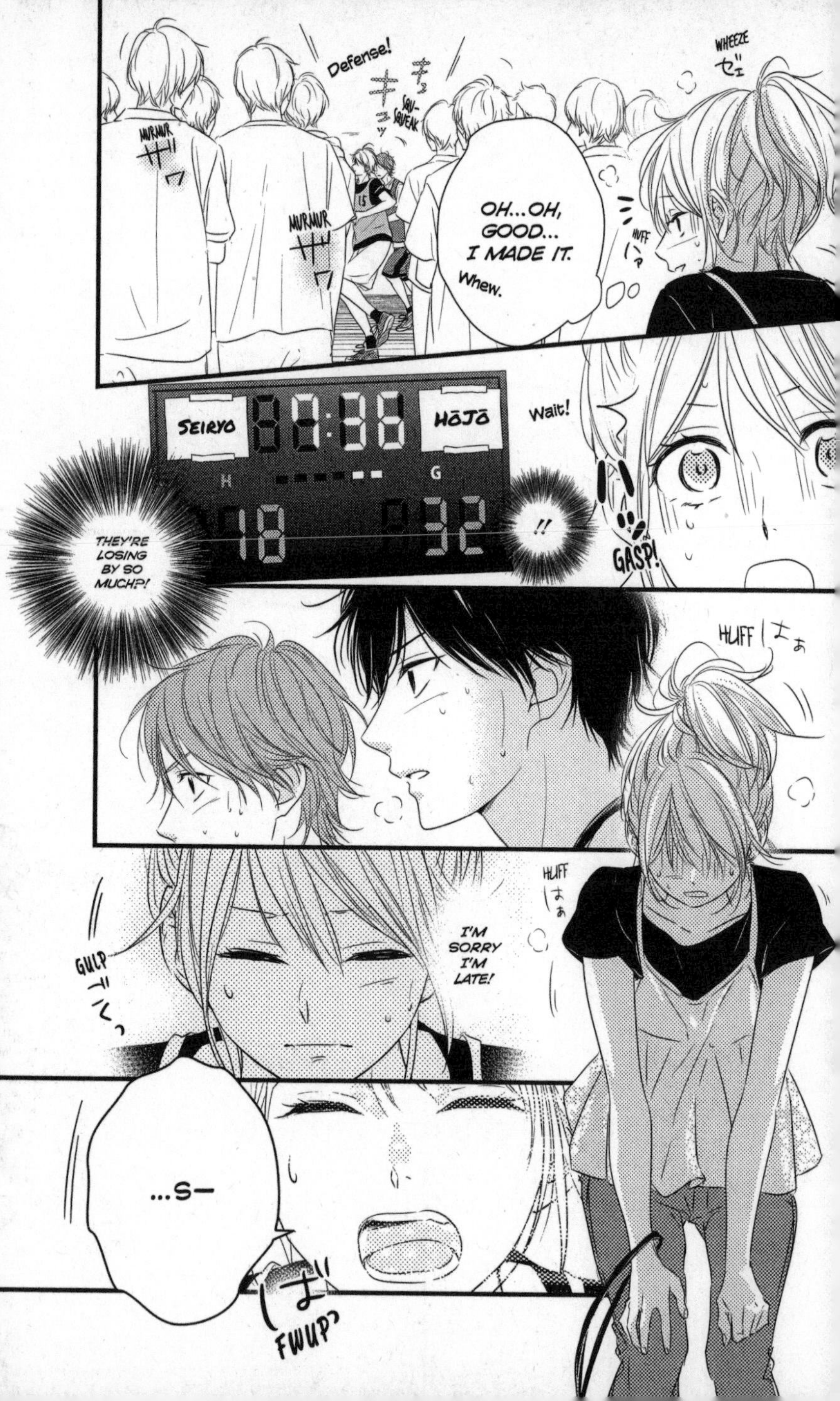
WHEEZE
セェ
HUFF
ハァ
OH...OH, GOOD... I MADE IT.
Whew.
Defense!
キュ
キュッ
SQU-SQUEAK
MURMUR
ザワ
MURMUR
ザワ
Wait!
GASP!
!!
SEIRYO
HŌJŌ
H
G
18
32
THEY'RE LOSING BY SO MUCH?!
HUFF
はぁ
HUFF
はぁ
I'M SORRY I'M LATE!
GULP
ごくっ
...S—
ぱ
FWUP

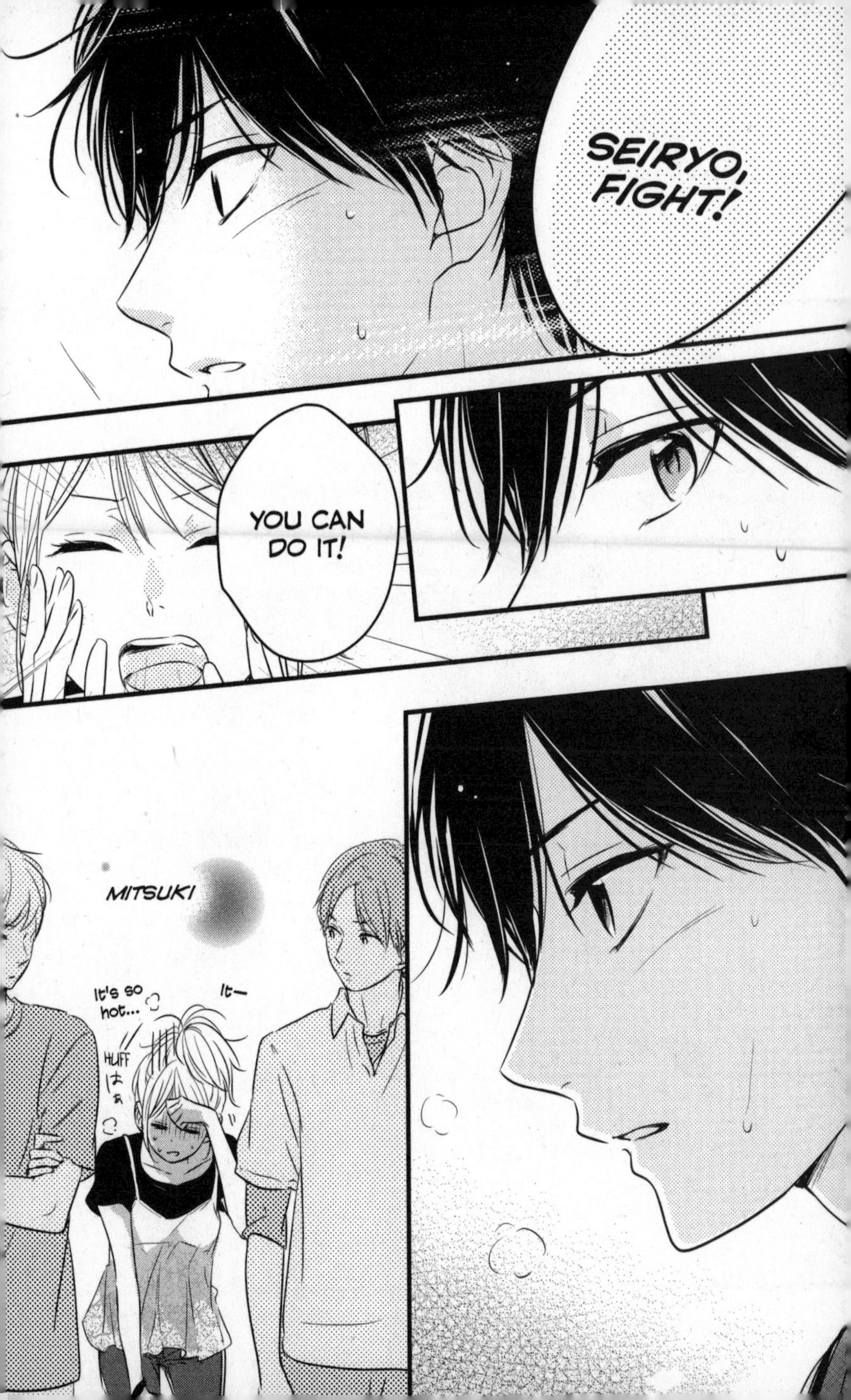
SEIRYO, FIGHT!
YOU CAN DO IT!
MITSUKI
ハー
It's so hot...
HUFF
はぁ

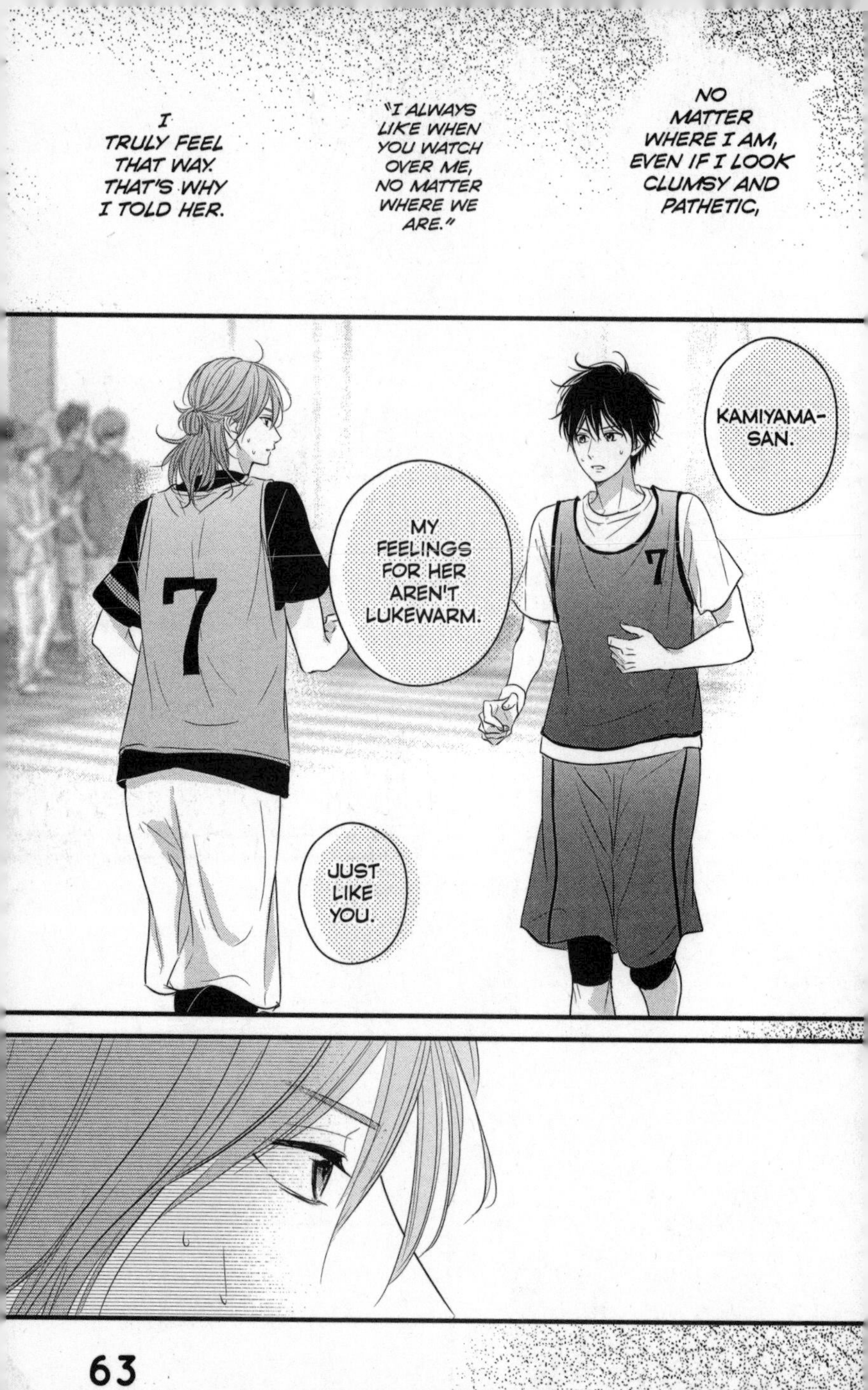
NO MATTER WHERE I AM, EVEN IF I LOOK CLUMSY AND PATHETIC,
"I ALWAYS LIKE WHEN YOU WATCH OVER ME, NO MATTER WHERE WE ARE."
I TRULY FEEL THAT WAY. THAT'S WHY I TOLD HER.
KAMIYAMA-SAN.
MY FEELINGS FOR HER AREN'T LUKEWARM.
JUST LIKE YOU.

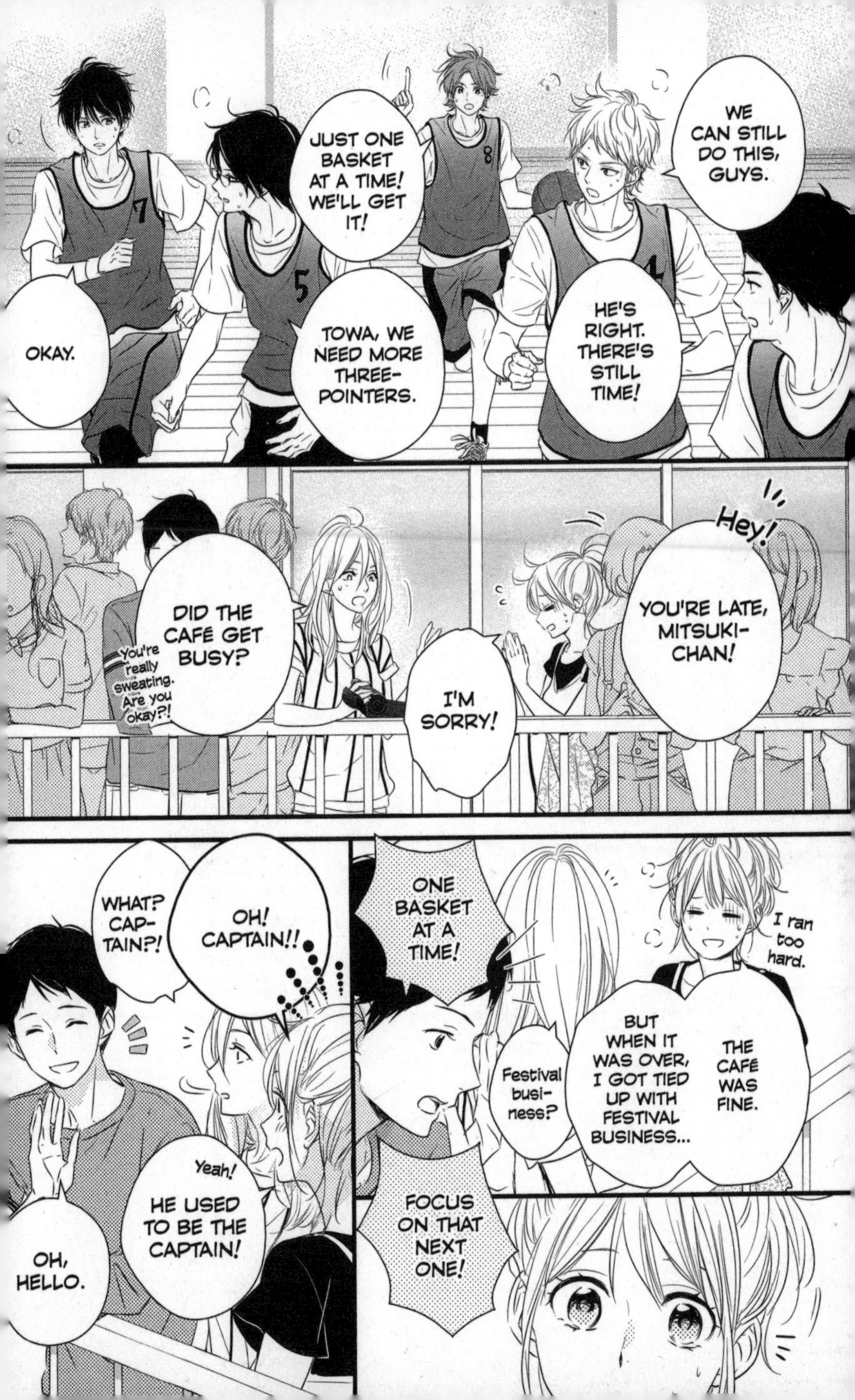
WE CAN STILL DO THIS, GUYS.
HE'S RIGHT. THERE'S STILL TIME!
JUST ONE BASKET AT A TIME! WE'LL GET IT!
TOWA, WE NEED MORE THREE-POINTERS.
OKAY.
Hey!
YOU'RE LATE, MITSUKI-CHAN!
I'M SORRY!
DID THE CAFÉ GET BUSY?
You're really sweating. Are you okay?!
I ran too hard.
THE CAFÉ WAS FINE.
BUT WHEN IT WAS OVER, I GOT TIED UP WITH FESTIVAL BUSINESS...
Festival business?
ONE BASKET AT A TIME!
FOCUS ON THAT NEXT ONE!
OH! CAPTAIN!!
WHAT? CAP-TAIN?!
Yeah!
HE USED TO BE THE CAPTAIN!
OH, HELLO.

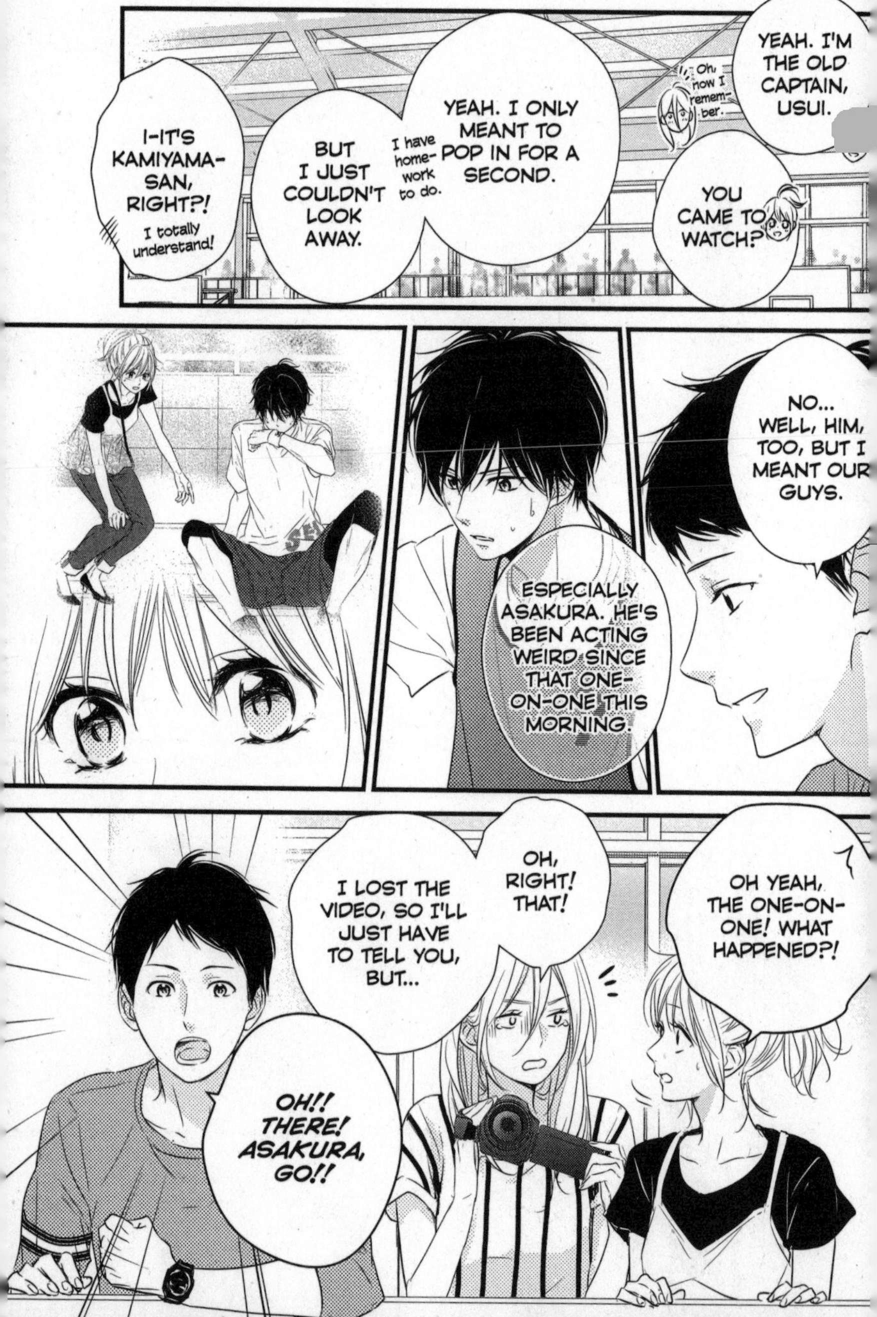

YEAH. I'M THE OLD CAPTAIN, USUI.
Oh, now I remember.
YOU CAME TO WATCH?
YEAH. I ONLY MEANT TO POP IN FOR A SECOND.
I have homework to do.
BUT I JUST COULDN'T LOOK AWAY.
I-IT'S KAMIYAMA-SAN, RIGHT?!
I totally understand!
NO... WELL, HIM, TOO, BUT I MEANT OUR GUYS.
ESPECIALLY ASAKURA. HE'S BEEN ACTING WEIRD SINCE THAT ONE-ON-ONE THIS MORNING.
OH YEAH, THE ONE-ON-ONE! WHAT HAPPENED?!
OH, RIGHT! THAT!
I LOST THE VIDEO, SO I'LL JUST HAVE TO TELL YOU, BUT...
OH!! THERE! ASAKURA, GO!!

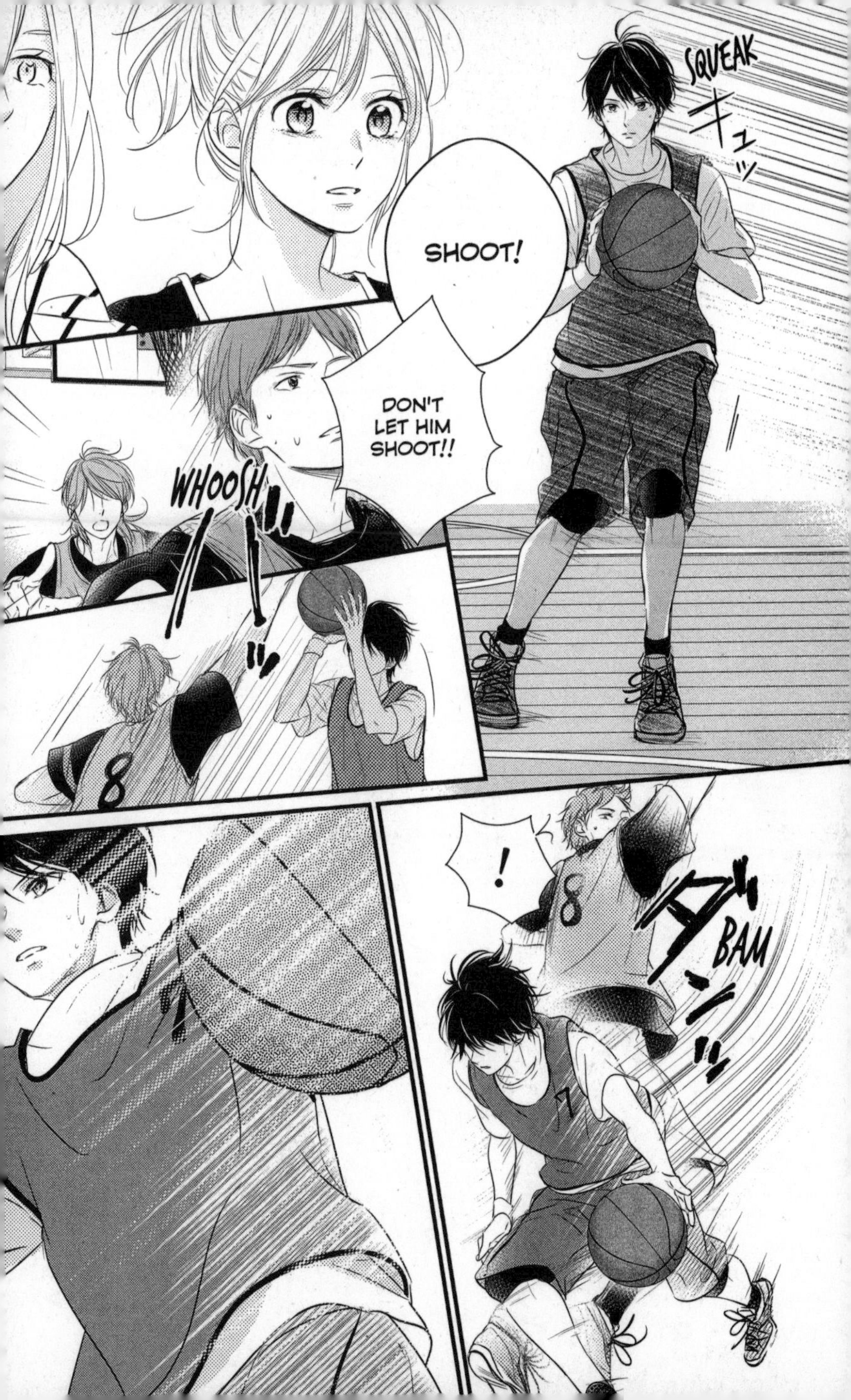
SQUEAK
キュッ
SHOOT!
DON'T LET HIM SHOOT!!
WHOOSH
!
BAM

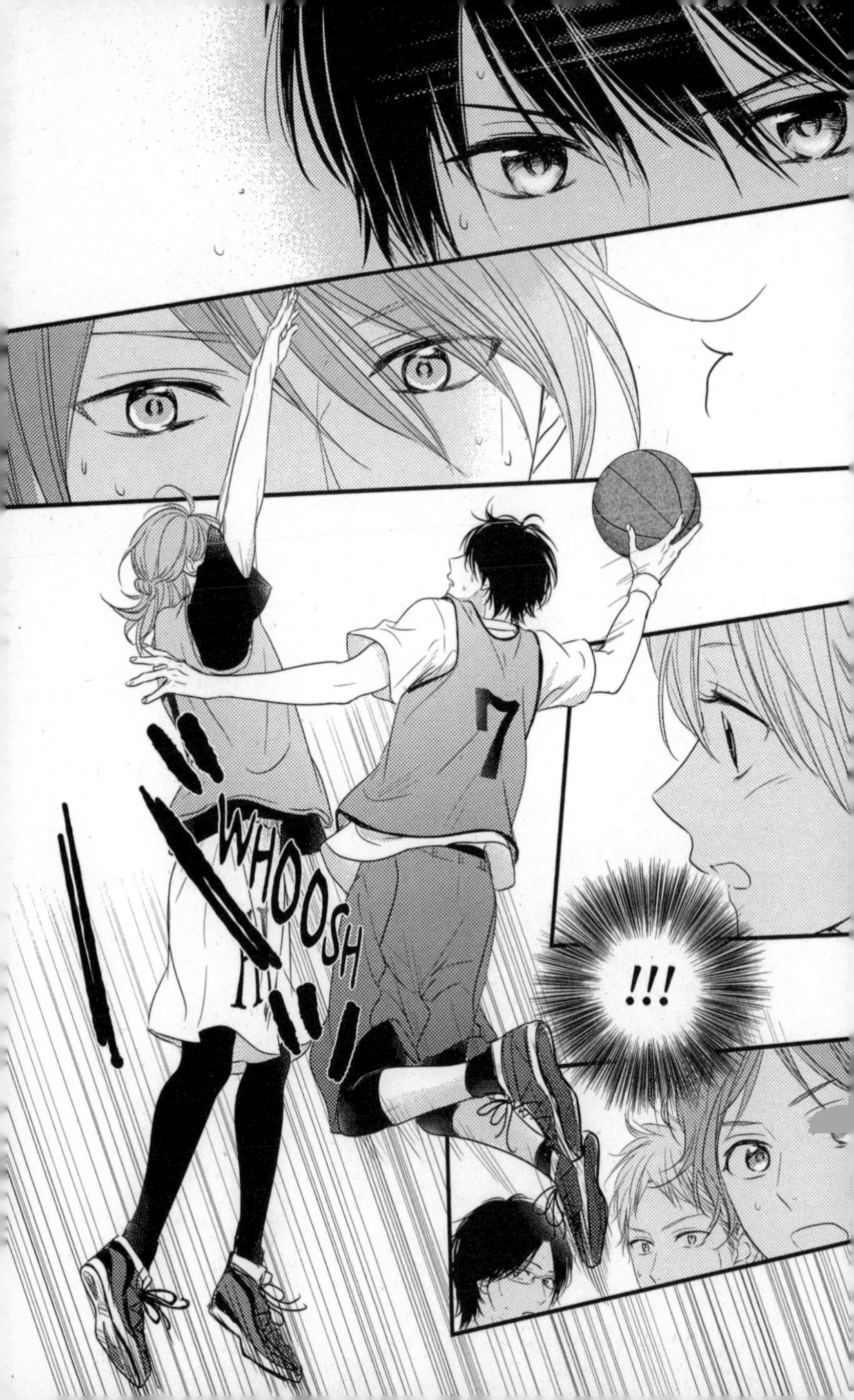
WHOOSH
!!!

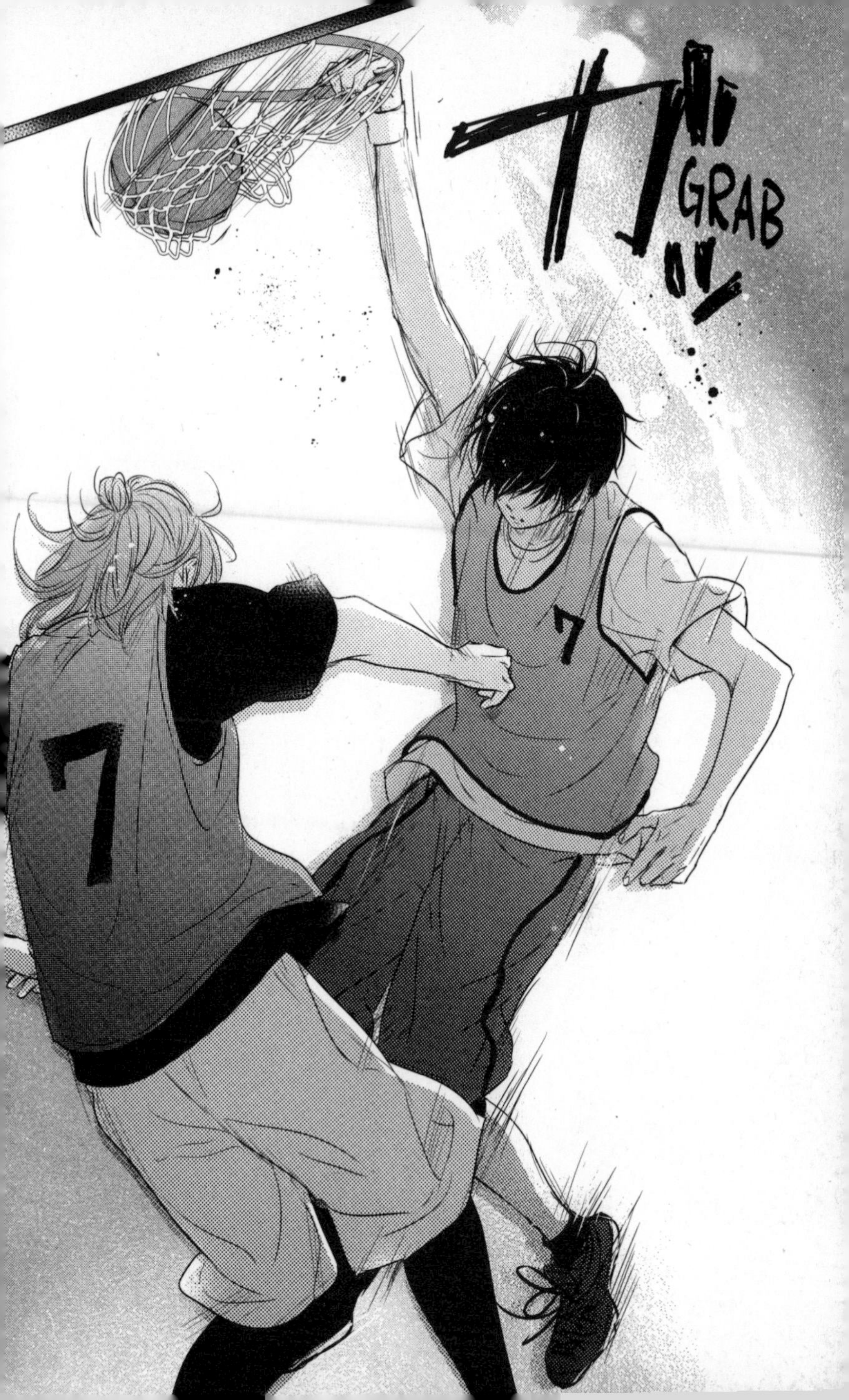
GRAB

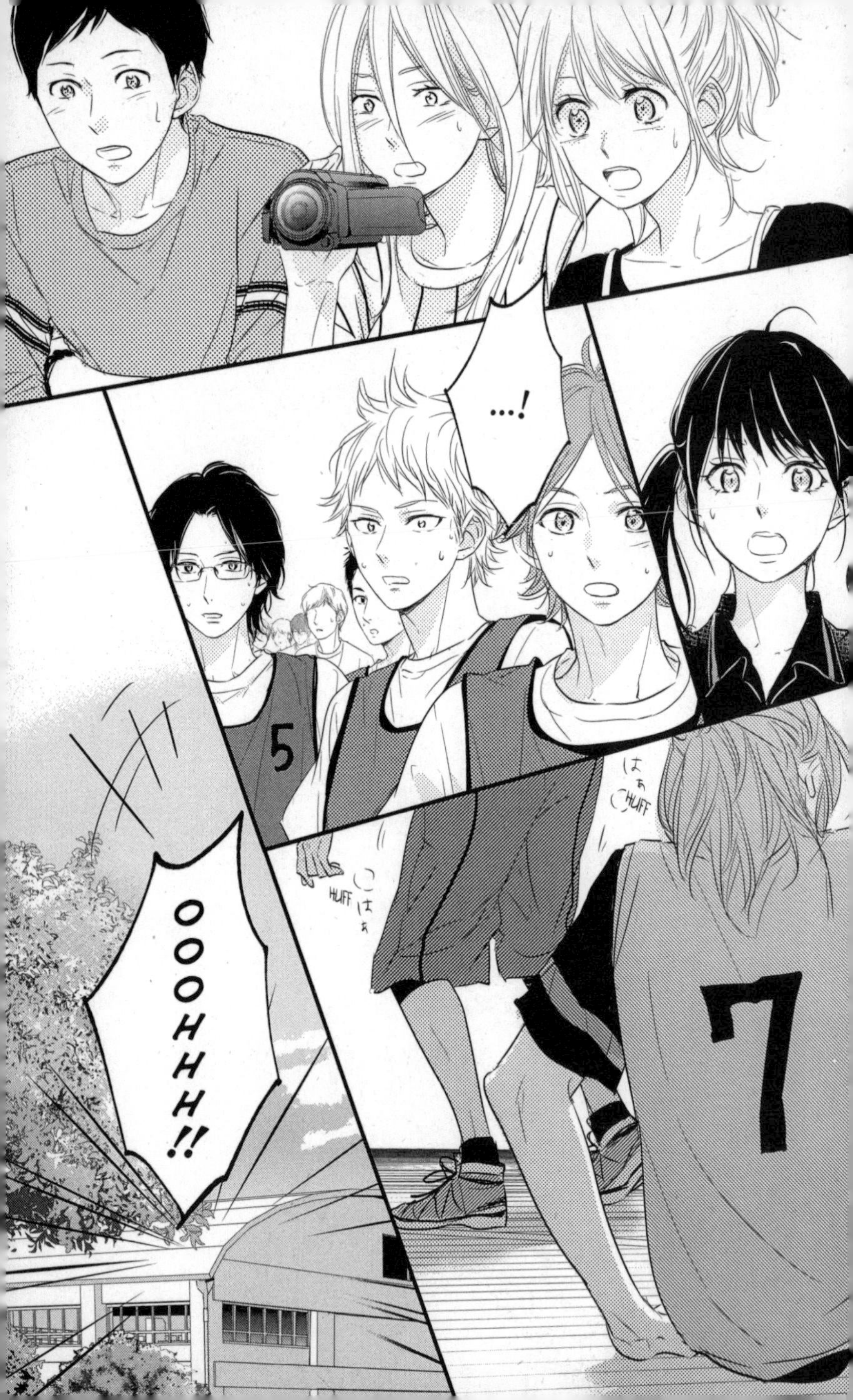

...!
HUFF
HUFF
OOOOHHHH!!

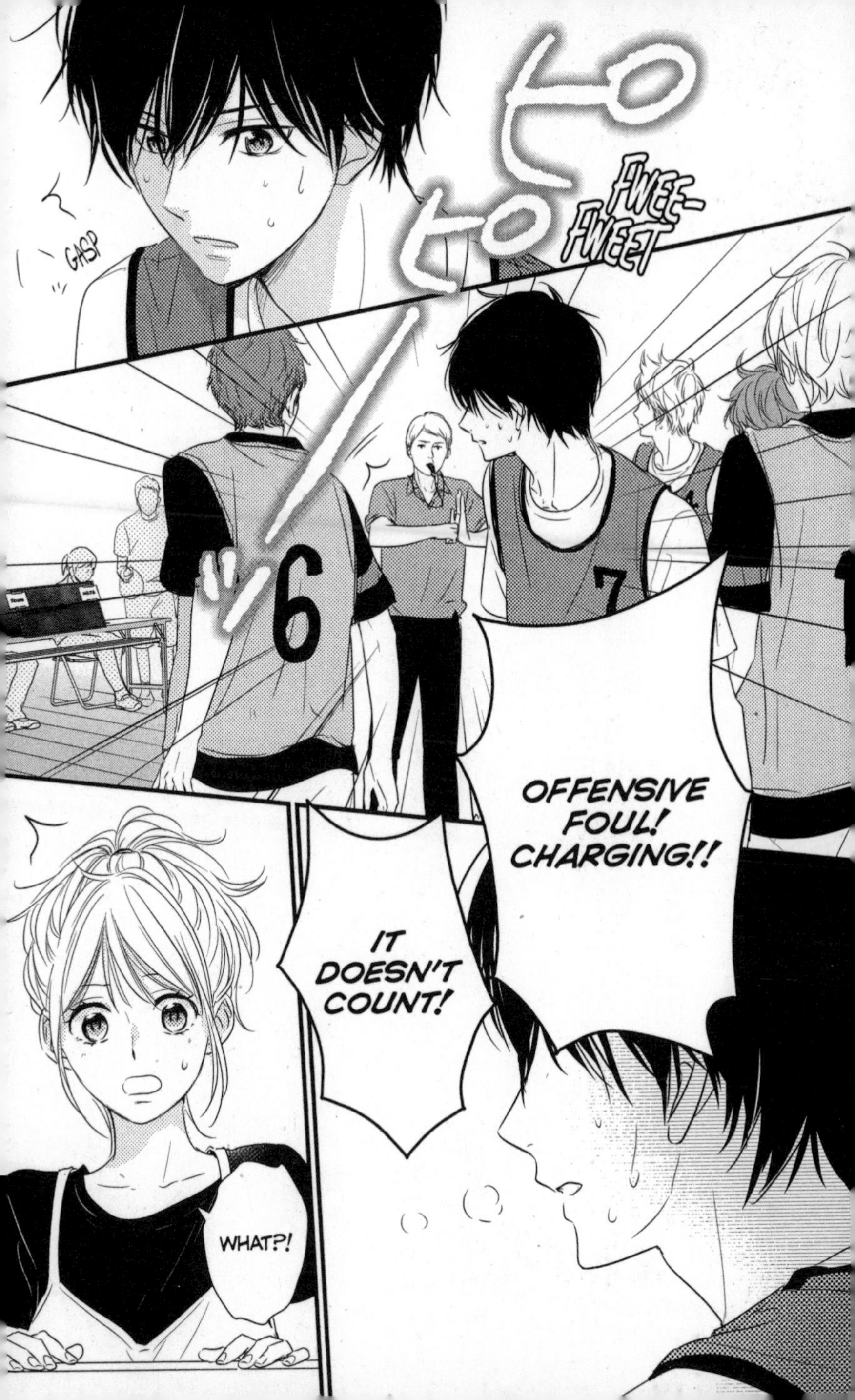
FWEE-FWEET
GASP
OFFENSIVE FOUL! CHARGING!!
IT DOESN'T COUNT!
WHAT?!

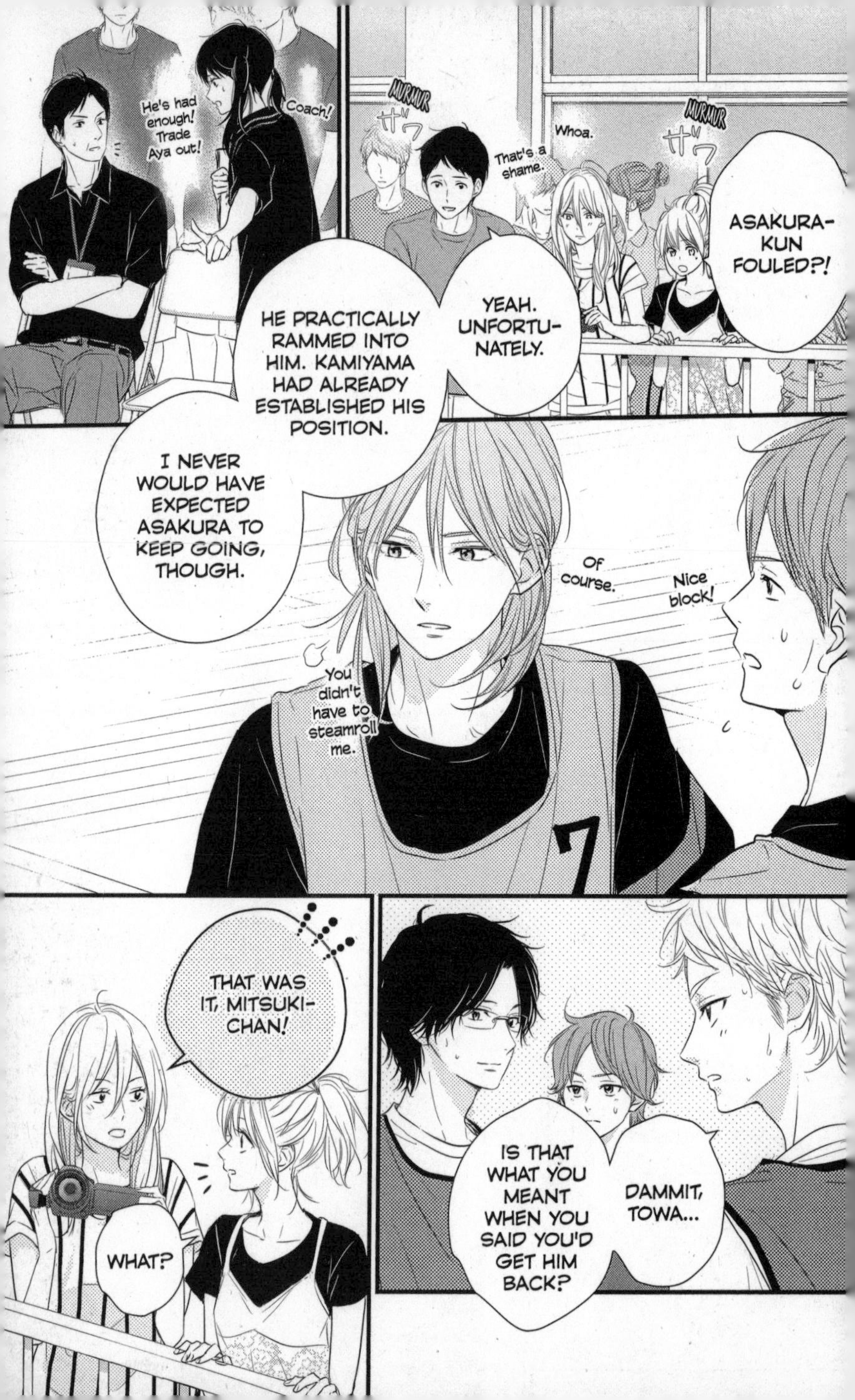
MURMUR
ザワ
MURMUR
ザワ
Whoa.
That's a shame.
ASAKURA-KUN FOULED?!
YEAH. UNFORTU-NATELY.
HE PRACTICALLY RAMMED INTO HIM. KAMIYAMA HAD ALREADY ESTABLISHED HIS POSITION.
Coach!
He's had enough! Trade Aya out!
Nice block!
Of course.
I NEVER WOULD HAVE EXPECTED ASAKURA TO KEEP GOING, THOUGH.
You didn't have to steamroll me.
DAMMIT, TOWA...
IS THAT WHAT YOU MEANT WHEN YOU SAID YOU'D GET HIM BACK?
THAT WAS IT, MITSUKI-CHAN!
WHAT?

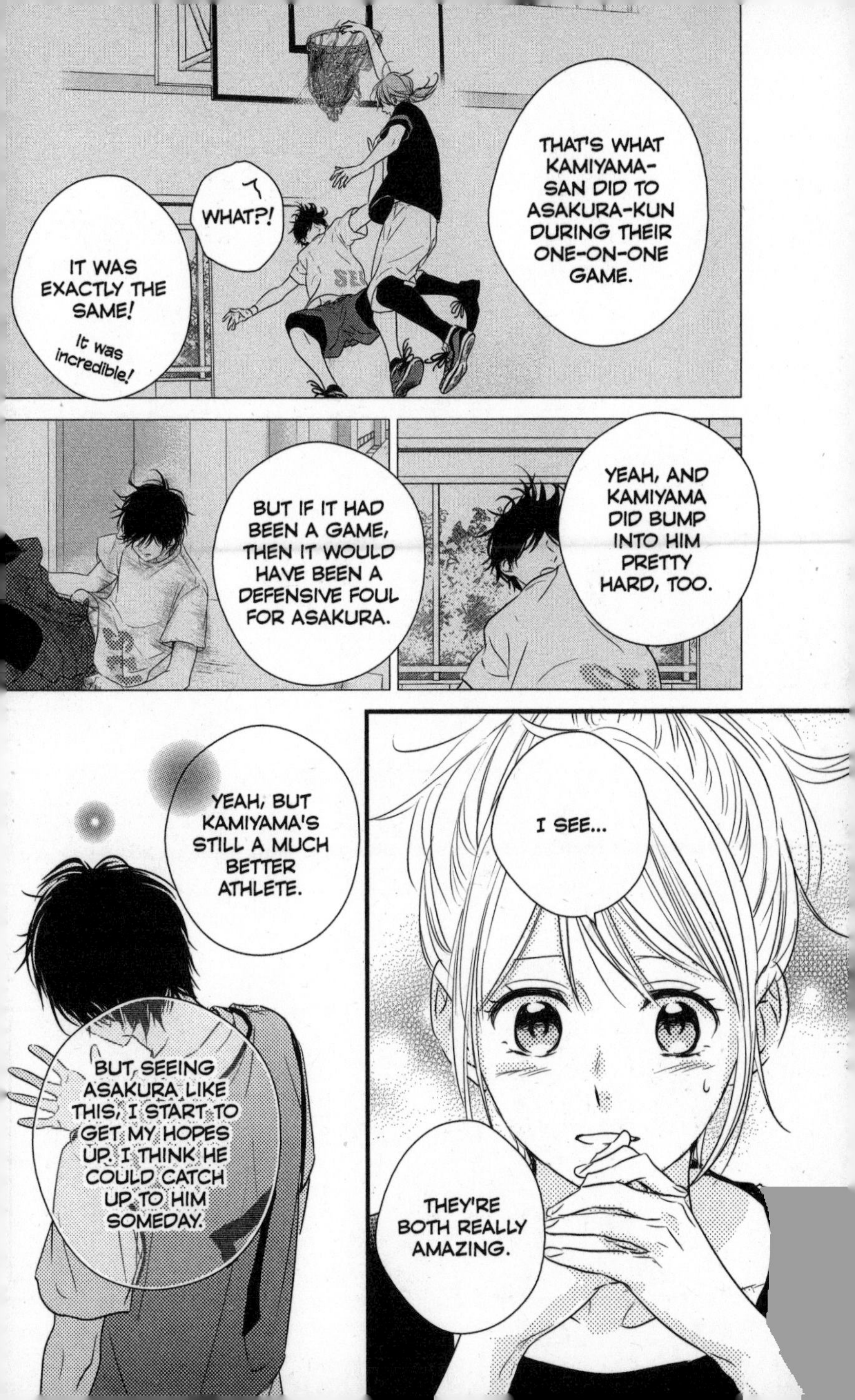
THAT'S WHAT KAMIYAMA-SAN DID TO ASAKURA-KUN DURING THEIR ONE-ON-ONE GAME.
WHAT?!
IT WAS EXACTLY THE SAME!
It was incredible!
YEAH, AND KAMIYAMA DID BUMP INTO HIM PRETTY HARD, TOO.
BUT IF IT HAD BEEN A GAME, THEN IT WOULD HAVE BEEN A DEFENSIVE FOUL FOR ASAKURA.
I SEE...
THEY'RE BOTH REALLY AMAZING.
YEAH, BUT KAMIYAMA'S STILL A MUCH BETTER ATHLETE.
BUT, SEEING ASAKURA LIKE THIS, I START TO GET MY HOPES UP. I THINK HE COULD CATCH UP TO HIM SOMEDAY.

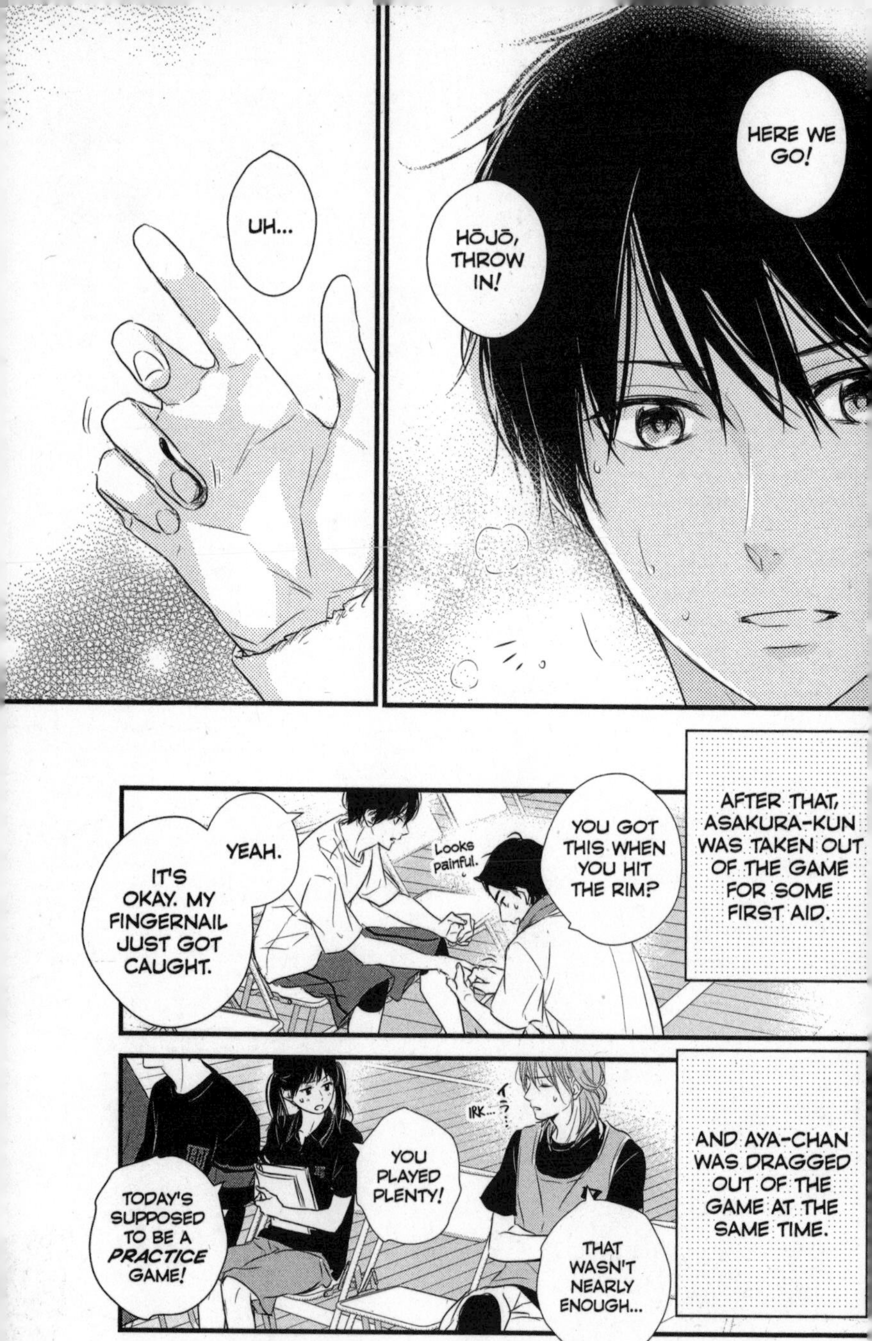
HERE WE GO!
HŌJŌ, THROW IN!
UH...
AFTER THAT, ASAKURA-KUN WAS TAKEN OUT OF THE GAME FOR SOME FIRST AID.
YOU GOT THIS WHEN YOU HIT THE RIM?
Looks painful.
YEAH.
IT'S OKAY. MY FINGERNAIL JUST GOT CAUGHT.
AND AYA-CHAN WAS DRAGGED OUT OF THE GAME AT THE SAME TIME.
IRK...
THAT WASN'T NEARLY ENOUGH...
YOU PLAYED PLENTY!
TODAY'S SUPPOSED TO BE A *PRACTICE* GAME!

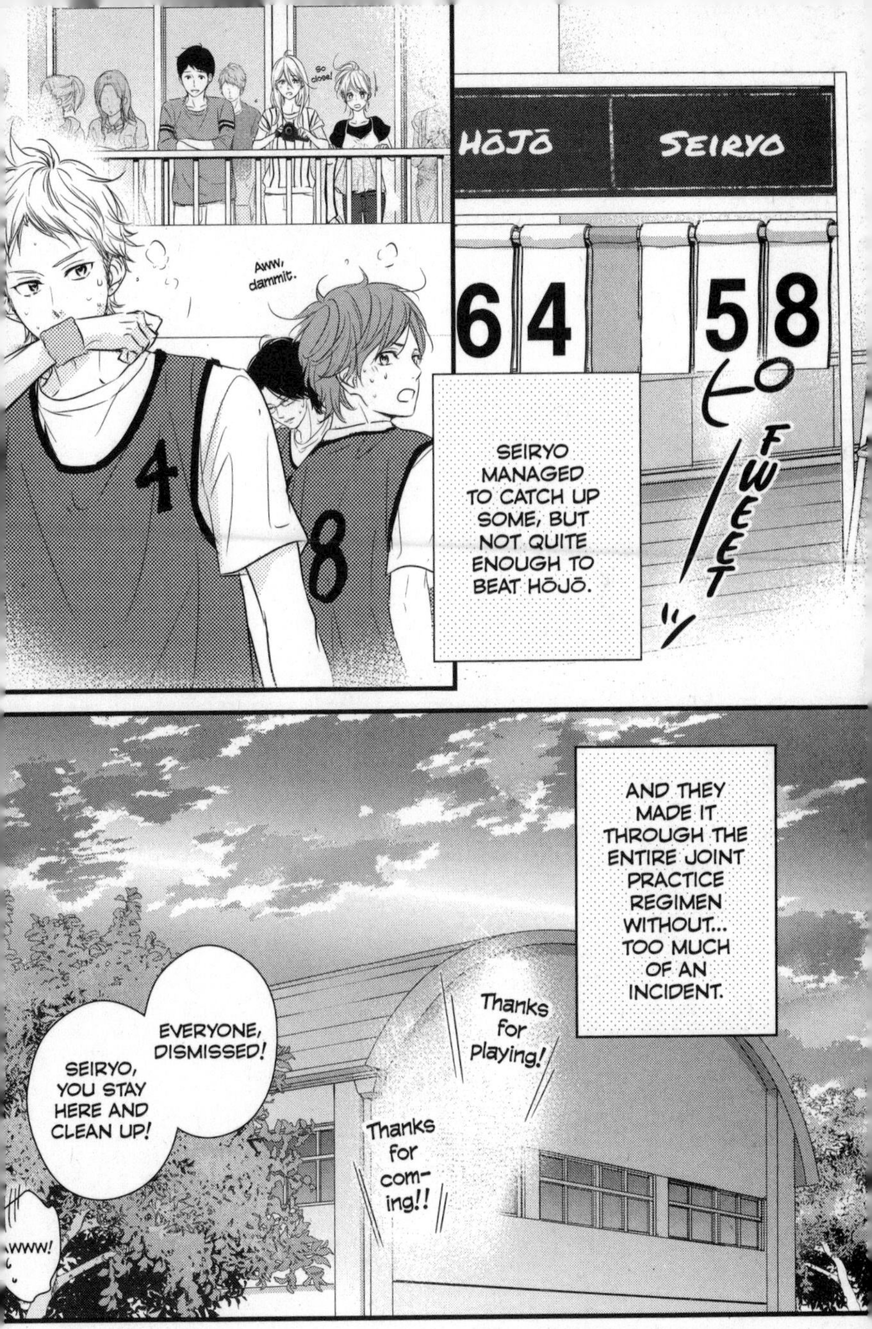
HŌJŌ
SEIRYO
64
58
FWEET
SEIRYO MANAGED TO CATCH UP SOME, BUT NOT QUITE ENOUGH TO BEAT HŌJŌ.
So close!
Aww, dammit.
AND THEY MADE IT THROUGH THE ENTIRE JOINT PRACTICE REGIMEN WITHOUT... TOO MUCH OF AN INCIDENT.
Thanks for playing!
Thanks for com-ing!!
EVERYONE, DISMISSED!
SEIRYO, YOU STAY HERE AND CLEAN UP!

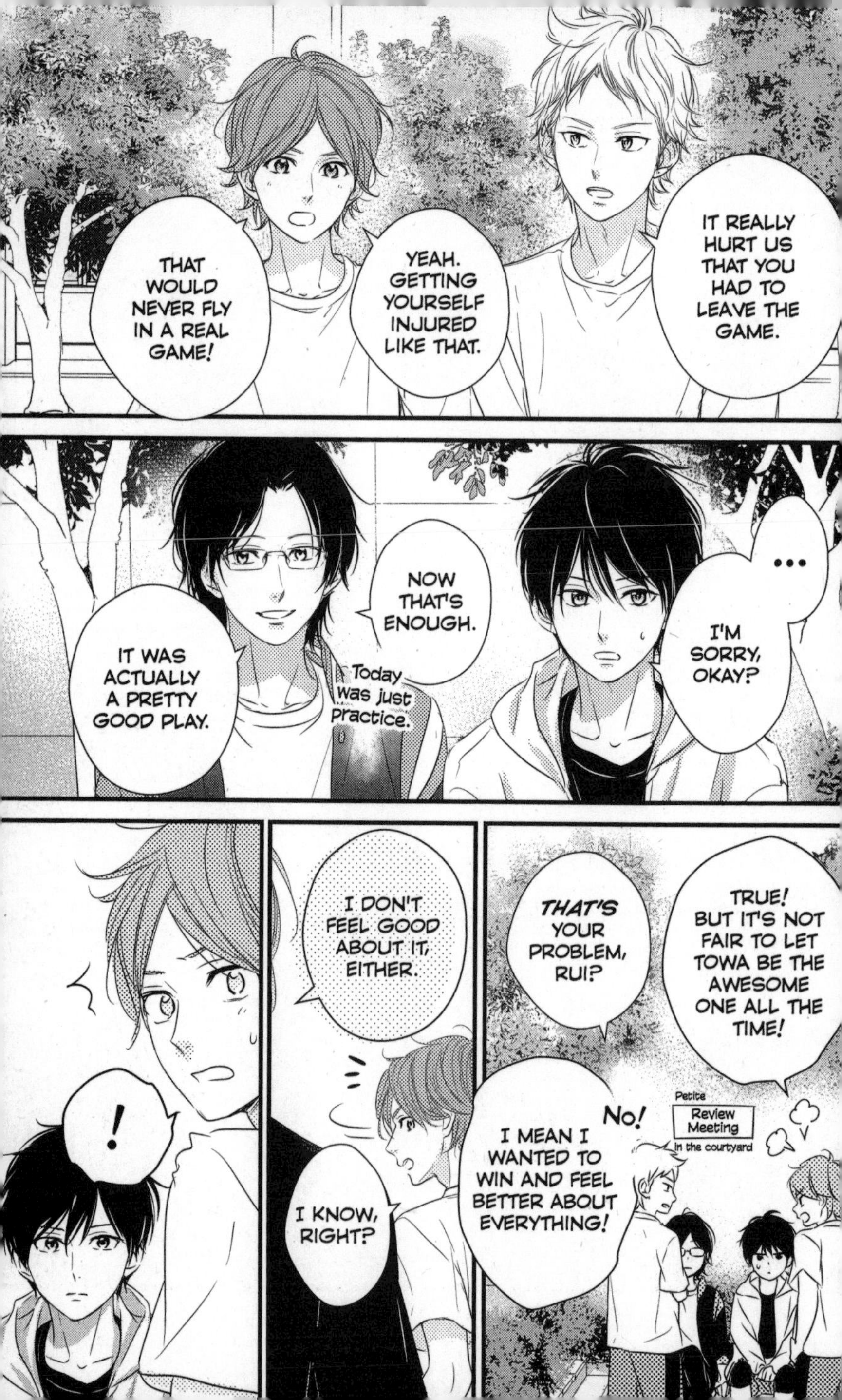
IT REALLY HURT US THAT YOU HAD TO LEAVE THE GAME.
YEAH. GETTING YOURSELF INJURED LIKE THAT.
THAT WOULD NEVER FLY IN A REAL GAME!
...
I'M SORRY, OKAY?
NOW THAT'S ENOUGH.
Today was just practice.
IT WAS ACTUALLY A PRETTY GOOD PLAY.
TRUE! BUT IT'S NOT FAIR TO LET TOWA BE THE AWESOME ONE ALL THE TIME!
THAT'S YOUR PROBLEM, RUI?
Petite Review Meeting in the courtyard
No!
I MEAN I WANTED TO WIN AND FEEL BETTER ABOUT EVERYTHING!
I DON'T FEEL GOOD ABOUT IT, EITHER.
I KNOW, RIGHT?
!

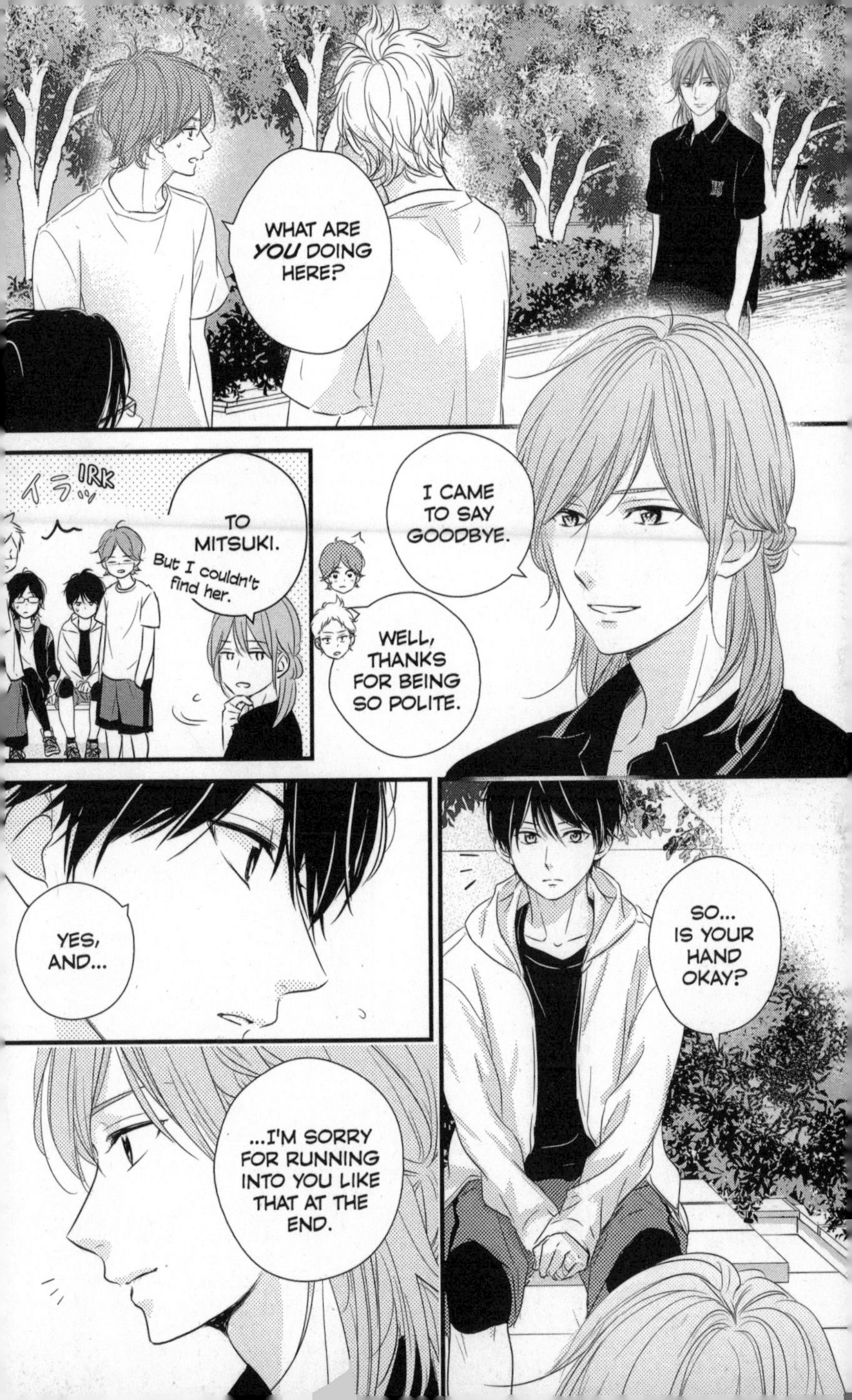
WHAT ARE *YOU* DOING HERE?
I CAME TO SAY GOODBYE.
WELL, THANKS FOR BEING SO POLITE.
イラッ IRK
TO MITSUKI. But I couldn't find her.
SO... IS YOUR HAND OKAY?
YES, AND...
...I'M SORRY FOR RUNNING INTO YOU LIKE THAT AT THE END.

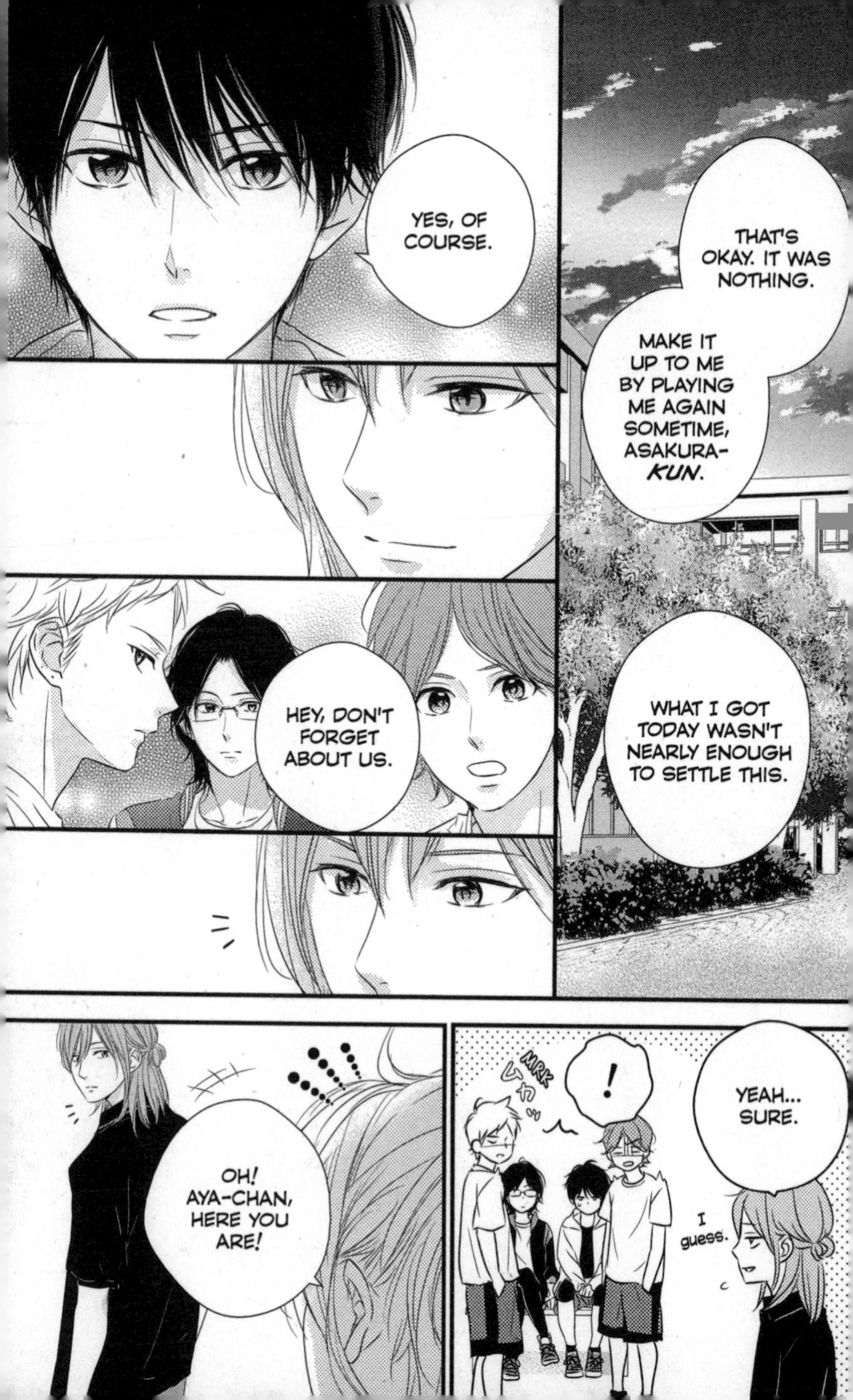

THAT'S OKAY. IT WAS NOTHING.
MAKE IT UP TO ME BY PLAYING ME AGAIN SOMETIME, ASAKURA-*KUN*.
WHAT I GOT TODAY WASN'T NEARLY ENOUGH TO SETTLE THIS.
YES, OF COURSE.
HEY, DON'T FORGET ABOUT US.
YEAH... SURE.
!
MRK
I guess.
OH! AYA-CHAN, HERE YOU ARE!

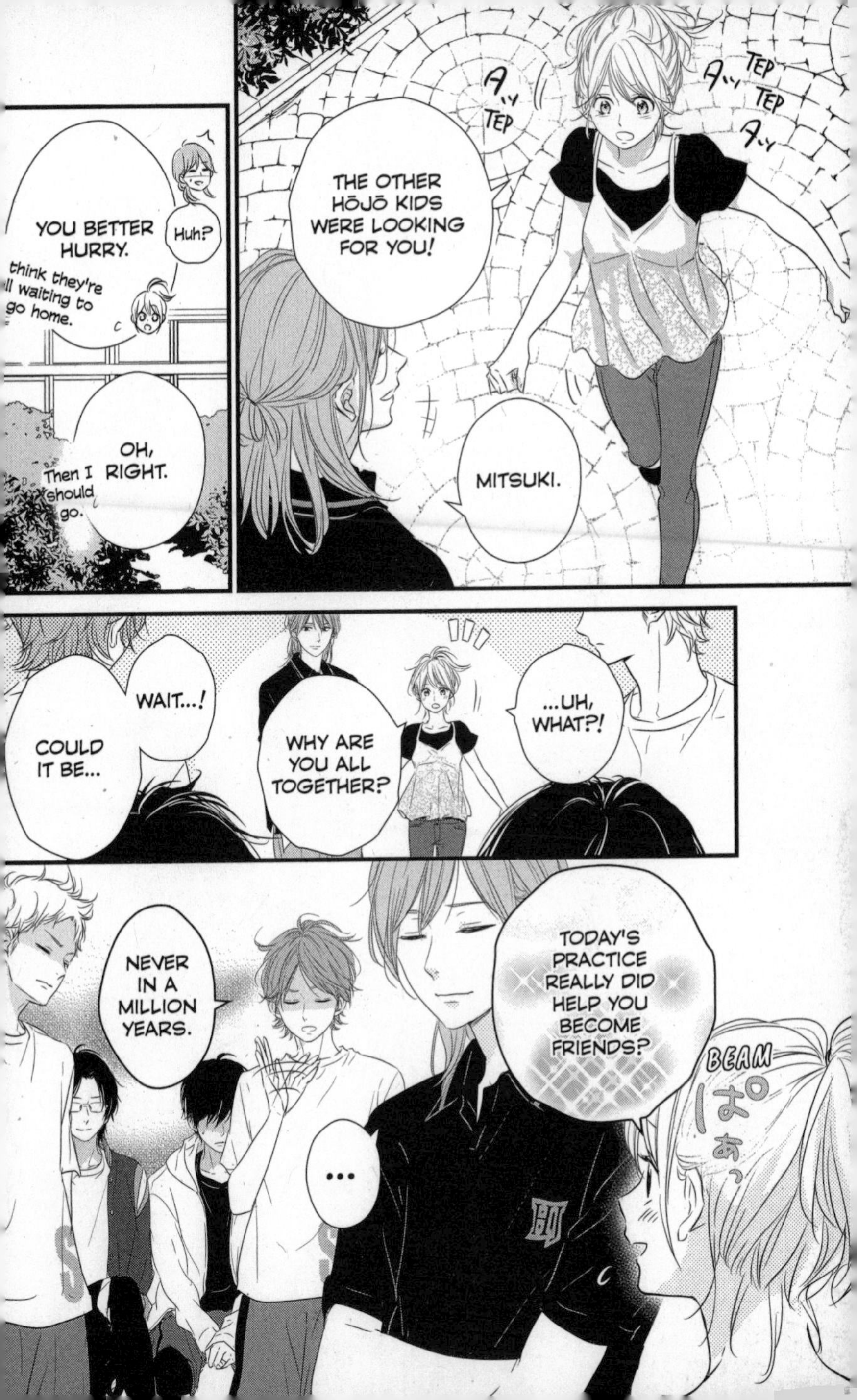
TEP
タッ
TEP
タッ
TEP
タッ
THE OTHER HŌJŌ KIDS WERE LOOKING FOR YOU!
MITSUKI.
Huh?
YOU BETTER HURRY.
think they're ll waiting to go home.
OH, RIGHT.
Then I should go.
...UH, WHAT?!
WHY ARE YOU ALL TOGETHER?
WAIT...!
COULD IT BE...
TODAY'S PRACTICE REALLY DID HELP YOU BECOME FRIENDS?
BEAM
ぱあっ
NEVER IN A MILLION YEARS.
...

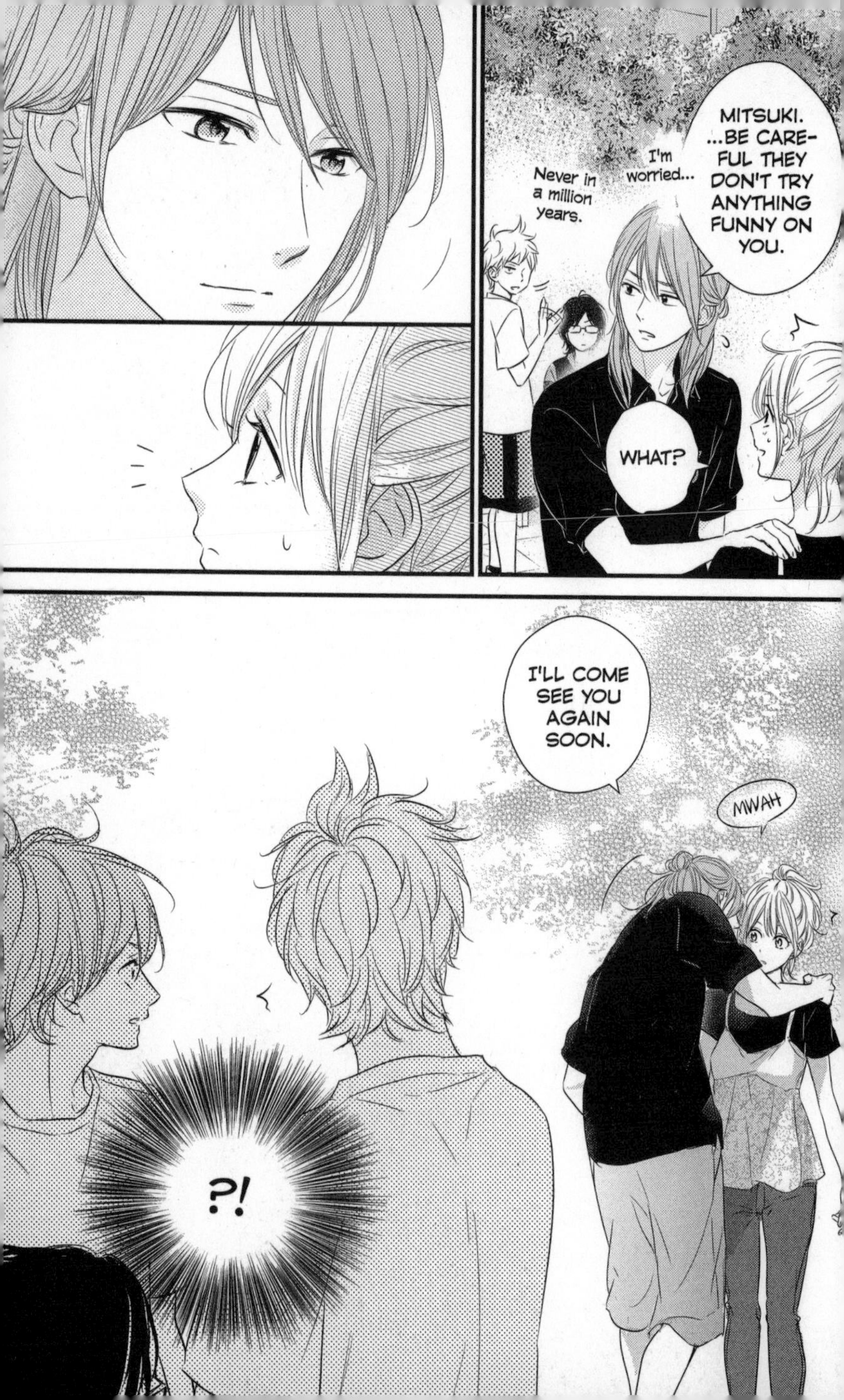
MITSUKI. ...BE CARE-FUL THEY DON'T TRY ANYTHING FUNNY ON YOU.
I'm worried...
Never in a million years.
WHAT?
I'LL COME SEE YOU AGAIN SOON.
MWAH
?!

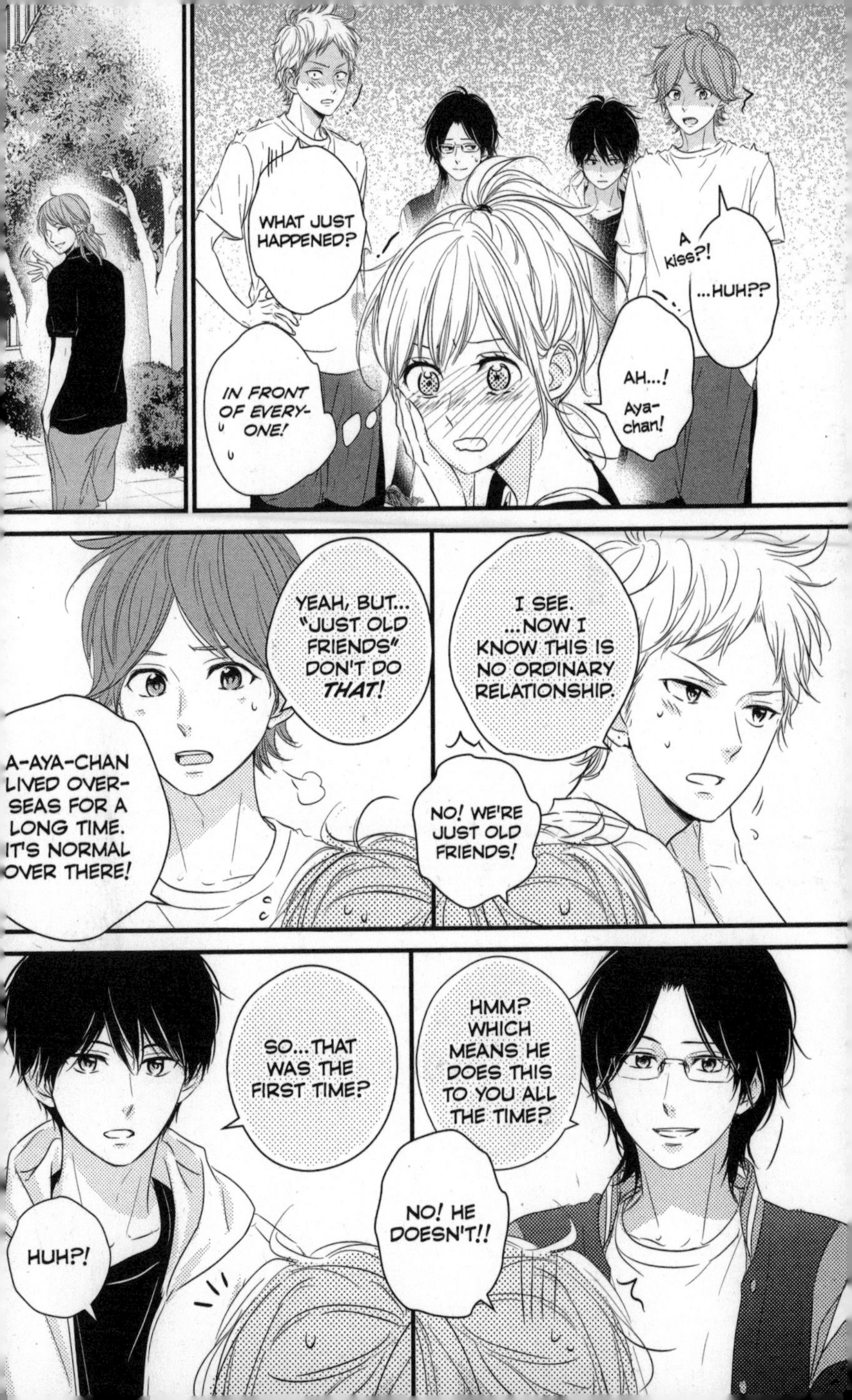
A kiss?!
WHAT JUST HAPPENED?
...HUH??
AH...! Aya-chan!
IN FRONT OF EVERY-ONE!
I SEE. ...NOW I KNOW THIS IS NO ORDINARY RELATIONSHIP.
NO! WE'RE JUST OLD FRIENDS!
YEAH, BUT... "JUST OLD FRIENDS" DON'T DO THAT!
A-AYA-CHAN LIVED OVER-SEAS FOR A LONG TIME. IT'S NORMAL OVER THERE!
HMM? WHICH MEANS HE DOES THIS TO YOU ALL THE TIME?
NO! HE DOESN'T!!
SO...THAT WAS THE FIRST TIME?
HUH?!

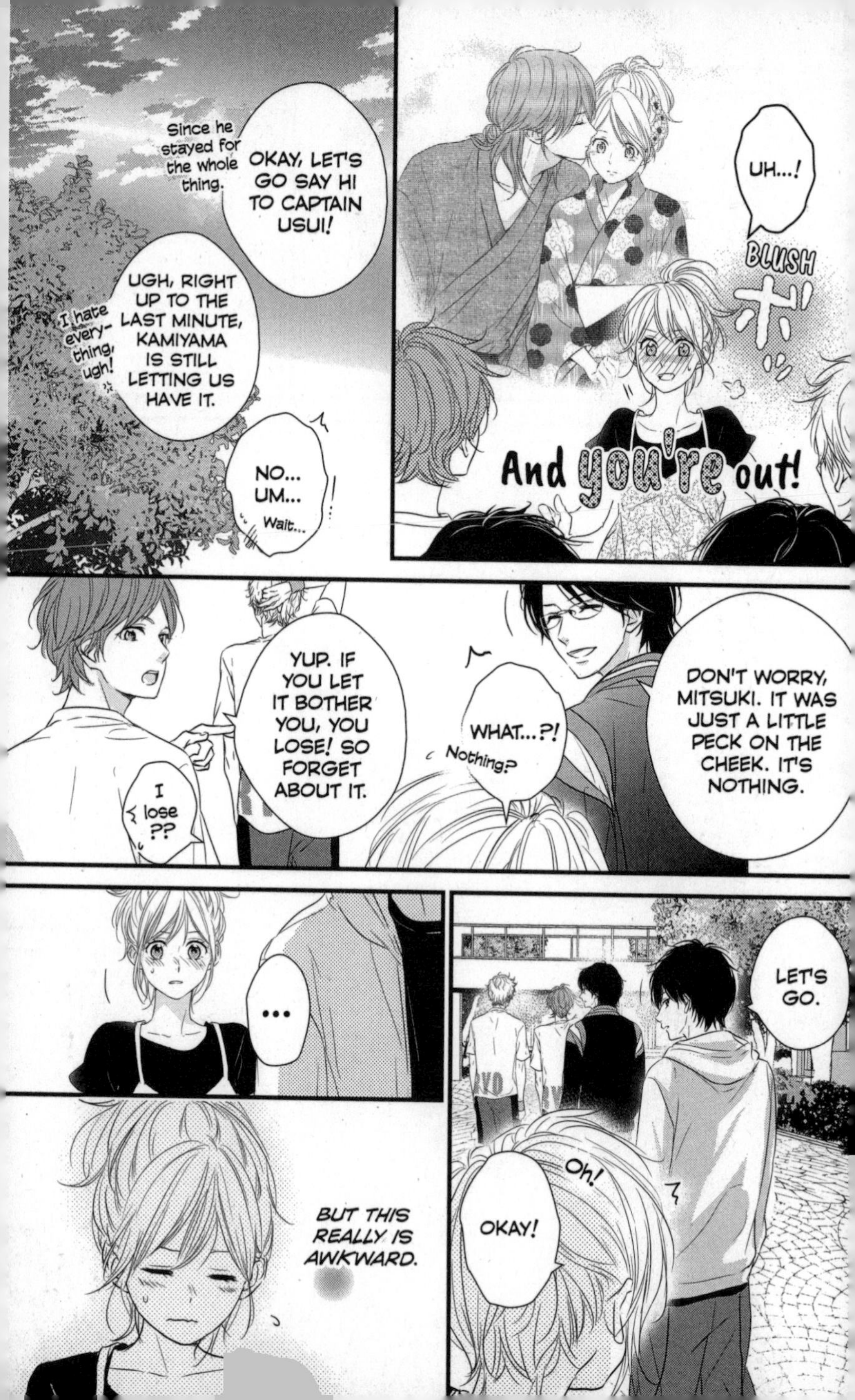
UH...!
BLUSH
ボッ
And you're out!
OKAY, LET'S GO SAY HI TO CAPTAIN USUI!
Since he stayed for the whole thing.
UGH, RIGHT UP TO THE LAST MINUTE, KAMIYAMA IS STILL LETTING US HAVE IT.
I hate everything, ugh!
NO... UM...
Wait...
DON'T WORRY, MITSUKI. IT WAS JUST A LITTLE PECK ON THE CHEEK. IT'S NOTHING.
WHAT...?!
Nothing?
YUP. IF YOU LET IT BOTHER YOU, YOU LOSE! SO FORGET ABOUT IT.
I lose ??
LET'S GO.
Oh!
OKAY!
...
BUT THIS REALLY IS AWKWARD.

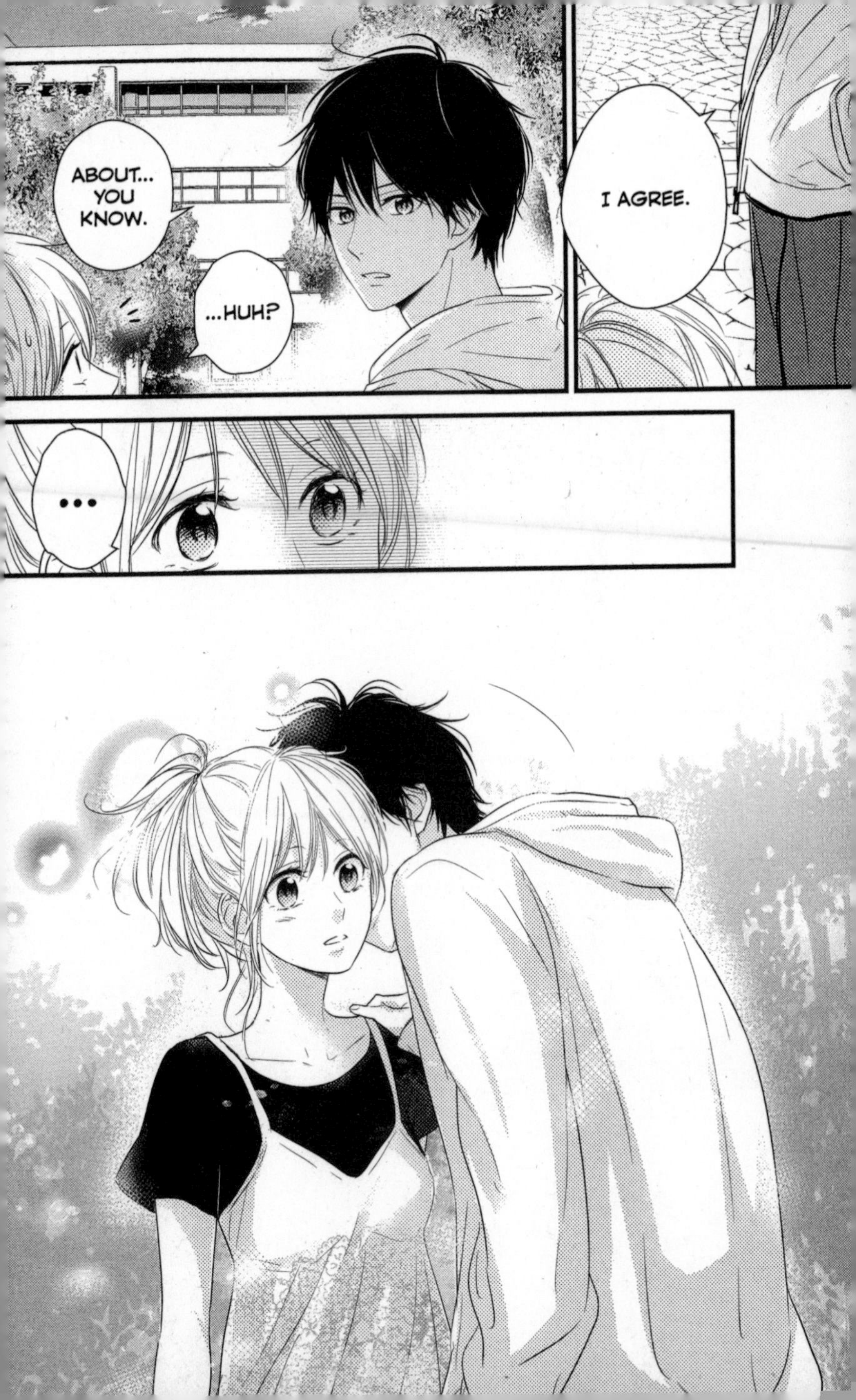
I AGREE.
ABOUT... YOU KNOW.
...HUH?
...

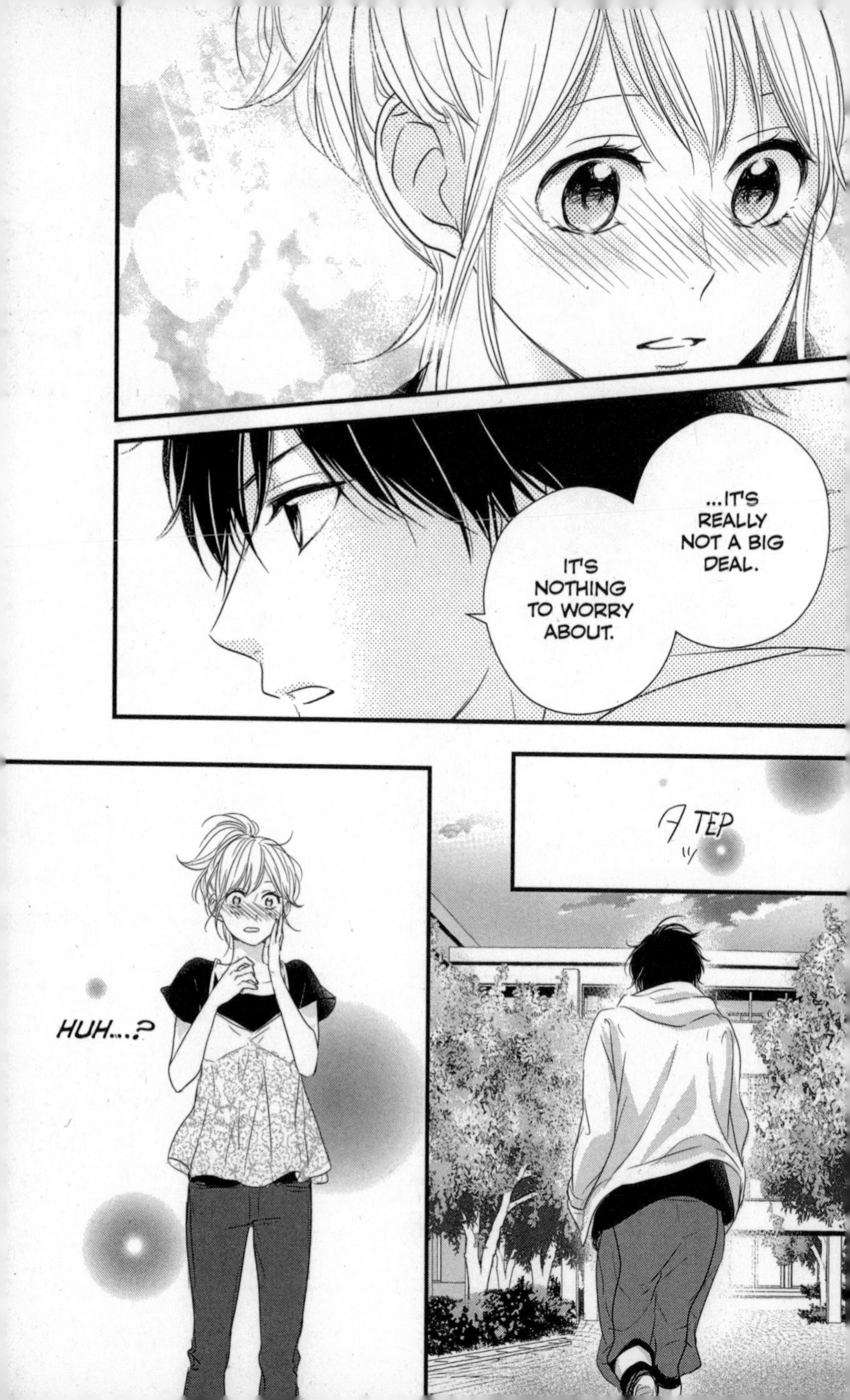
...IT'S REALLY NOT A BIG DEAL.
IT'S NOTHING TO WORRY ABOUT.
TEP
HUH...?

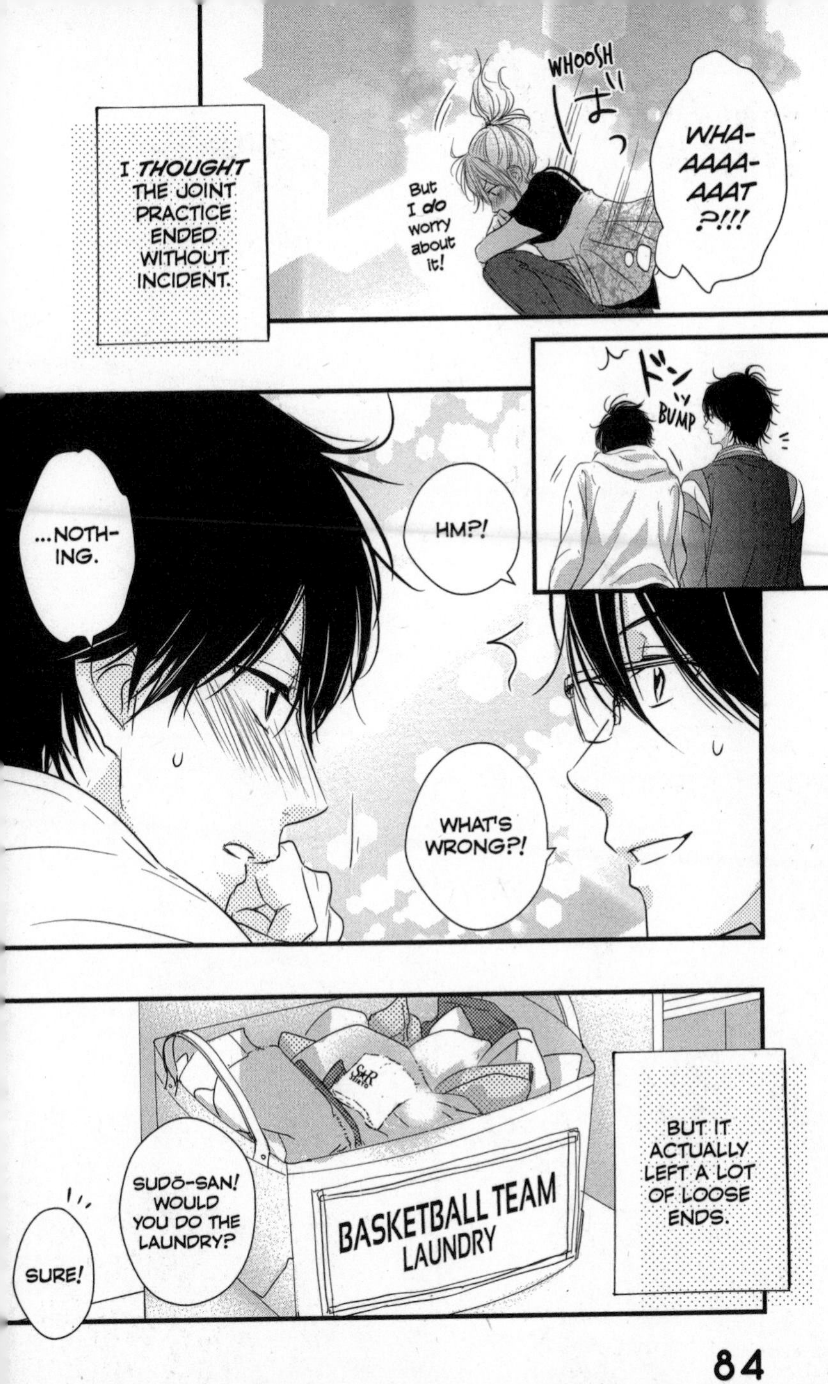
WHA-AAAA-AAAT?!!!
WHOOSH
But I do worry about it!
I THOUGHT THE JOINT PRACTICE ENDED WITHOUT INCIDENT.
BUMP
HM?!
WHAT'S WRONG?!
...NOTH-ING.
BUT IT ACTUALLY LEFT A LOT OF LOOSE ENDS.
BASKETBALL TEAM LAUNDRY
SUDŌ-SAN! WOULD YOU DO THE LAUNDRY?
SURE!

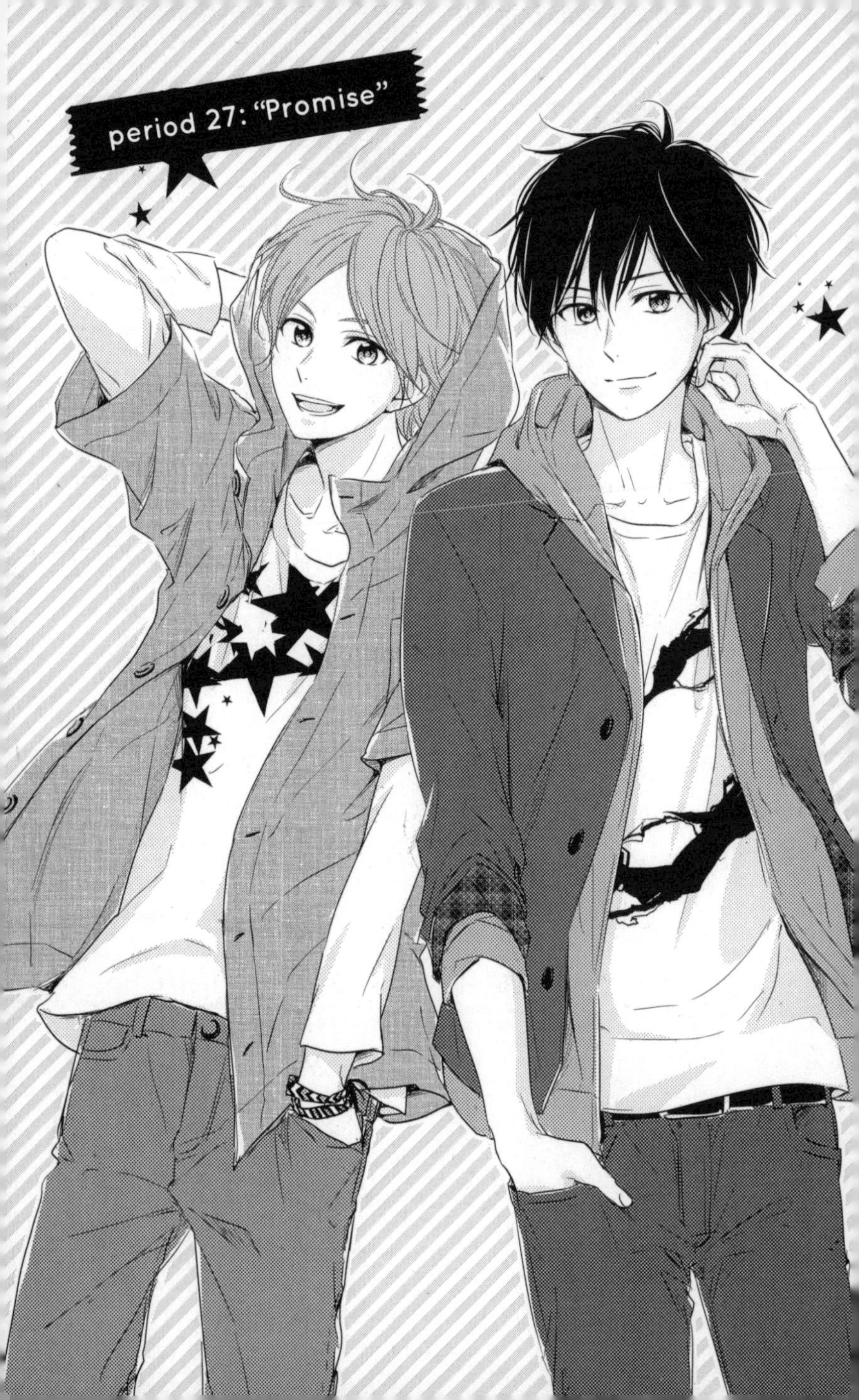
period 27: "Promise"

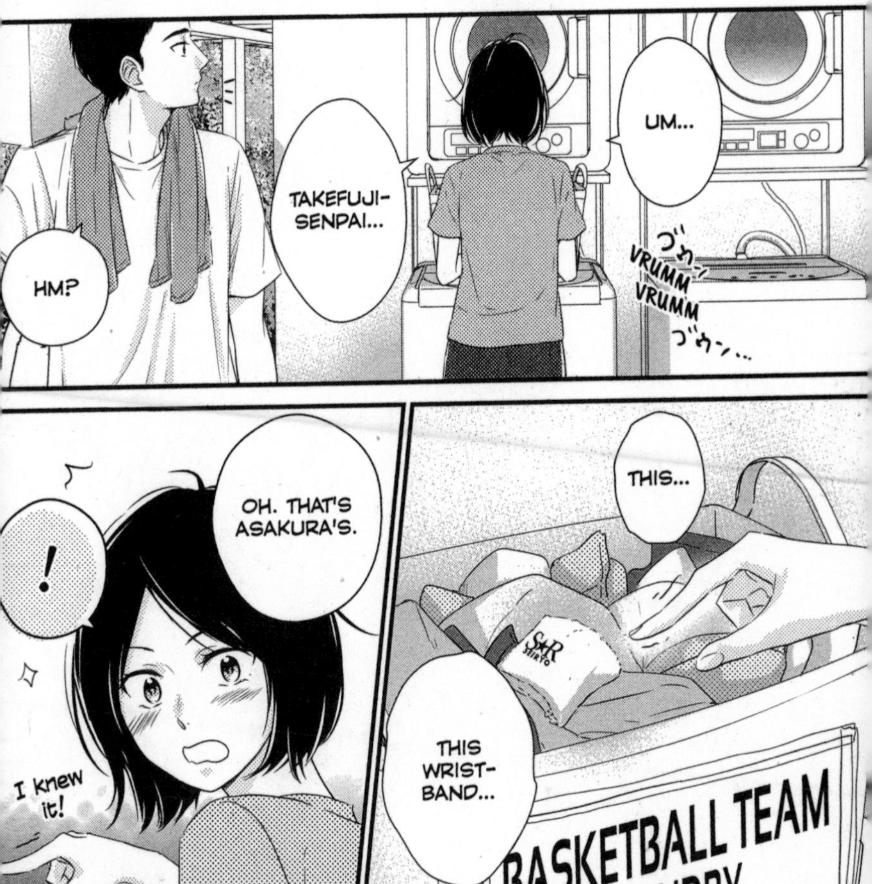
UM...
TAKEFUJI-SENPAI...
HM?
VRUMM VRUMM
THIS...
THIS WRIST-BAND...
BASKETBALL TEAM LAUNDRY
OH. THAT'S ASAKURA'S.
!
I knew it!

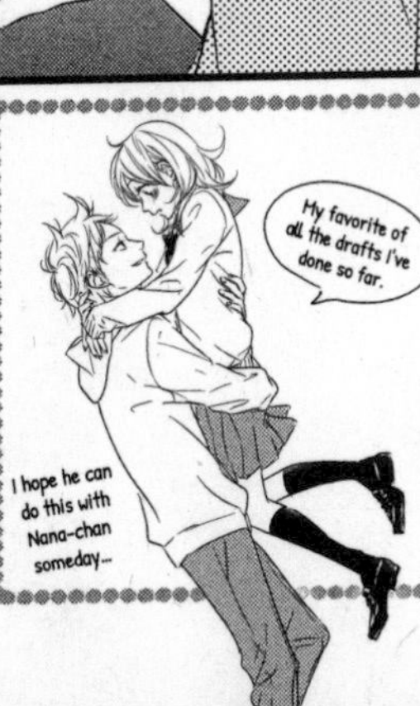
My favorite of all the drafts I've done so far.
I hope he can do this with Nana-chan someday...

And the answer to the Mini Silhouette Quiz is Ryūji-kun!

Popularity Ranking: 6!! (ha ha)

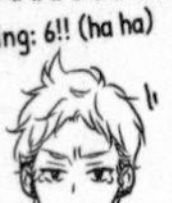
Don't laugh!

The truth is, when I think about a favorite, I like them all for different reasons, and I look at them all the same, so I don't have an answer. But if I think of myself as a reader and nothing else, I think I would like Ryūji.

I want to keep working hard so that someday I can draw what makes Ryūji so cool...

Just you wait, Ryūji!

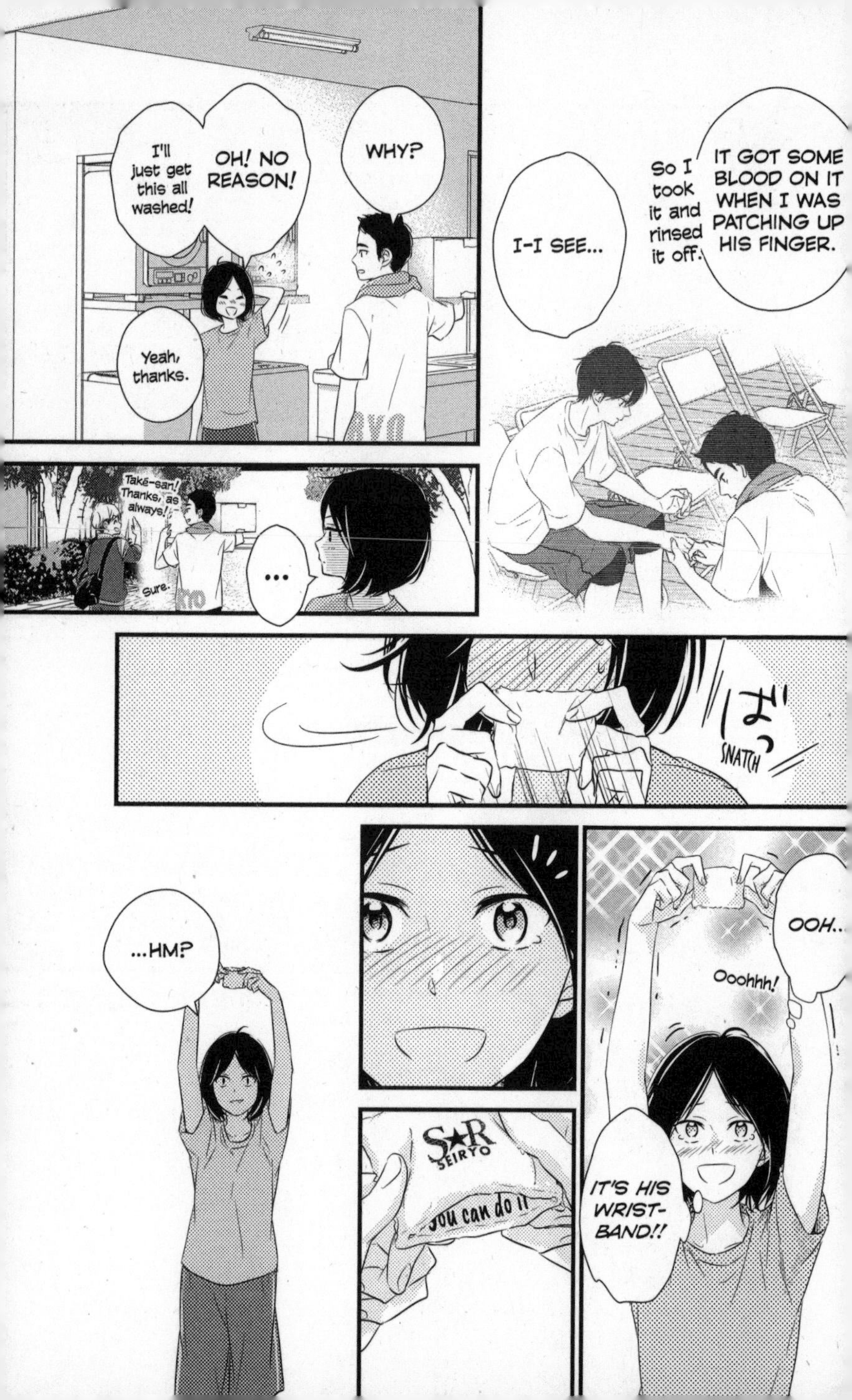
IT GOT SOME BLOOD ON IT WHEN I WAS PATCHING UP HIS FINGER.
So I took it and rinsed it off.
I-I SEE...
WHY?
OH! NO REASON!
I'll just get this all washed!
Yeah, thanks.
Také-san! Thanks, as always!
Sure.
...
ぱっ
SNATCH
OOH...
Ooohhh!
IT'S HIS WRIST-BAND!!
S★R
SEIRYO
...HM?

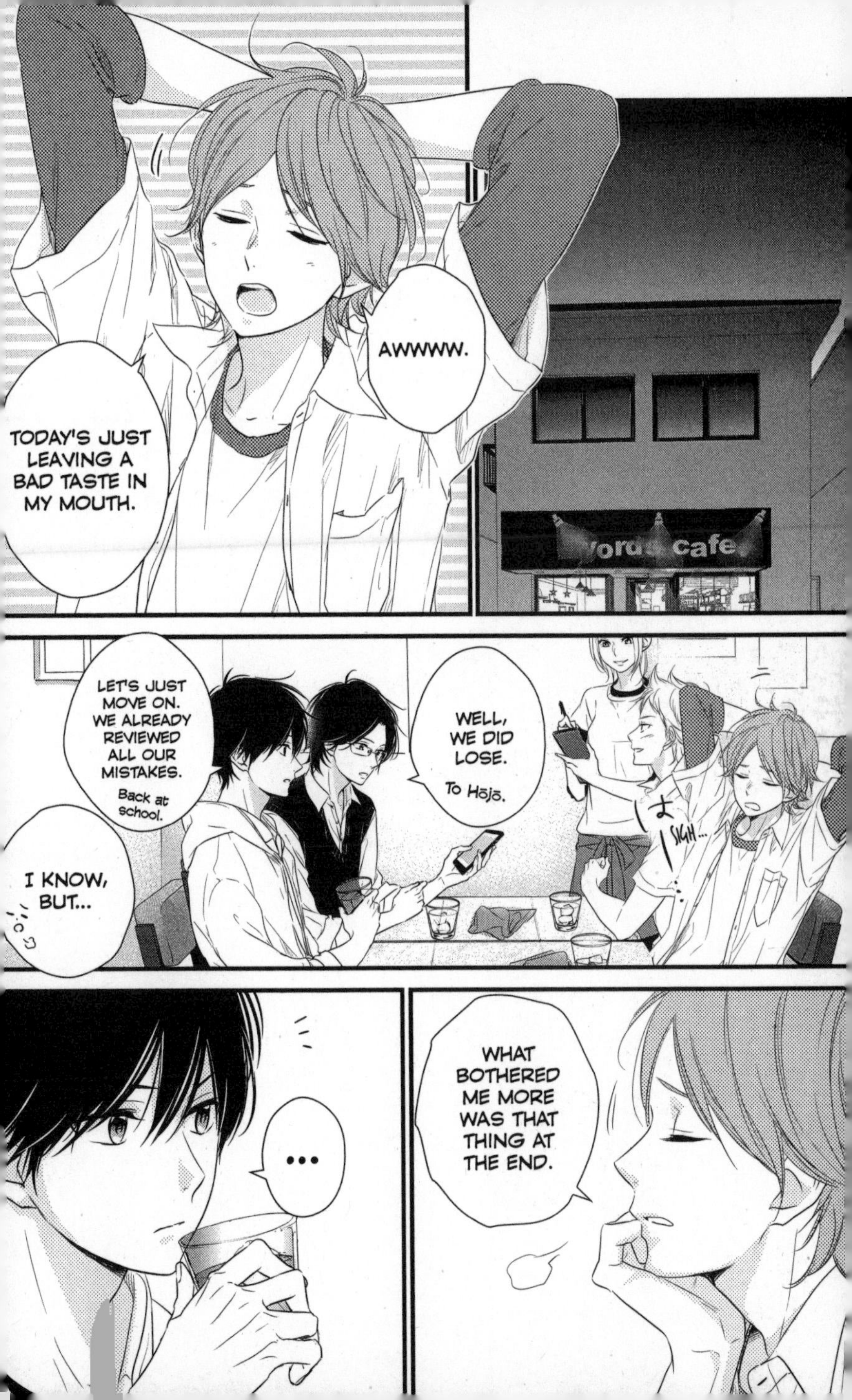
AWWWW.
TODAY'S JUST LEAVING A BAD TASTE IN MY MOUTH.
SIGH...
WELL, WE DID LOSE.
To Hōjō.
LET'S JUST MOVE ON. WE ALREADY REVIEWED ALL OUR MISTAKES.
Back at school.
I KNOW, BUT...
WHAT BOTHERED ME MORE WAS THAT THING AT THE END.
...

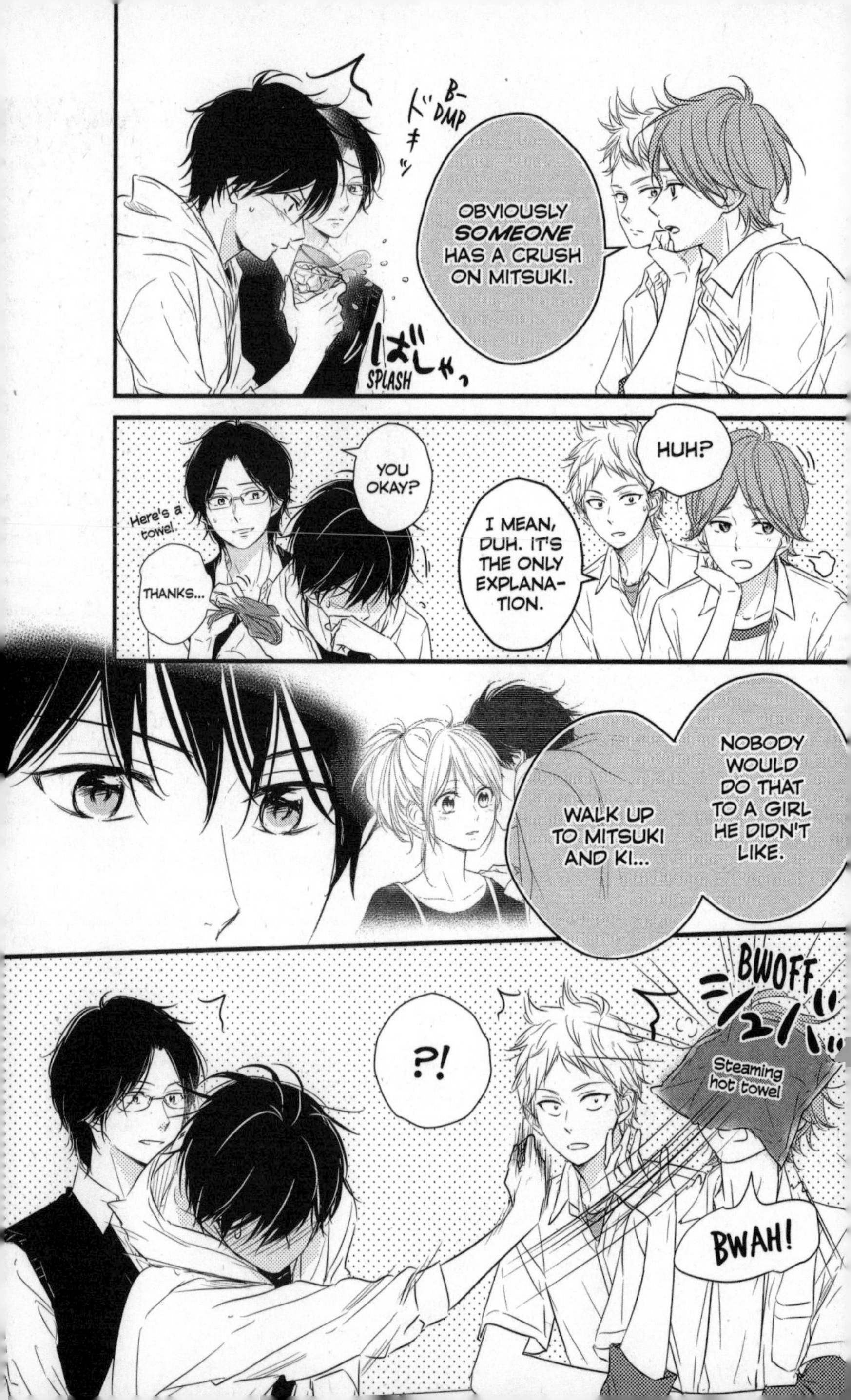
OBVIOUSLY *SOMEONE* HAS A CRUSH ON MITSUKI.
ドキッ
B-DMP
ばしゃっ
SPLASH
HUH?
I MEAN, DUH. IT'S THE ONLY EXPLANATION.
YOU OKAY?
Here's a towel.
THANKS...
NOBODY WOULD DO THAT TO A GIRL HE DIDN'T LIKE.
WALK UP TO MITSUKI AND KI...
BWOFF
Steaming hot towel
BWAH!
?!

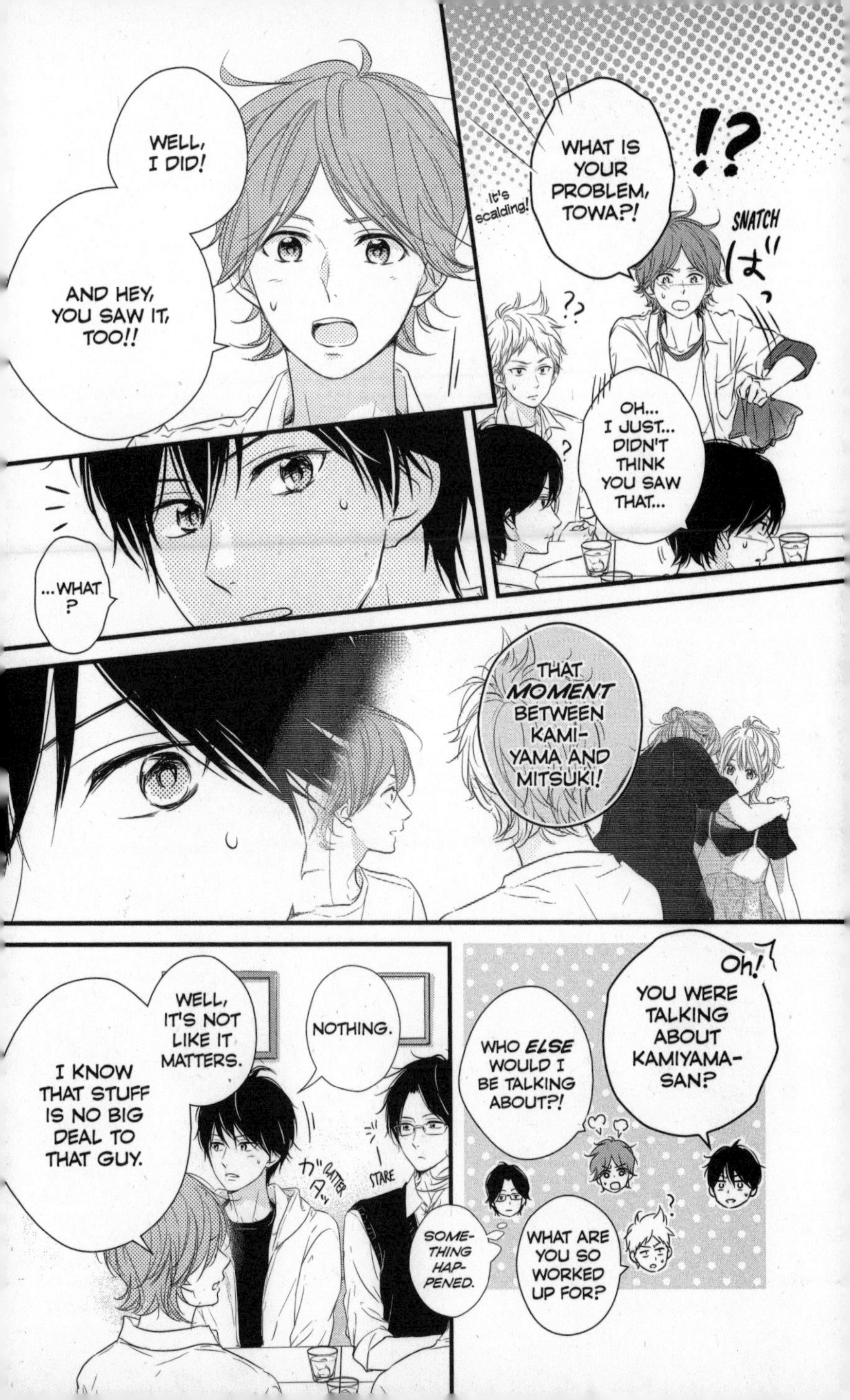
WHAT IS YOUR PROBLEM, TOWA?!
It's scalding!
!?
SNATCH
OH... I JUST... DIDN'T THINK YOU SAW THAT...
WELL, I DID!
AND HEY, YOU SAW IT, TOO!!
...WHAT?
THAT MOMENT BETWEEN KAMI-YAMA AND MITSUKI!
Oh!
YOU WERE TALKING ABOUT KAMIYAMA-SAN?
WHO ELSE WOULD I BE TALKING ABOUT?!
WHAT ARE YOU SO WORKED UP FOR?
NOTHING.
WELL, IT'S NOT LIKE IT MATTERS.
I KNOW THAT STUFF IS NO BIG DEAL TO THAT GUY.
CLATTER
STARE
SOME-THING HAP-PENED.

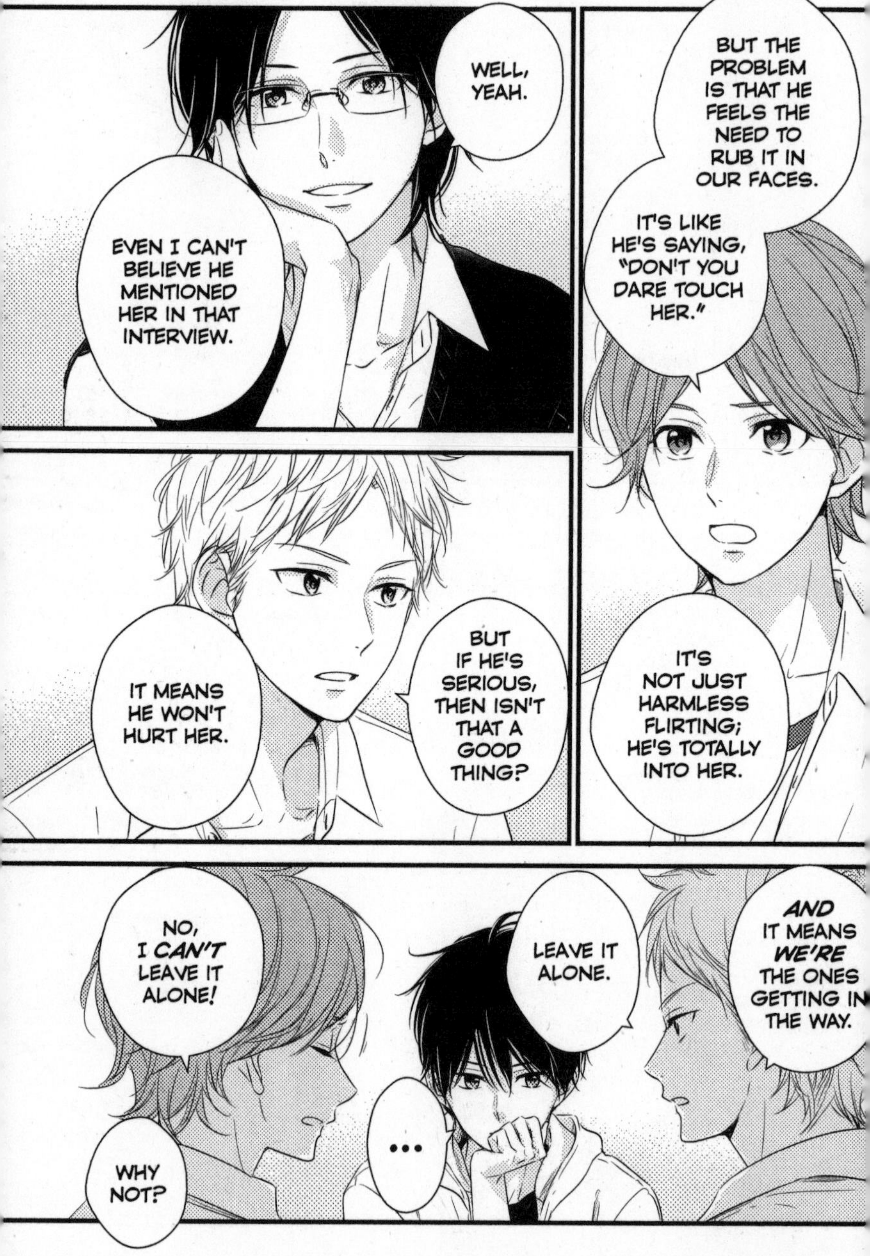
BUT THE PROBLEM IS THAT HE FEELS THE NEED TO RUB IT IN OUR FACES.
IT'S LIKE HE'S SAYING, "DON'T YOU DARE TOUCH HER."
IT'S NOT JUST HARMLESS FLIRTING; HE'S TOTALLY INTO HER.
WELL, YEAH.
EVEN I CAN'T BELIEVE HE MENTIONED HER IN THAT INTERVIEW.
BUT IF HE'S SERIOUS, THEN ISN'T THAT A GOOD THING?
IT MEANS HE WON'T HURT HER.
AND IT MEANS *WE'RE* THE ONES GETTING IN THE WAY.
LEAVE IT ALONE.
NO, I *CAN'T* LEAVE IT ALONE!
...
WHY NOT?

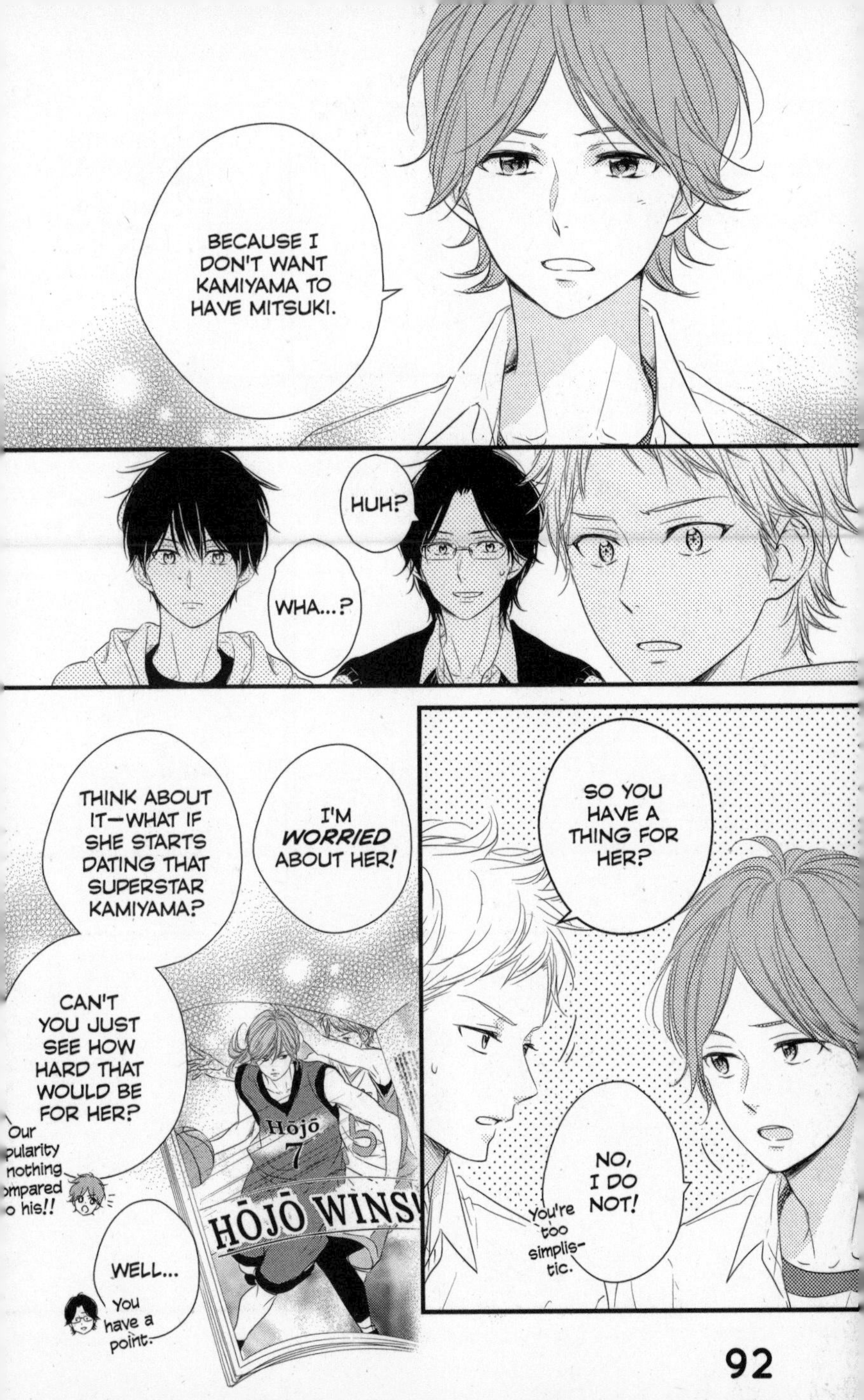
BECAUSE I DON'T WANT KAMIYAMA TO HAVE MITSUKI.
HUH?
WHA...?
SO YOU HAVE A THING FOR HER?
NO, I DO NOT!
You're too simplis-tic.
I'M *WORRIED* ABOUT HER!
THINK ABOUT IT—WHAT IF SHE STARTS DATING THAT SUPERSTAR KAMIYAMA?
CAN'T YOU JUST SEE HOW HARD THAT WOULD BE FOR HER?
Hōjō 7
HŌJŌ WINS
Our pularity nothing ompared o his!!
WELL...
You have a point.

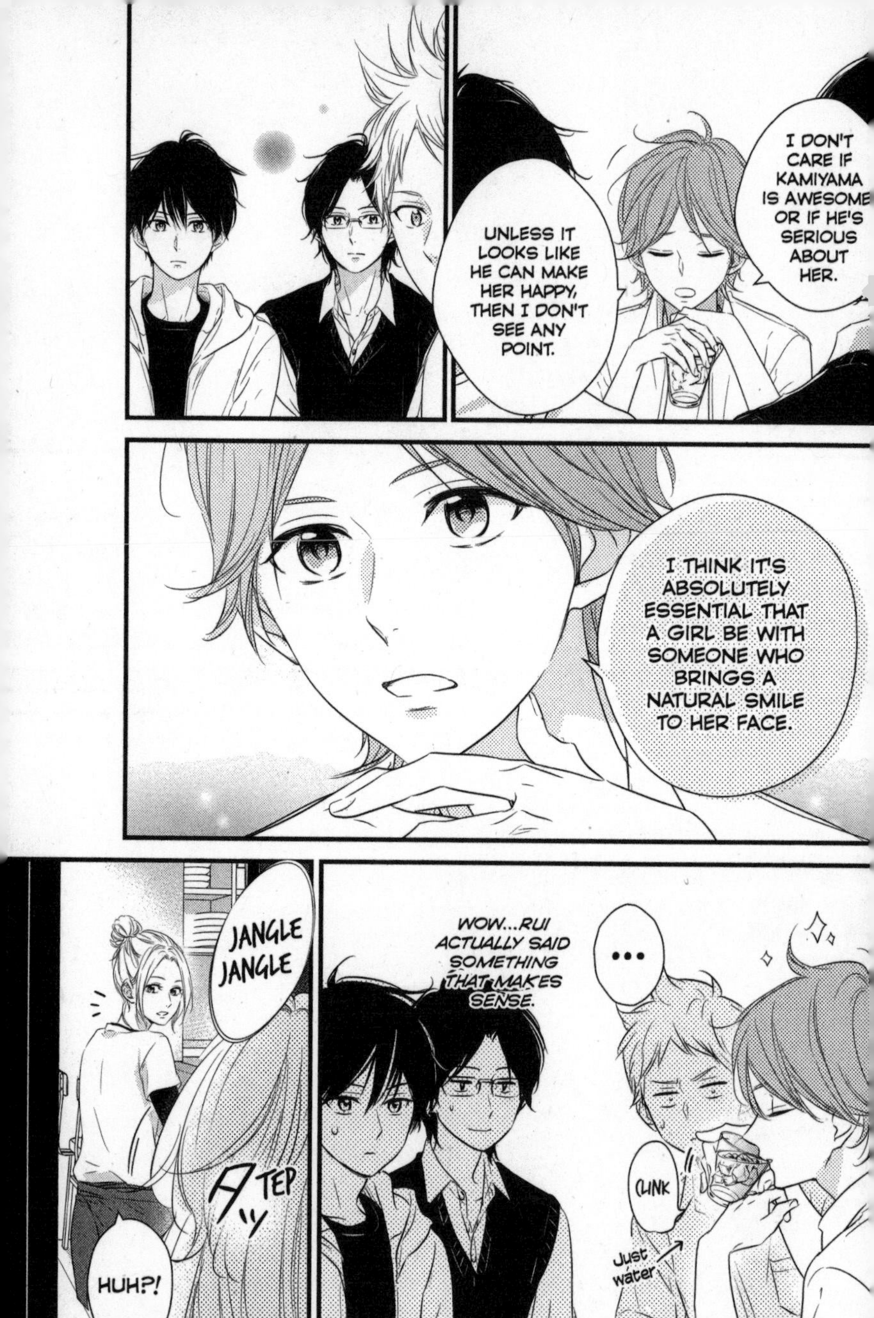
I DON'T CARE IF KAMIYAMA IS AWESOME OR IF HE'S SERIOUS ABOUT HER.
UNLESS IT LOOKS LIKE HE CAN MAKE HER HAPPY, THEN I DON'T SEE ANY POINT.
I THINK IT'S ABSOLUTELY ESSENTIAL THAT A GIRL BE WITH SOMEONE WHO BRINGS A NATURAL SMILE TO HER FACE.
...
WOW...RUI ACTUALLY SAID SOMETHING THAT MAKES SENSE.
CLINK
Just water
JANGLE JANGLE
TEP
HUH?!

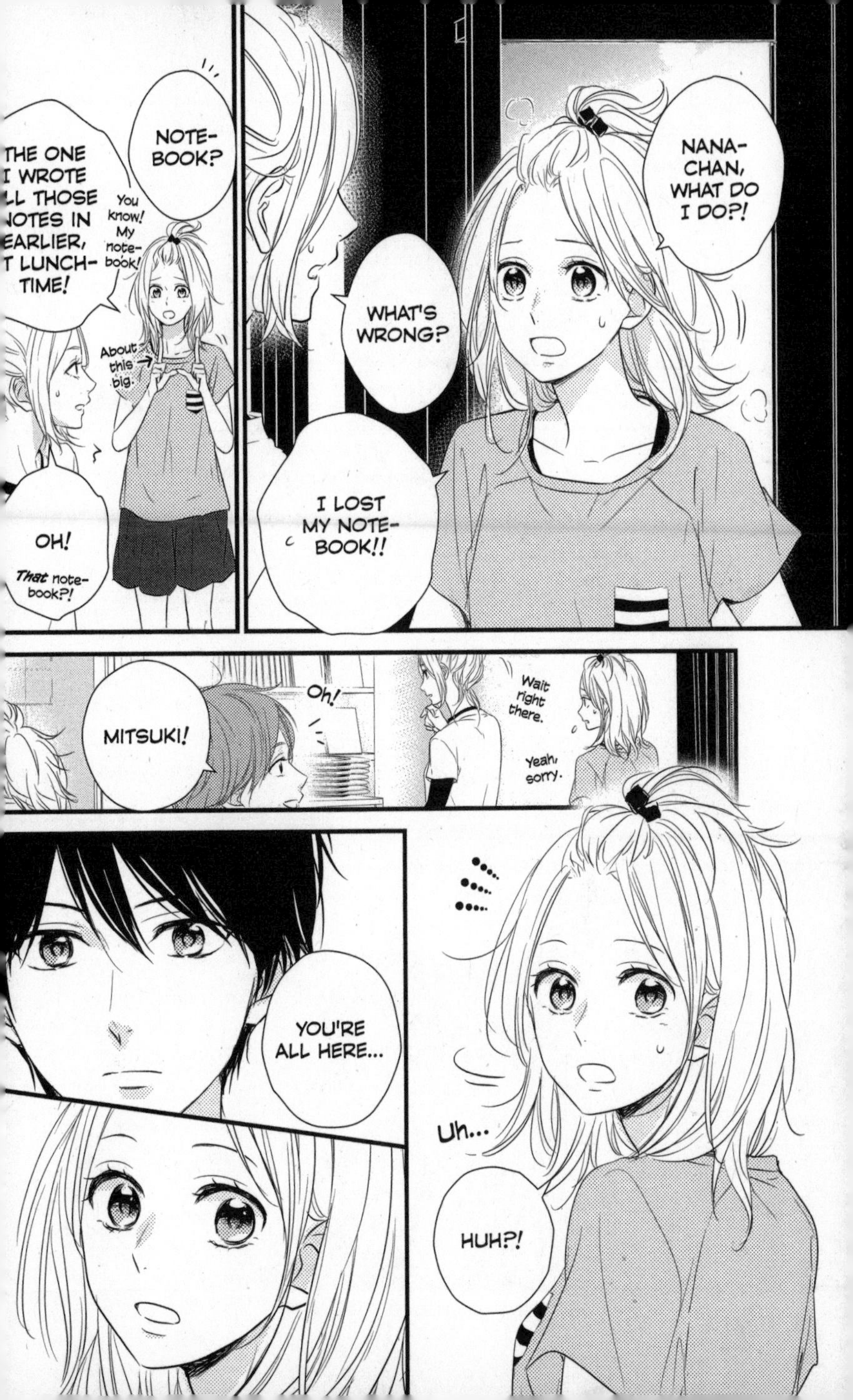
NANA-CHAN, WHAT DO I DO?!
WHAT'S WRONG?
I LOST MY NOTE-BOOK!!
NOTE-BOOK?
THE ONE I WROTE LL THOSE NOTES IN EARLIER, T LUNCH-TIME!
You know! My note-book!
About this big.
OH!
That note-book?!
Wait right there.
Yeah, sorry.
Oh!
MITSUKI!
......
YOU'RE ALL HERE...
Uh...
HUH?!

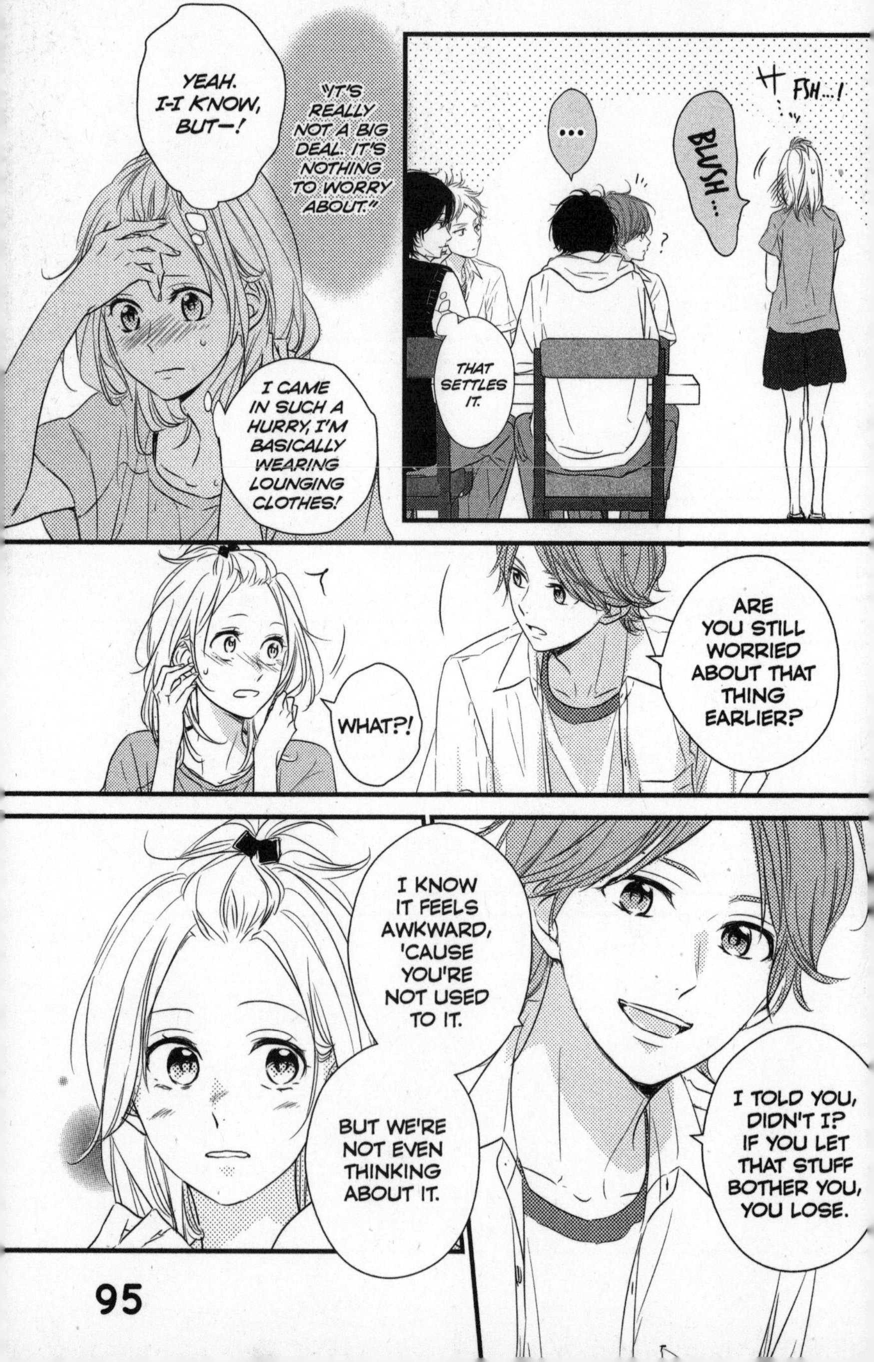
FSH...!
BLUSH...
...
THAT SETTLES IT.
"IT'S REALLY NOT A BIG DEAL. IT'S NOTHING TO WORRY ABOUT."
YEAH. I-I KNOW, BUT—!
I CAME IN SUCH A HURRY, I'M BASICALLY WEARING LOUNGING CLOTHES!
ARE YOU STILL WORRIED ABOUT THAT THING EARLIER?
WHAT?!
I KNOW IT FEELS AWKWARD, 'CAUSE YOU'RE NOT USED TO IT.
BUT WE'RE NOT EVEN THINKING ABOUT IT.
I TOLD YOU, DIDN'T I? IF YOU LET THAT STUFF BOTHER YOU, YOU LOSE.

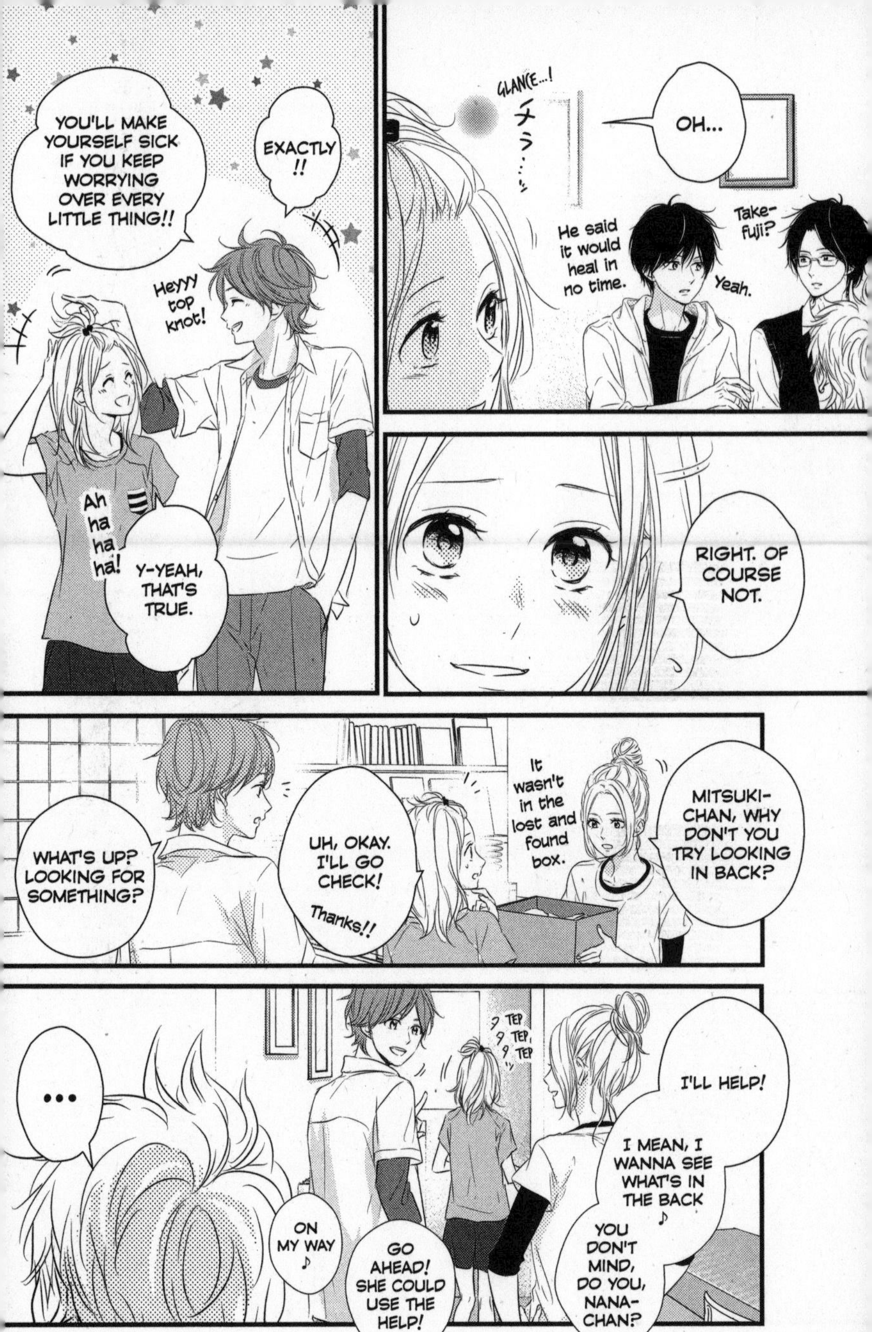
OH...
Take-fuji?
Yeah.
He said it would heal in no time.
GLANCE...!
RIGHT. OF COURSE NOT.
EXACTLY!!
YOU'LL MAKE YOURSELF SICK IF YOU KEEP WORRYING OVER EVERY LITTLE THING!!
Heyyy top knot!
Y-YEAH, THAT'S TRUE.
Ah ha ha ha!
MITSUKI-CHAN, WHY DON'T YOU TRY LOOKING IN BACK?
It wasn't in the lost and found box.
UH, OKAY. I'LL GO CHECK!
Thanks!!
WHAT'S UP? LOOKING FOR SOMETHING?
I'LL HELP!
I MEAN, I WANNA SEE WHAT'S IN THE BACK ♪
YOU DON'T MIND, DO YOU, NANA-CHAN?
TEP TEP, TEP
GO AHEAD! SHE COULD USE THE HELP!
ON MY WAY ♪
...

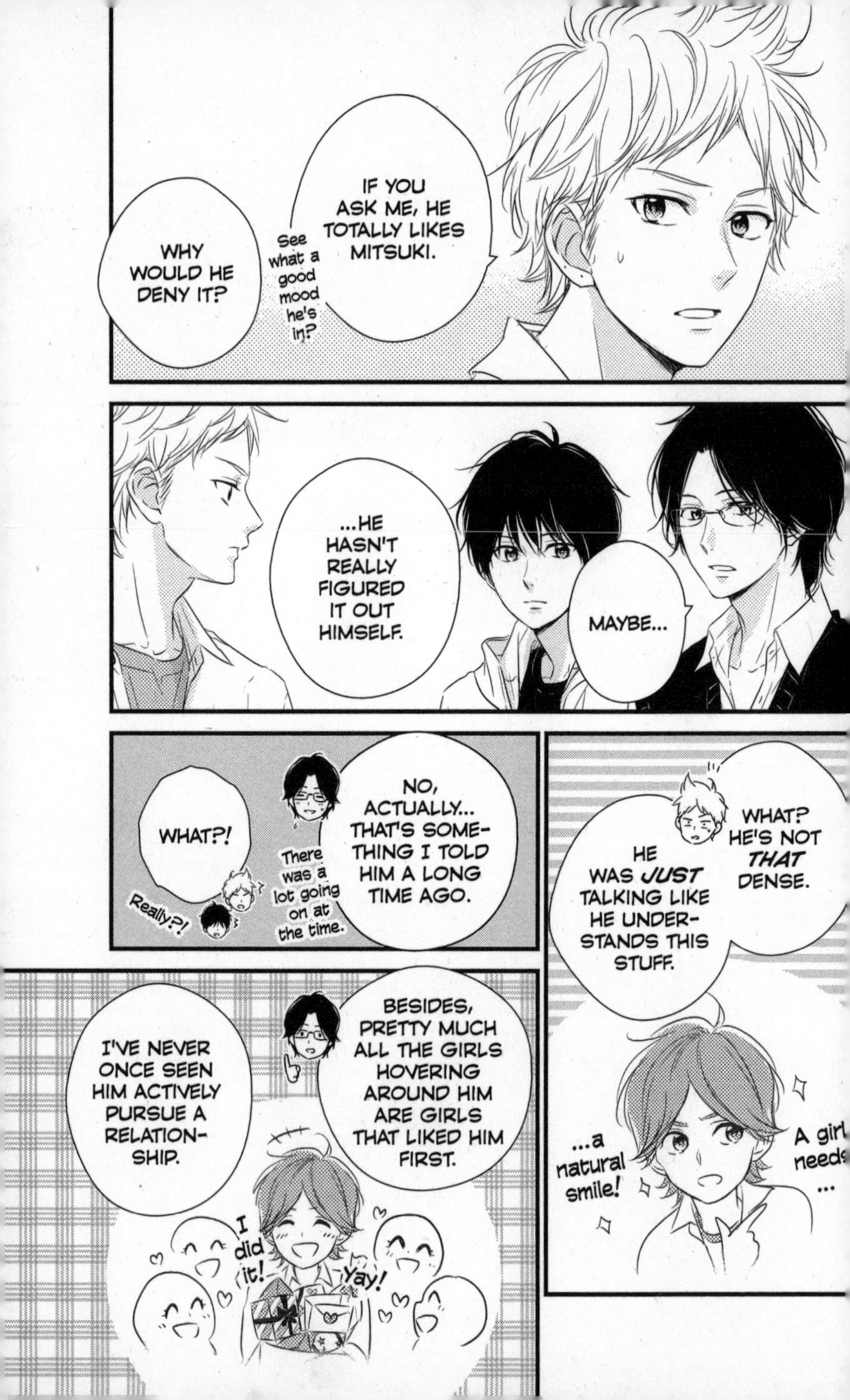
IF YOU ASK ME, HE TOTALLY LIKES MITSUKI.
See what a good mood he's in?
WHY WOULD HE DENY IT?
MAYBE...
...HE HASN'T REALLY FIGURED IT OUT HIMSELF.
WHAT? HE'S NOT *THAT* DENSE.
HE WAS *JUST* TALKING LIKE HE UNDERSTANDS THIS STUFF.
A girl needs...
...a natural smile!
NO, ACTUALLY... THAT'S SOMETHING I TOLD HIM A LONG TIME AGO.
There was a lot going on at the time.
WHAT?!
Really?!
BESIDES, PRETTY MUCH ALL THE GIRLS HOVERING AROUND HIM ARE GIRLS THAT LIKED HIM FIRST.
I'VE NEVER ONCE SEEN HIM ACTIVELY PURSUE A RELATIONSHIP.
Yay!
I did it!

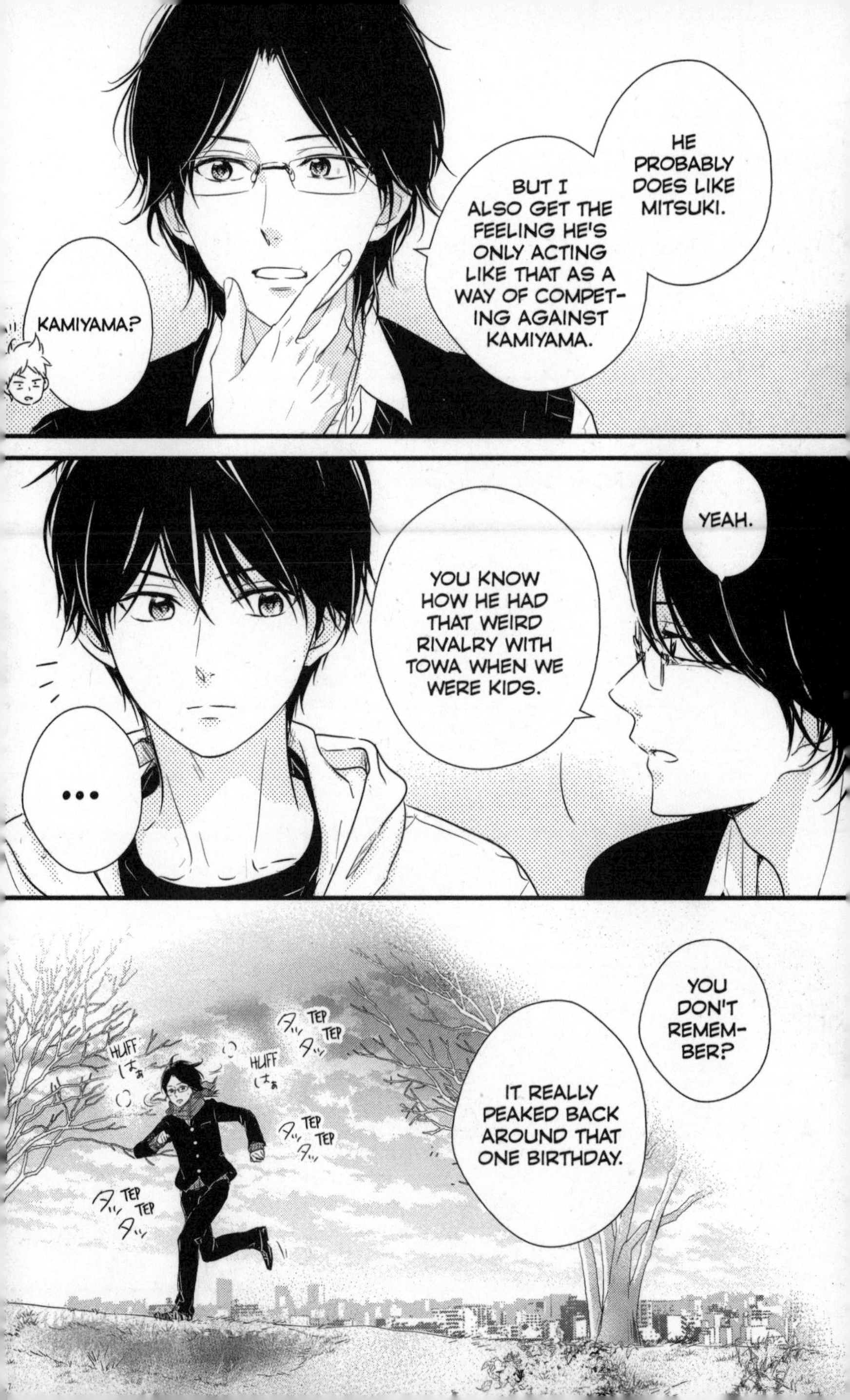
HE PROBABLY DOES LIKE MITSUKI.
BUT I ALSO GET THE FEELING HE'S ONLY ACTING LIKE THAT AS A WAY OF COMPET-ING AGAINST KAMIYAMA.
KAMIYAMA?
YEAH.
YOU KNOW HOW HE HAD THAT WEIRD RIVALRY WITH TOWA WHEN WE WERE KIDS.
...
YOU DON'T REMEMBER?
IT REALLY PEAKED BACK AROUND THAT ONE BIRTHDAY.
TEP TEP
HUFF
HUFF
TEP TEP
TEP TEP

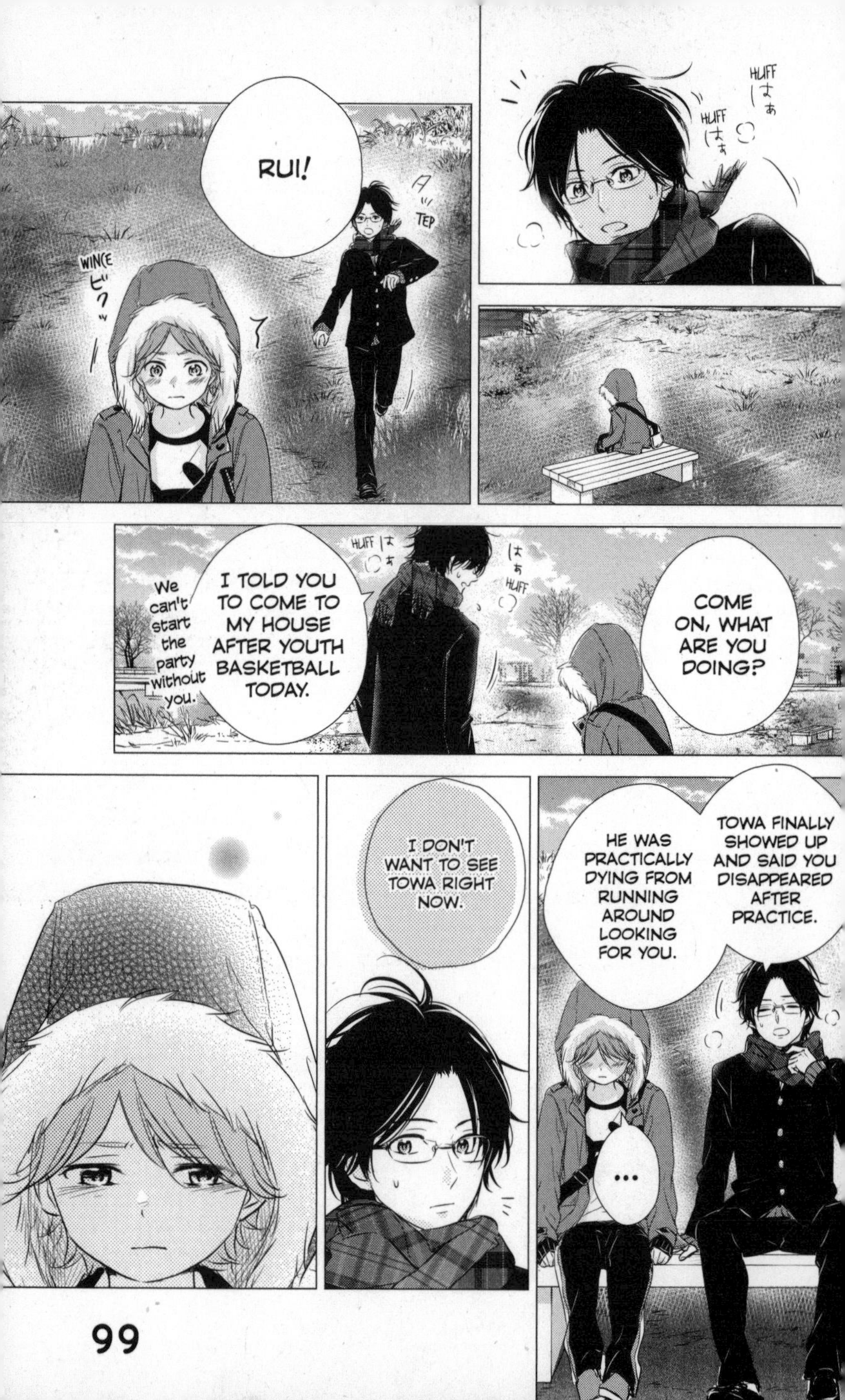
HUFF はぁ
HUFF はぁ
RUI!
タッ TEP
WINCE ビクッ
COME ON, WHAT ARE YOU DOING?
はぁ HUFF
HUFF はぁ
I TOLD YOU TO COME TO MY HOUSE AFTER YOUTH BASKETBALL TODAY.
We can't start the party without you.
TOWA FINALLY SHOWED UP AND SAID YOU DISAPPEARED AFTER PRACTICE.
HE WAS PRACTICALLY DYING FROM RUNNING AROUND LOOKING FOR YOU.
...
I DON'T WANT TO SEE TOWA RIGHT NOW.

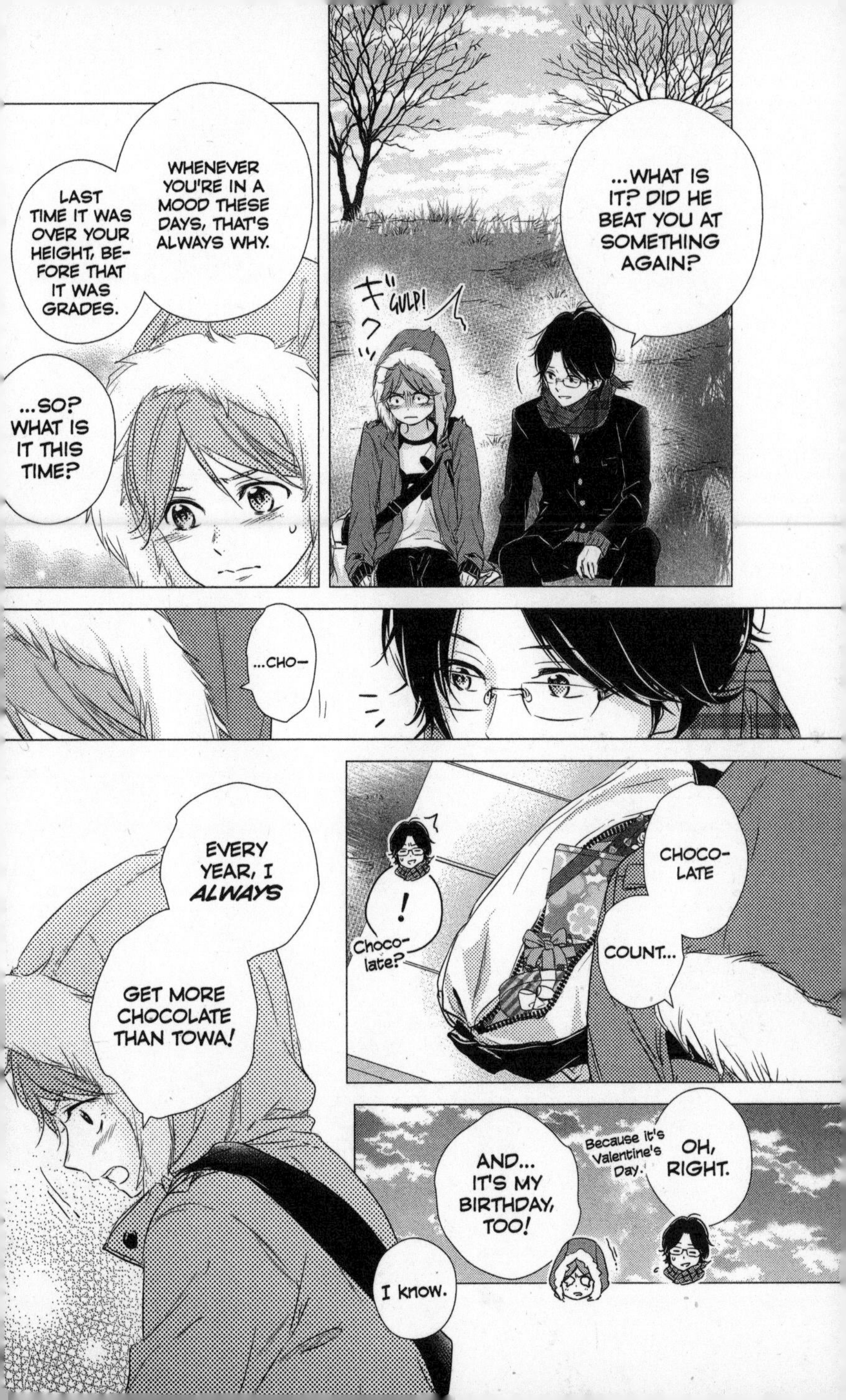
...WHAT IS IT? DID HE BEAT YOU AT SOMETHING AGAIN?
ギク GULP!
WHENEVER YOU'RE IN A MOOD THESE DAYS, THAT'S ALWAYS WHY.
LAST TIME IT WAS OVER YOUR HEIGHT, BEFORE THAT IT WAS GRADES.
...SO? WHAT IS IT THIS TIME?
...CHO-
CHOCO-LATE
COUNT...
!
Chocolate?
OH, RIGHT.
Because it's Valentine's Day.
AND... IT'S MY BIRTHDAY, TOO!
I know.
EVERY YEAR, I *ALWAYS*
GET MORE CHOCOLATE THAN TOWA!

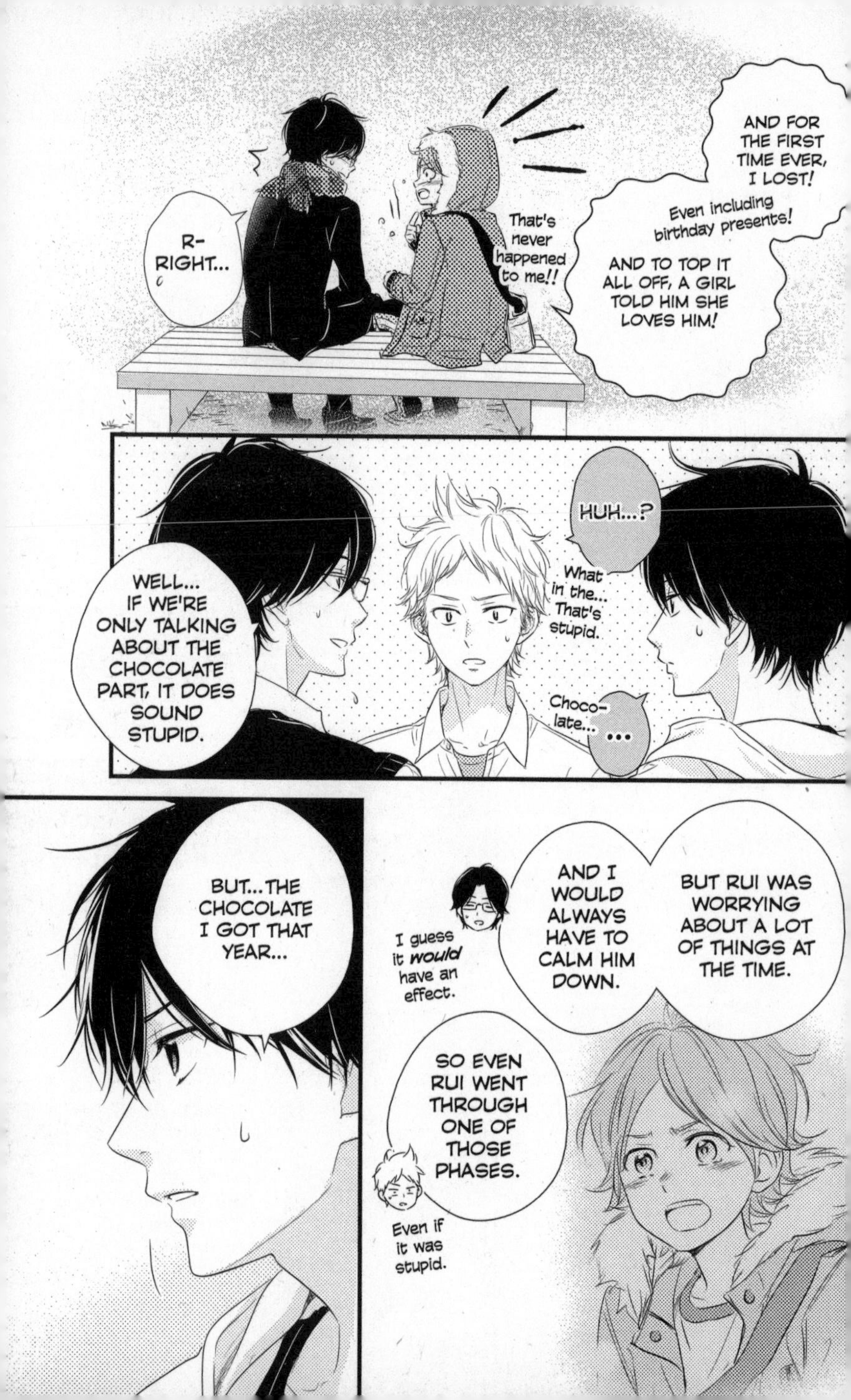
AND FOR THE FIRST TIME EVER, I LOST!
Even including birthday presents!
AND TO TOP IT ALL OFF, A GIRL TOLD HIM SHE LOVES HIM!
That's never happened to me!!
R-RIGHT...
HUH...?
What in the... That's stupid.
Choco-late...
...
WELL... IF WE'RE ONLY TALKING ABOUT THE CHOCOLATE PART, IT DOES SOUND STUPID.
BUT RUI WAS WORRYING ABOUT A LOT OF THINGS AT THE TIME.
AND I WOULD ALWAYS HAVE TO CALM HIM DOWN.
I guess it *would* have an effect.
SO EVEN RUI WENT THROUGH ONE OF THOSE PHASES.
Even if it was stupid.
BUT... THE CHOCOLATE I GOT THAT YEAR...

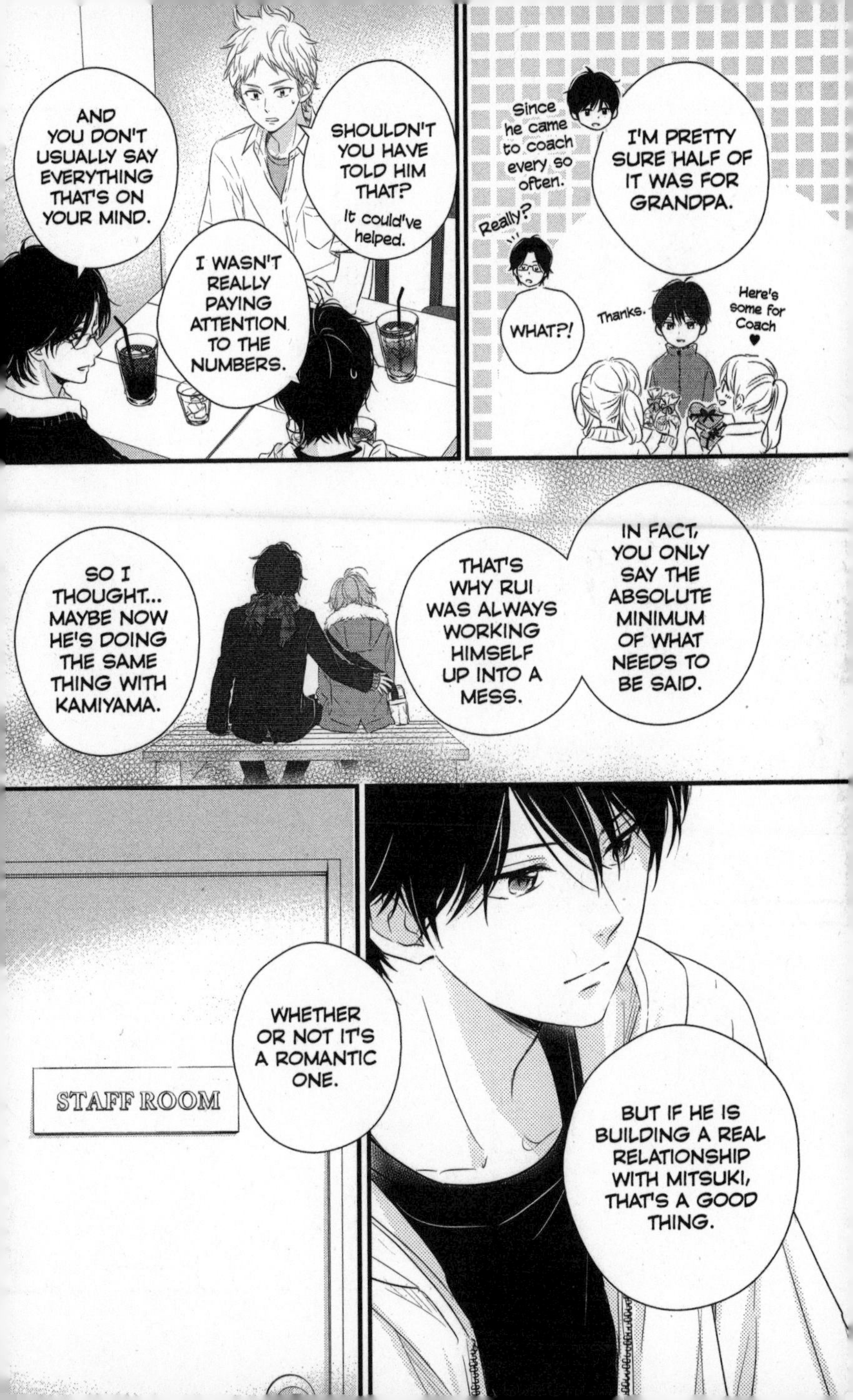
I'M PRETTY SURE HALF OF IT WAS FOR GRANDPA.
Since he came to coach every so often.
Here's some for Coach ♥
Thanks.
Really?
WHAT?!
SHOULDN'T YOU HAVE TOLD HIM THAT?
It could've helped.
AND YOU DON'T USUALLY SAY EVERYTHING THAT'S ON YOUR MIND.
I WASN'T REALLY PAYING ATTENTION TO THE NUMBERS.
IN FACT, YOU ONLY SAY THE ABSOLUTE MINIMUM OF WHAT NEEDS TO BE SAID.
THAT'S WHY RUI WAS ALWAYS WORKING HIMSELF UP INTO A MESS.
SO I THOUGHT... MAYBE NOW HE'S DOING THE SAME THING WITH KAMIYAMA.
WHETHER OR NOT IT'S A ROMANTIC ONE.
BUT IF HE IS BUILDING A REAL RELATIONSHIP WITH MITSUKI, THAT'S A GOOD THING.
STAFF ROOM

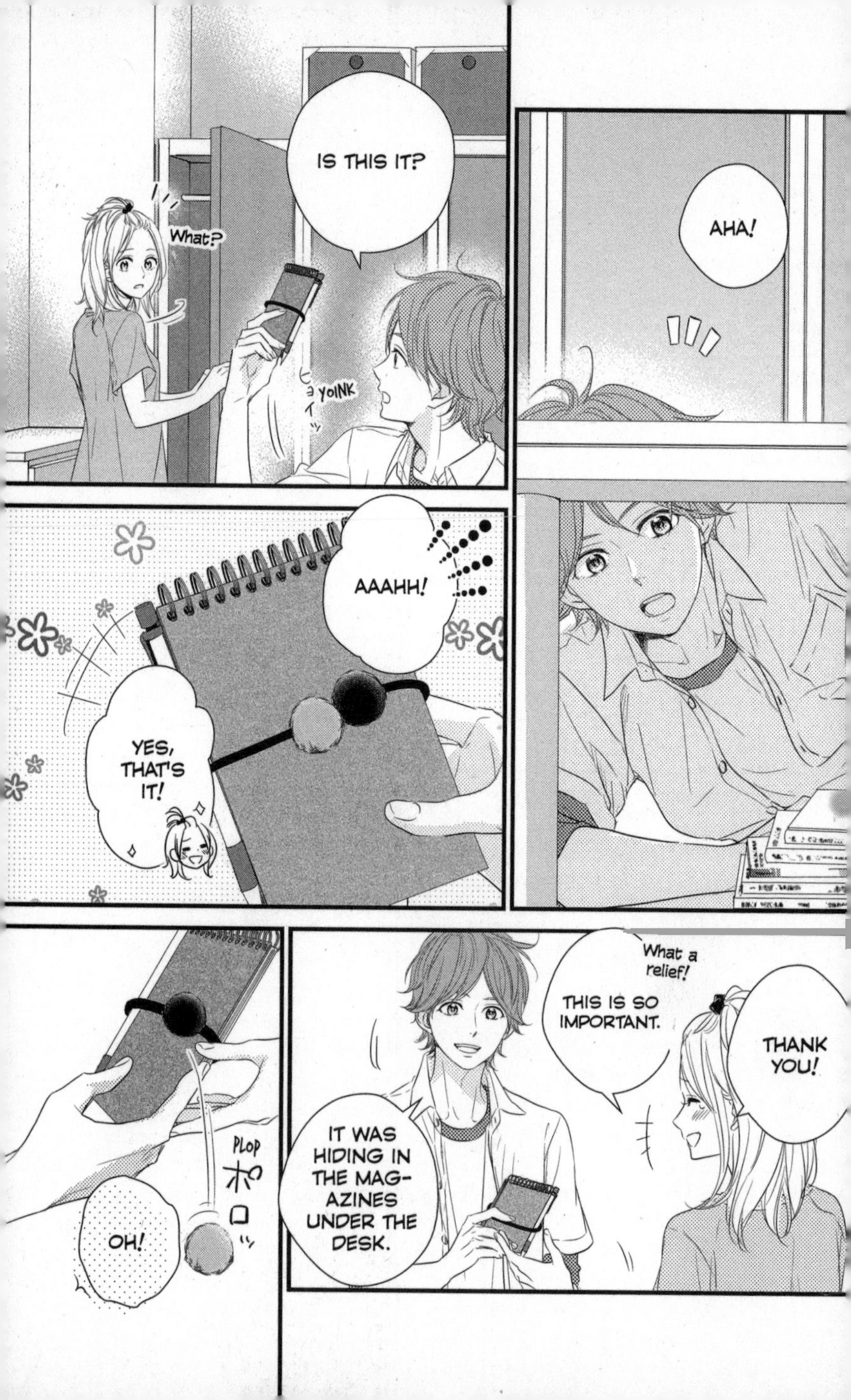
AHA!
IS THIS IT?
What?
ヒョイッ
YOINK
AAAHH!
YES, THAT'S IT!
THANK YOU!
What a relief!
THIS IS SO IMPORTANT.
IT WAS HIDING IN THE MAG-AZINES UNDER THE DESK.
PLOP
ポロッ
OH!

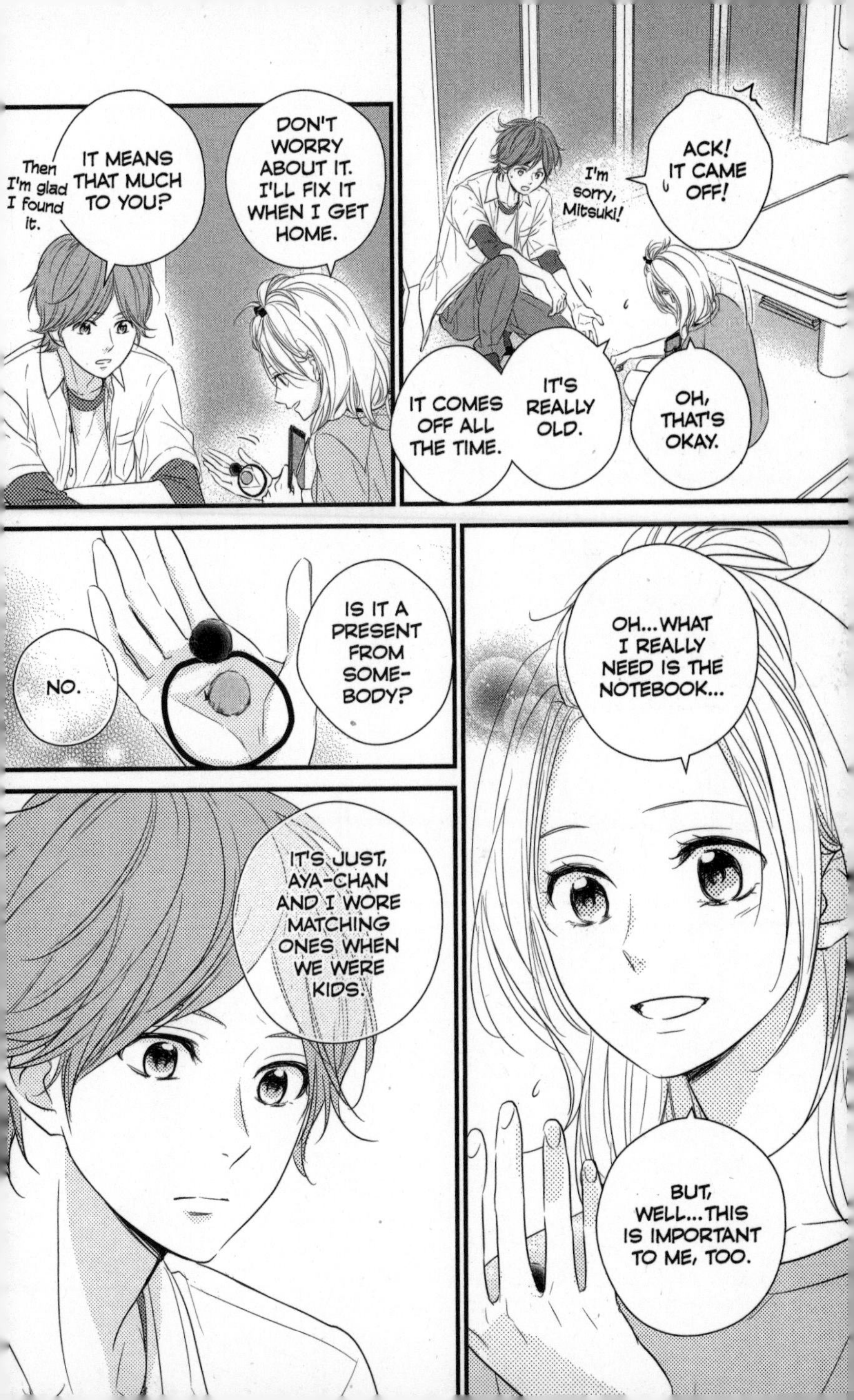
ACK! IT CAME OFF!
I'm sorry, Mitsuki!
OH, THAT'S OKAY.
IT'S REALLY OLD.
IT COMES OFF ALL THE TIME.
DON'T WORRY ABOUT IT. I'LL FIX IT WHEN I GET HOME.
IT MEANS THAT MUCH TO YOU?
Then I'm glad I found it.
OH...WHAT I REALLY NEED IS THE NOTEBOOK...
BUT, WELL...THIS IS IMPORTANT TO ME, TOO.
IS IT A PRESENT FROM SOME-BODY?
NO.
IT'S JUST, AYA-CHAN AND I WORE MATCHING ONES WHEN WE WERE KIDS.

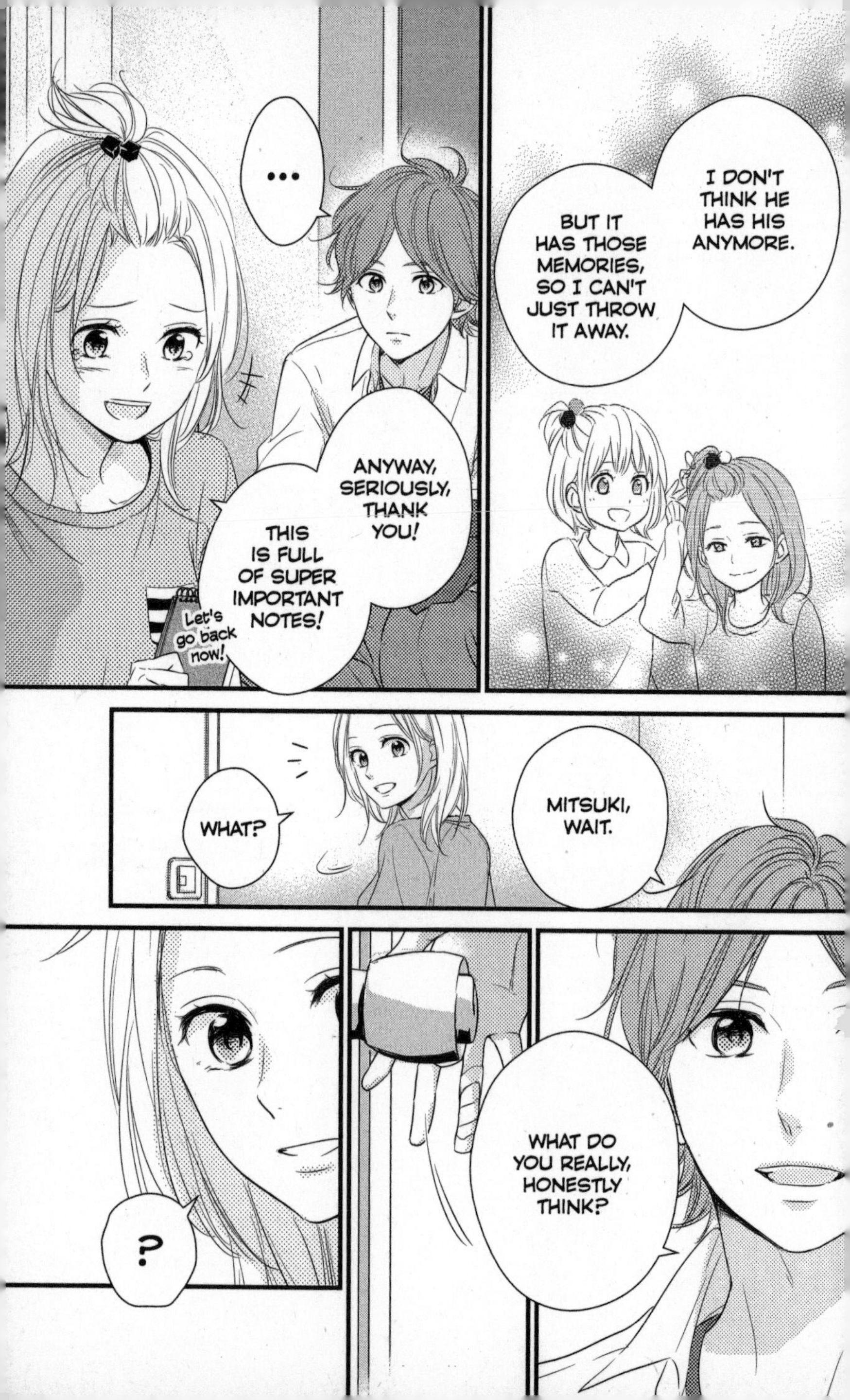
I DON'T THINK HE HAS HIS ANYMORE.
BUT IT HAS THOSE MEMORIES, SO I CAN'T JUST THROW IT AWAY.
...
ANYWAY, SERIOUSLY, THANK YOU!
THIS IS FULL OF SUPER IMPORTANT NOTES!
Let's go back now!
MITSUKI, WAIT.
WHAT?
WHAT DO YOU REALLY, HONESTLY THINK?
?

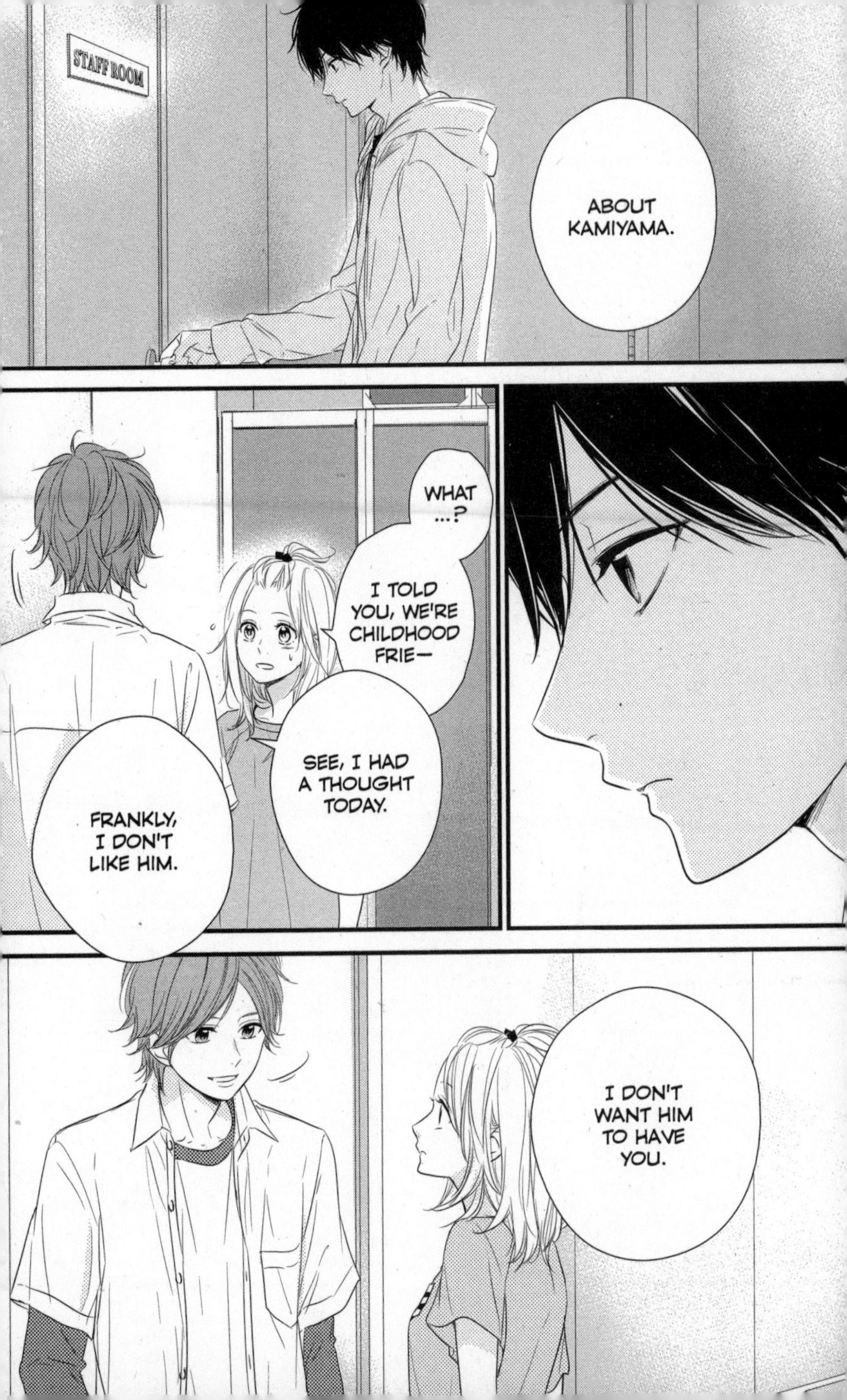
STAFF ROOM
ABOUT KAMIYAMA.
WHAT ...?
I TOLD YOU, WE'RE CHILDHOOD FRIE—
SEE, I HAD A THOUGHT TODAY.
FRANKLY, I DON'T LIKE HIM.
I DON'T WANT HIM TO HAVE YOU.

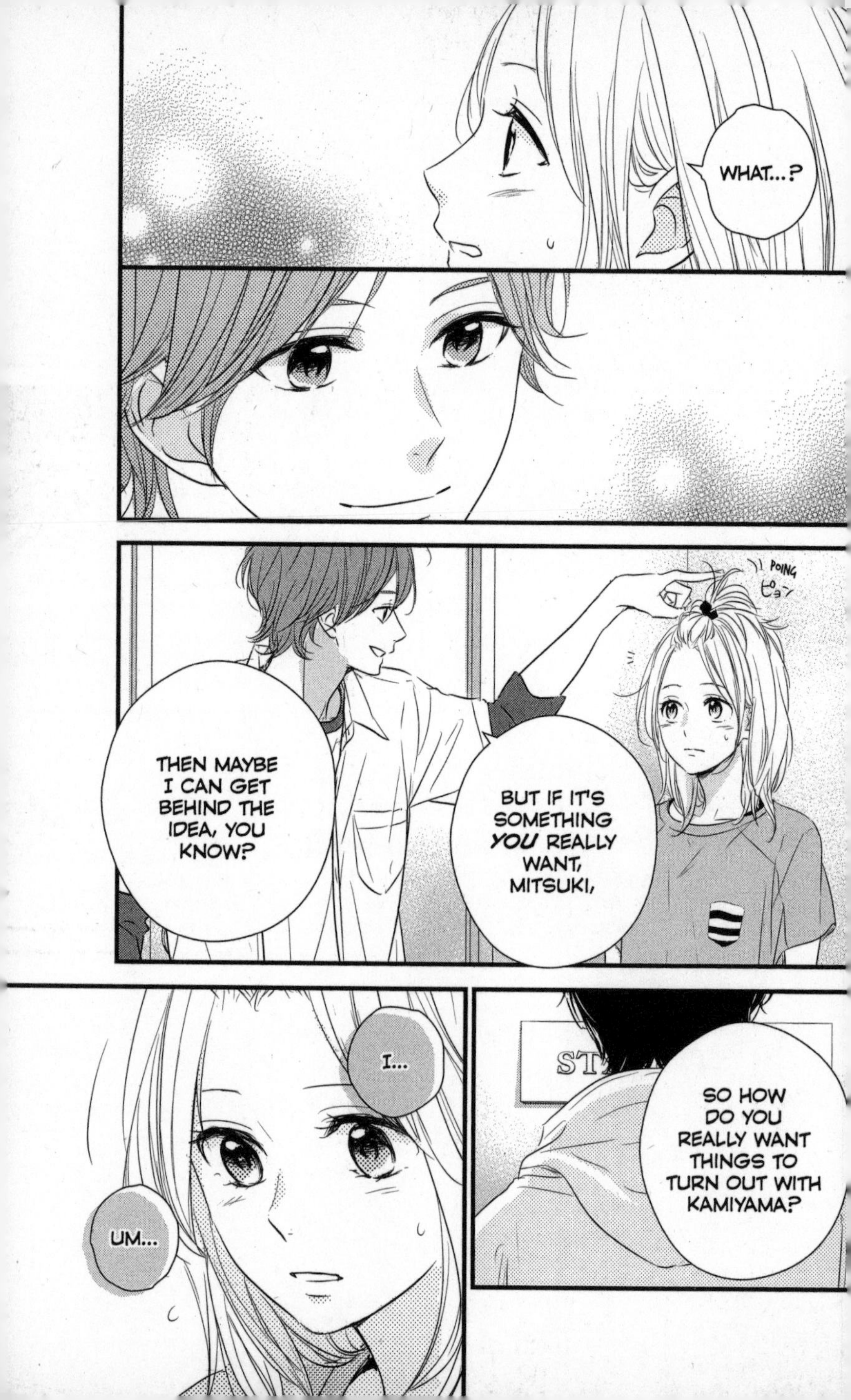
WHAT...?
POING
BUT IF IT'S SOMETHING *YOU* REALLY WANT, MITSUKI,
THEN MAYBE I CAN GET BEHIND THE IDEA, YOU KNOW?
SO HOW DO YOU REALLY WANT THINGS TO TURN OUT WITH KAMIYAMA?
I...
UM...

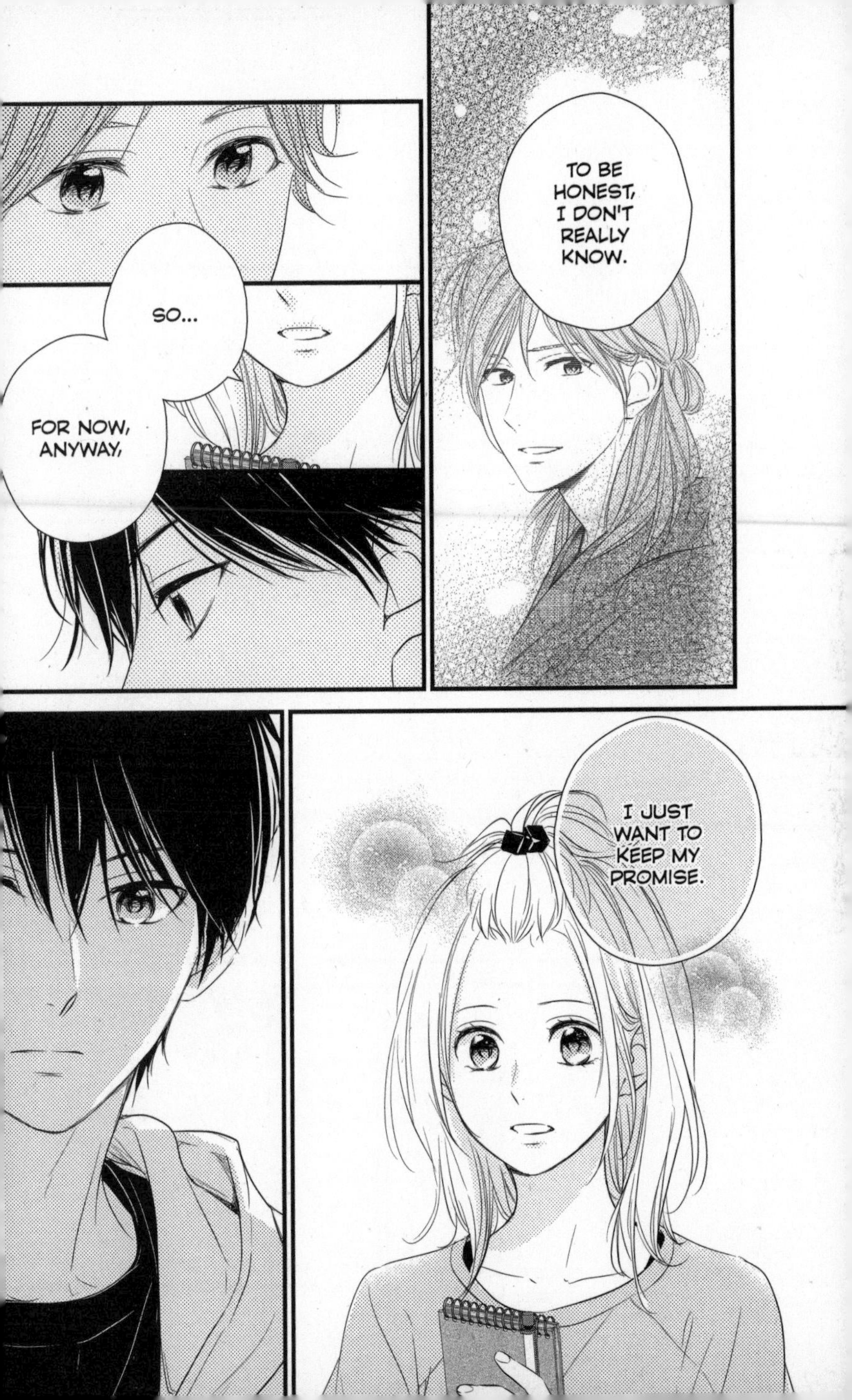
TO BE HONEST, I DON'T REALLY KNOW.
SO...
FOR NOW, ANYWAY,
I JUST WANT TO KEEP MY PROMISE.

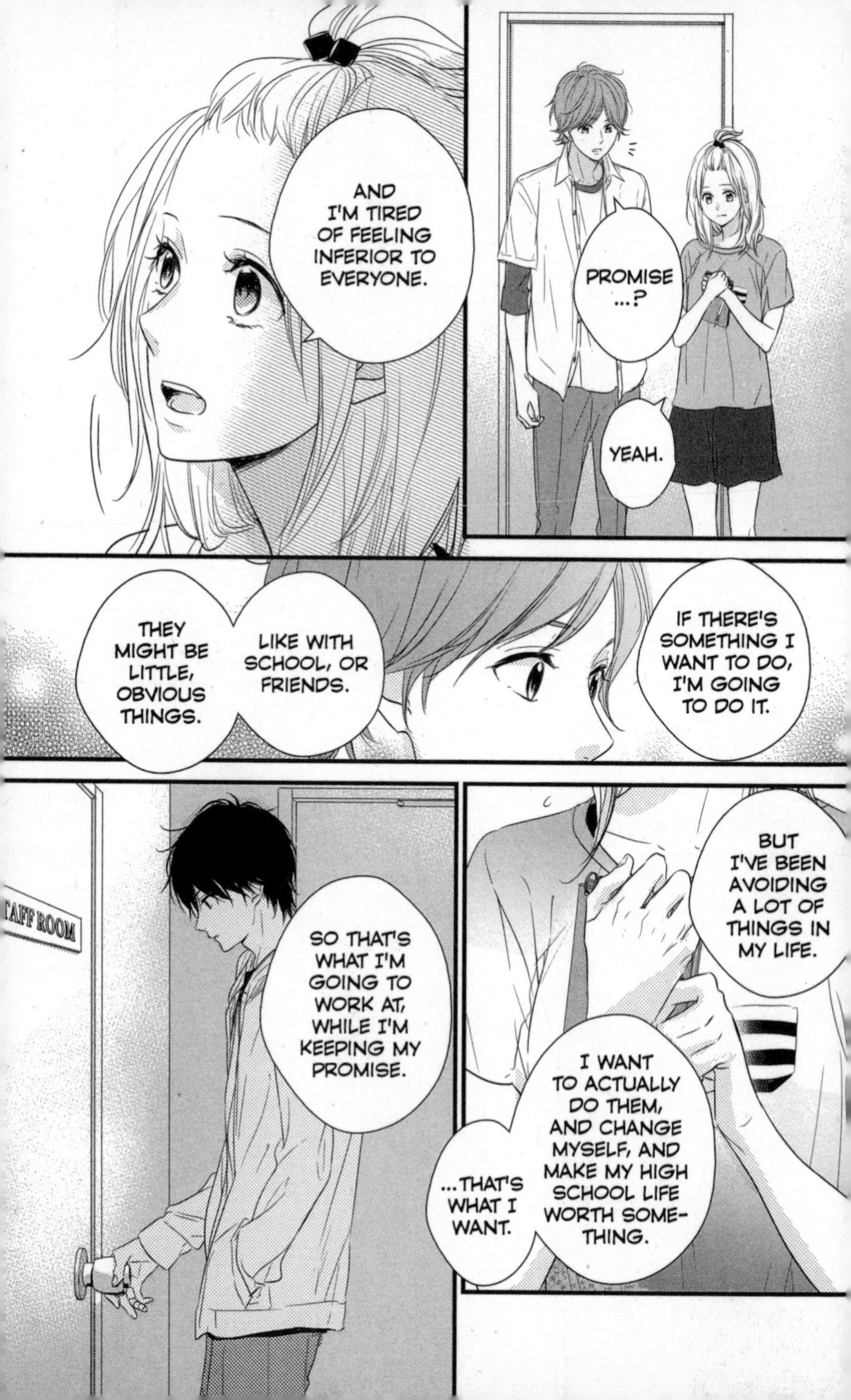
PROMISE ...?
YEAH.
AND I'M TIRED OF FEELING INFERIOR TO EVERYONE.
IF THERE'S SOMETHING I WANT TO DO, I'M GOING TO DO IT.
LIKE WITH SCHOOL, OR FRIENDS.
THEY MIGHT BE LITTLE, OBVIOUS THINGS.
BUT I'VE BEEN AVOIDING A LOT OF THINGS IN MY LIFE.
I WANT TO ACTUALLY DO THEM, AND CHANGE MYSELF, AND MAKE MY HIGH SCHOOL LIFE WORTH SOME-THING.
...THAT'S WHAT I WANT.
TAFF ROOM
SO THAT'S WHAT I'M GOING TO WORK AT, WHILE I'M KEEPING MY PROMISE.

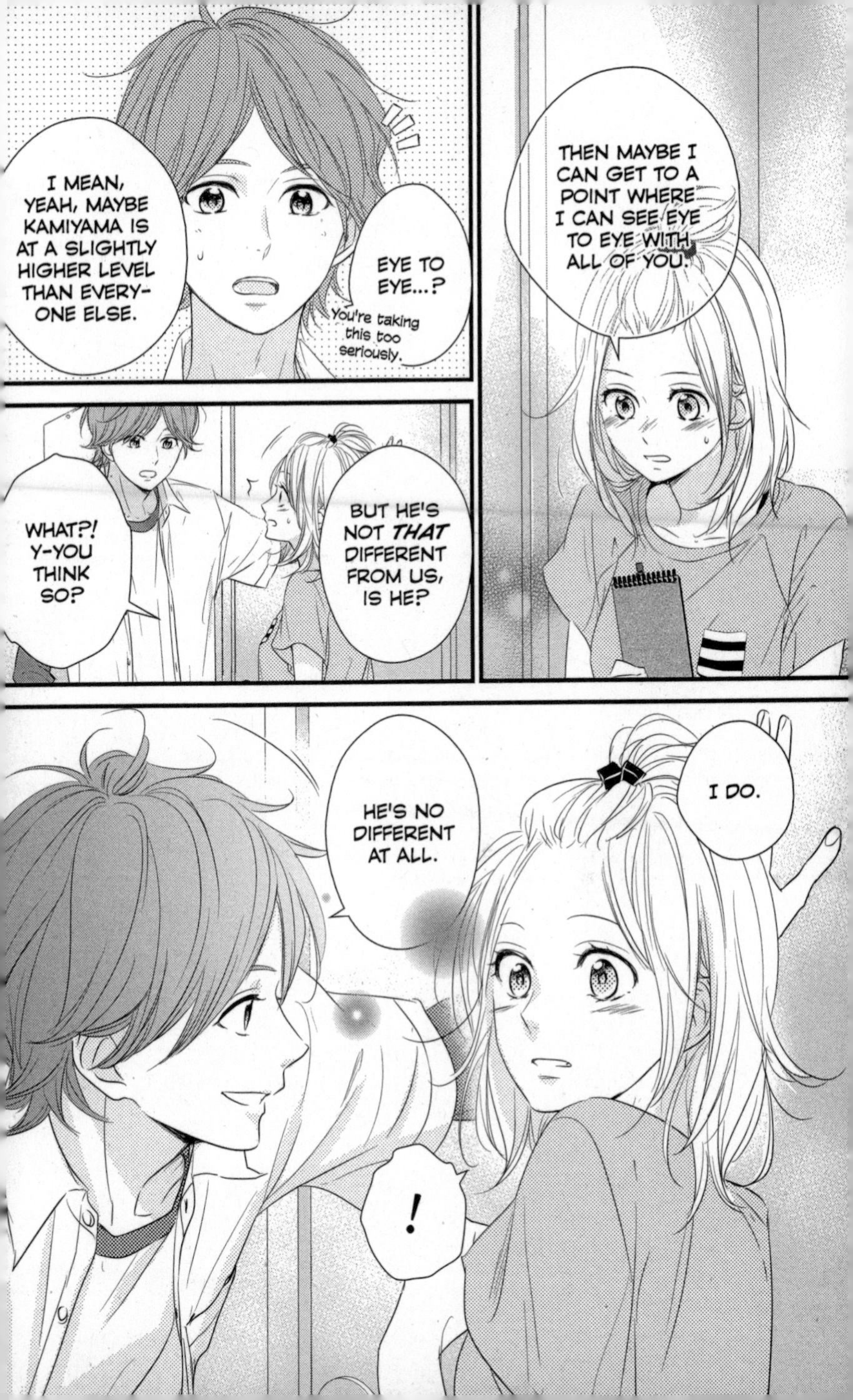
THEN MAYBE I CAN GET TO A POINT WHERE I CAN SEE EYE TO EYE WITH ALL OF YOU.
EYE TO EYE...?
You're taking this too seriously.
I MEAN, YEAH, MAYBE KAMIYAMA IS AT A SLIGHTLY HIGHER LEVEL THAN EVERY-ONE ELSE.
BUT HE'S NOT *THAT* DIFFERENT FROM US, IS HE?
WHAT?! Y-YOU THINK SO?
I DO.
HE'S NO DIFFERENT AT ALL.
!

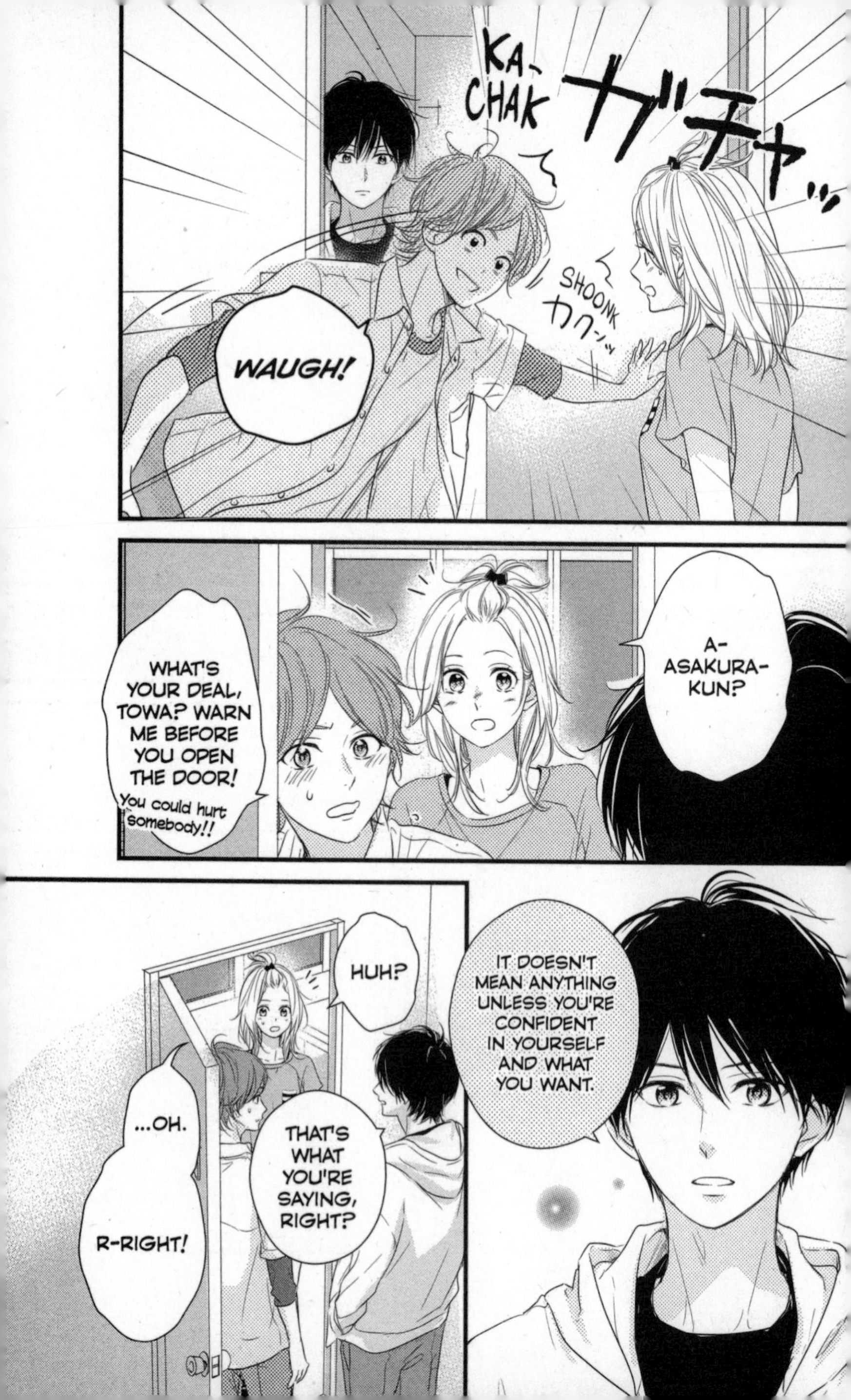
KA-CHAK
ガチャッ
SHOONK
カクーッ
WAUGH!
A-ASAKURA-KUN?
WHAT'S YOUR DEAL, TOWA? WARN ME BEFORE YOU OPEN THE DOOR! You could hurt somebody!!
IT DOESN'T MEAN ANYTHING UNLESS YOU'RE CONFIDENT IN YOURSELF AND WHAT YOU WANT.
HUH?
THAT'S WHAT YOU'RE SAYING, RIGHT?
...OH.
R-RIGHT!

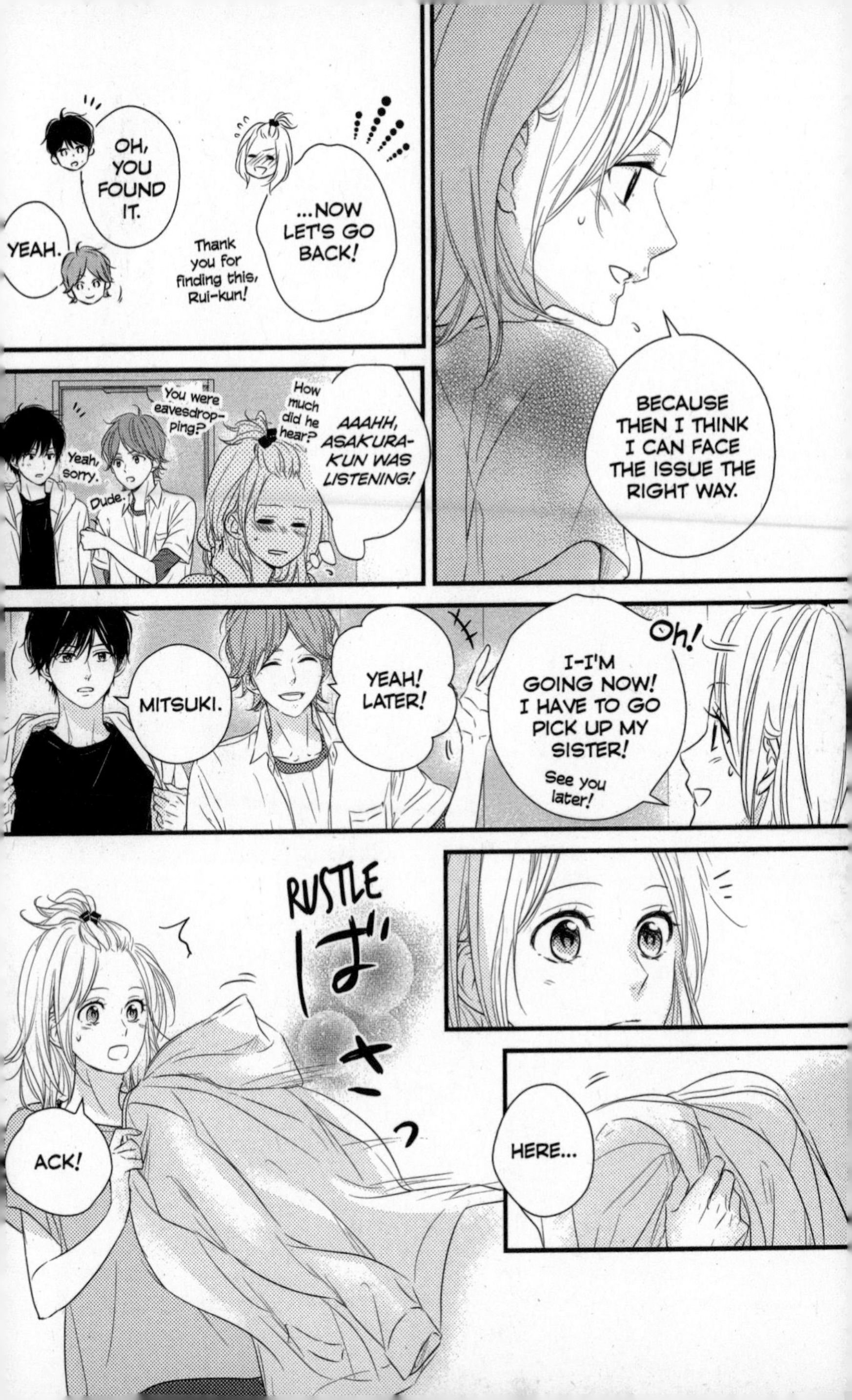

BECAUSE THEN I THINK I CAN FACE THE ISSUE THE RIGHT WAY.
...NOW LET'S GO BACK!
Thank you for finding this, Rui-kun!
OH, YOU FOUND IT.
YEAH.
AAAHH, ASAKURA-KUN WAS LISTENING!
How much did he hear?
You were eavesdropping?
Yeah, sorry.
Dude.
Oh!
I-I'M GOING NOW! I HAVE TO GO PICK UP MY SISTER!
See you later!
YEAH! LATER!
MITSUKI.
HERE...
RUSTLE
ACK!

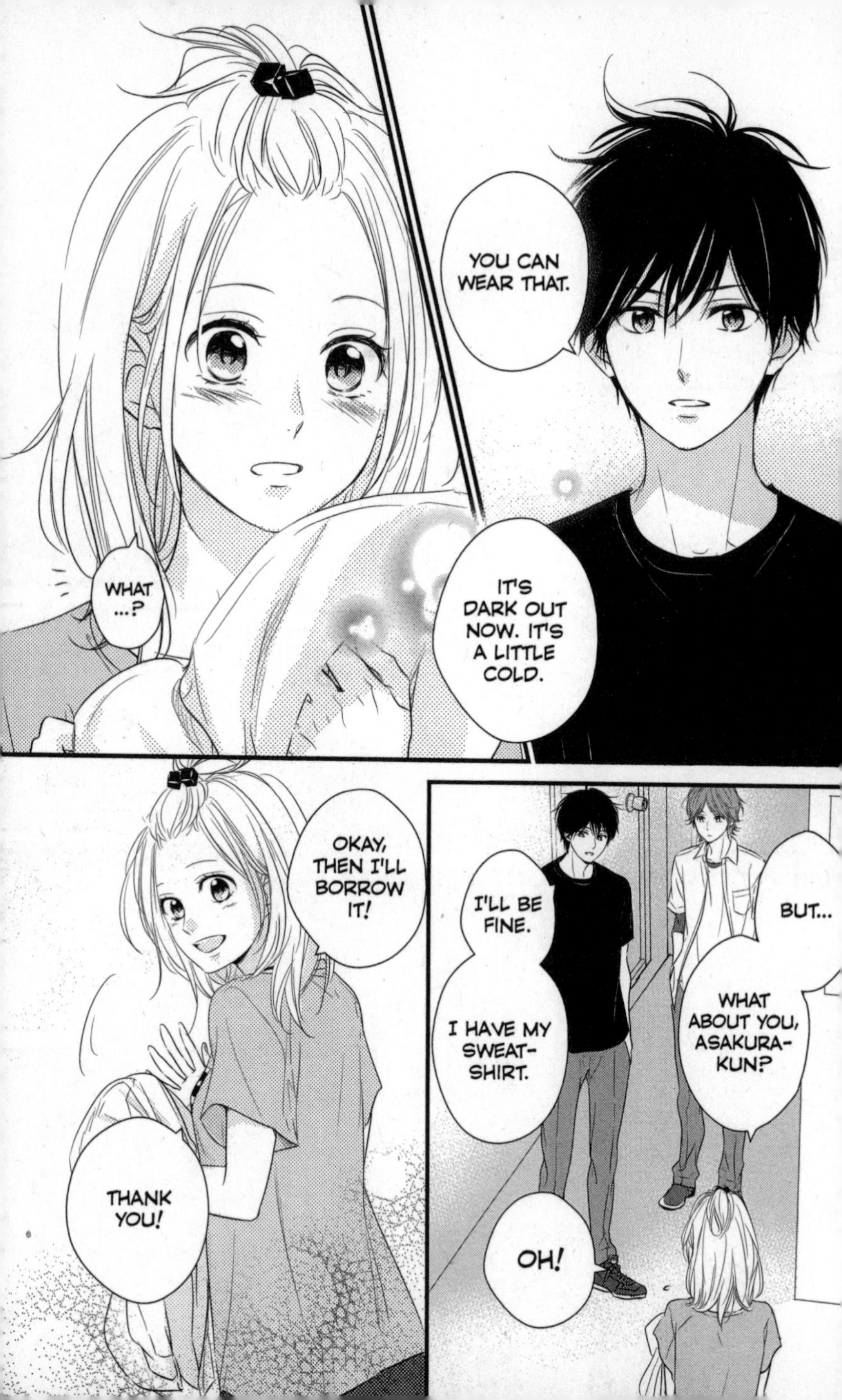
YOU CAN WEAR THAT.
IT'S DARK OUT NOW. IT'S A LITTLE COLD.
WHAT ...?
BUT...
WHAT ABOUT YOU, ASAKURA-KUN?
I'LL BE FINE.
I HAVE MY SWEAT-SHIRT.
OH!
OKAY, THEN I'LL BORROW IT!
THANK YOU!

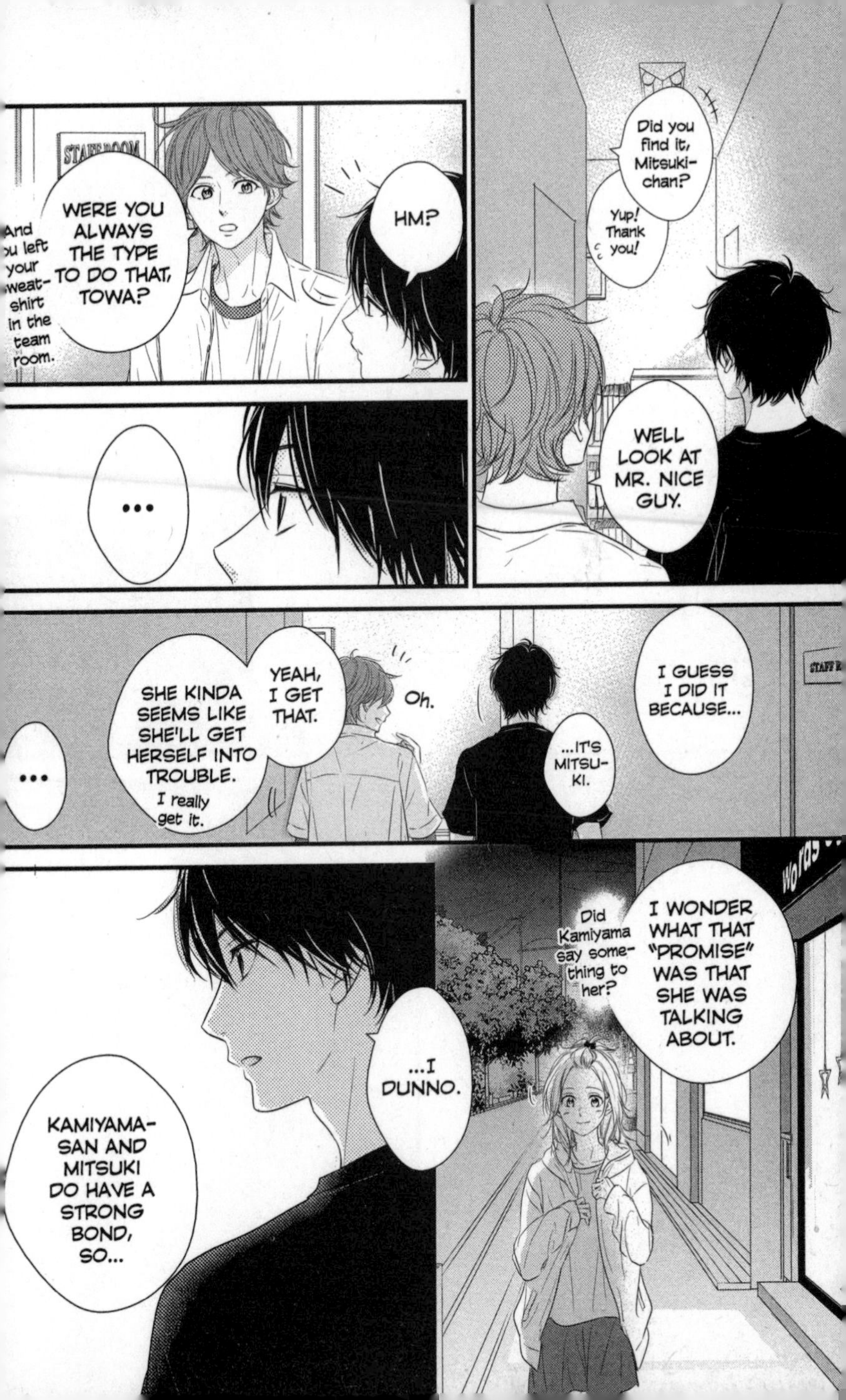
Did you find it, Mitsuki-chan?
Yup! Thank you!
WELL LOOK AT MR. NICE GUY.
STAFF ROOM
WERE YOU ALWAYS THE TYPE TO DO THAT, TOWA?
And you left your sweat-shirt in the team room.
HM?
...
I GUESS I DID IT BECAUSE...
...IT'S MITSU-KI.
Oh.
YEAH, I GET THAT.
SHE KINDA SEEMS LIKE SHE'LL GET HERSELF INTO TROUBLE.
I really get it.
...
I WONDER WHAT THAT "PROMISE" WAS THAT SHE WAS TALKING ABOUT.
Did Kamiyama say some-thing to her?
...I DUNNO.
KAMIYAMA-SAN AND MITSUKI DO HAVE A STRONG BOND, SO...

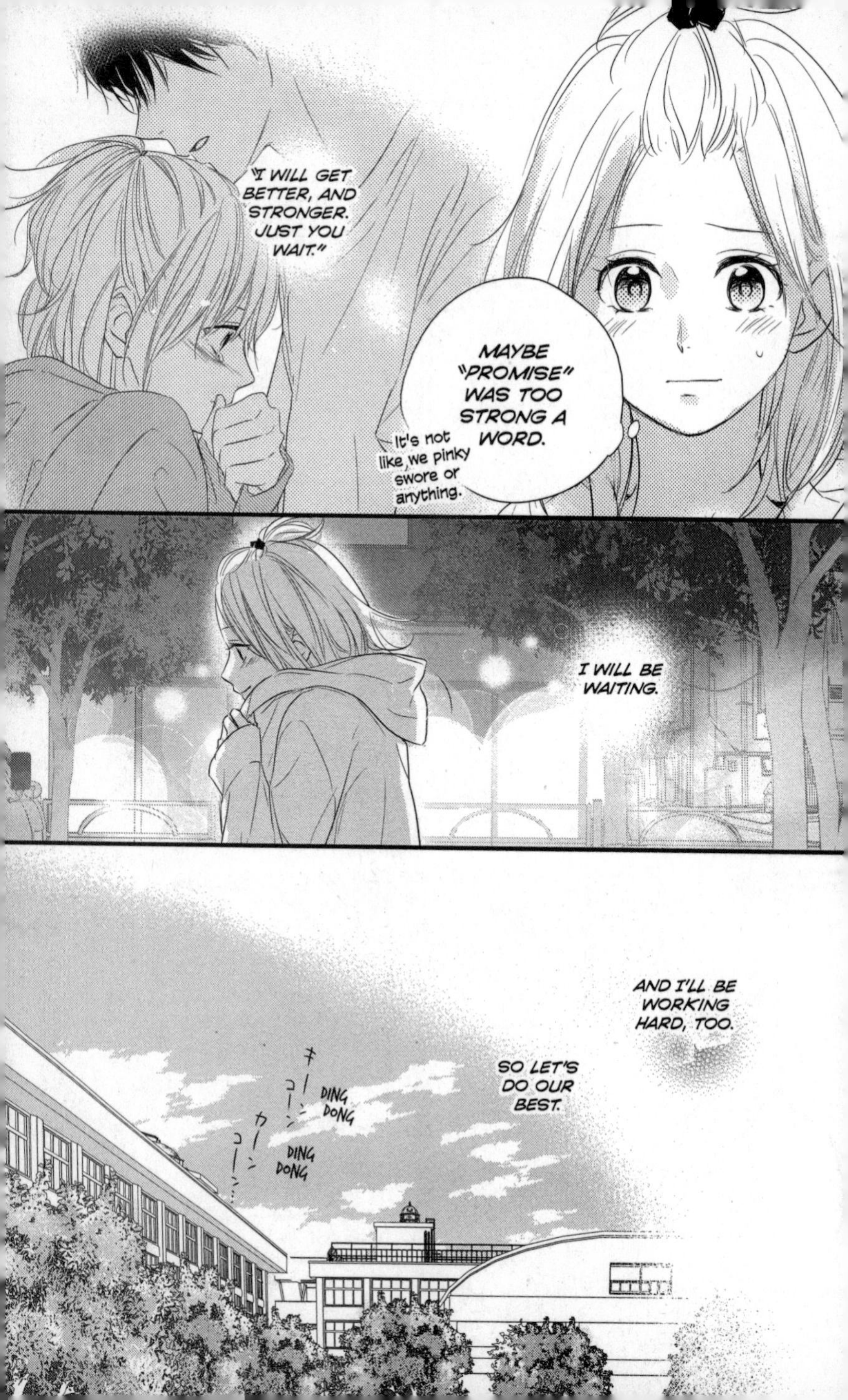

"I WILL GET BETTER, AND STRONGER. JUST YOU WAIT."
MAYBE "PROMISE" WAS TOO STRONG A WORD.
It's not like we pinky swore or anything.
I WILL BE WAITING.
AND I'LL BE WORKING HARD, TOO.
SO LET'S DO OUR BEST.
キーンコーン
DING DONG
カーンコーン
DING DONG

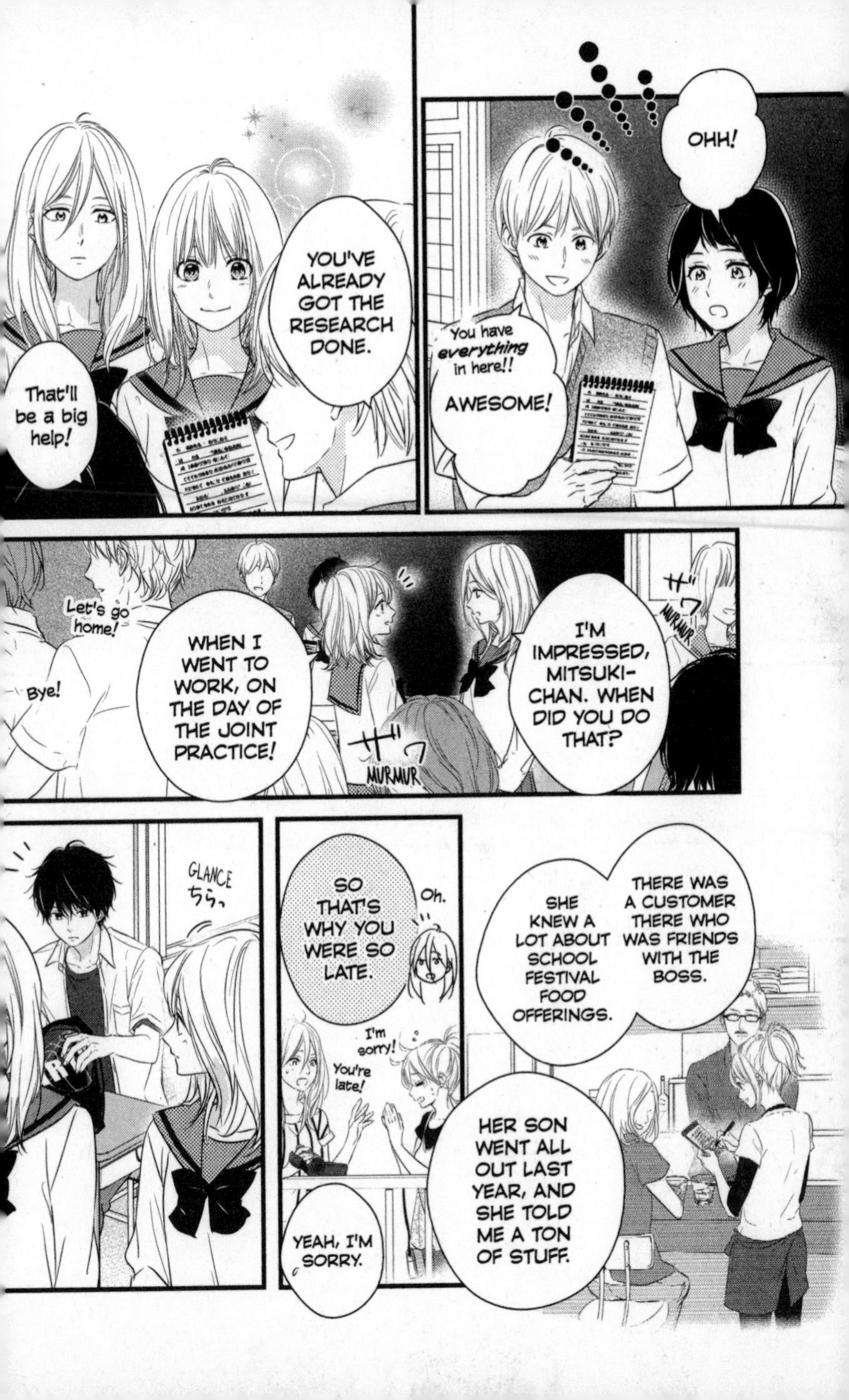
OHH!
You have everything in here!!
AWESOME!
YOU'VE ALREADY GOT THE RESEARCH DONE.
That'll be a big help!
ザワ MURMUR
I'M IMPRESSED, MITSUKI-CHAN. WHEN DID YOU DO THAT?
ザワ MURMUR
WHEN I WENT TO WORK, ON THE DAY OF THE JOINT PRACTICE!
Let's go home!
Bye!
THERE WAS A CUSTOMER THERE WHO WAS FRIENDS WITH THE BOSS.
SHE KNEW A LOT ABOUT SCHOOL FESTIVAL FOOD OFFERINGS.
HER SON WENT ALL OUT LAST YEAR, AND SHE TOLD ME A TON OF STUFF.
Oh.
SO THAT'S WHY YOU WERE SO LATE.
I'm sorry!
You're late!
YEAH, I'M SORRY.
GLANCE ちらっ

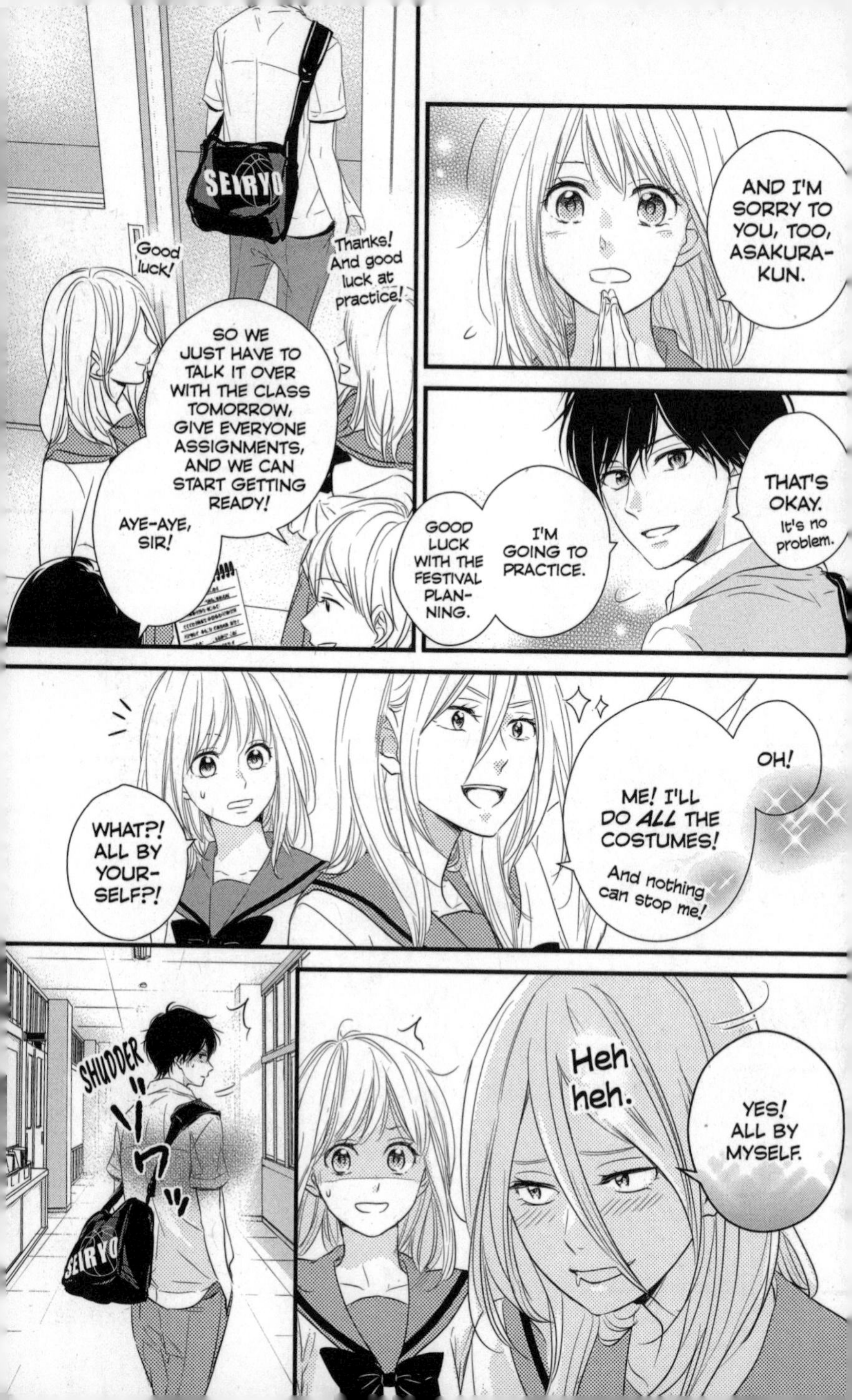
AND I'M SORRY TO YOU, TOO, ASAKURA-KUN.
THAT'S OKAY. It's no problem.
I'M GOING TO PRACTICE.
GOOD LUCK WITH THE FESTIVAL PLANNING.
Thanks! And good luck at practice!
Good luck!
SO WE JUST HAVE TO TALK IT OVER WITH THE CLASS TOMORROW, GIVE EVERYONE ASSIGNMENTS, AND WE CAN START GETTING READY!
AYE-AYE, SIR!
SEIRYO
OH!
ME! I'LL DO ALL THE COSTUMES!
And nothing can stop me!
WHAT?! ALL BY YOURSELF?!
YES! ALL BY MYSELF.
Heh heh.
SHUDDER
SEIRYO

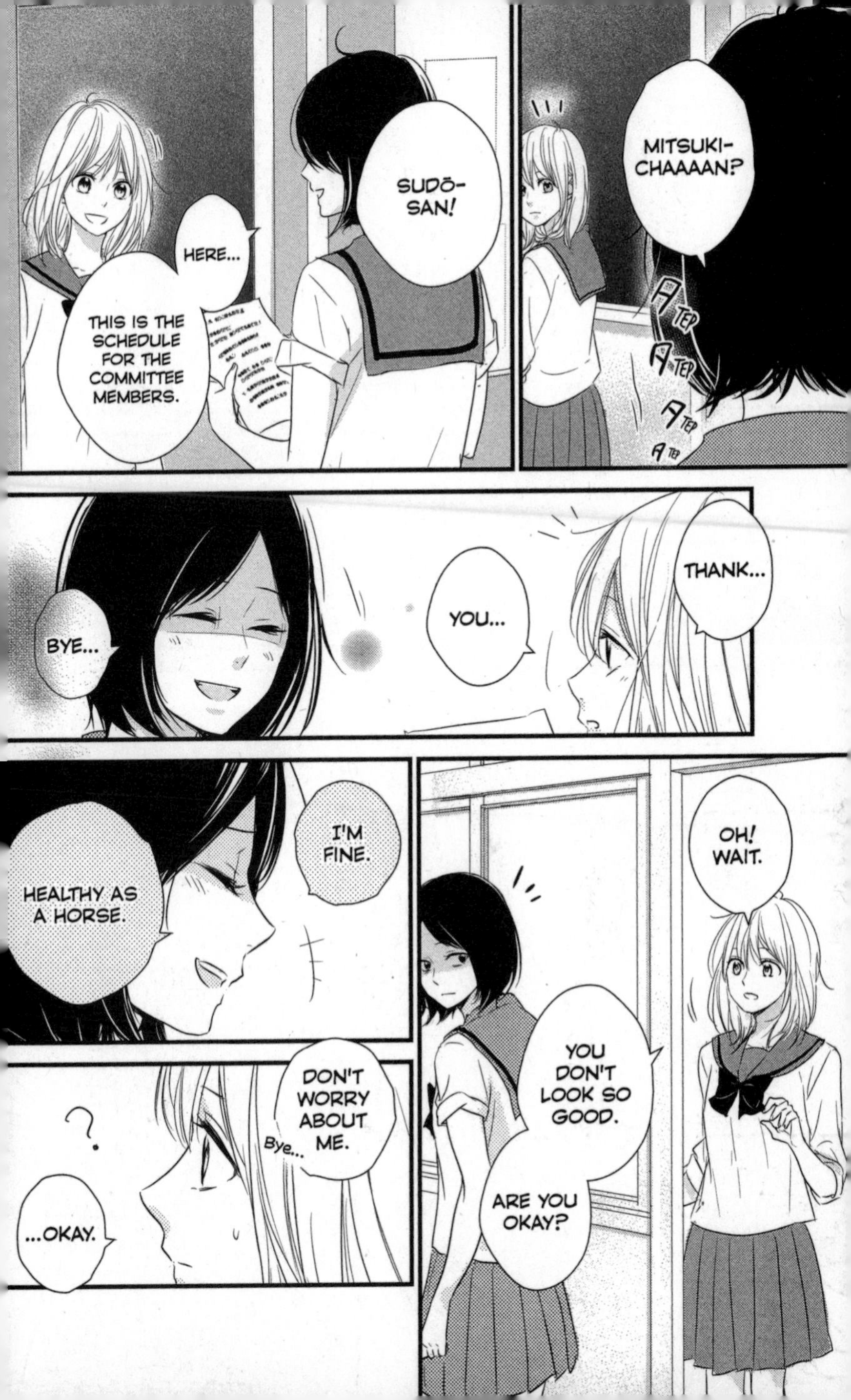
MITSUKI-CHAAAAN?
TEP
TEP
TEP
TEP
SUDŌ-SAN!
HERE...
THIS IS THE SCHEDULE FOR THE COMMITTEE MEMBERS.
THANK...
YOU...
BYE...
OH! WAIT.
YOU DON'T LOOK SO GOOD.
ARE YOU OKAY?
I'M FINE.
HEALTHY AS A HORSE.
DON'T WORRY ABOUT ME.
Bye...
?
...OKAY.

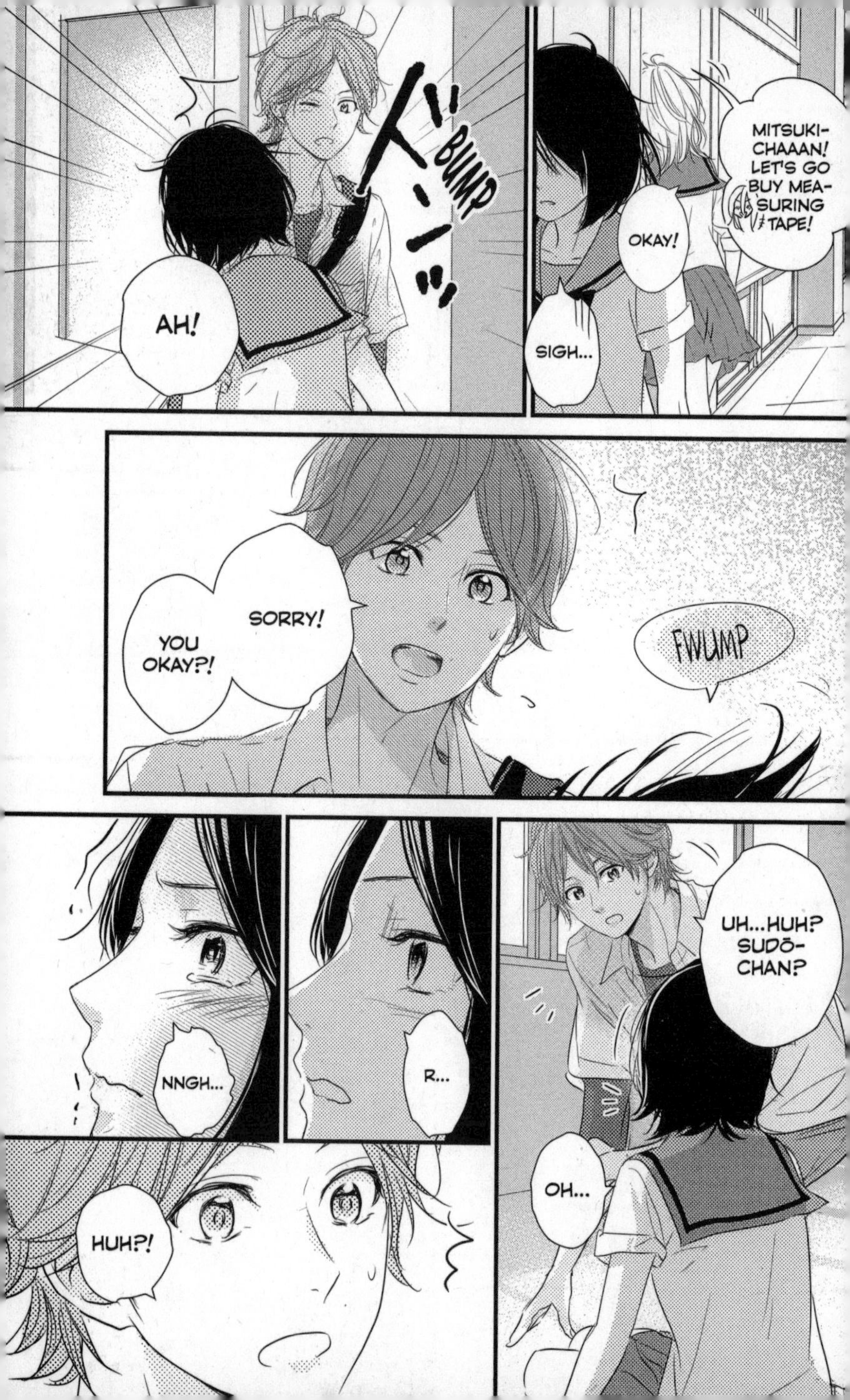
MITSUKI-CHAAAN! LET'S GO BUY MEA-SURING TAPE!
OKAY!
SIGH...
BUMP
AH!
FWUMP
SORRY!
YOU OKAY?!
UH...HUH? SUDŌ-CHAN?
OH...
R...
NNGH...
HUH?!

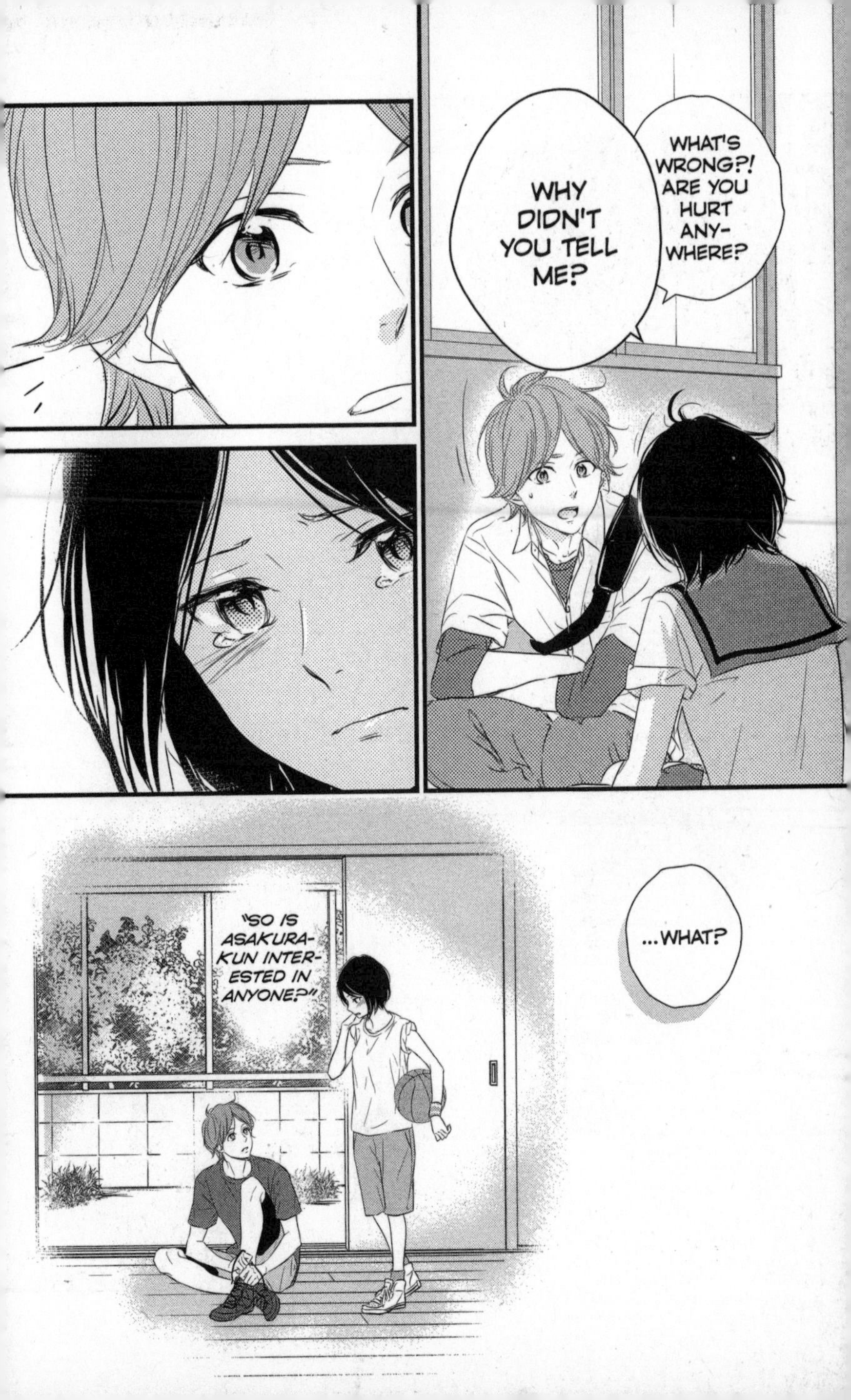
WHAT'S WRONG?! ARE YOU HURT ANY-WHERE?
WHY DIDN'T YOU TELL ME?
...WHAT?
"SO IS ASAKURA-KUN INTER-ESTED IN ANYONE?"

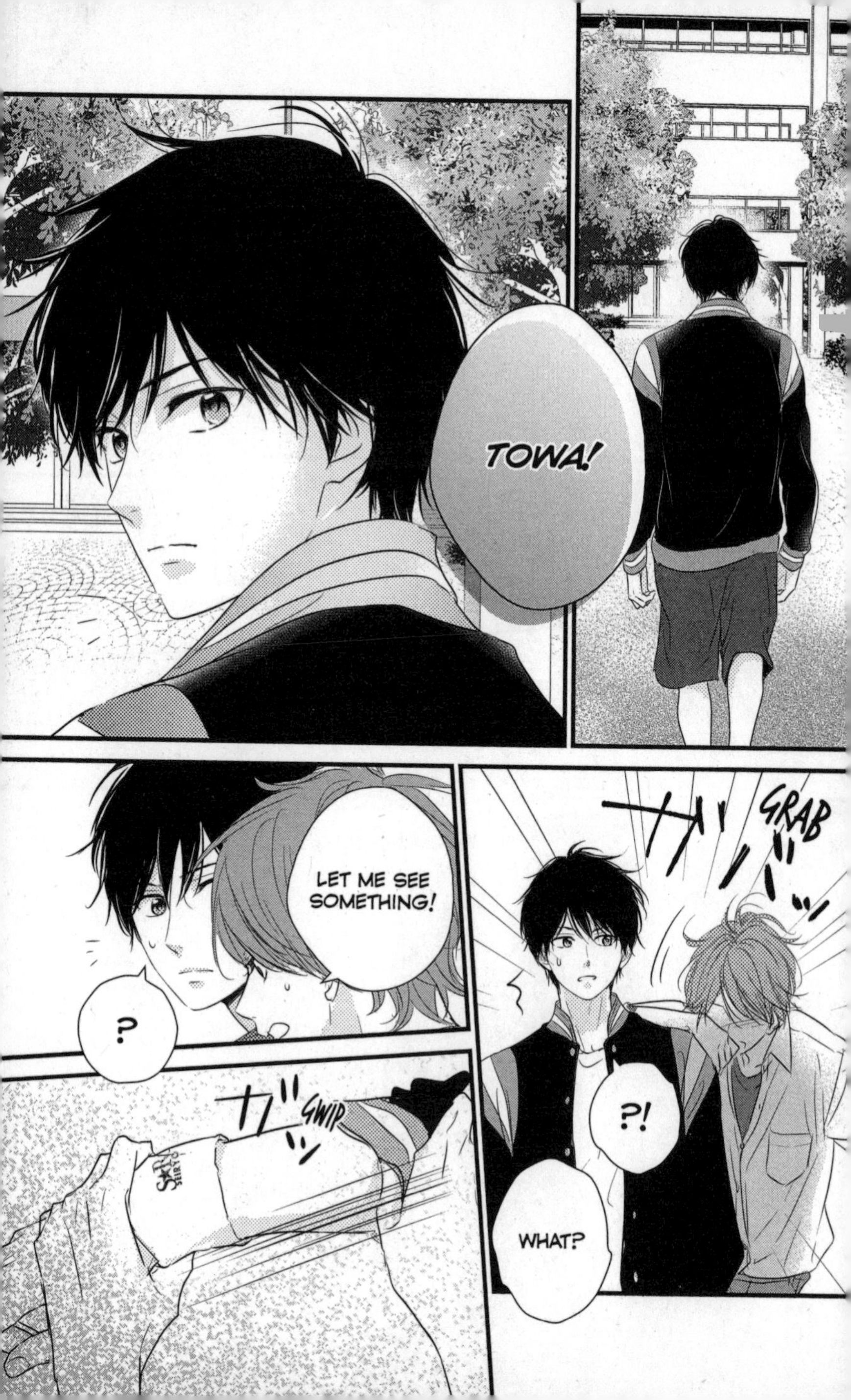
TOWA!
GRAB
?!
WHAT?
LET ME SEE SOMETHING!
?
GWIP

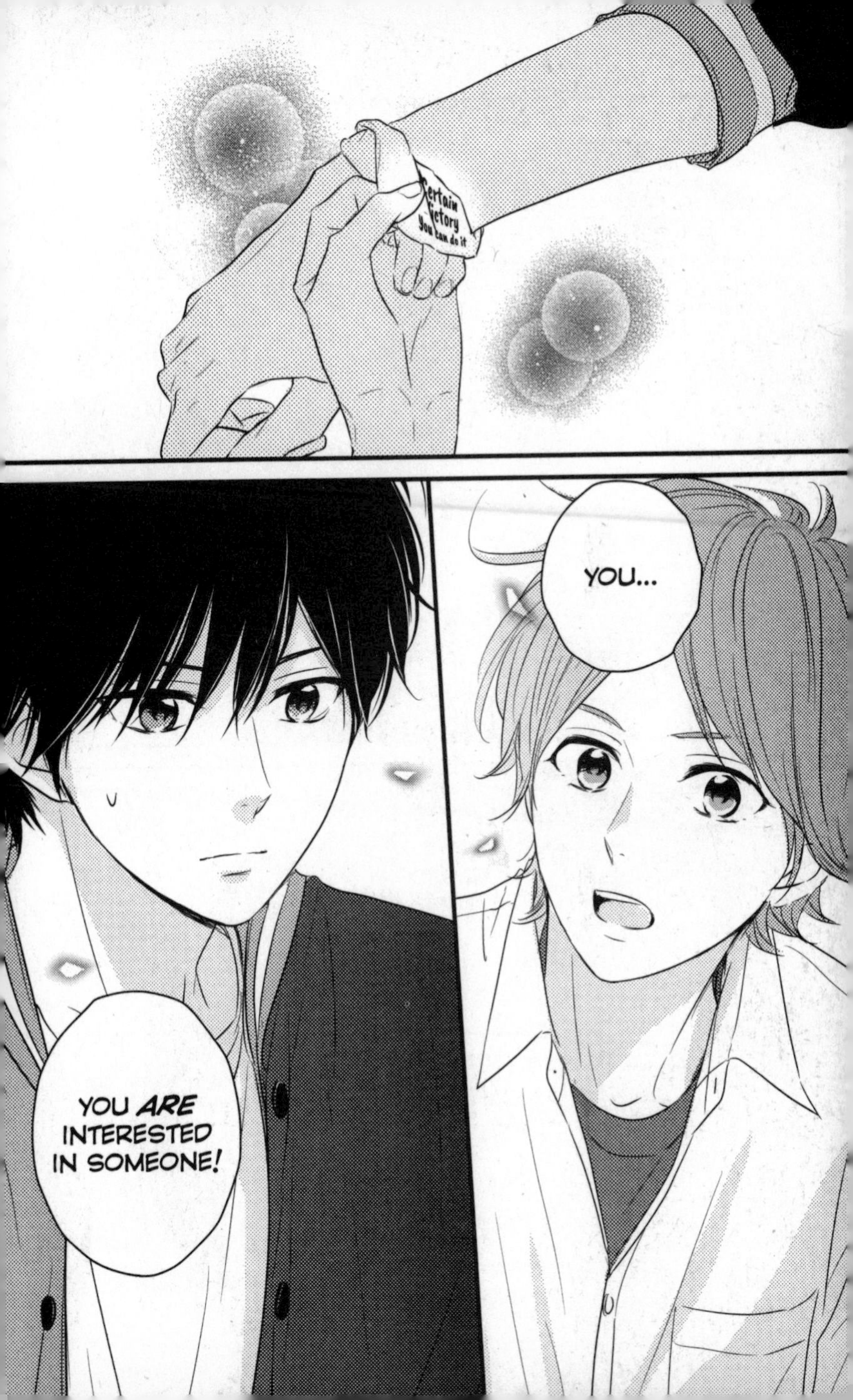
Certain Victory
You can do it
YOU...
YOU ARE INTERESTED IN SOMEONE!

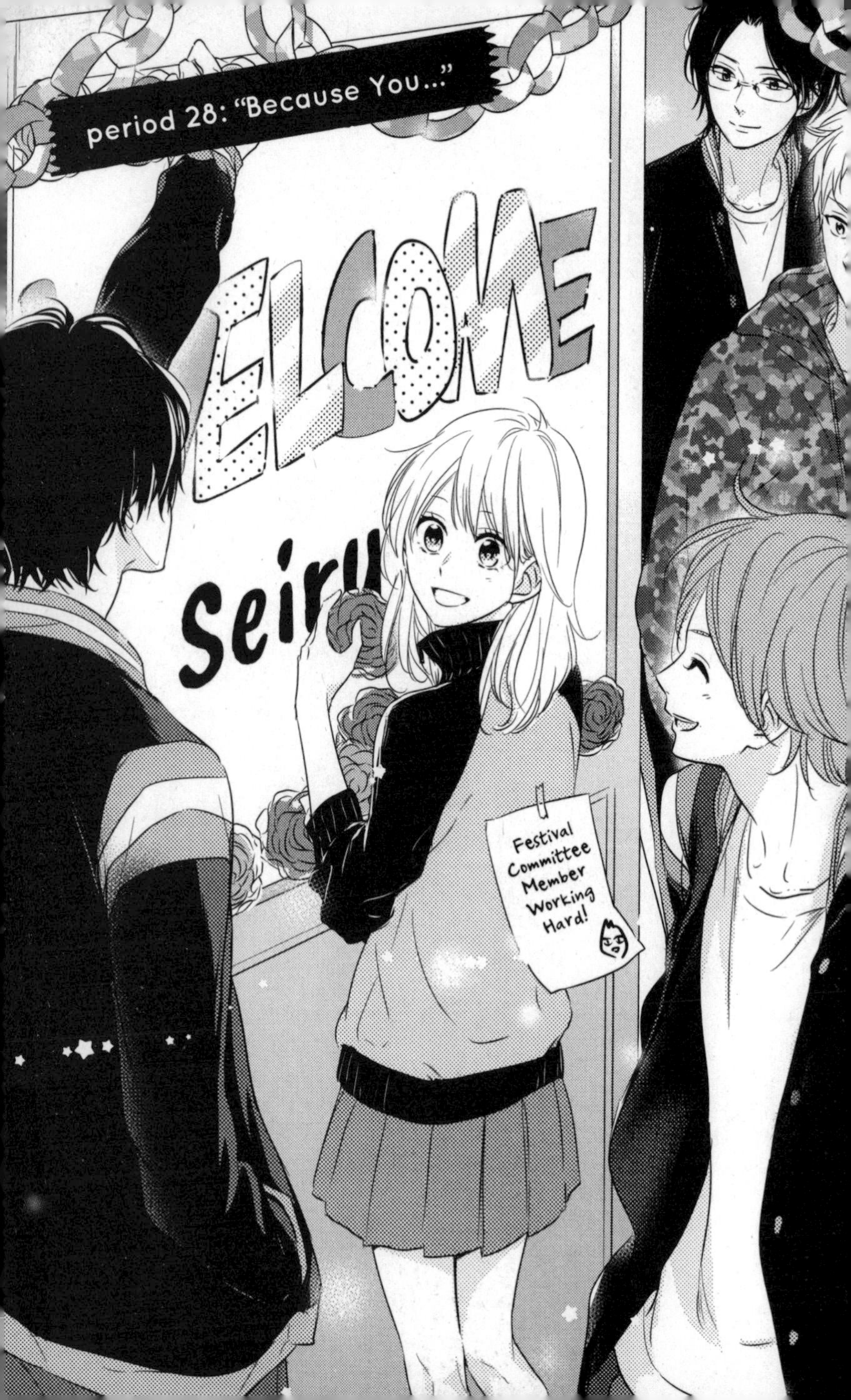
period 28: "Because You..."
ELCOME
Seiru
Festival Committee Member Working Hard!

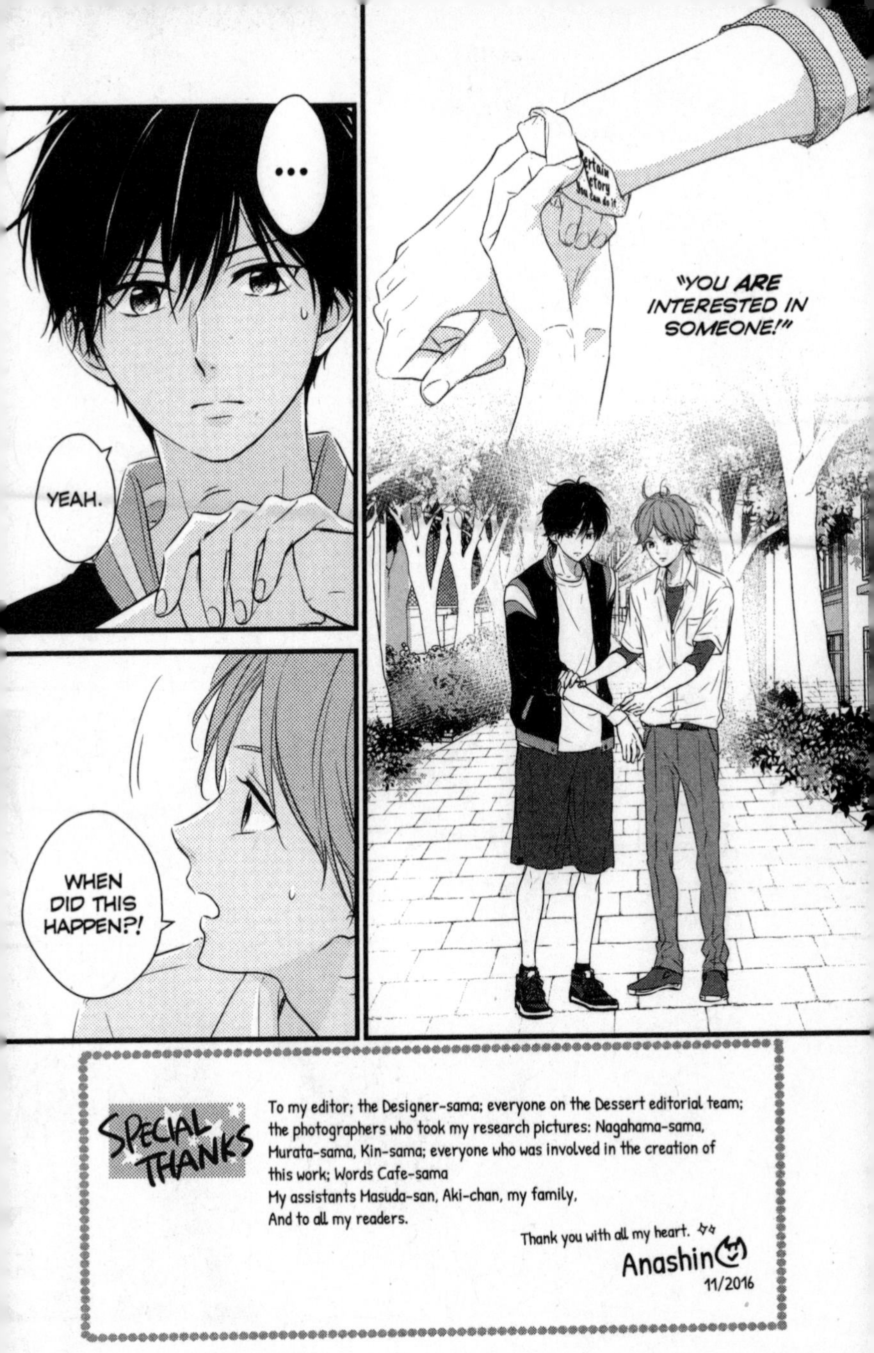
"YOU ARE INTERESTED IN SOMEONE!"
...
YEAH.
WHEN DID THIS HAPPEN?!

SPECIAL THANKS

To my editor; the Designer-sama; everyone on the Dessert editorial team; the photographers who took my research pictures: Nagahama-sama, Murata-sama, Kin-sama; everyone who was involved in the creation of this work; Words Cafe-sama
My assistants Masuda-san, Aki-chan, my family,
And to all my readers.

Thank you with all my heart.
Anashin
11/2016

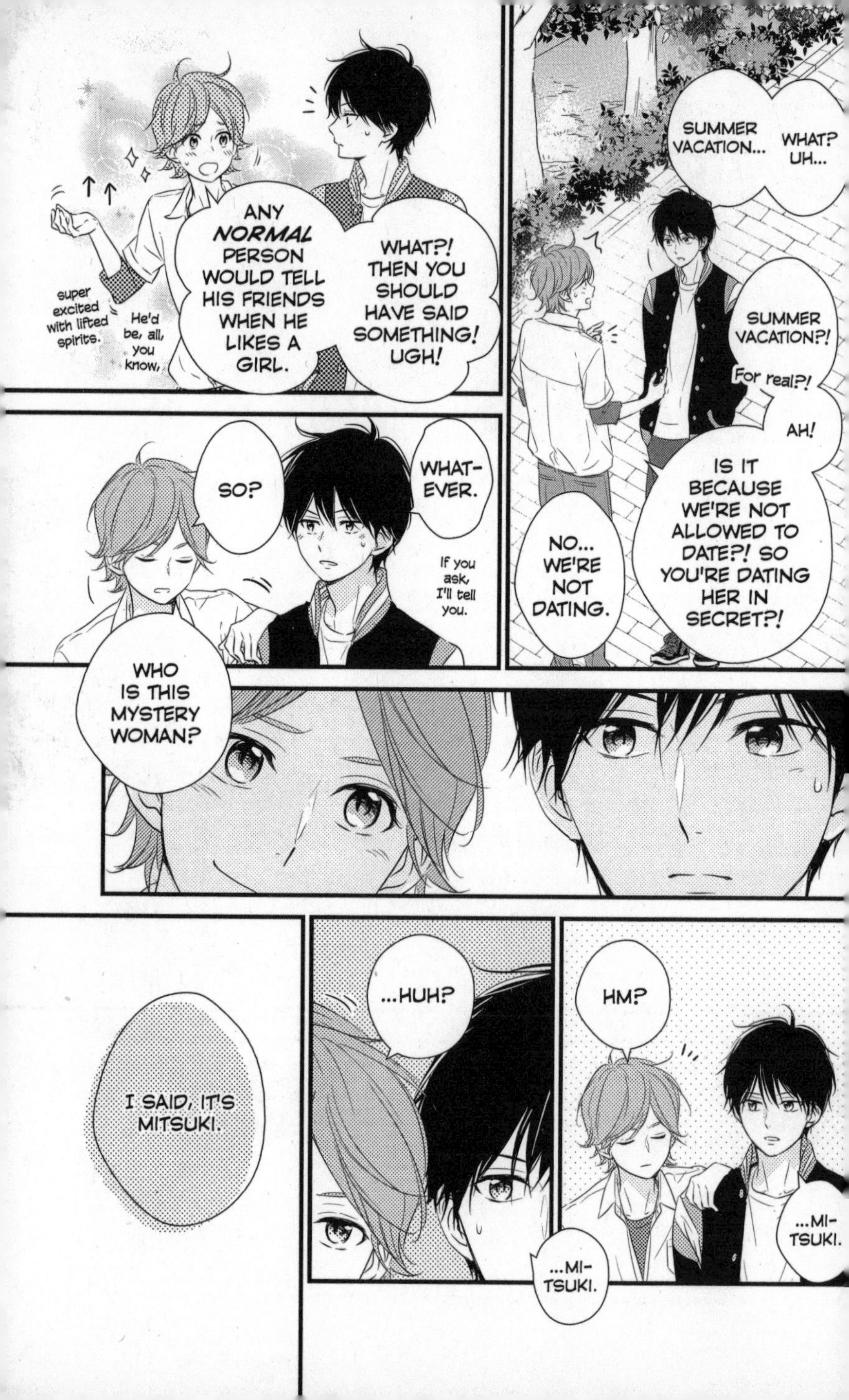
WHAT? UH...
SUMMER VACATION...
SUMMER VACATION?!
For real?!
AH!
IS IT BECAUSE WE'RE NOT ALLOWED TO DATE?! SO YOU'RE DATING HER IN SECRET?!
NO... WE'RE NOT DATING.
WHAT?! THEN YOU SHOULD HAVE SAID SOMETHING! UGH!
ANY NORMAL PERSON WOULD TELL HIS FRIENDS WHEN HE LIKES A GIRL.
He'd be, all, you know,
super excited with lifted spirits.
WHAT-EVER.
If you ask, I'll tell you.
SO?
WHO IS THIS MYSTERY WOMAN?
HM?
...MI-TSUKI.
...HUH?
...MI-TSUKI.
I SAID, IT'S MITSUKI.

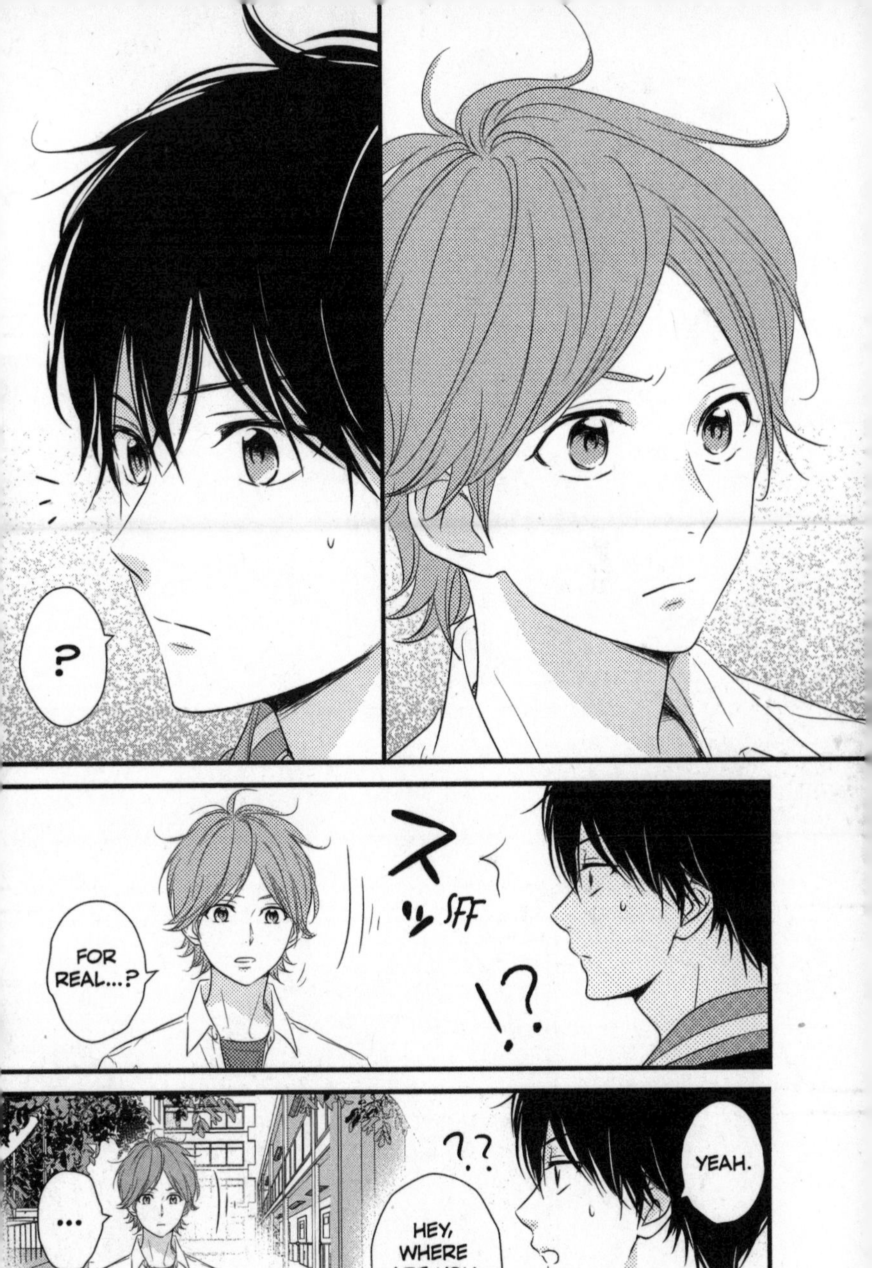
?
ス
ッ SFF
!?
FOR REAL...?
YEAH.
??
HEY, WHERE ARE YOU GOING?
Hey!
...

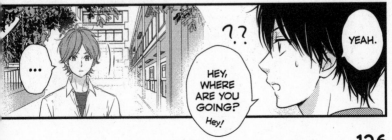

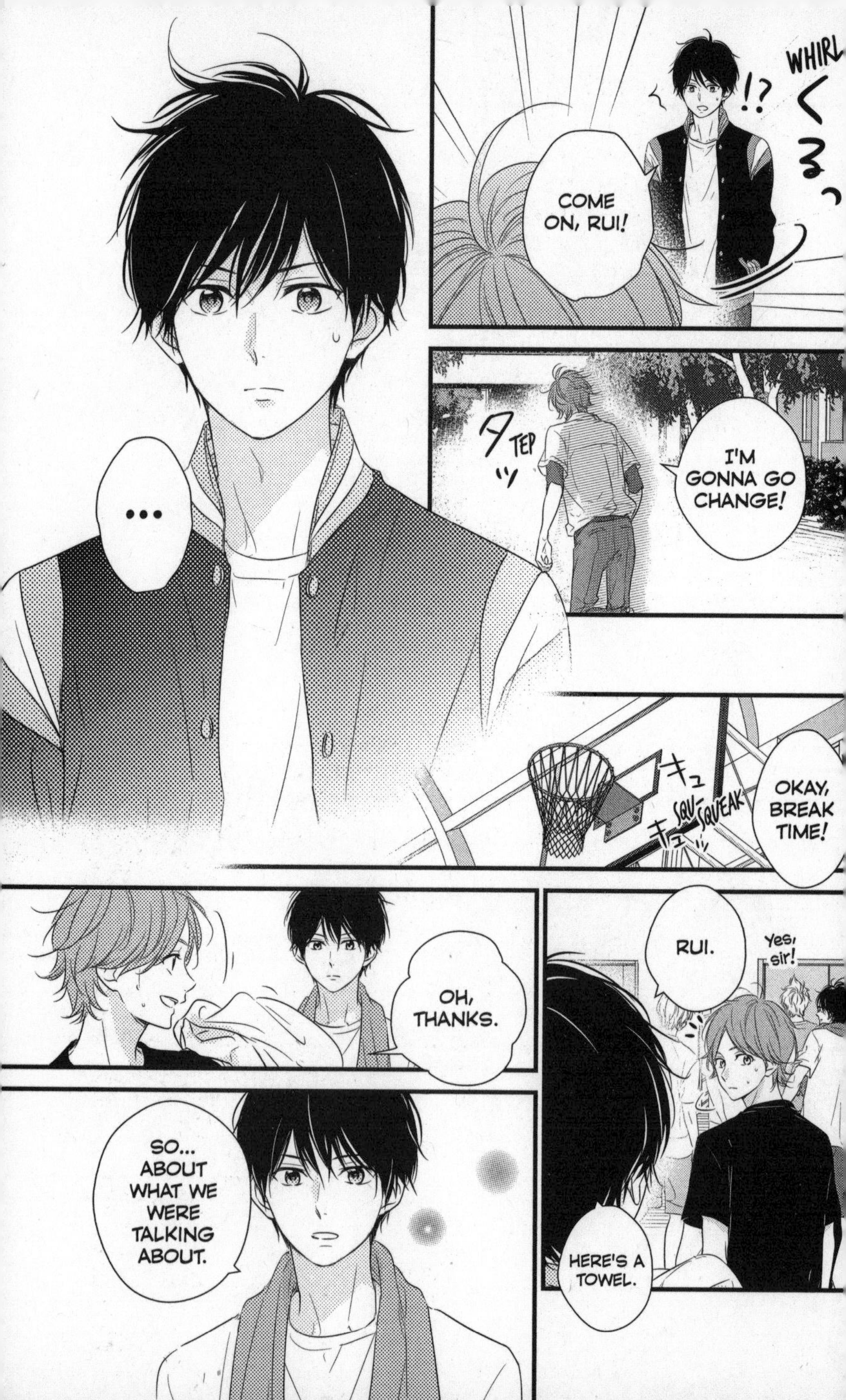
WHIRL
くるっ
!?
COME ON, RUI!
タッ
TEP
I'M GONNA GO CHANGE!
キュ
SQUEAK
キュ
SQU-
OKAY, BREAK TIME!
...
RUI.
Yes, sir!
HERE'S A TOWEL.
OH, THANKS.
SO... ABOUT WHAT WE WERE TALKING ABOUT.

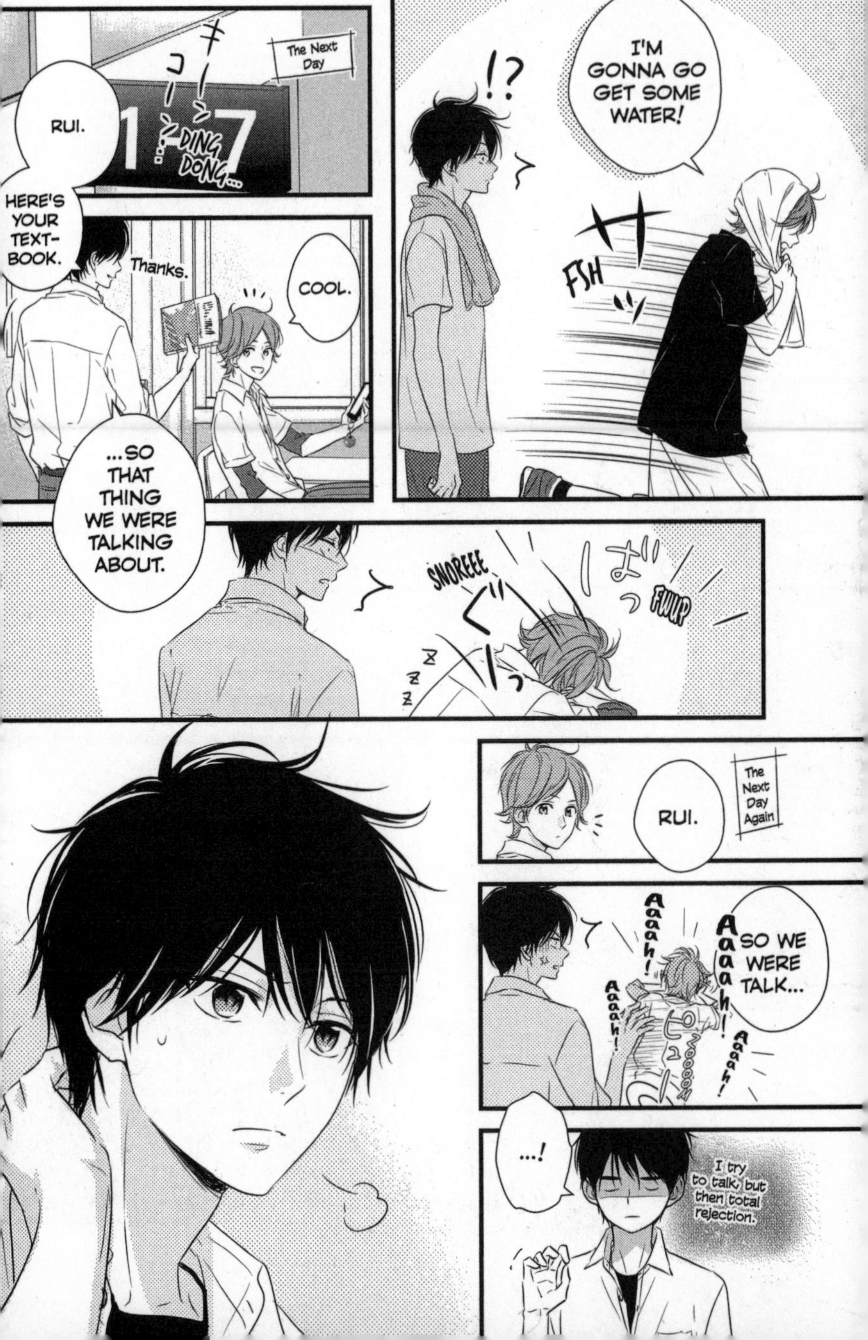
!?
I'M GONNA GO GET SOME WATER!
FSH
The Next Day
DING DONG...
RUI.
HERE'S YOUR TEXT-BOOK.
Thanks.
COOL.
...SO THAT THING WE WERE TALKING ABOUT.
SNOREEE
FWUP
The Next Day Again
RUI.
SO WE WERE TALK...
Aaaah!
Aaaah!
Aaaah!
Aaaah!
ZOOOOM
...!
I try to talk, but then total rejection.

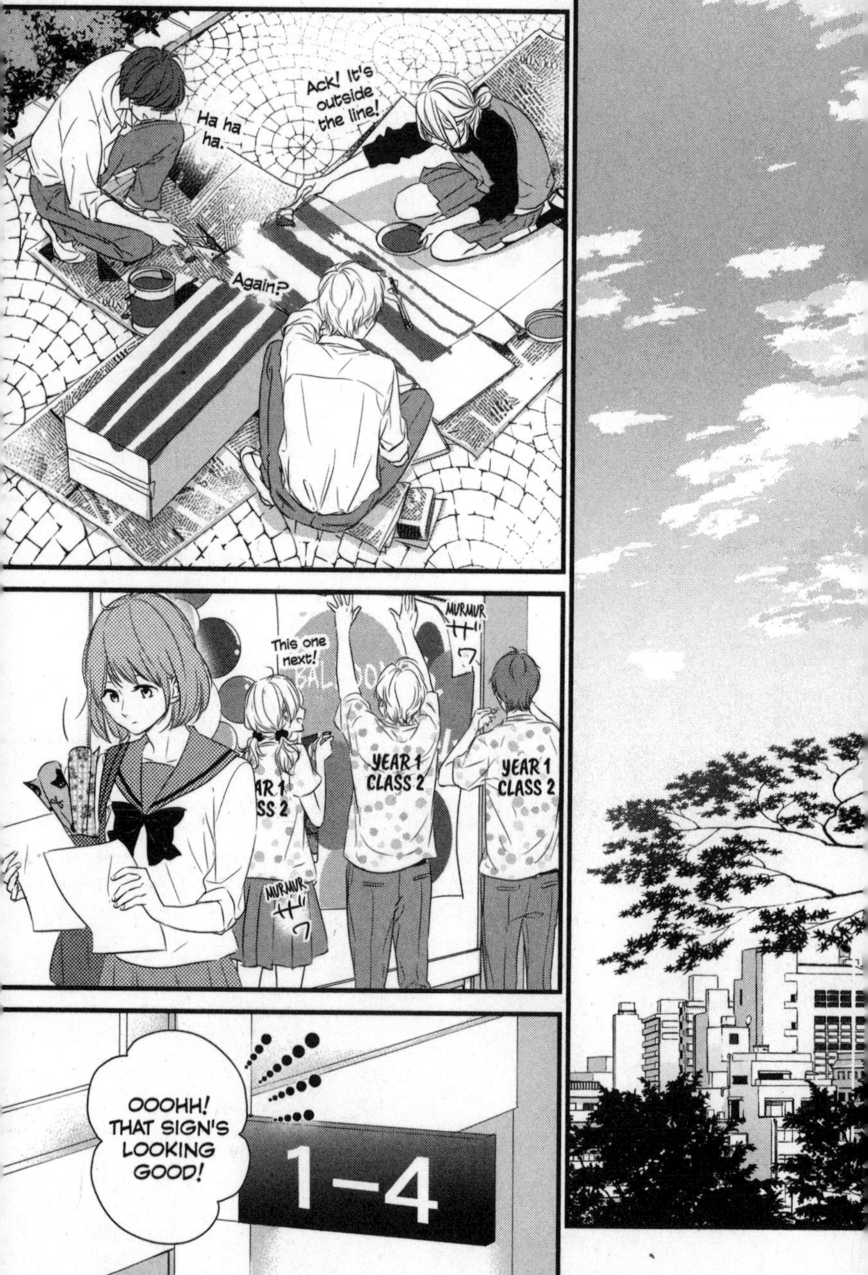

Ack! It's outside the line!
Ha ha ha.
Again?
MURMUR
ザワ
This one next!
YEAR 1 CLASS 2
YEAR 1 CLASS 2
AR 1 SS 2
MURMUR
ザワ
OOOHH! THAT SIGN'S LOOKING GOOD!
1-4

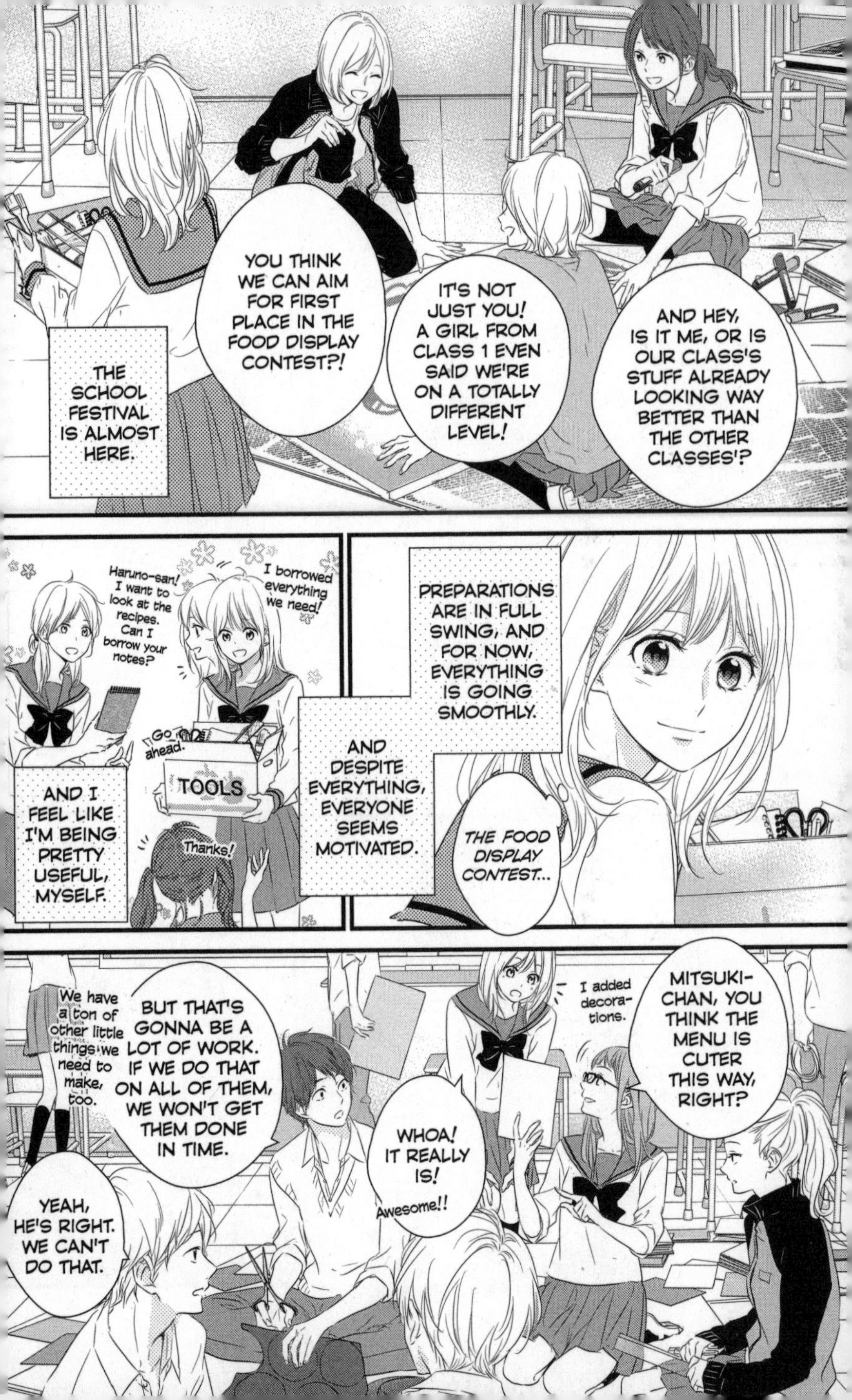
AND HEY, IS IT ME, OR IS OUR CLASS'S STUFF ALREADY LOOKING WAY BETTER THAN THE OTHER CLASSES'?
IT'S NOT JUST YOU! A GIRL FROM CLASS 1 EVEN SAID WE'RE ON A TOTALLY DIFFERENT LEVEL!
YOU THINK WE CAN AIM FOR FIRST PLACE IN THE FOOD DISPLAY CONTEST?!
THE SCHOOL FESTIVAL IS ALMOST HERE.
PREPARATIONS ARE IN FULL SWING, AND FOR NOW, EVERYTHING IS GOING SMOOTHLY.
AND DESPITE EVERYTHING, EVERYONE SEEMS MOTIVATED.
THE FOOD DISPLAY CONTEST...
I borrowed everything we need!
Haruno-san! I want to look at the recipes. Can I borrow your notes?
Go ahead.
TOOLS
Thanks!
AND I FEEL LIKE I'M BEING PRETTY USEFUL, MYSELF.
MITSUKI-CHAN, YOU THINK THE MENU IS CUTER THIS WAY, RIGHT?
I added decorations.
WHOA! IT REALLY IS!
Awesome!!
BUT THAT'S GONNA BE A LOT OF WORK. IF WE DO THAT ON ALL OF THEM, WE WON'T GET THEM DONE IN TIME.
We have a ton of other little things we need to make, too.
YEAH, HE'S RIGHT. WE CAN'T DO THAT.

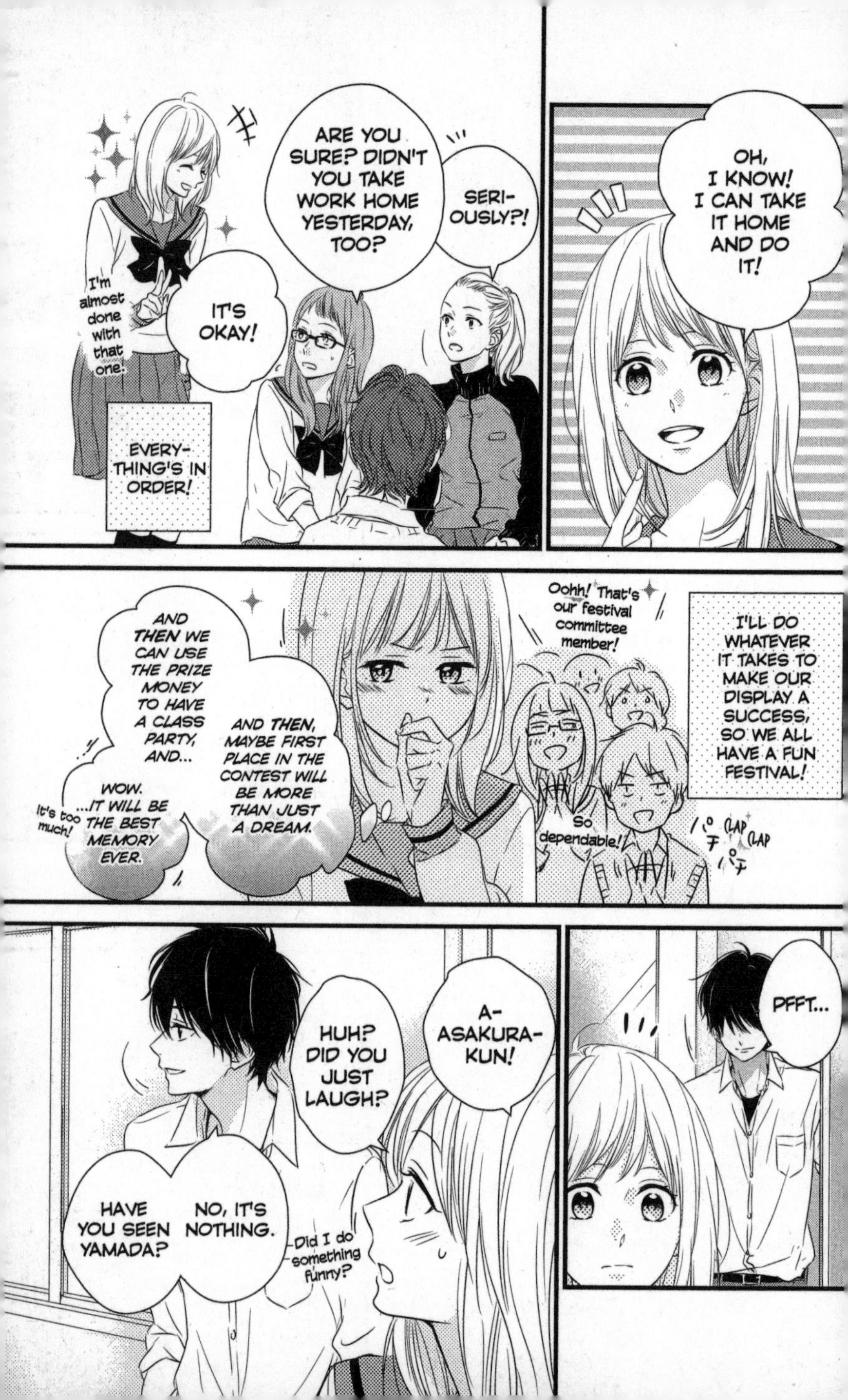
OH, I KNOW! I CAN TAKE IT HOME AND DO IT!
SERI-OUSLY?!
ARE YOU SURE? DIDN'T YOU TAKE WORK HOME YESTERDAY, TOO?
IT'S OKAY!
I'm almost done with that one.
EVERY-THING'S IN ORDER!
I'LL DO WHATEVER IT TAKES TO MAKE OUR DISPLAY A SUCCESS, SO WE ALL HAVE A FUN FESTIVAL!
Oohh! That's our festival committee member!
CLAP CLAP
So dependable!
AND THEN, MAYBE FIRST PLACE IN THE CONTEST WILL BE MORE THAN JUST A DREAM.
AND THEN WE CAN USE THE PRIZE MONEY TO HAVE A CLASS PARTY, AND...
WOW. ...IT WILL BE THE BEST MEMORY EVER.
It's too much!
PFFT...
A-ASAKURA-KUN!
HUH? DID YOU JUST LAUGH?
NO, IT'S NOTHING.
Did I do something funny?
HAVE YOU SEEN YAMADA?

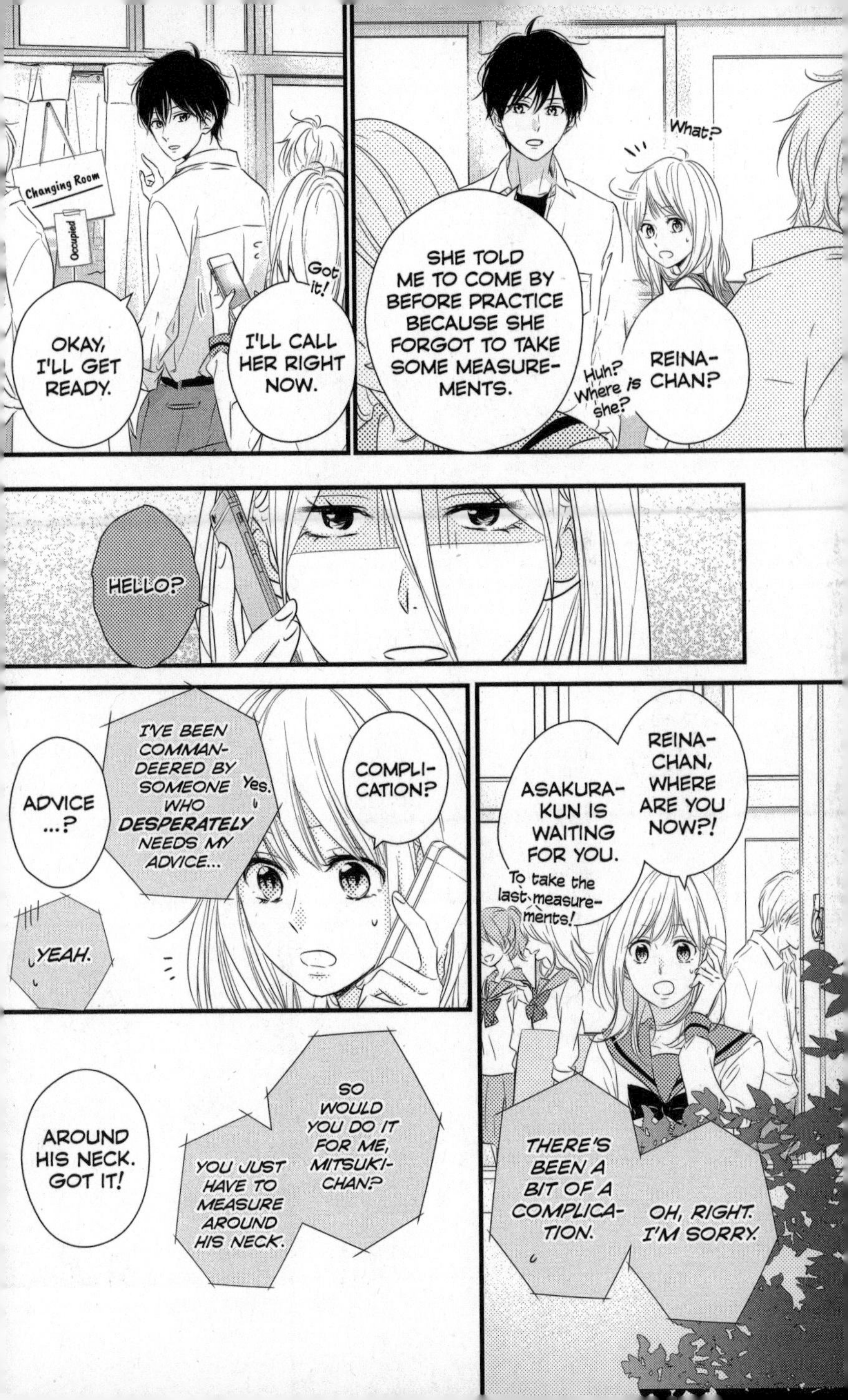
What?
SHE TOLD ME TO COME BY BEFORE PRACTICE BECAUSE SHE FORGOT TO TAKE SOME MEASUREMENTS.
REINA-CHAN?
Huh? Where is she?
Changing Room
Occupied
Got it!
I'LL CALL HER RIGHT NOW.
OKAY, I'LL GET READY.
HELLO?
REINA-CHAN, WHERE ARE YOU NOW?!
ASAKURA-KUN IS WAITING FOR YOU.
To take the last measurements!
OH, RIGHT. I'M SORRY.
THERE'S BEEN A BIT OF A COMPLICATION.
COMPLICATION?
Yes.
I'VE BEEN COMMANDEERED BY SOMEONE WHO DESPERATELY NEEDS MY ADVICE...
ADVICE ...?
YEAH.
SO WOULD YOU DO IT FOR ME, MITSUKI-CHAN?
YOU JUST HAVE TO MEASURE AROUND HIS NECK.
AROUND HIS NECK. GOT IT!

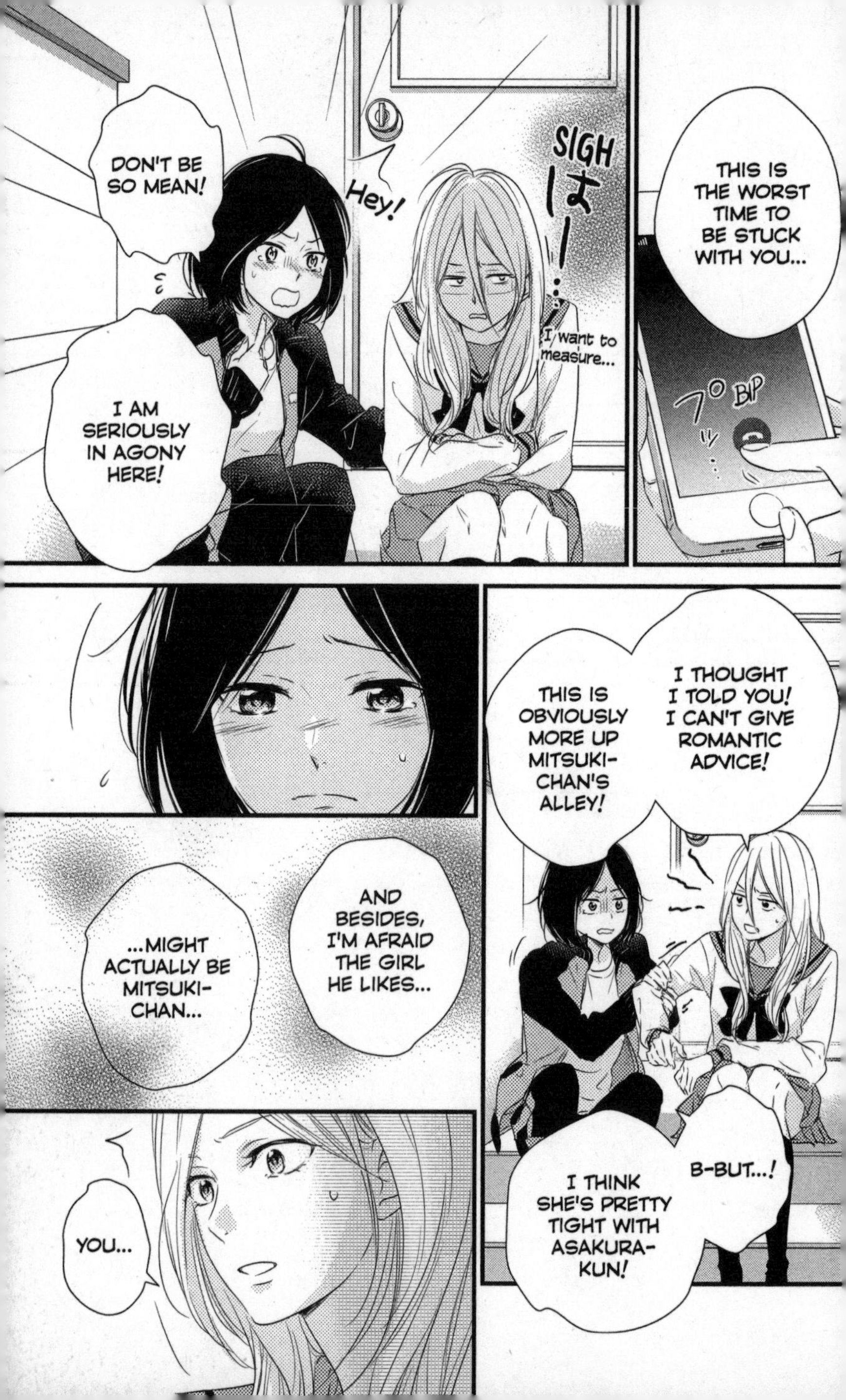
THIS IS THE WORST TIME TO BE STUCK WITH YOU...
BIP
SIGH
I want to measure...
Hey!
DON'T BE SO MEAN!
I AM SERIOUSLY IN AGONY HERE!
I THOUGHT I TOLD YOU! I CAN'T GIVE ROMANTIC ADVICE!
THIS IS OBVIOUSLY MORE UP MITSUKI-CHAN'S ALLEY!
B-BUT...!
I THINK SHE'S PRETTY TIGHT WITH ASAKURA-KUN!
AND BESIDES, I'M AFRAID THE GIRL HE LIKES...
...MIGHT ACTUALLY BE MITSUKI-CHAN...
YOU...

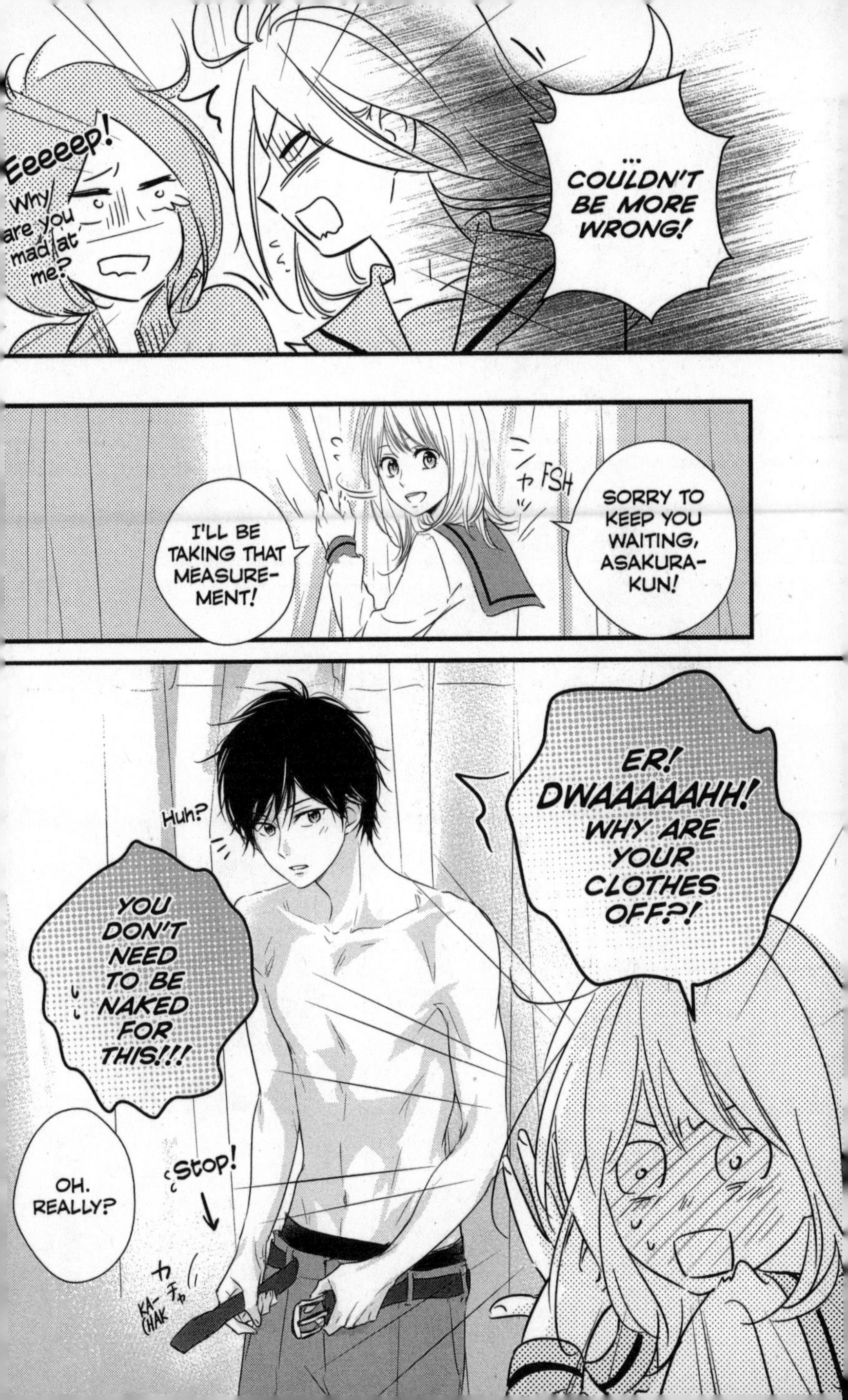
...COULDN'T BE MORE WRONG!
Eeeeep!
Why are you mad at me?
SORRY TO KEEP YOU WAITING, ASAKURA-KUN!
FSH
I'LL BE TAKING THAT MEASUREMENT!
ER! DWAAAAAHH! WHY ARE YOUR CLOTHES OFF?!
Huh?
YOU DON'T NEED TO BE NAKED FOR THIS!!!
Stop!
OH. REALLY?
KA-CHAK

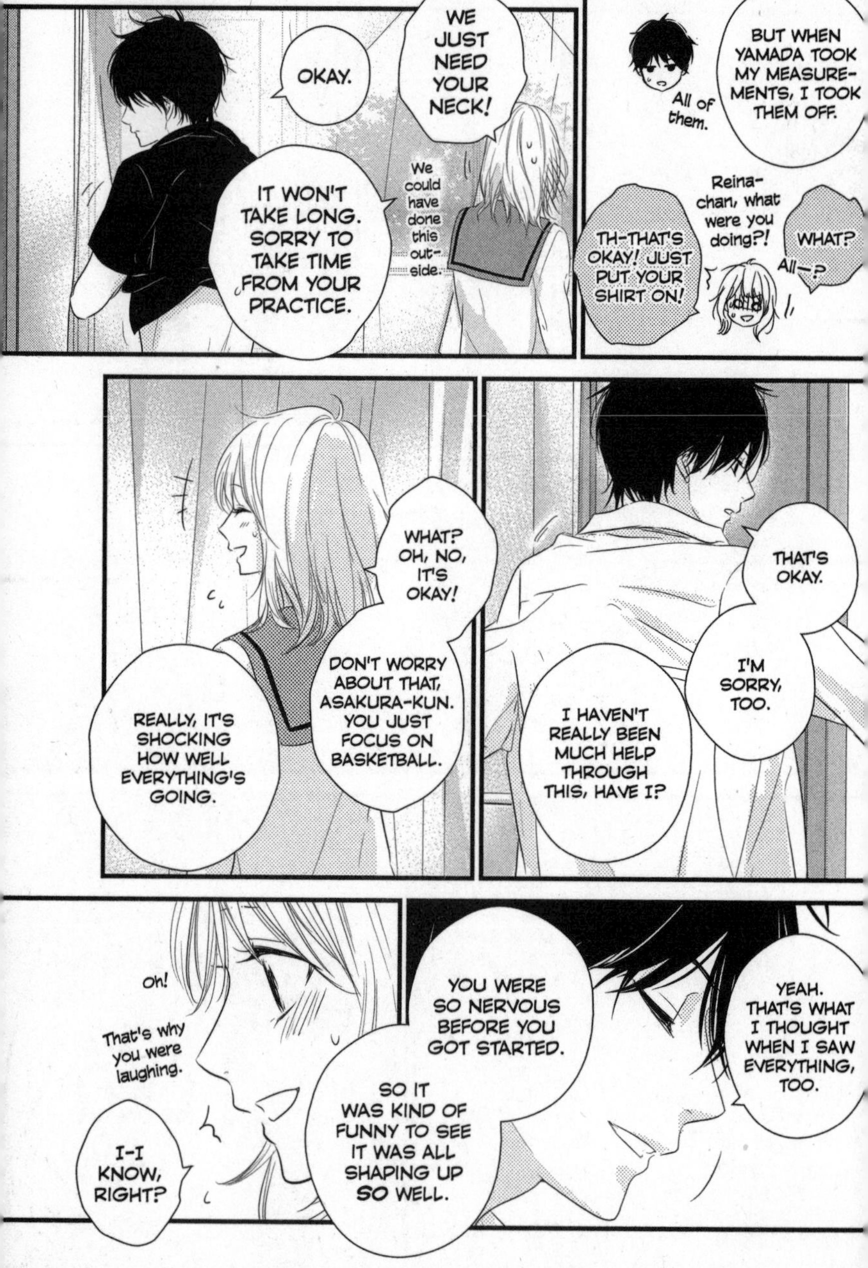
BUT WHEN YAMADA TOOK MY MEASUREMENTS, I TOOK THEM OFF.
All of them.
WHAT? All—?
Reina-chan, what were you doing?!
TH-THAT'S OKAY! JUST PUT YOUR SHIRT ON!
WE JUST NEED YOUR NECK!
OKAY.
We could have done this outside.
IT WON'T TAKE LONG. SORRY TO TAKE TIME FROM YOUR PRACTICE.
THAT'S OKAY.
I'M SORRY, TOO.
I HAVEN'T REALLY BEEN MUCH HELP THROUGH THIS, HAVE I?
WHAT? OH, NO, IT'S OKAY!
DON'T WORRY ABOUT THAT, ASAKURA-KUN. YOU JUST FOCUS ON BASKETBALL.
REALLY, IT'S SHOCKING HOW WELL EVERYTHING'S GOING.
YEAH. THAT'S WHAT I THOUGHT WHEN I SAW EVERYTHING, TOO.
YOU WERE SO NERVOUS BEFORE YOU GOT STARTED.
SO IT WAS KIND OF FUNNY TO SEE IT WAS ALL SHAPING UP SO WELL.
Oh!
That's why you were laughing.
I-I KNOW, RIGHT?

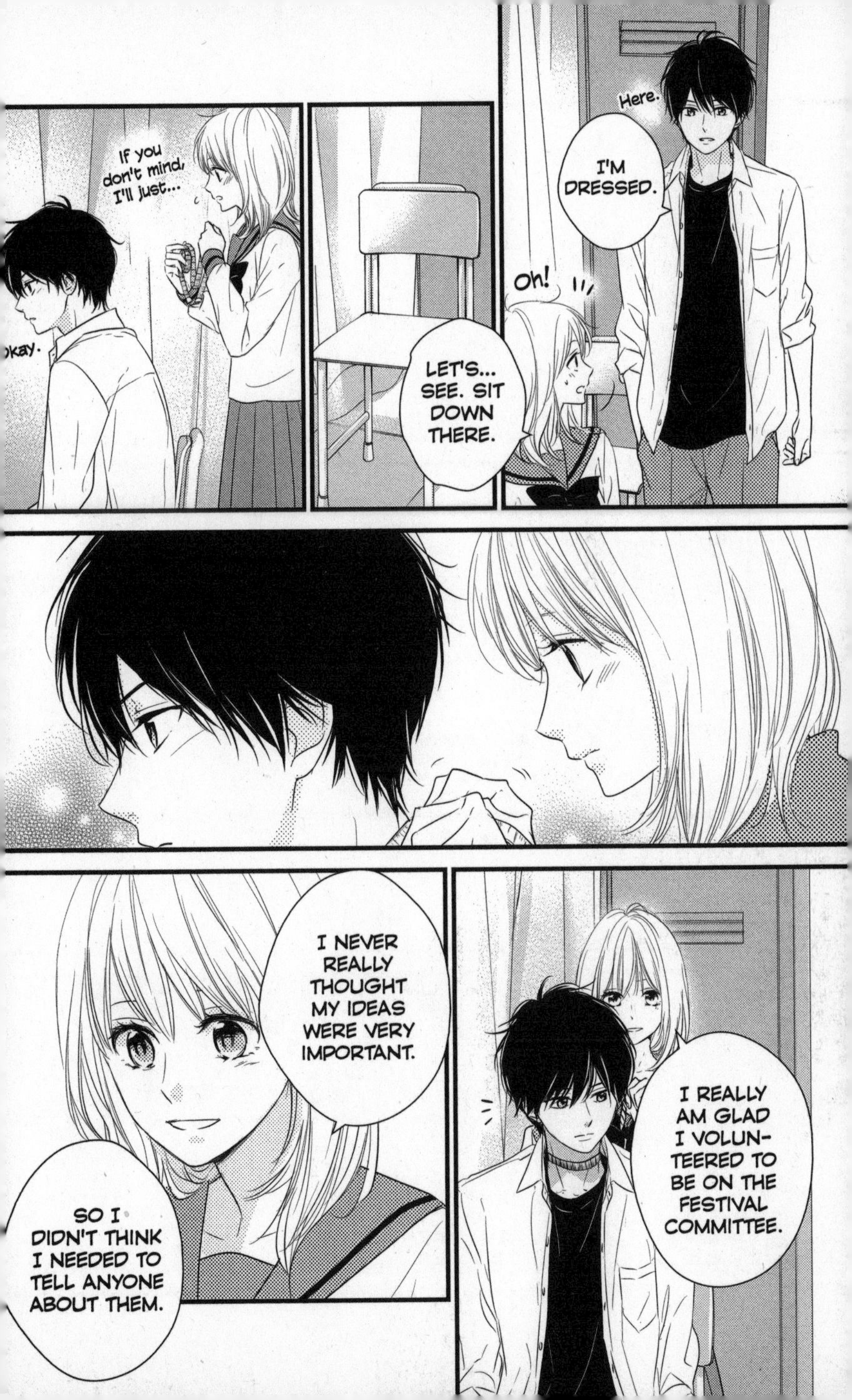
Here.
I'M DRESSED.
Oh!
LET'S... SEE. SIT DOWN THERE.
If you don't mind, I'll just...
okay.
I REALLY AM GLAD I VOLUN-TEERED TO BE ON THE FESTIVAL COMMITTEE.
I NEVER REALLY THOUGHT MY IDEAS WERE VERY IMPORTANT.
SO I DIDN'T THINK I NEEDED TO TELL ANYONE ABOUT THEM.

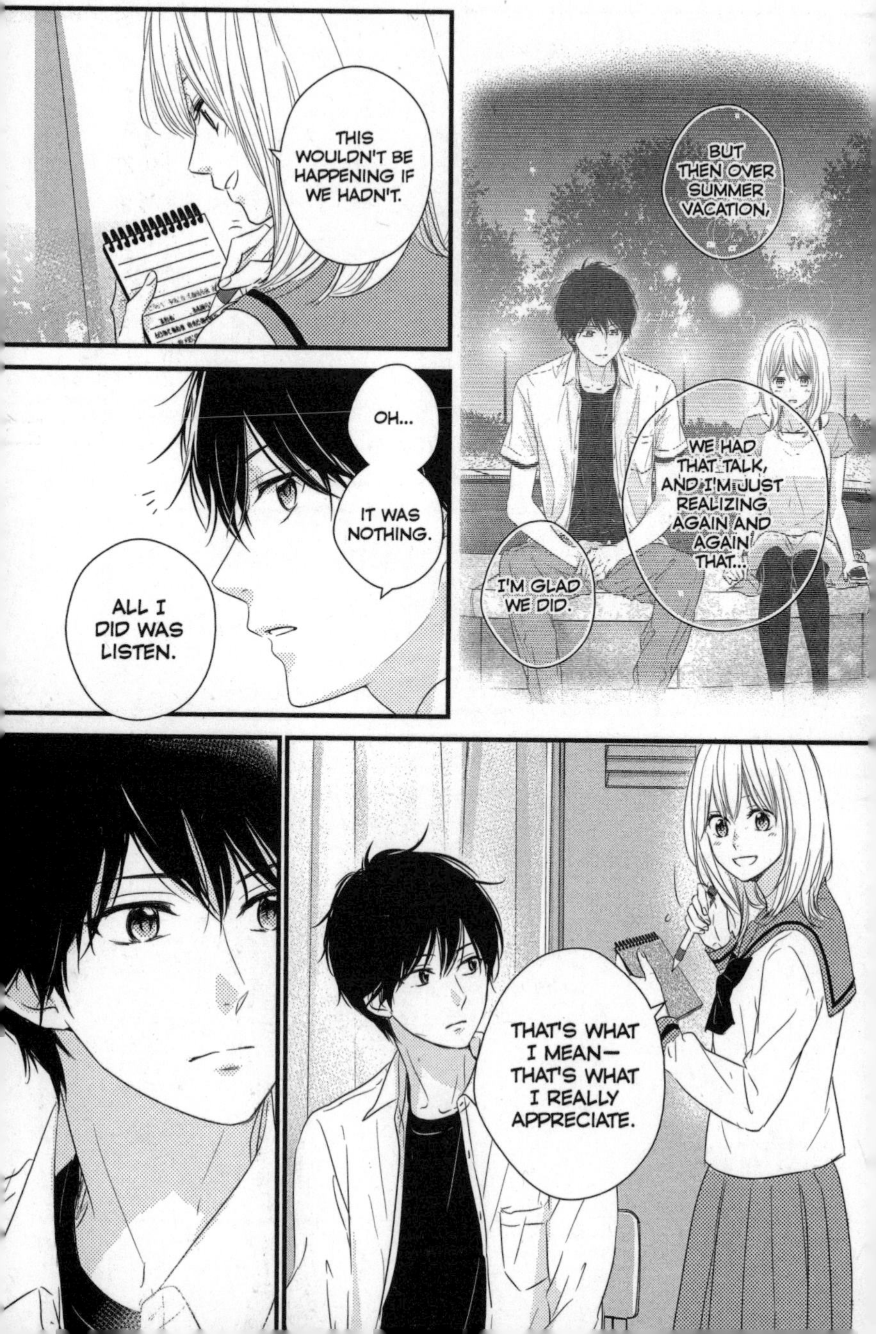
BUT THEN OVER SUMMER VACATION,
WE HAD THAT TALK, AND I'M JUST REALIZING AGAIN AND AGAIN THAT...
I'M GLAD WE DID.
THIS WOULDN'T BE HAPPENING IF WE HADN'T.
OH...
IT WAS NOTHING.
ALL I DID WAS LISTEN.
THAT'S WHAT I MEAN—THAT'S WHAT I REALLY APPRECIATE.

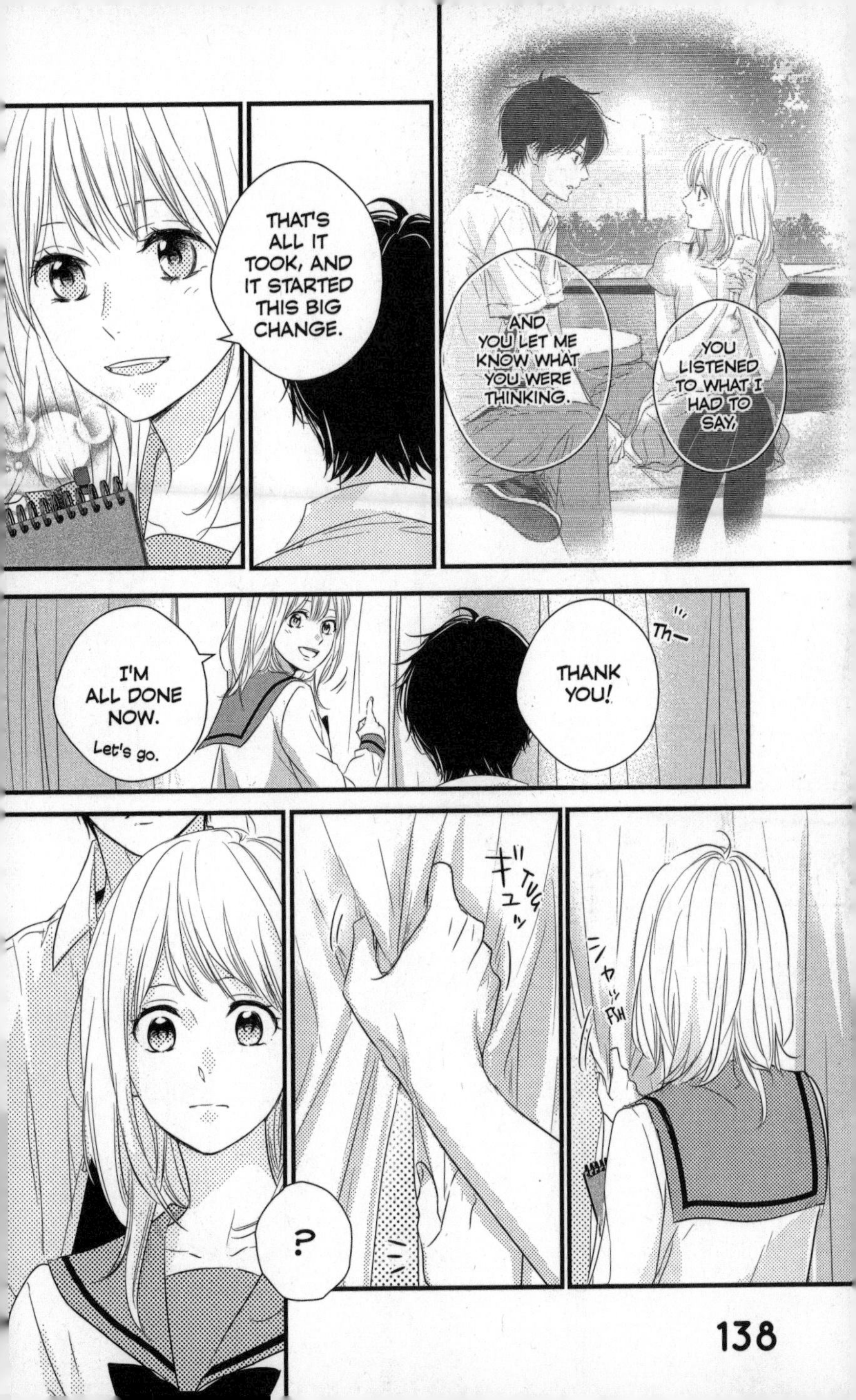
YOU LISTENED TO WHAT I HAD TO SAY,
AND YOU LET ME KNOW WHAT YOU WERE THINKING.
THAT'S ALL IT TOOK, AND IT STARTED THIS BIG CHANGE.
Th—
THANK YOU!
I'M ALL DONE NOW.
Let's go.
シャッ
FSH
ギュッ
TUG
?

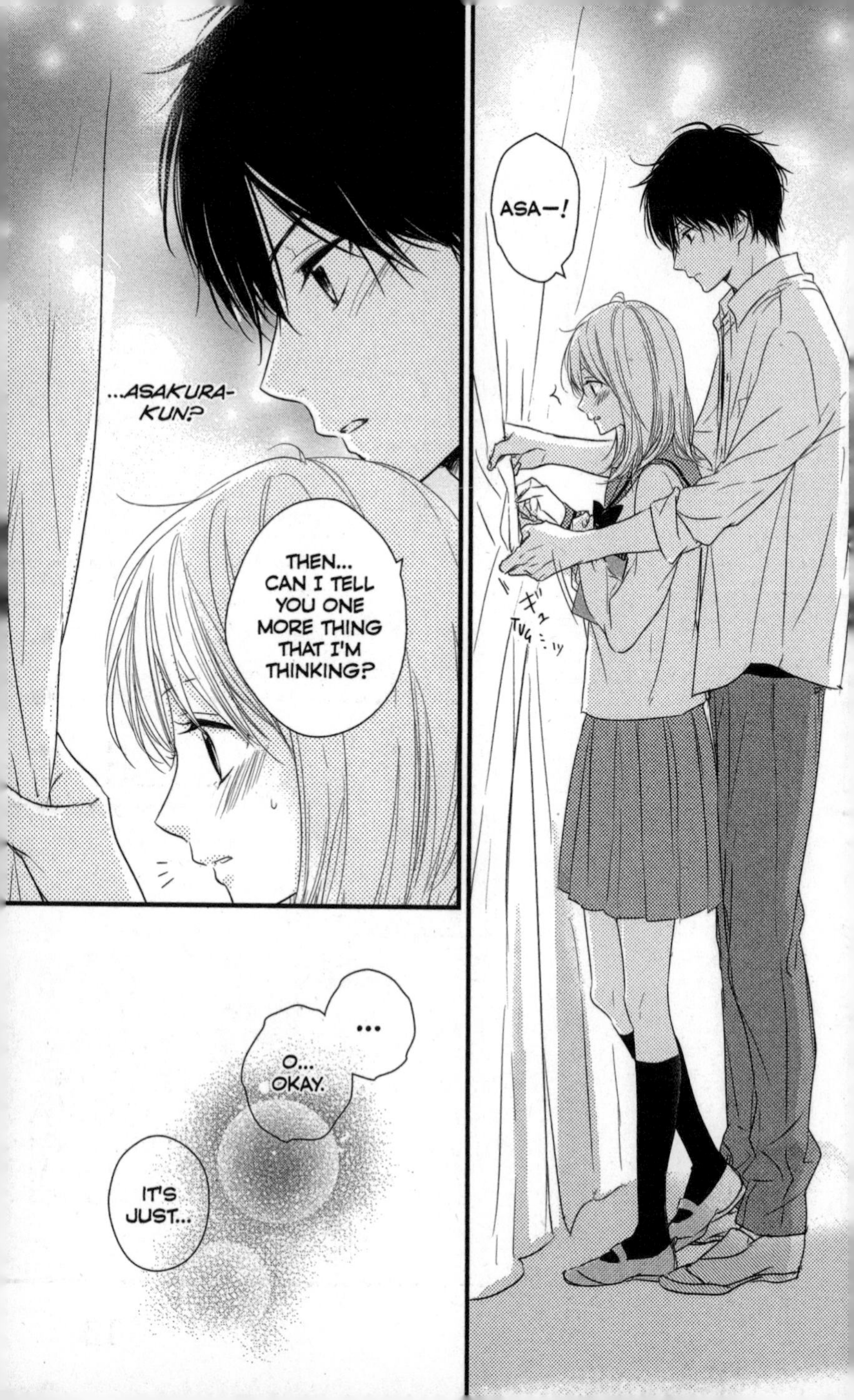
ASA—!
TUG
...ASAKURA-KUN?
THEN... CAN I TELL YOU ONE MORE THING THAT I'M THINKING?
...
O... OKAY.
IT'S JUST...

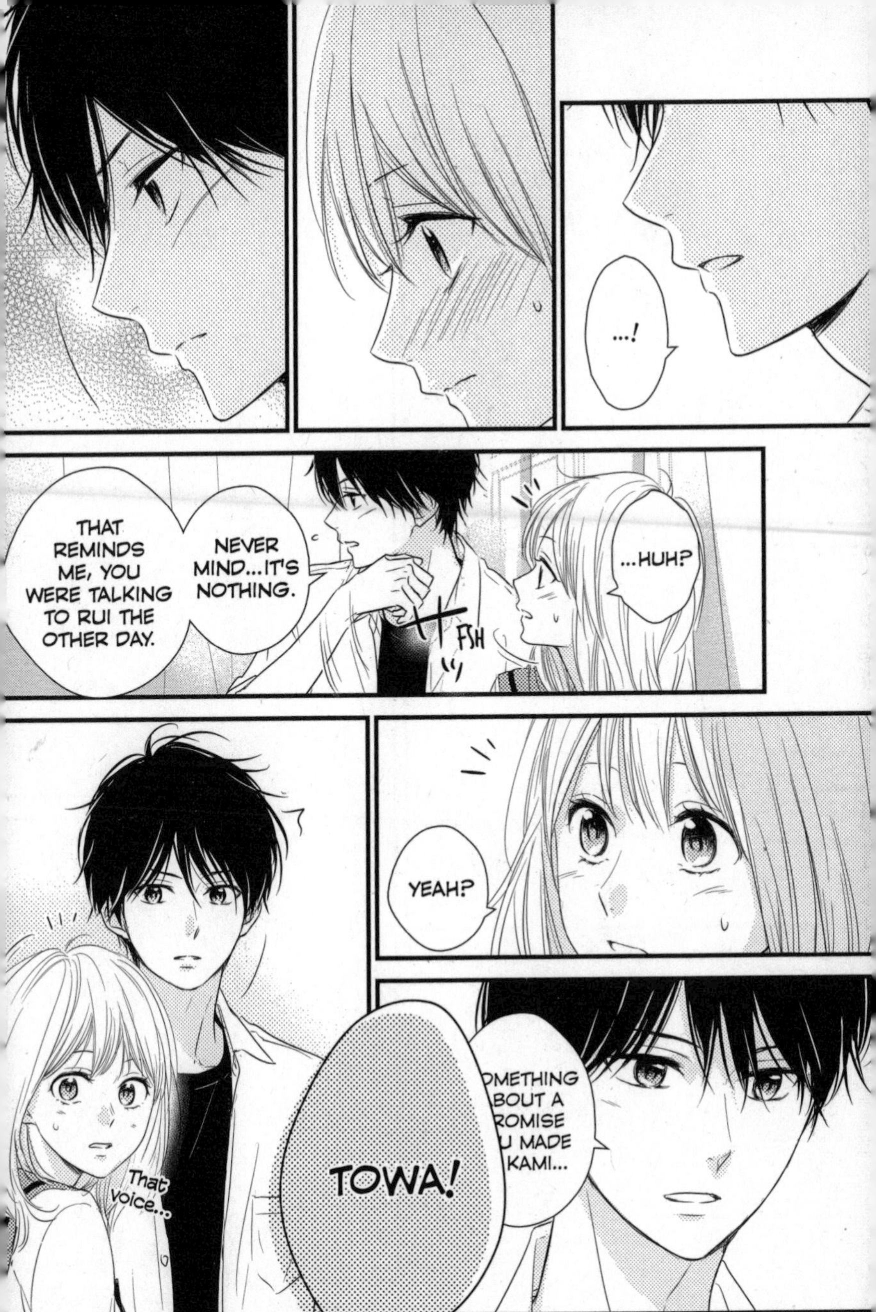
...!
...HUH?
NEVER MIND...IT'S NOTHING.
FSH
THAT REMINDS ME, YOU WERE TALKING TO RUI THE OTHER DAY.
YEAH?
OMETHING BOUT A ROMISE U MADE KAMI...
TOWA!
That voice...

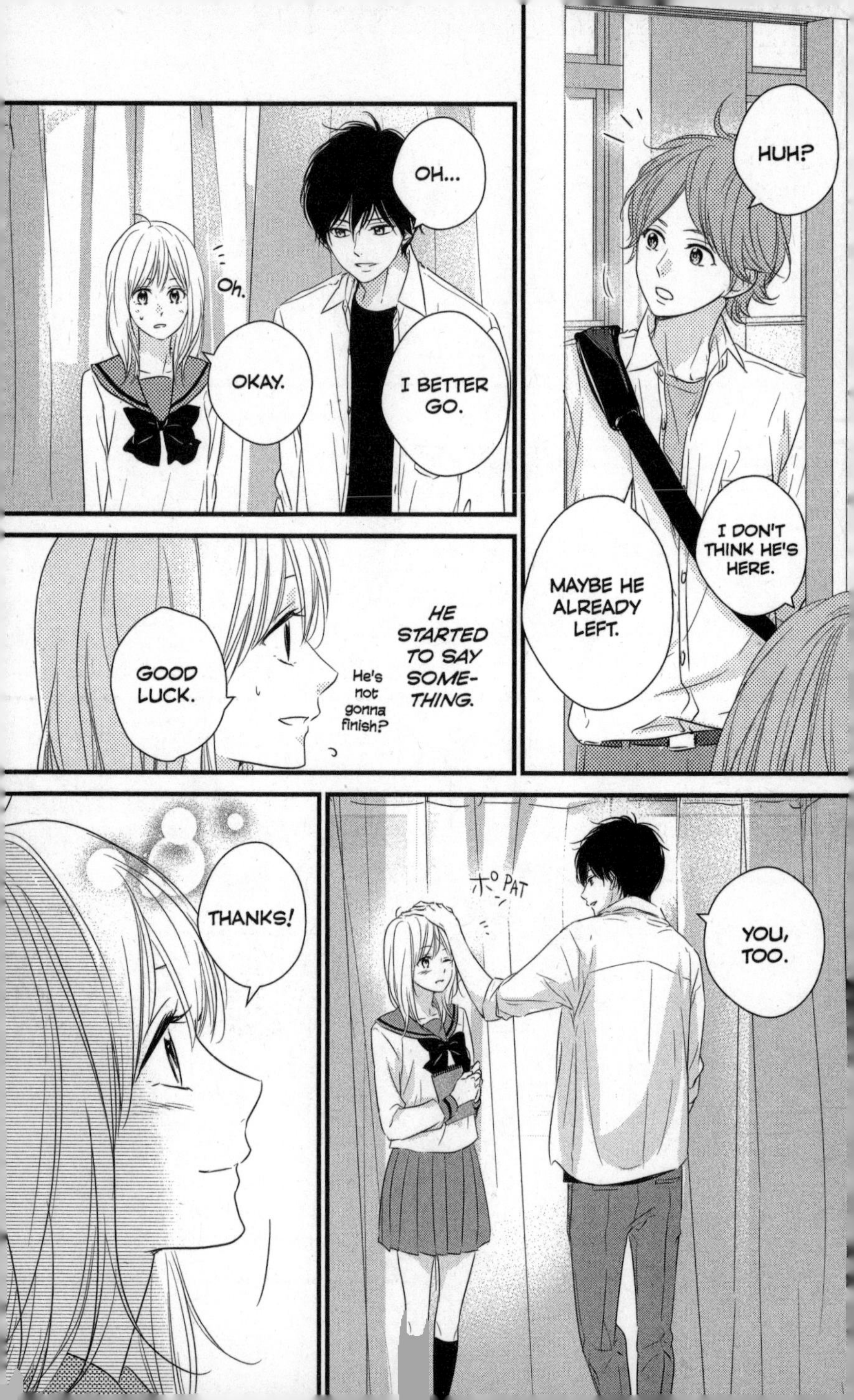
HUH?
I DON'T THINK HE'S HERE.
MAYBE HE ALREADY LEFT.
OH...
I BETTER GO.
Oh.
OKAY.
HE STARTED TO SAY SOME-THING.
He's not gonna finish?
GOOD LUCK.
YOU, TOO.
PAT
THANKS!

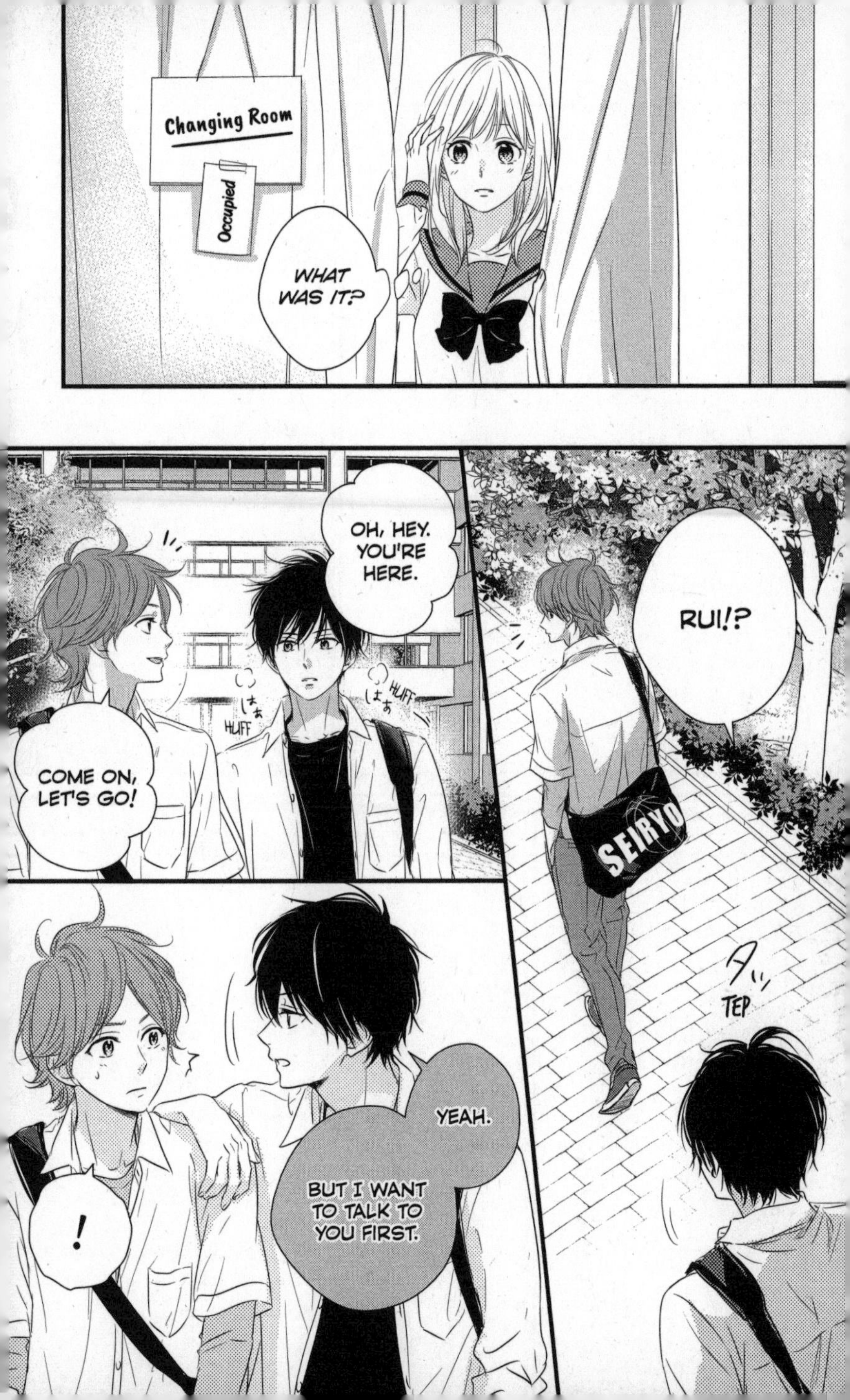
Changing Room
Occupied
WHAT WAS IT?
RUI!?
TEP
OH, HEY. YOU'RE HERE.
HUFF
HUFF
COME ON, LET'S GO!
YEAH.
BUT I WANT TO TALK TO YOU FIRST.
!

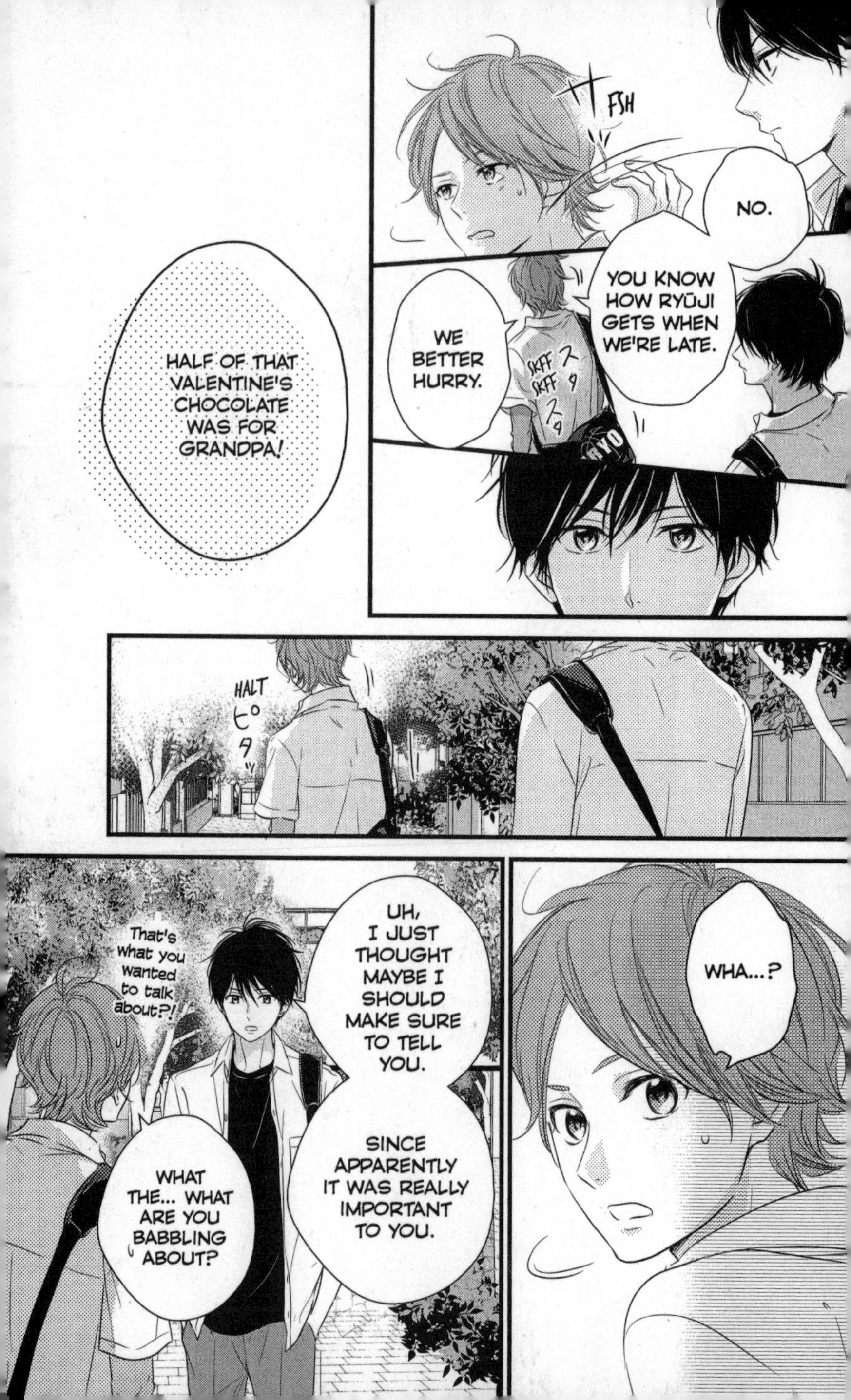
FSH
NO.
YOU KNOW HOW RYŪJI GETS WHEN WE'RE LATE.
WE BETTER HURRY.
SKFF SKFF
HALF OF THAT VALENTINE'S CHOCOLATE WAS FOR GRANDPA!
HALT
WHA...?
UH, I JUST THOUGHT MAYBE I SHOULD MAKE SURE TO TELL YOU.
SINCE APPARENTLY IT WAS REALLY IMPORTANT TO YOU.
That's what you wanted to talk about?!
WHAT THE... WHAT ARE YOU BABBLING ABOUT?

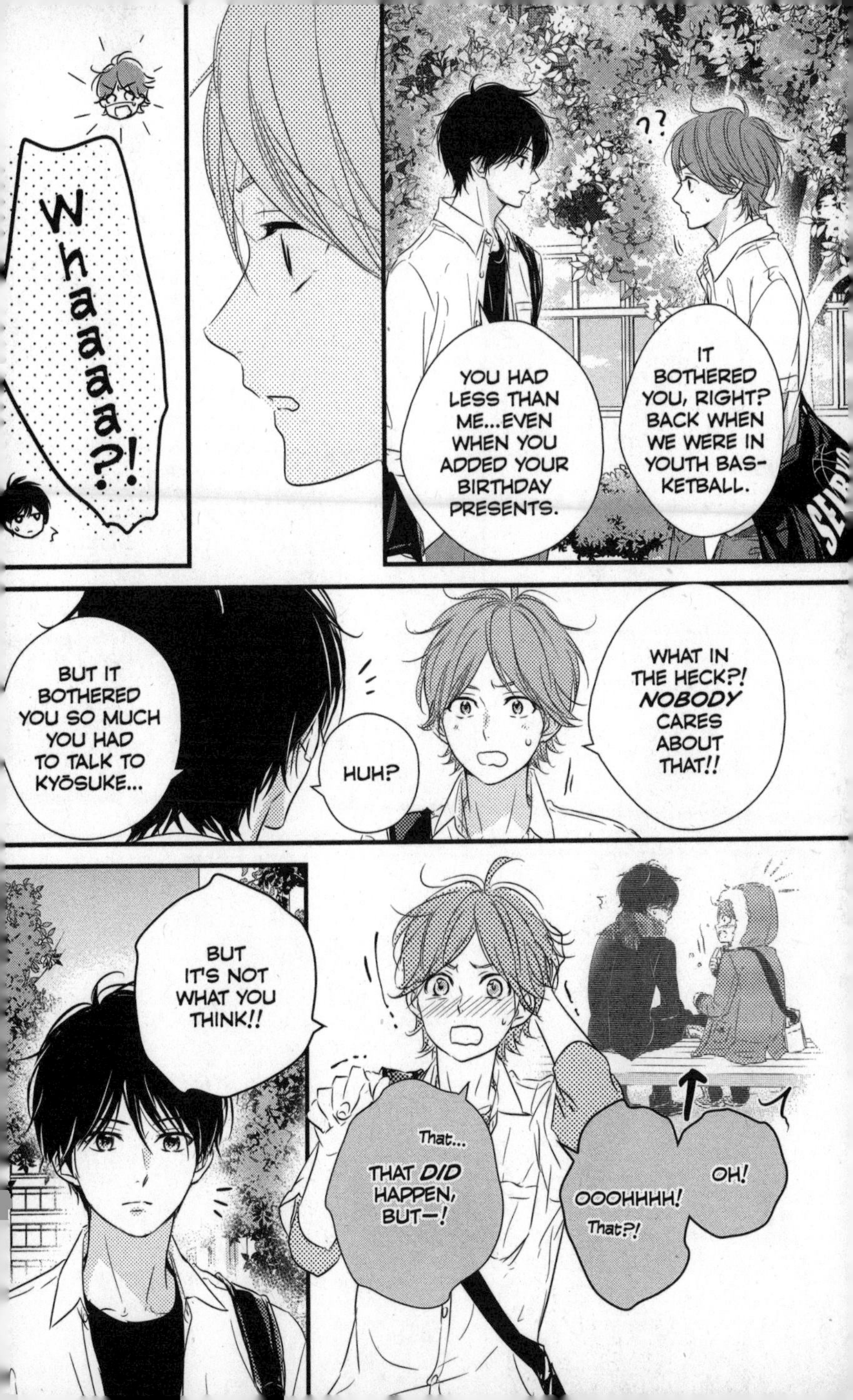
IT BOTHERED YOU, RIGHT? BACK WHEN WE WERE IN YOUTH BAS-KETBALL.
YOU HAD LESS THAN ME...EVEN WHEN YOU ADDED YOUR BIRTHDAY PRESENTS.
Whaaaaa?!
WHAT IN THE HECK?! NOBODY CARES ABOUT THAT!!
HUH?
BUT IT BOTHERED YOU SO MUCH YOU HAD TO TALK TO KYŌSUKE...
OH!
OOOHHHH! That?!
That... THAT DID HAPPEN, BUT—!
BUT IT'S NOT WHAT YOU THINK!!

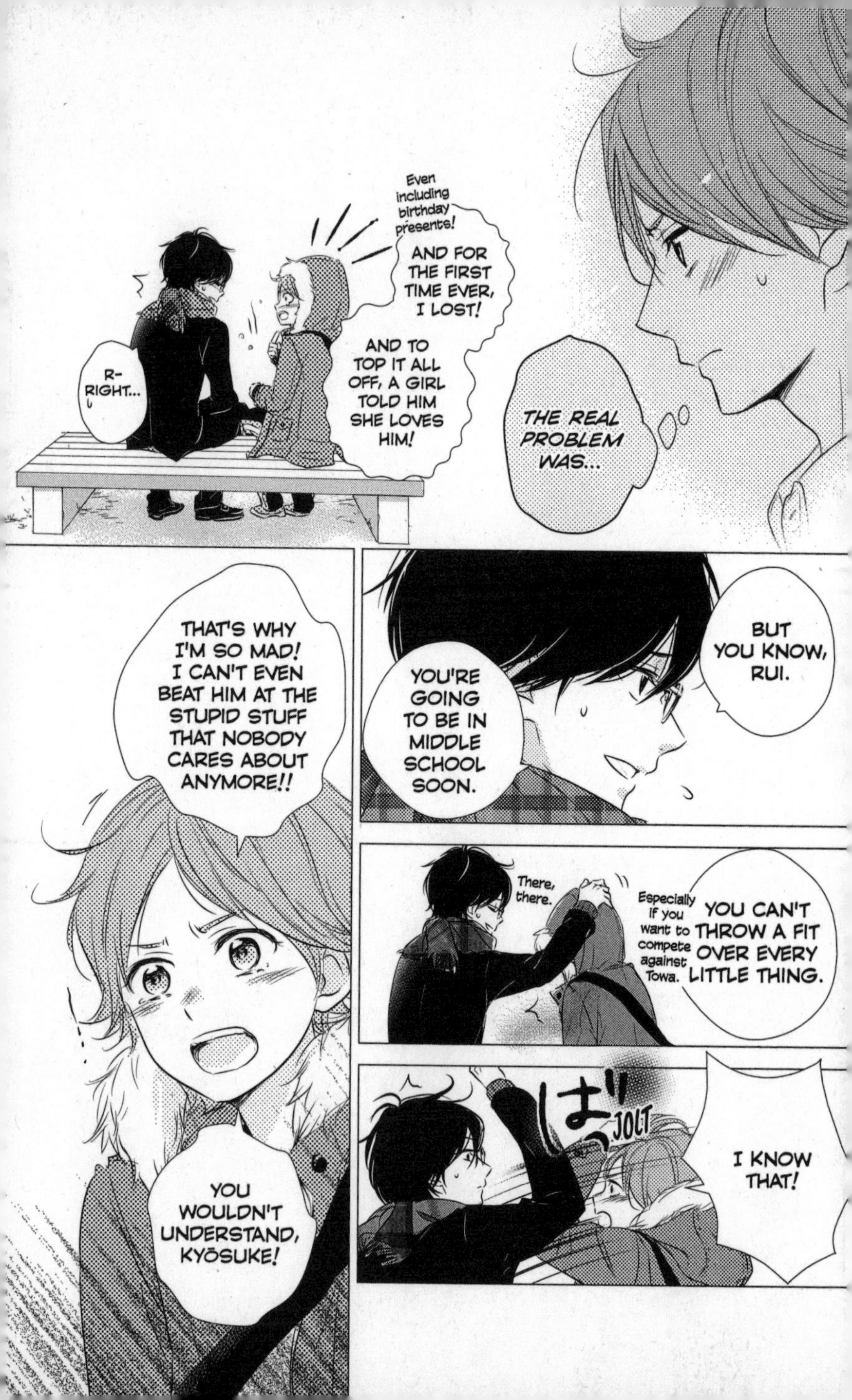
THE REAL PROBLEM WAS...
Even including birthday presents!
AND FOR THE FIRST TIME EVER, I LOST!
AND TO TOP IT ALL OFF, A GIRL TOLD HIM SHE LOVES HIM!
R-RIGHT...
BUT YOU KNOW, RUI.
YOU'RE GOING TO BE IN MIDDLE SCHOOL SOON.
YOU CAN'T THROW A FIT OVER EVERY LITTLE THING.
Especially if you want to compete against Towa.
There, there.
I KNOW THAT!
JOLT
THAT'S WHY I'M SO MAD! I CAN'T EVEN BEAT HIM AT THE STUPID STUFF THAT NOBODY CARES ABOUT ANYMORE!!
YOU WOULDN'T UNDERSTAND, KYŌSUKE!

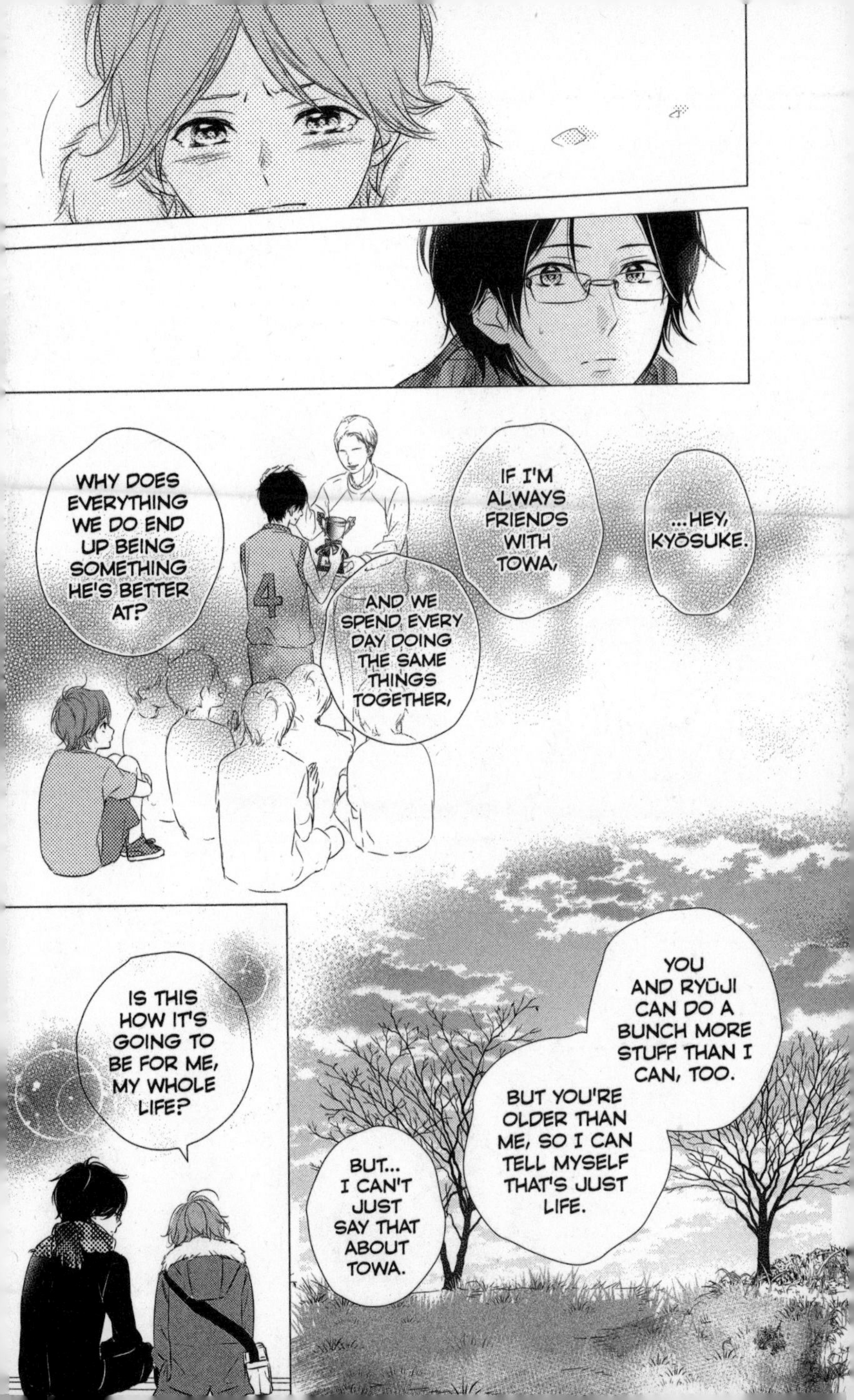
...HEY, KYŌSUKE.
IF I'M ALWAYS FRIENDS WITH TOWA,
AND WE SPEND EVERY DAY DOING THE SAME THINGS TOGETHER,
WHY DOES EVERYTHING WE DO END UP BEING SOMETHING HE'S BETTER AT?
YOU AND RYŪJI CAN DO A BUNCH MORE STUFF THAN I CAN, TOO.
BUT YOU'RE OLDER THAN ME, SO I CAN TELL MYSELF THAT'S JUST LIFE.
BUT... I CAN'T JUST SAY THAT ABOUT TOWA.
IS THIS HOW IT'S GOING TO BE FOR ME, MY WHOLE LIFE?

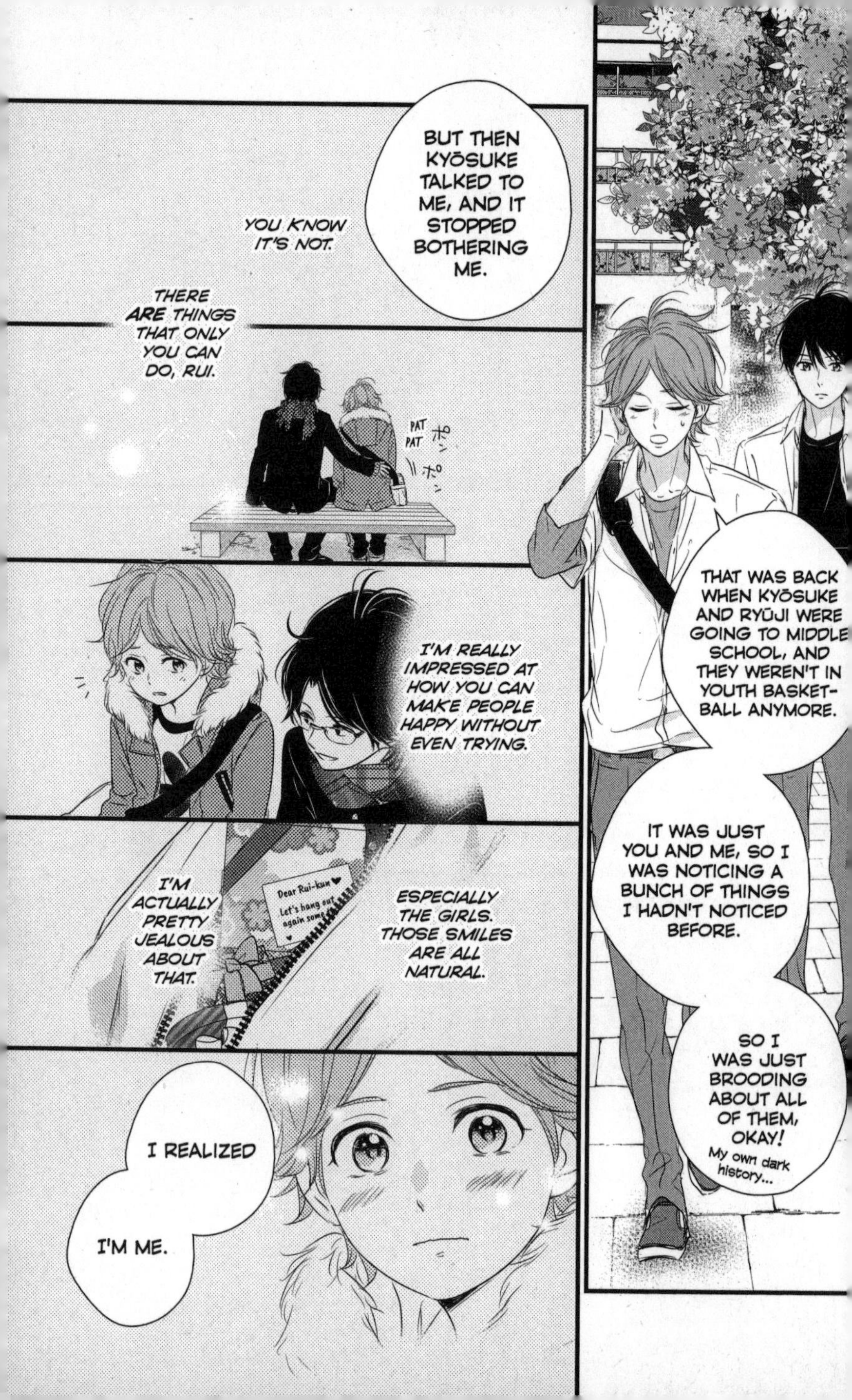
THAT WAS BACK WHEN KYŌSUKE AND RYŪJI WERE GOING TO MIDDLE SCHOOL, AND THEY WEREN'T IN YOUTH BASKET-BALL ANYMORE.
IT WAS JUST YOU AND ME, SO I WAS NOTICING A BUNCH OF THINGS I HADN'T NOTICED BEFORE.
SO I WAS JUST BROODING ABOUT ALL OF THEM, OKAY!
My own dark history...
BUT THEN KYŌSUKE TALKED TO ME, AND IT STOPPED BOTHERING ME.
YOU KNOW IT'S NOT.
THERE ARE THINGS THAT ONLY YOU CAN DO, RUI.
PAT PAT
ポン ポン
I'M REALLY IMPRESSED AT HOW YOU CAN MAKE PEOPLE HAPPY WITHOUT EVEN TRYING.
ESPECIALLY THE GIRLS. THOSE SMILES ARE ALL NATURAL.
Dear Rui-kun
Let's hang out again some
I'M ACTUALLY PRETTY JEALOUS ABOUT THAT.
I REALIZED
I'M ME.

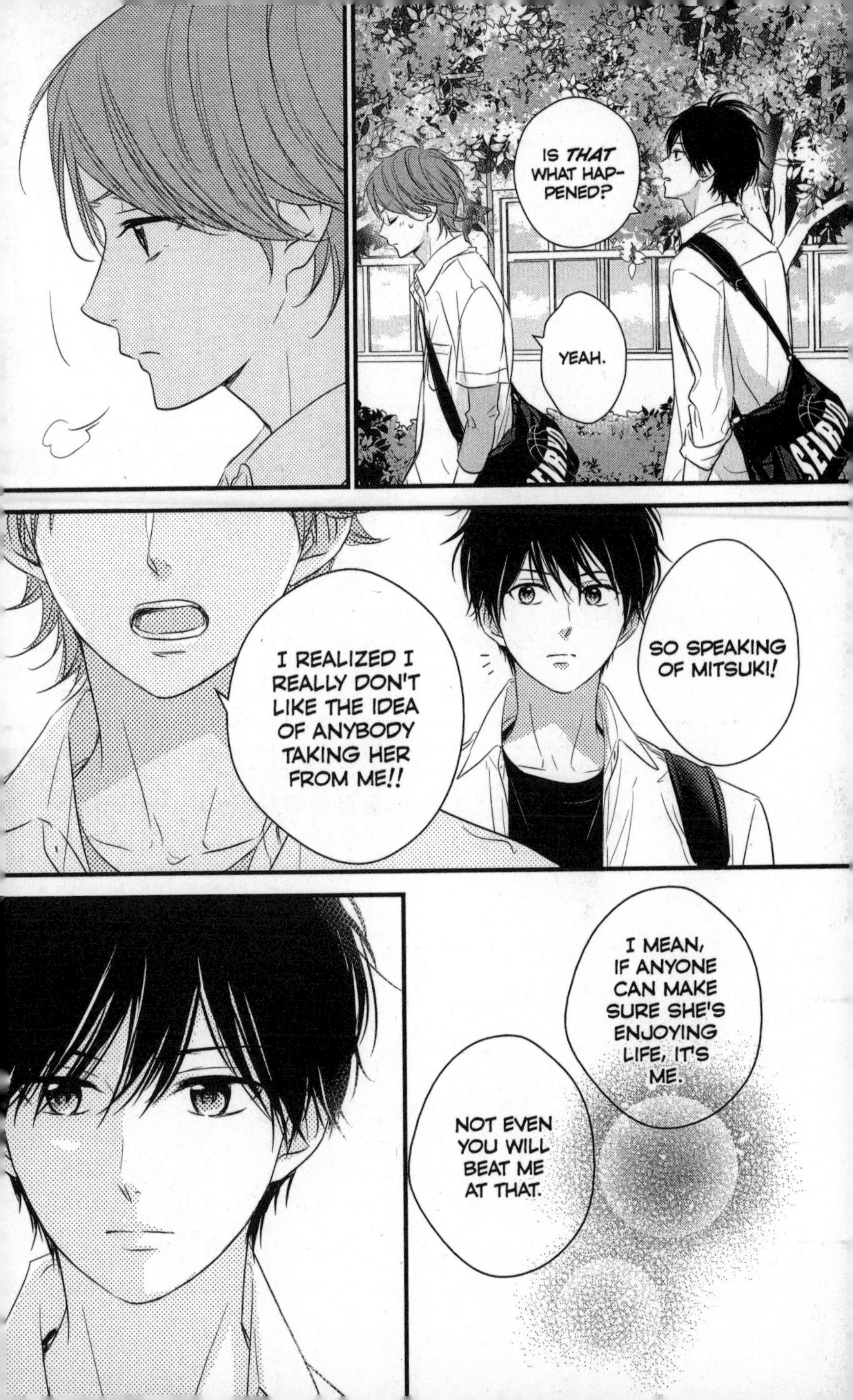
IS *THAT* WHAT HAP-PENED?
YEAH.
SO SPEAKING OF MITSUKI!
I REALIZED I REALLY DON'T LIKE THE IDEA OF ANYBODY TAKING HER FROM ME!!
I MEAN, IF ANYONE CAN MAKE SURE SHE'S ENJOYING LIFE, IT'S ME.
NOT EVEN YOU WILL BEAT ME AT THAT.

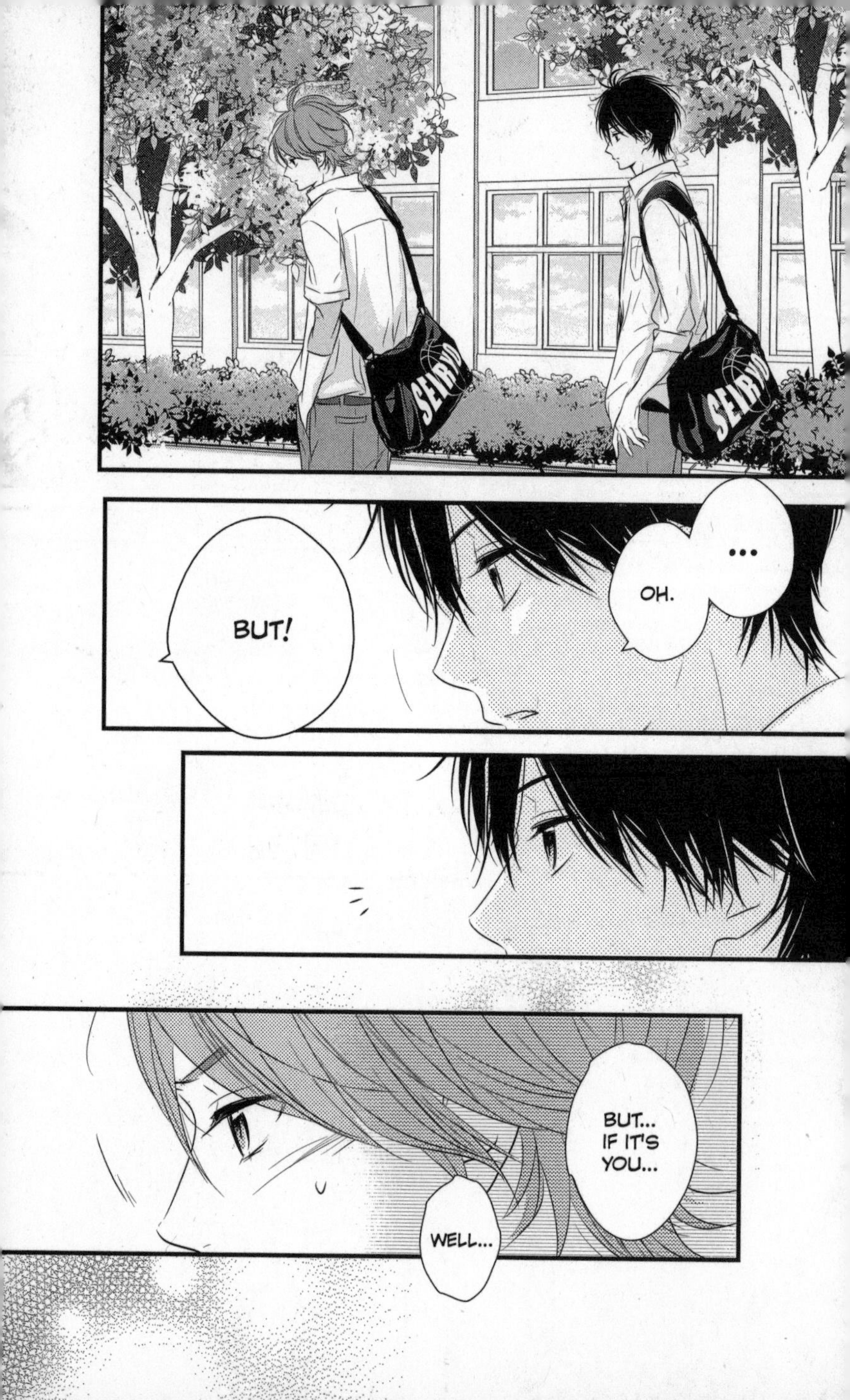
...
OH.
BUT!
BUT... IF IT'S YOU...
WELL...

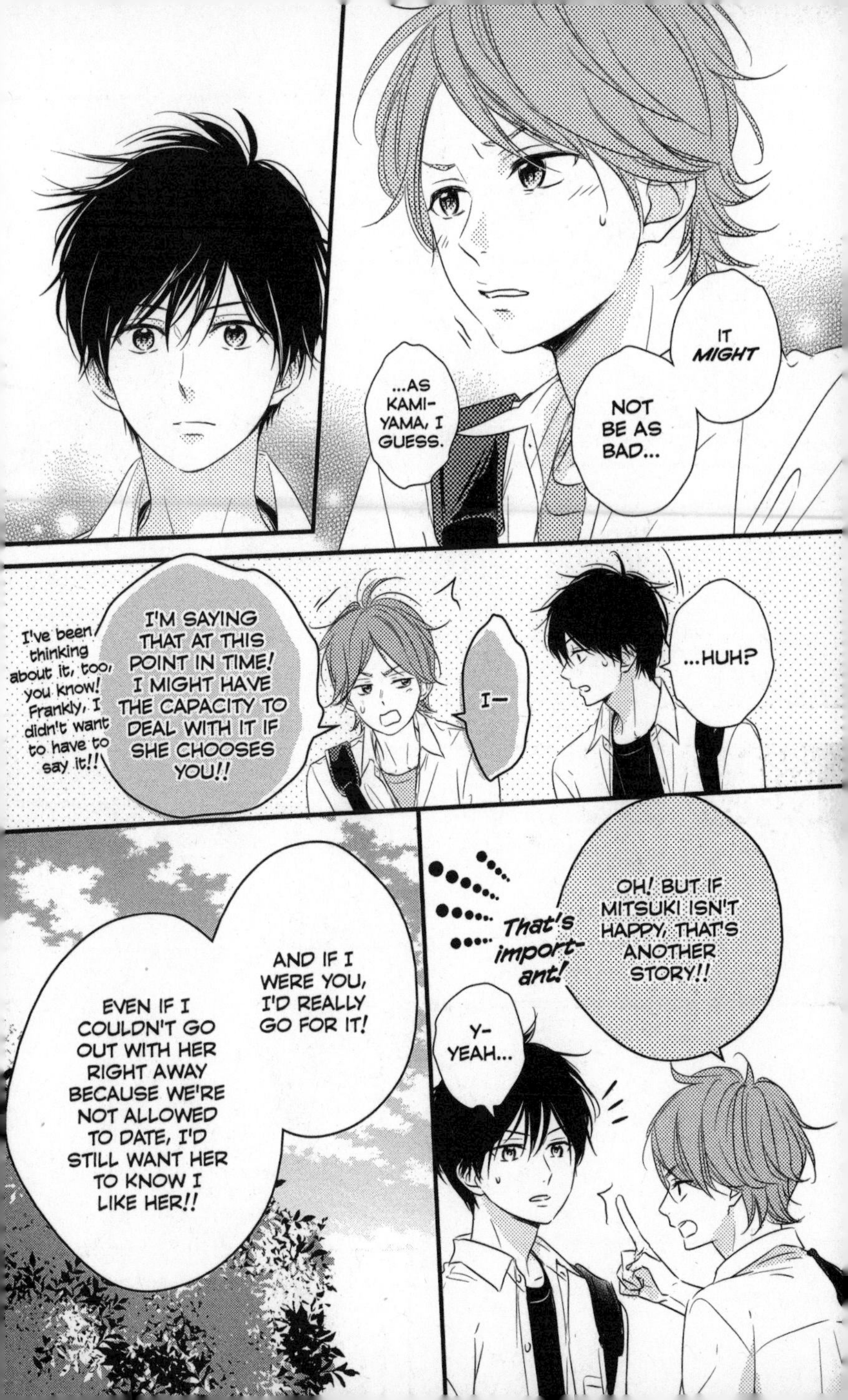
IT MIGHT NOT BE AS BAD...
...AS KAMI-YAMA, I GUESS.
...HUH?
I—
I'M SAYING THAT AT THIS POINT IN TIME! I MIGHT HAVE THE CAPACITY TO DEAL WITH IT IF SHE CHOOSES YOU!!
I've been thinking about it, too, you know! Frankly, I didn't want to have to say it!!
OH! BUT IF MITSUKI ISN'T HAPPY, THAT'S ANOTHER STORY!!
That's import-ant!
•••• •••••• ••••• ••••
Y-YEAH...
AND IF I WERE YOU, I'D REALLY GO FOR IT!
EVEN IF I COULDN'T GO OUT WITH HER RIGHT AWAY BECAUSE WE'RE NOT ALLOWED TO DATE, I'D STILL WANT HER TO KNOW I LIKE HER!!

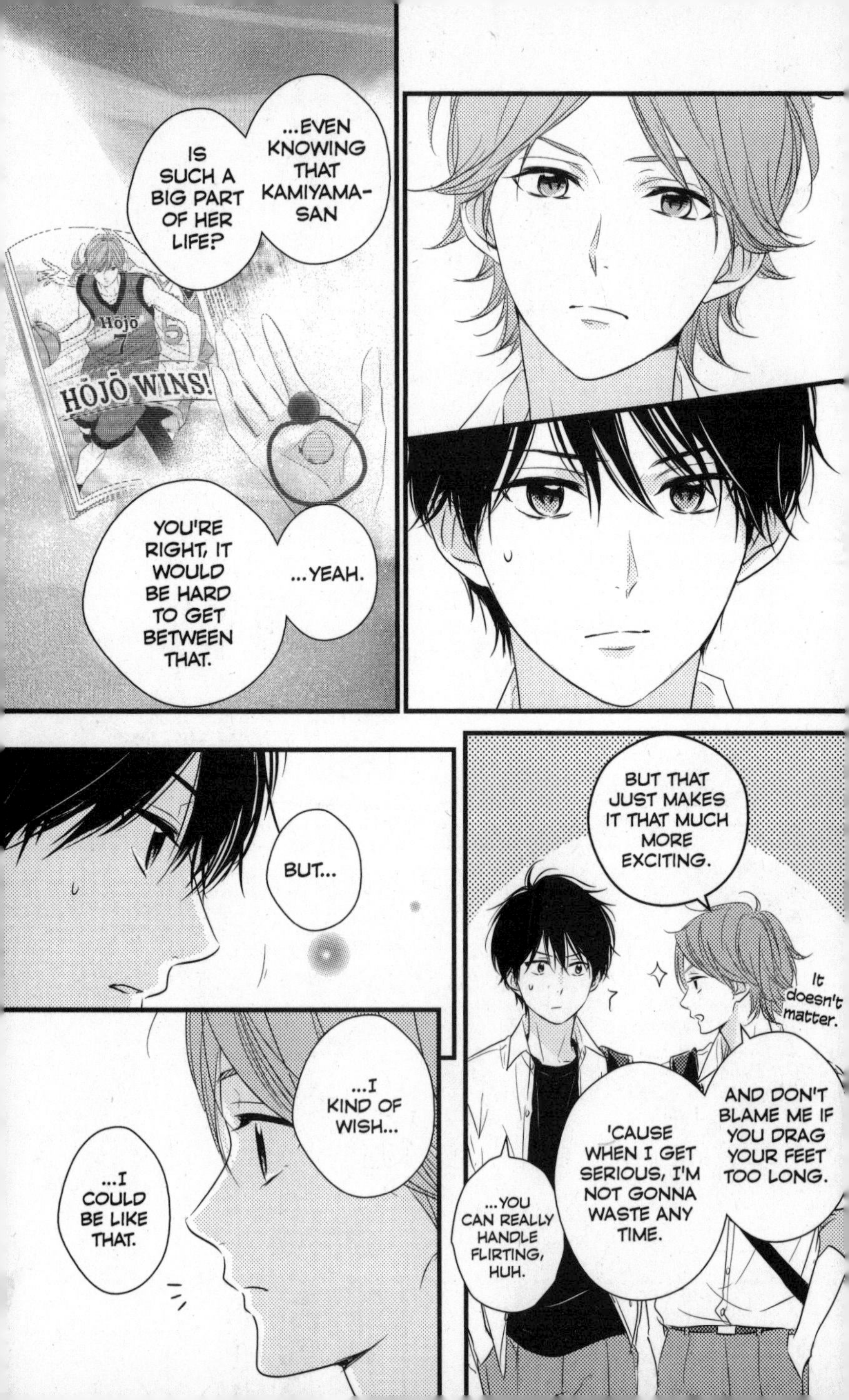
...EVEN KNOWING THAT KAMIYAMA-SAN
IS SUCH A BIG PART OF HER LIFE?
HŌJŌ WINS!
...YEAH.
YOU'RE RIGHT, IT WOULD BE HARD TO GET BETWEEN THAT.
BUT THAT JUST MAKES IT THAT MUCH MORE EXCITING.
It doesn't matter.
AND DON'T BLAME ME IF YOU DRAG YOUR FEET TOO LONG.
'CAUSE WHEN I GET SERIOUS, I'M NOT GONNA WASTE ANY TIME.
...YOU CAN REALLY HANDLE FLIRTING, HUH.
BUT...
...I KIND OF WISH...
...I COULD BE LIKE THAT.

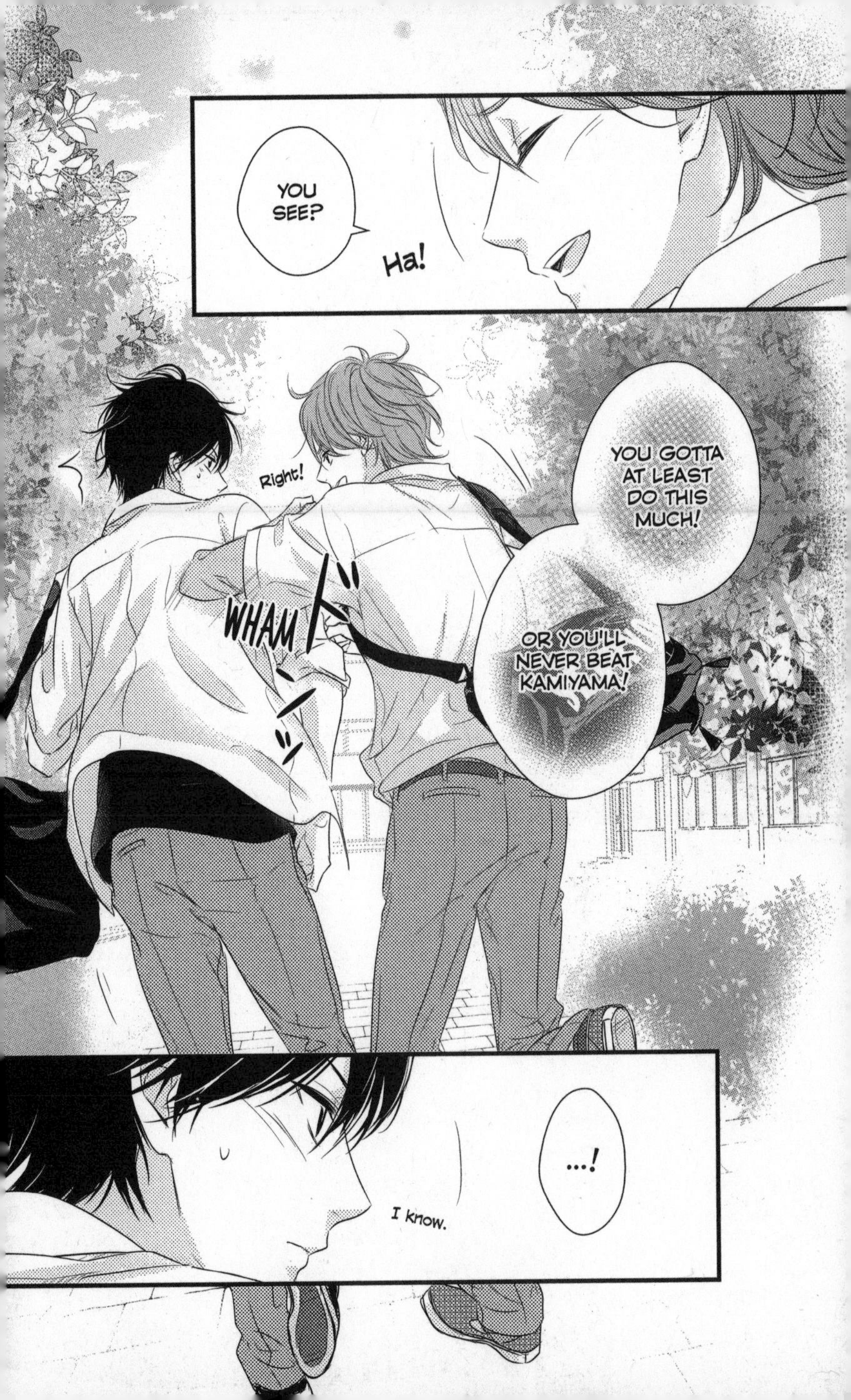

Ha!
YOU SEE?
YOU GOTTA AT LEAST DO THIS MUCH!
OR YOU'LL NEVER BEAT KAMIYAMA!
WHAM
Right!
...!
I know.

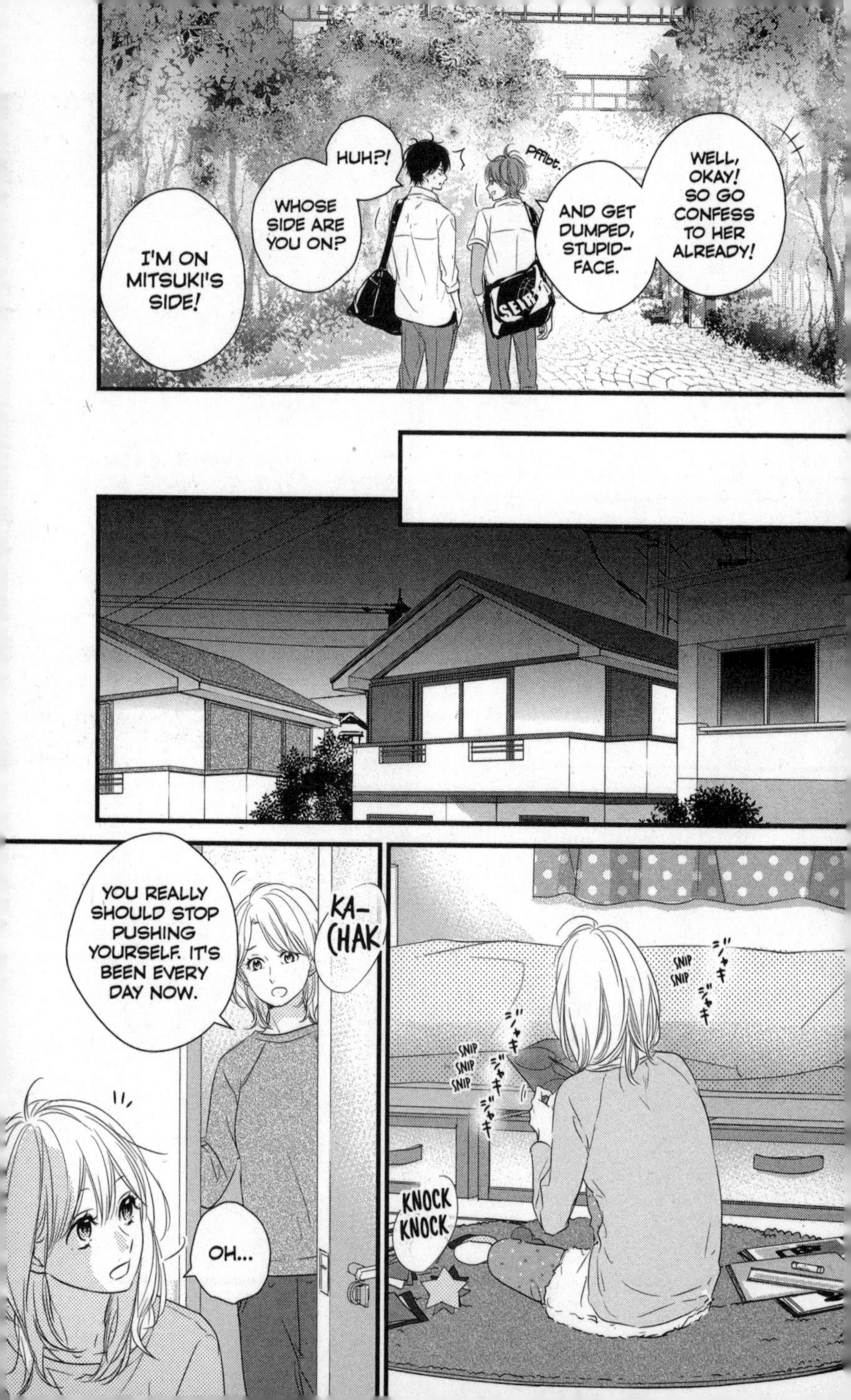
WELL, OKAY! SO GO CONFESS TO HER ALREADY!
Pfflbt.
AND GET DUMPED, STUPID-FACE.
HUH?!
WHOSE SIDE ARE YOU ON?
I'M ON MITSUKI'S SIDE!
ジャキ ジャキ
SNIP SNIP
ジャキ ジャキ ジャキ
SNIP SNIP SNIP
KNOCK KNOCK
KA-CHAK
YOU REALLY SHOULD STOP PUSHING YOURSELF. IT'S BEEN EVERY DAY NOW.
OH...

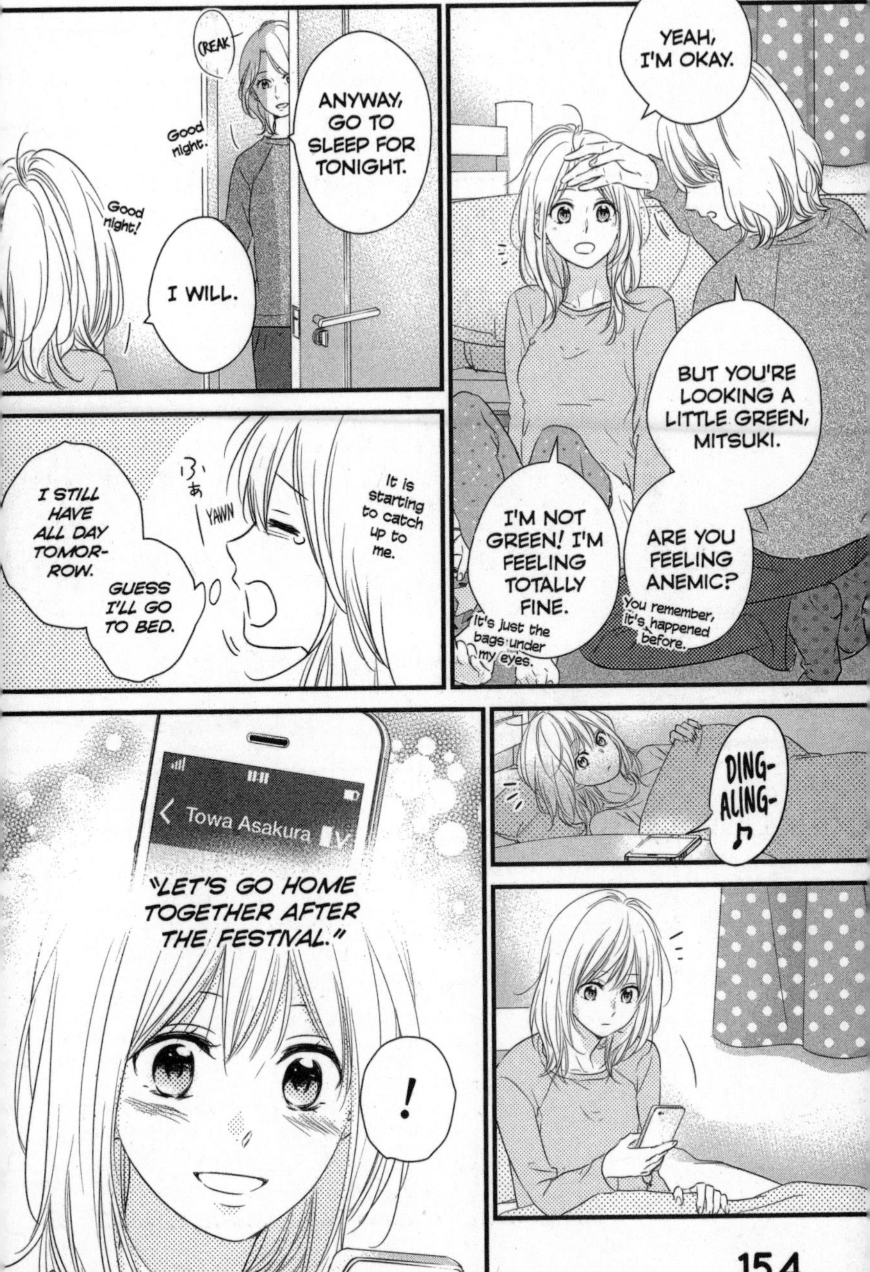
YEAH, I'M OKAY.
BUT YOU'RE LOOKING A LITTLE GREEN, MITSUKI.
ARE YOU FEELING ANEMIC?
You remember, it's happened before.
I'M NOT GREEN! I'M FEELING TOTALLY FINE.
It's just the bags under my eyes.
CREAK
ANYWAY, GO TO SLEEP FOR TONIGHT.
Good night.
Good night!
I WILL.
It is starting to catch up to me.
ふぁ
YAWN
I STILL HAVE ALL DAY TOMORROW.
GUESS I'LL GO TO BED.
DING-ALING-♪
Towa Asakura
"LET'S GO HOME TOGETHER AFTER THE FESTIVAL."
!

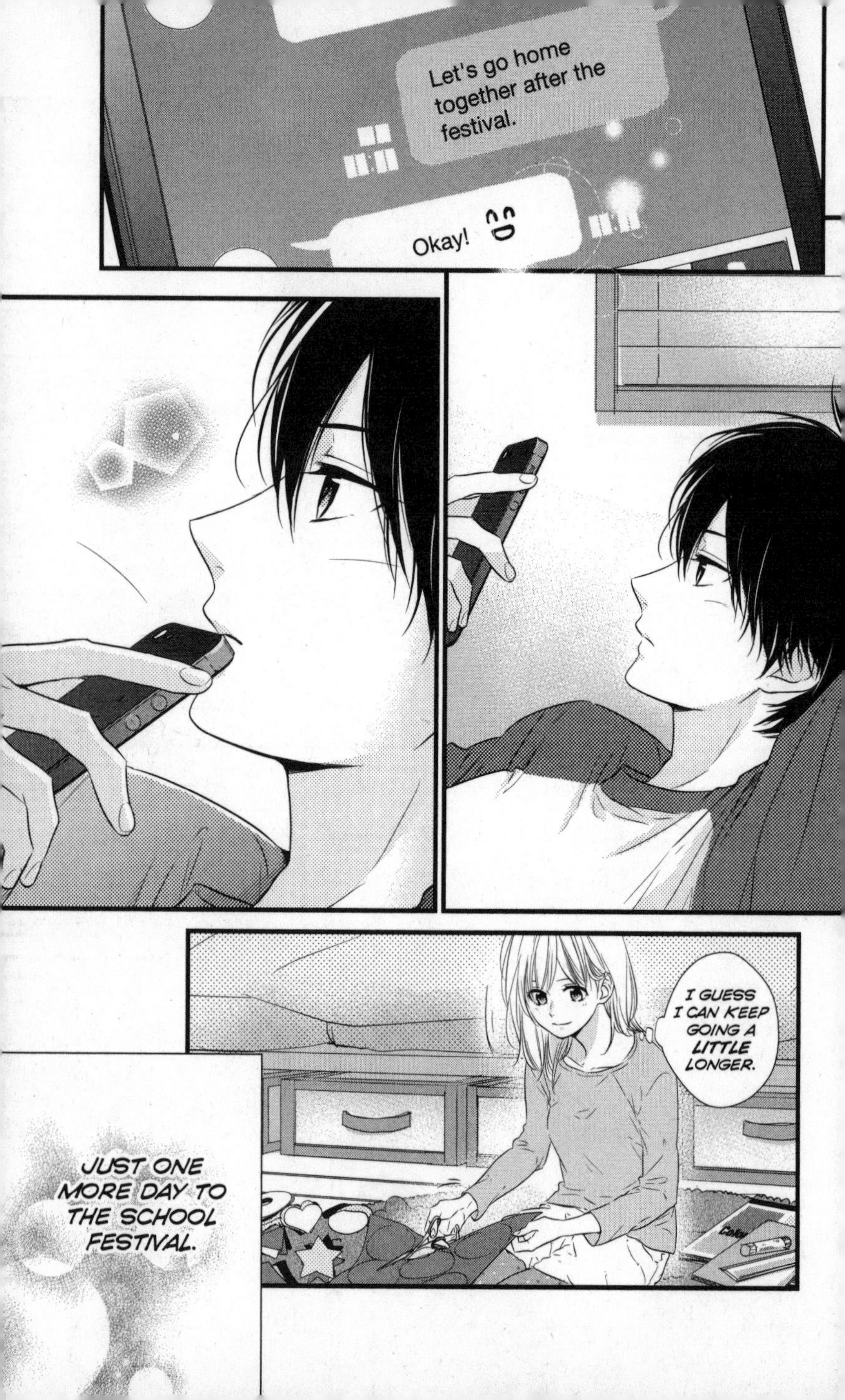
Let's go home together after the festival.
Okay!
I GUESS I CAN KEEP GOING A LITTLE LONGER.
JUST ONE MORE DAY TO THE SCHOOL FESTIVAL.

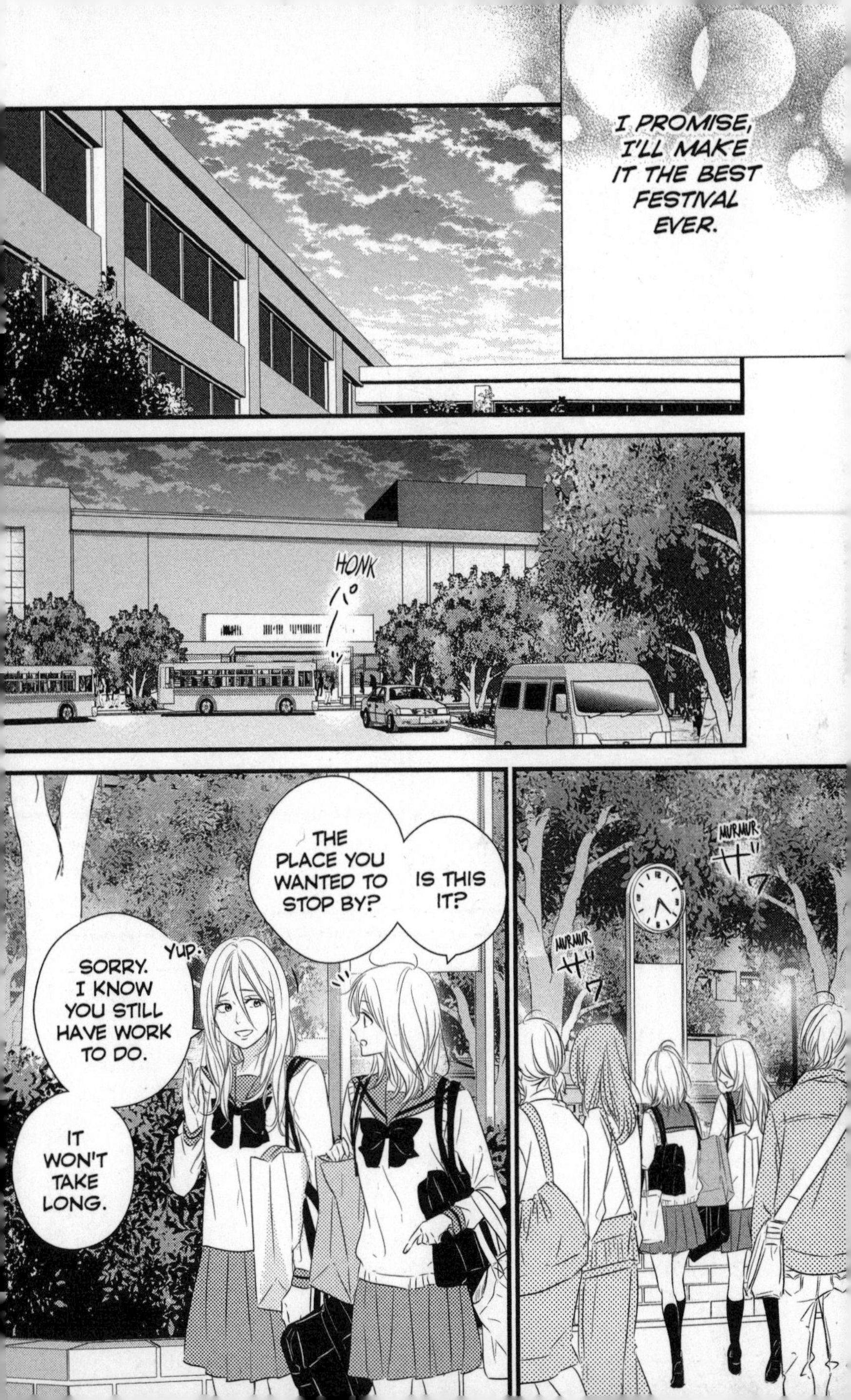
I PROMISE, I'LL MAKE IT THE BEST FESTIVAL EVER.
HONK
パーッ
MURMUR
ザワ
MURMUR
ザワ
IS THIS IT?
THE PLACE YOU WANTED TO STOP BY?
YUP.
SORRY. I KNOW YOU STILL HAVE WORK TO DO.
IT WON'T TAKE LONG.

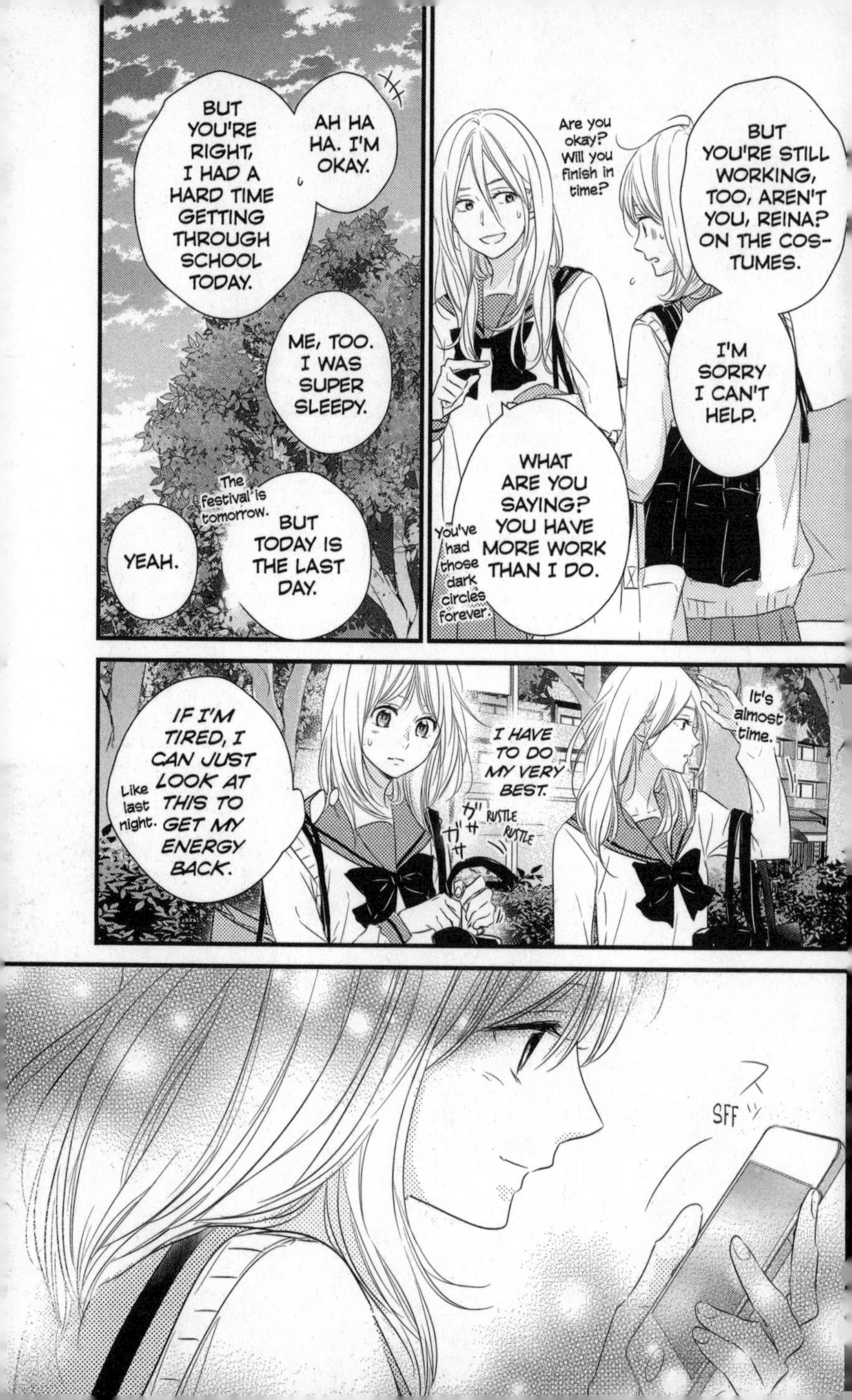
BUT YOU'RE STILL WORKING, TOO, AREN'T YOU, REINA? ON THE COSTUMES.
Are you okay? Will you finish in time?
I'M SORRY I CAN'T HELP.
WHAT ARE YOU SAYING? YOU HAVE MORE WORK THAN I DO.
You've had those dark circles forever.
AH HA HA. I'M OKAY.
BUT YOU'RE RIGHT, I HAD A HARD TIME GETTING THROUGH SCHOOL TODAY.
ME, TOO. I WAS SUPER SLEEPY.
The festival is tomorrow.
BUT TODAY IS THE LAST DAY.
YEAH.
It's almost time.
I HAVE TO DO MY VERY BEST.
RUSTLE RUSTLE
IF I'M TIRED, I CAN JUST LOOK AT THIS TO GET MY ENERGY BACK.
Like last night.
SFF

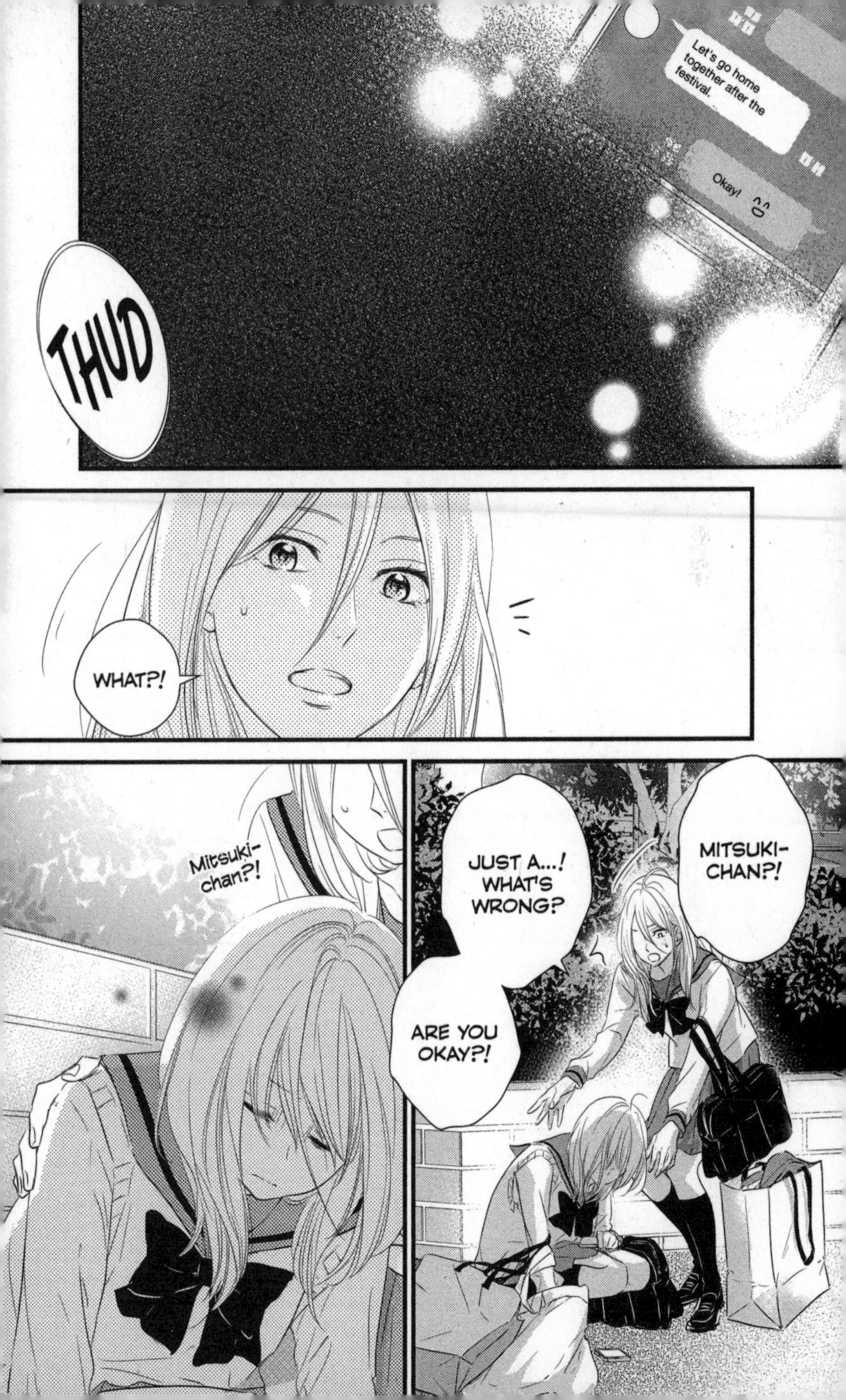
Let's go home together after the festival.
Okay!
THUD
WHAT?!
MITSUKI-CHAN?!
JUST A...! WHAT'S WRONG?
ARE YOU OKAY?!
Mitsuki-chan?!

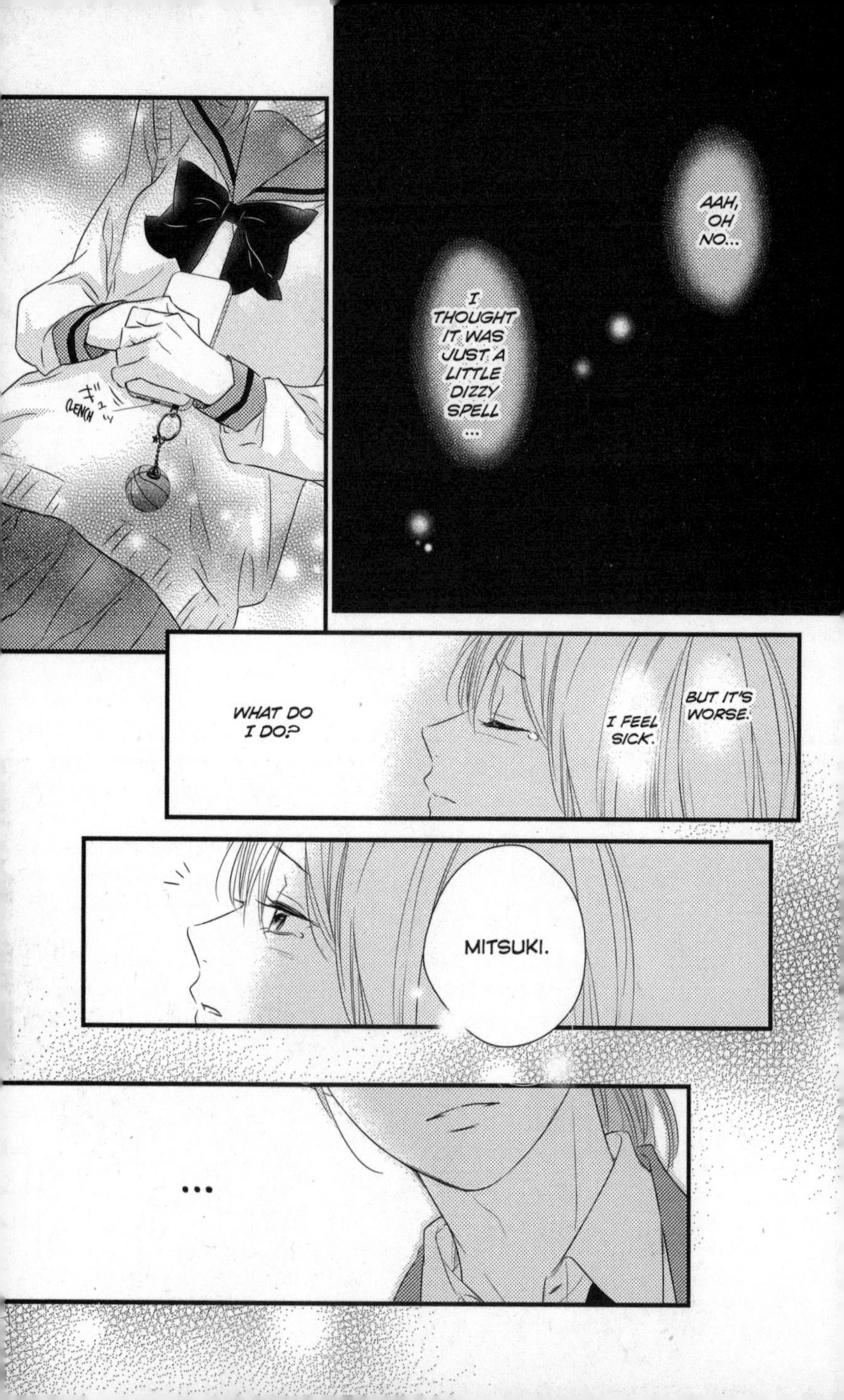
AAH, OH NO...
I THOUGHT IT WAS JUST A LITTLE DIZZY SPELL...
CLENCH
BUT IT'S WORSE.
I FEEL SICK.
WHAT DO I DO?
MITSUKI.
...

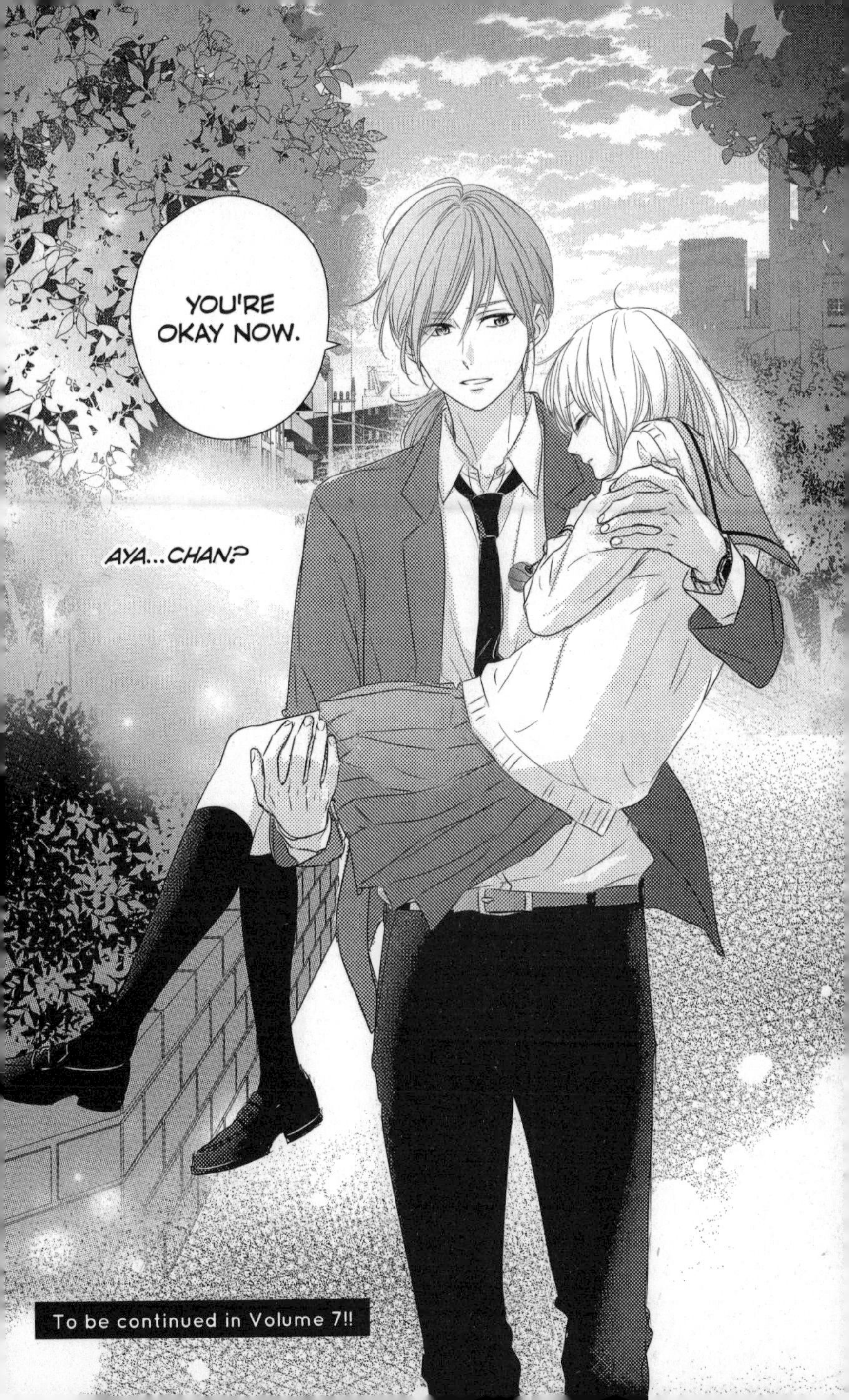
YOU'RE OKAY NOW.
AYA...CHAN?
To be continued in Volume 7!!

Bonus Extra Manga

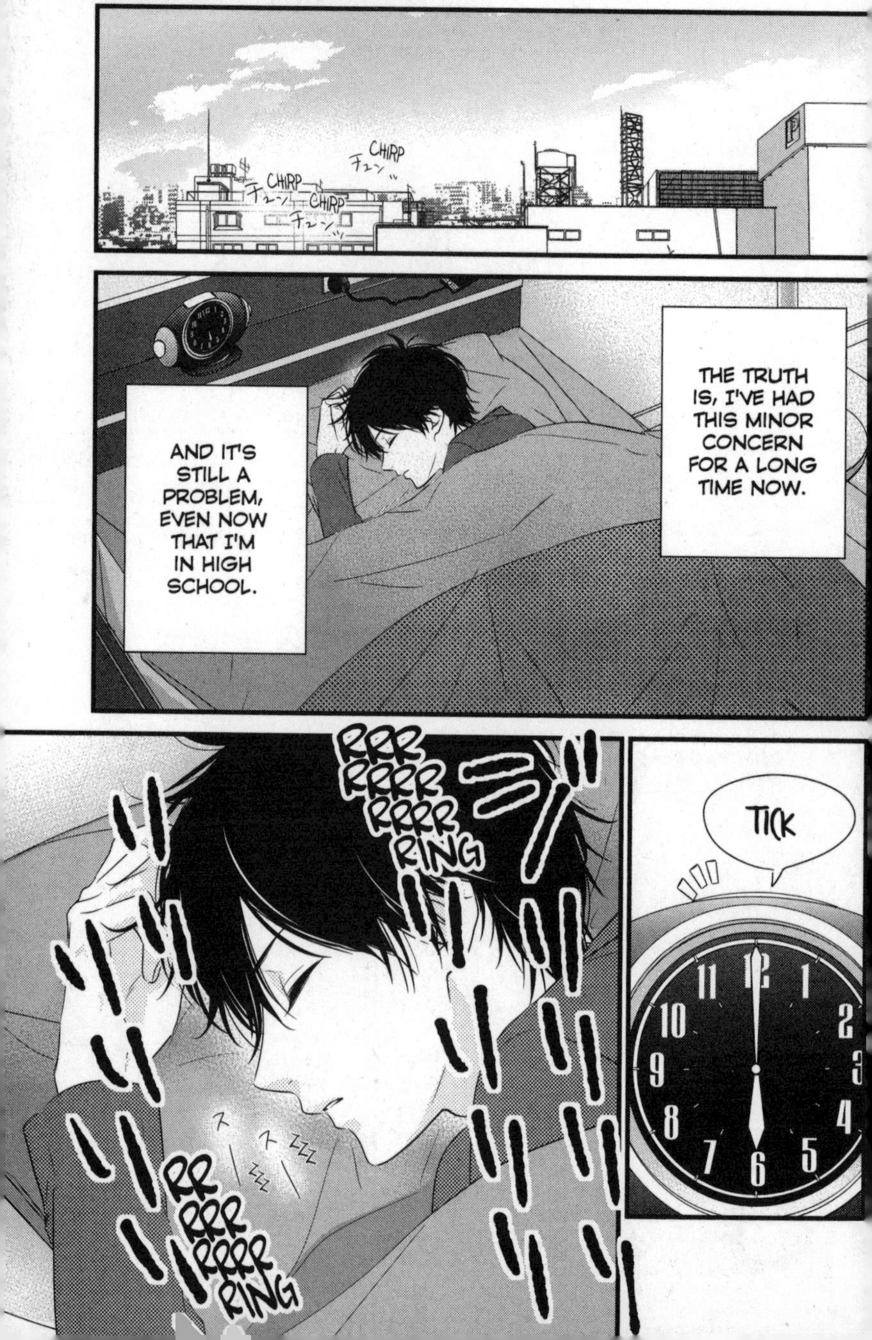
CHIRP
チュン
CHIRP
チュン
CHIRP
チュン
THE TRUTH IS, I'VE HAD THIS MINOR CONCERN FOR A LONG TIME NOW.
AND IT'S STILL A PROBLEM, EVEN NOW THAT I'M IN HIGH SCHOOL.
TICK
RRR RRRR RRRR RING
RR RRR RRRR RING

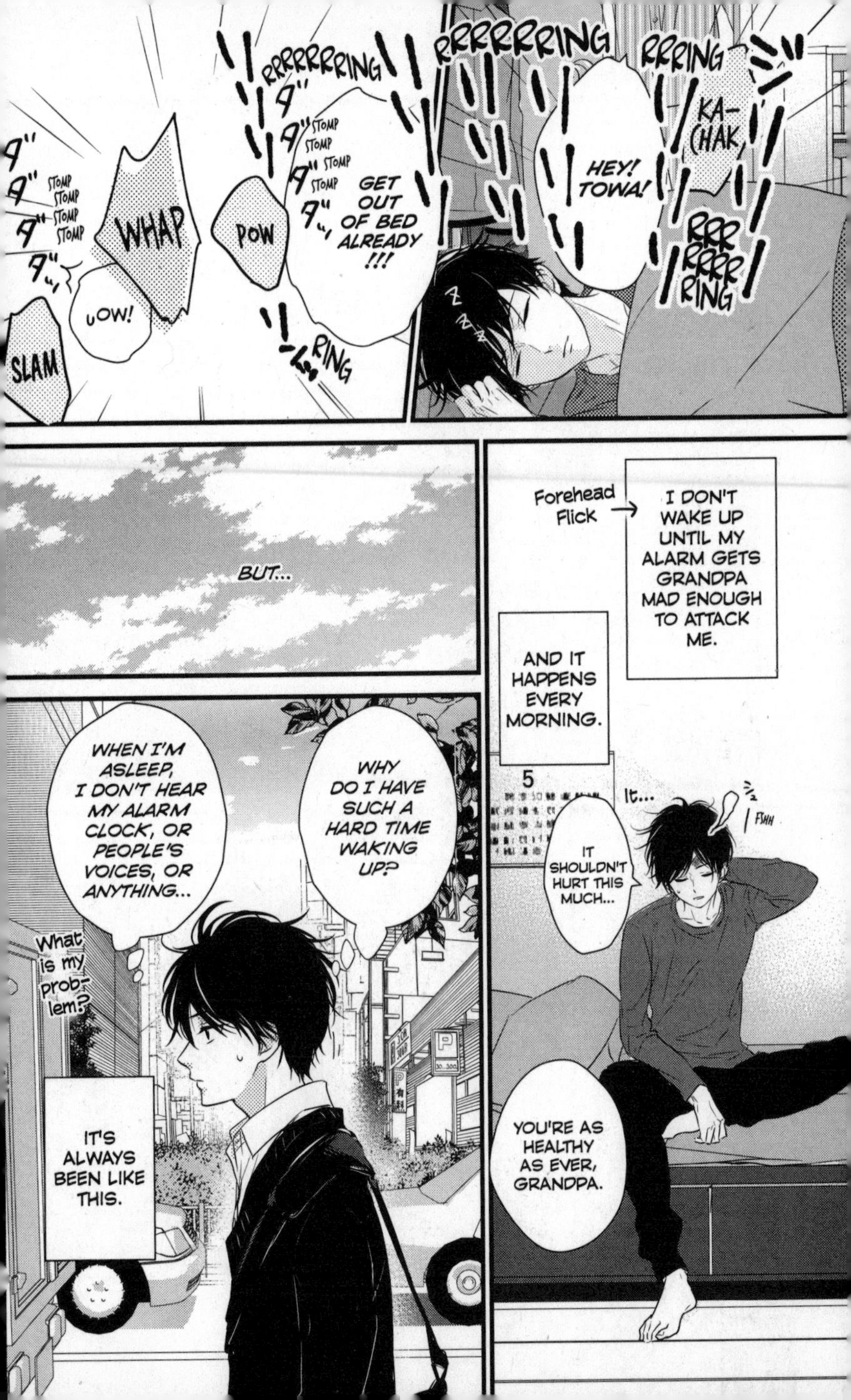
RRRING
KA-CHAK
HEY! TOWA!
RRRRRRRING
RRRRRRRRING
STOMP STOMP STOMP STOMP
RRR RRRR RING
GET OUT OF BED ALREADY!!!
RING
POW
STOMP STOMP STOMP STOMP
WHAP
OW!
SLAM
Forehead Flick
I DON'T WAKE UP UNTIL MY ALARM GETS GRANDPA MAD ENOUGH TO ATTACK ME.
AND IT HAPPENS EVERY MORNING.
It...
FSHH
IT SHOULDN'T HURT THIS MUCH...
YOU'RE AS HEALTHY AS EVER, GRANDPA.
BUT...
WHY DO I HAVE SUCH A HARD TIME WAKING UP?
WHEN I'M ASLEEP, I DON'T HEAR MY ALARM CLOCK, OR PEOPLE'S VOICES, OR ANYTHING...
What is my prob-lem?
IT'S ALWAYS BEEN LIKE THIS.

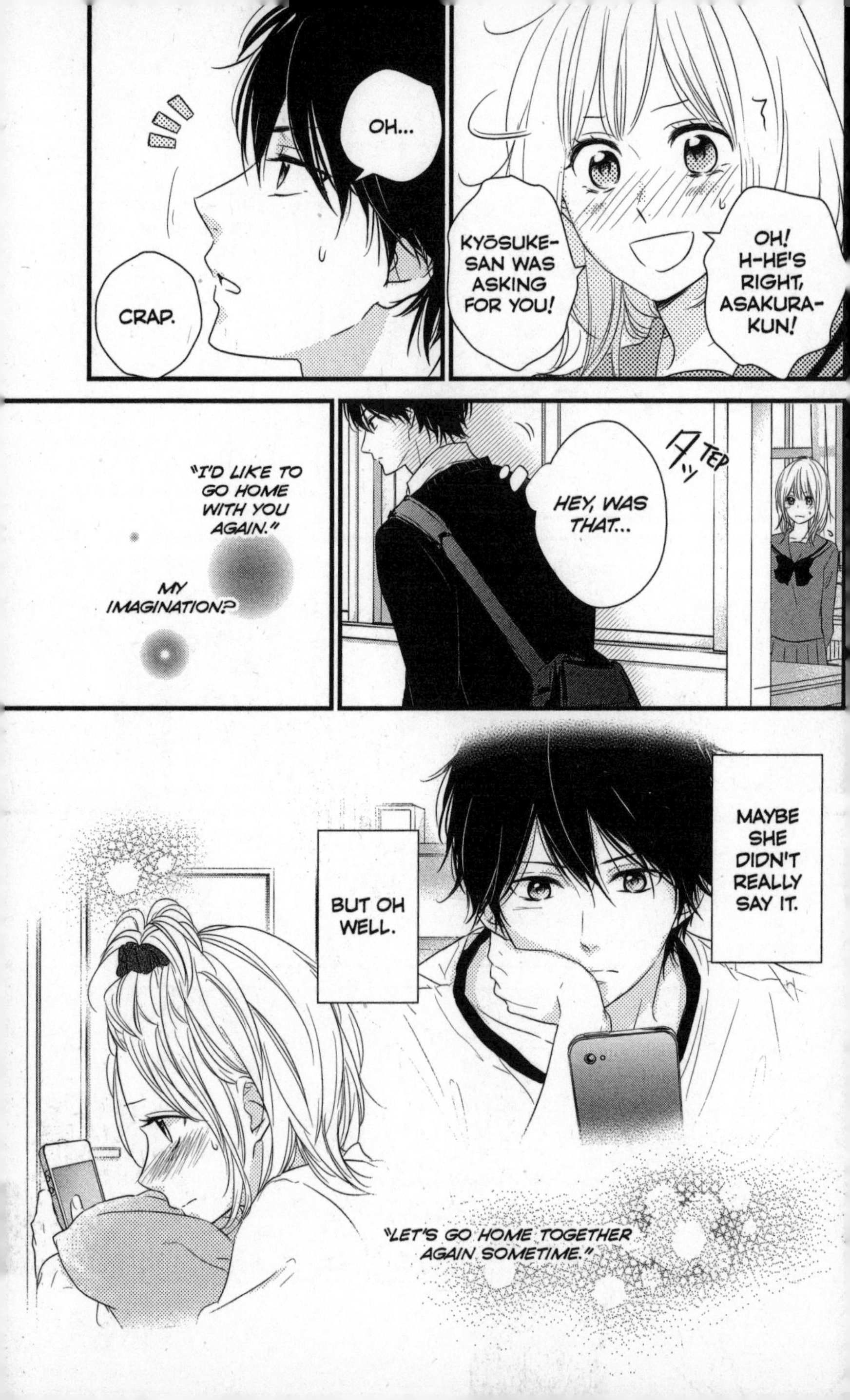
OH! H-HE'S RIGHT, ASAKURA-KUN!
KYŌSUKE-SAN WAS ASKING FOR YOU!
OH...
CRAP.
タッ TEP
HEY, WAS THAT...
"I'D LIKE TO GO HOME WITH YOU AGAIN."
MY IMAGINATION?
MAYBE SHE DIDN'T REALLY SAY IT.
BUT OH WELL.
"LET'S GO HOME TOGETHER AGAIN SOMETIME."

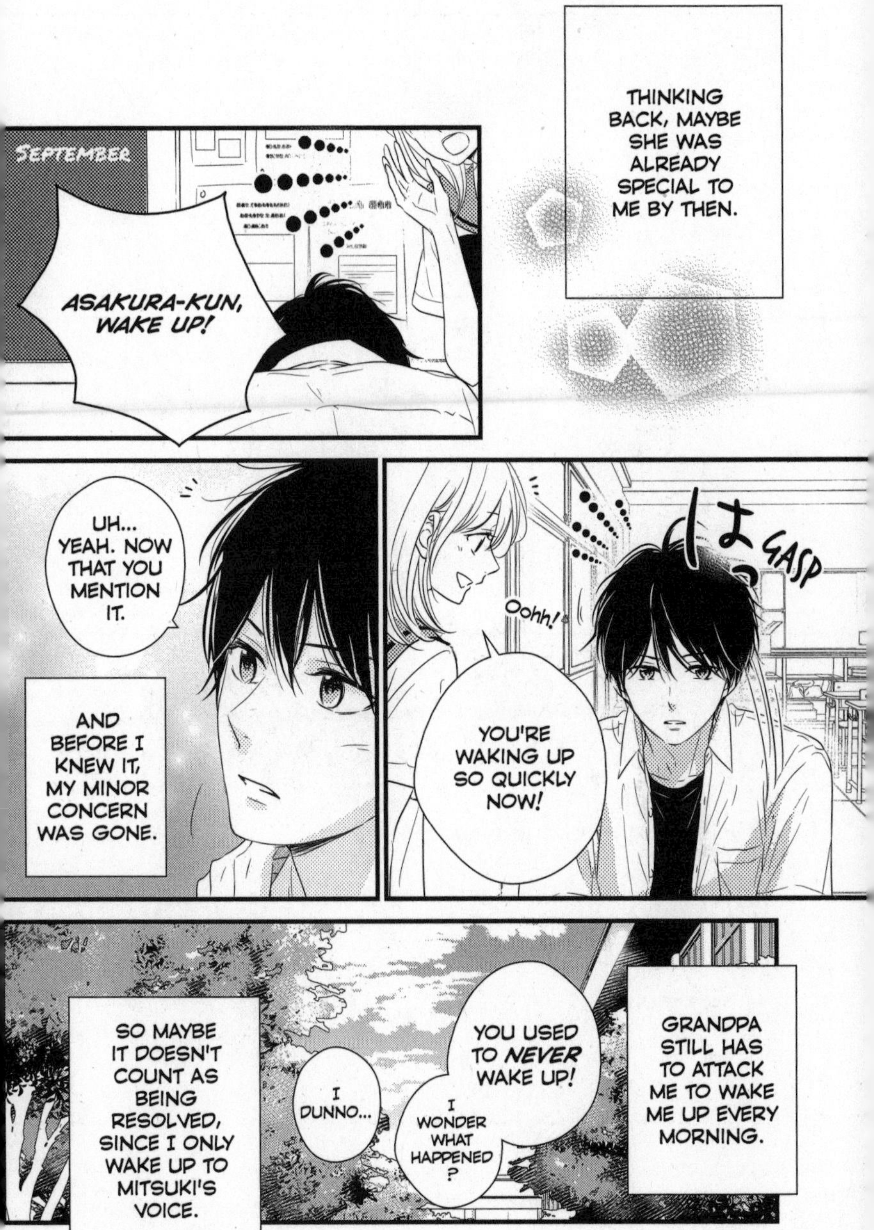
THINKING BACK, MAYBE SHE WAS ALREADY SPECIAL TO ME BY THEN.
SEPTEMBER
ASAKURA-KUN, WAKE UP!
GASP
Oohh!
YOU'RE WAKING UP SO QUICKLY NOW!
UH... YEAH. NOW THAT YOU MENTION IT.
AND BEFORE I KNEW IT, MY MINOR CONCERN WAS GONE.
GRANDPA STILL HAS TO ATTACK ME TO WAKE ME UP EVERY MORNING.
YOU USED TO *NEVER* WAKE UP!
I WONDER WHAT HAPPENED?
I DUNNO...
SO MAYBE IT DOESN'T COUNT AS BEING RESOLVED, SINCE I ONLY WAKE UP TO MITSUKI'S VOICE.

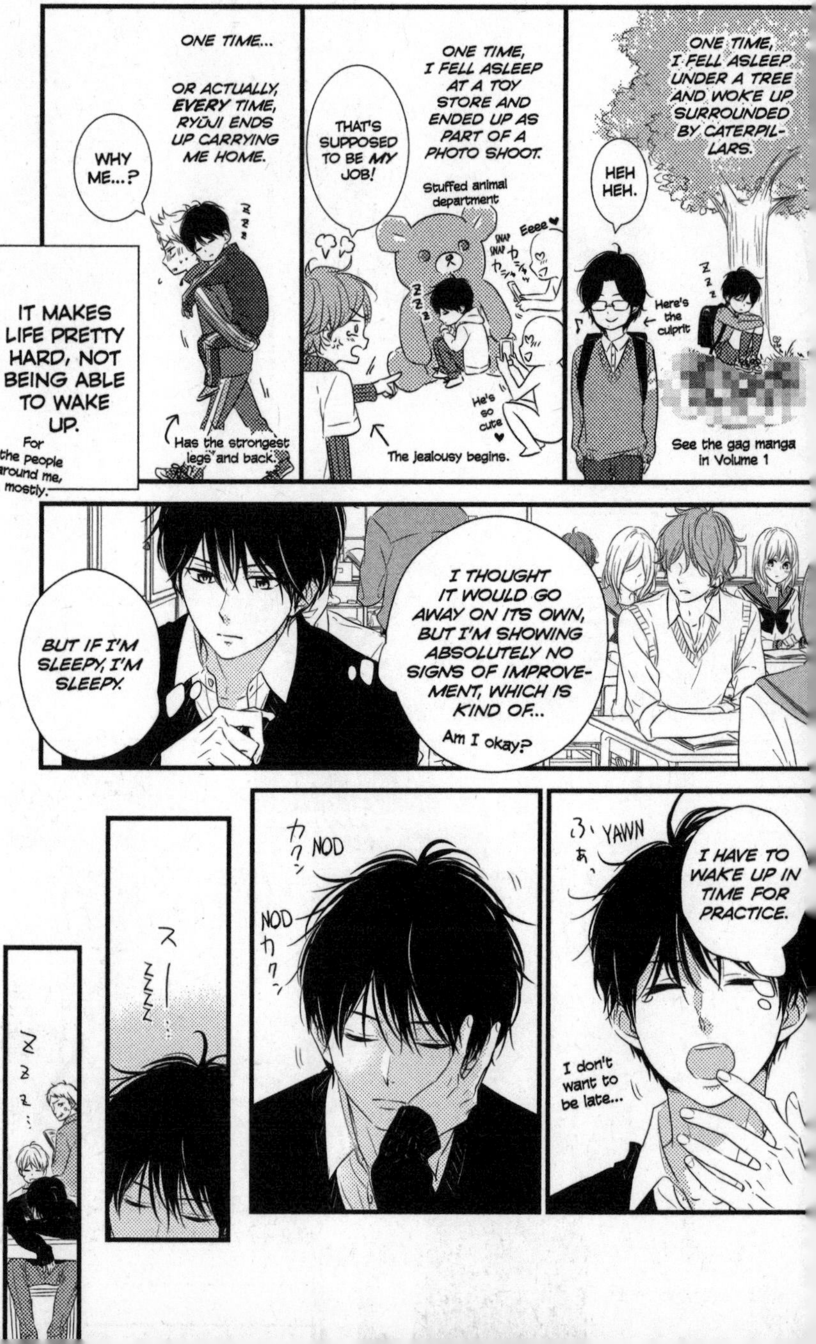
ONE TIME, I FELL ASLEEP UNDER A TREE AND WOKE UP SURROUNDED BY CATERPIL-LARS.
HEH HEH.
Here's the culprit
See the gag manga in Volume 1
ONE TIME, I FELL ASLEEP AT A TOY STORE AND ENDED UP AS PART OF A PHOTO SHOOT.
THAT'S SUPPOSED TO BE MY JOB!
Stuffed animal department
Eeee♥
SNAP SNAP
He's so cute♥
The jealousy begins.
ONE TIME...
OR ACTUALLY, EVERY TIME, RYŪJI ENDS UP CARRYING ME HOME.
WHY ME...?
Has the strongest legs and back.
IT MAKES LIFE PRETTY HARD, NOT BEING ABLE TO WAKE UP.
For the people around me, mostly.
I THOUGHT IT WOULD GO AWAY ON ITS OWN, BUT I'M SHOWING ABSOLUTELY NO SIGNS OF IMPROVE-MENT, WHICH IS KIND OF...
Am I okay?
BUT IF I'M SLEEPY, I'M SLEEPY.
YAWN
I HAVE TO WAKE UP IN TIME FOR PRACTICE.
I don't want to be late...
NOD
NOD
ZZZ
Z Z Z...

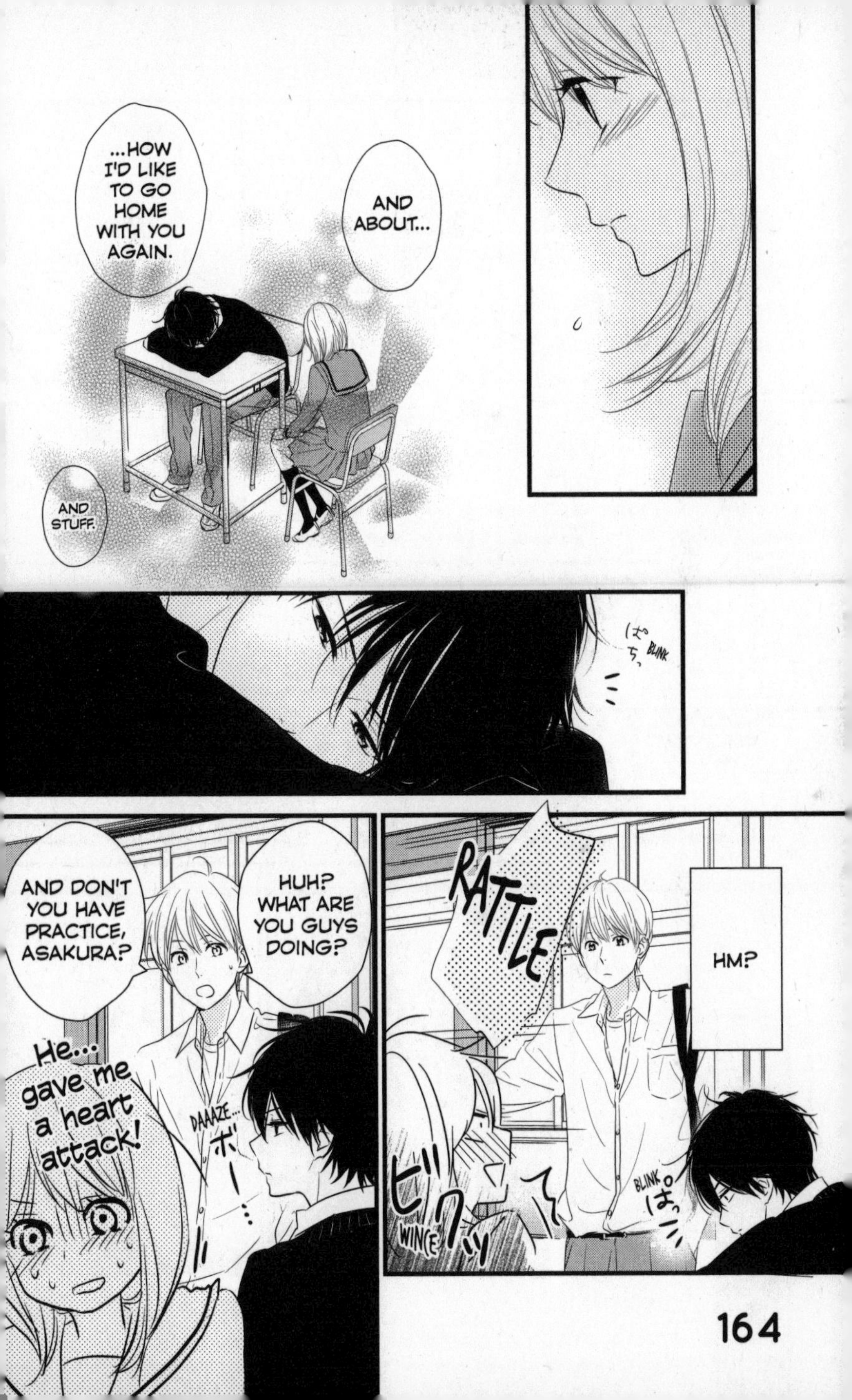
AND ABOUT...
...HOW I'D LIKE TO GO HOME WITH YOU AGAIN.
AND STUFF.
ぱちっ BLINK
HM?
RATTLE
ビクッ WINCE
ぱっ BLINK
HUH? WHAT ARE YOU GUYS DOING?
AND DON'T YOU HAVE PRACTICE, ASAKURA?
He... gave me a heart attack!
ボー DAAAZE...

"An emotional and artistic tour de force! We see incredible triumph, and crushing defeat... each panel [is] a thrill!"
—Anitay

"A journey that's instantly compelling."
—Anime News Network

WELCOME TO THE BALLROOM

By Tomo Takeuchi

Feckless high school student Tatara Fujita wants to be good at something—anything. Unfortunately, he's about as average as a slouchy teen can be. The local bullies know this, and make it a habit to hit him up for cash, but all that changes when the debonair Kaname Sengoku sends them packing. Sengoku's not the neighborhood watch, though. He's a professional ballroom dancer. And once Tatara Fujita gets pulled into the world of ballroom, his life will never be the same.

KC KODANSHA COMICS

Waiting for Spring

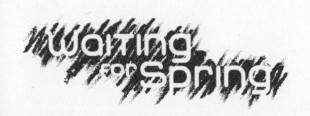

Translation Notes

School festival vote, page 7

The *kanji* seen on the blackboard under all of the suggestions for the class's school festival options is the word "correct." It is commonly used for keeping score. The Japanese character has exactly five strokes, so every complete character can be counted by five to tally the score more quickly.

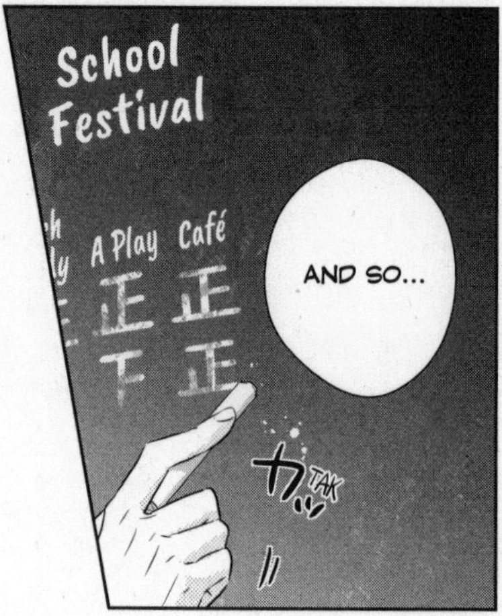
School Festival
A Play
Café
AND SO...
TAK

The Ex-Captain's Love♡

Former Captain
MAN, I CAN'T BELIEVE YOU'RE IN LOVE, RYŪJI.
Ha ha.
IT WAS LOVE AT FIRST SIGHT.
LOVE AT FIRST SIGHT, EH?
YOU KNOW, I SORT OF FELL IN LOVE AT FIRST SIGHT ONCE.
Oohh!
Just like me!!
REALLY?!
YEAH. I DON'T KNOW WHO SHE WAS OR WHERE SHE CAME FROM, THOUGH.
WHEN OUR EYES MET, SHE ACTED SO EMBARRASSED, AND SHE GREETED ME IN THE POLITEST WAY YOU CAN IMAGINE...
BOW
IT KIND OF GOT ME RIGHT IN THE HEART.
BUMP
IT WAS ON THE DAY OF THE SCHOOL FESTIVAL, SO MAYBE SHE WAS FROM ANOTHER SCHOOL?
I'd like to see her again.
SENPAI, THAT WAS...
UGH, HOW EMBARRASSING! SENPAI SAW ME!
...ME!!

Note: Last year's festival

YOU KNOW, I DON'T HAVE ANY GOOD MEMORIES OF SCHOOL FESTIVALS.
They always make me wear weird clothes.
SAME...
I don't want to dress in girls' clothes anymore.

So what will they be forced to do this year?

To be continued in Volume 7!!

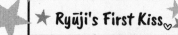

★ Ryūji's First Kiss♡

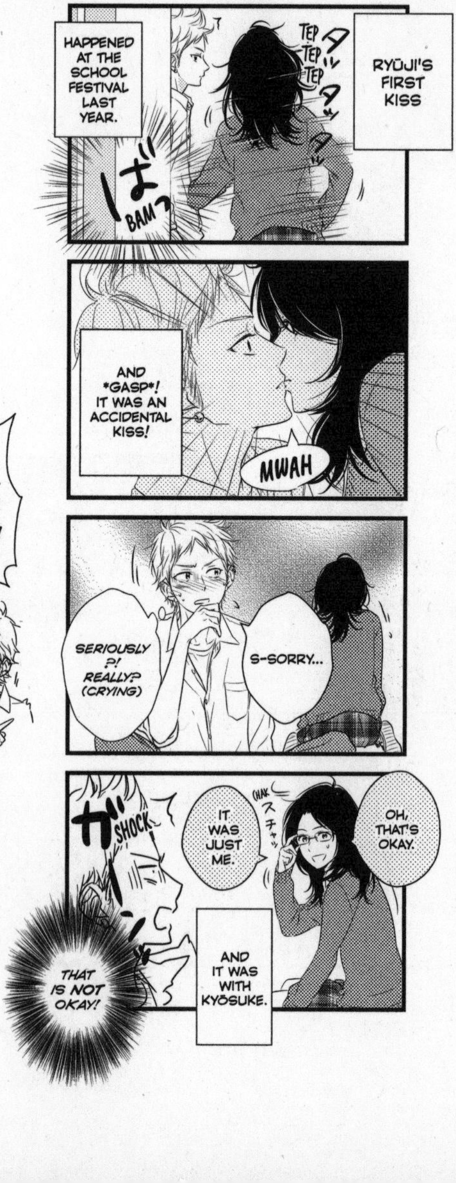
RYŪJI'S FIRST KISS
TEP TEP TEP
HAPPENED AT THE SCHOOL FESTIVAL LAST YEAR.
BAM
AND *GASP*! IT WAS AN ACCIDENTAL KISS!
MWAH
S-SORRY...
SERIOUSLY?! REALLY? (CRYING)
OH, THAT'S OKAY.
CHAK
IT WAS JUST ME.
SHOCK
AND IT WAS WITH KYŌSUKE.
THAT IS NOT OKAY!

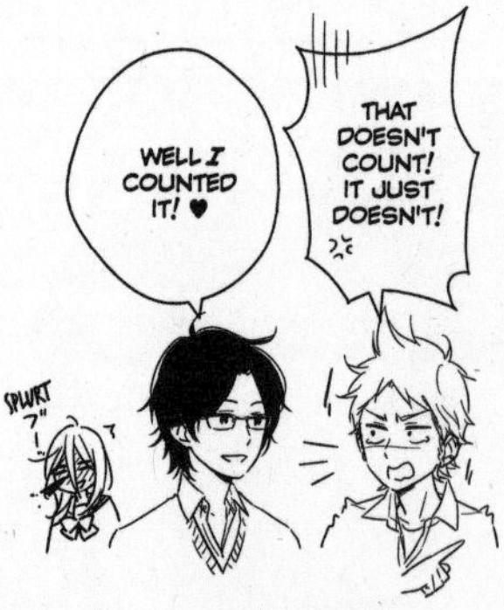
THAT DOESN'T COUNT! IT JUST DOESN'T!
WELL I COUNTED IT! ♥
SPLURT

Both forced to dress in girl's clothes at their last school festival.

(See Volume 5, Chapter 24)

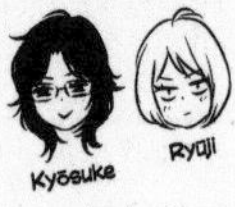
Kyōsuke
Ryūji

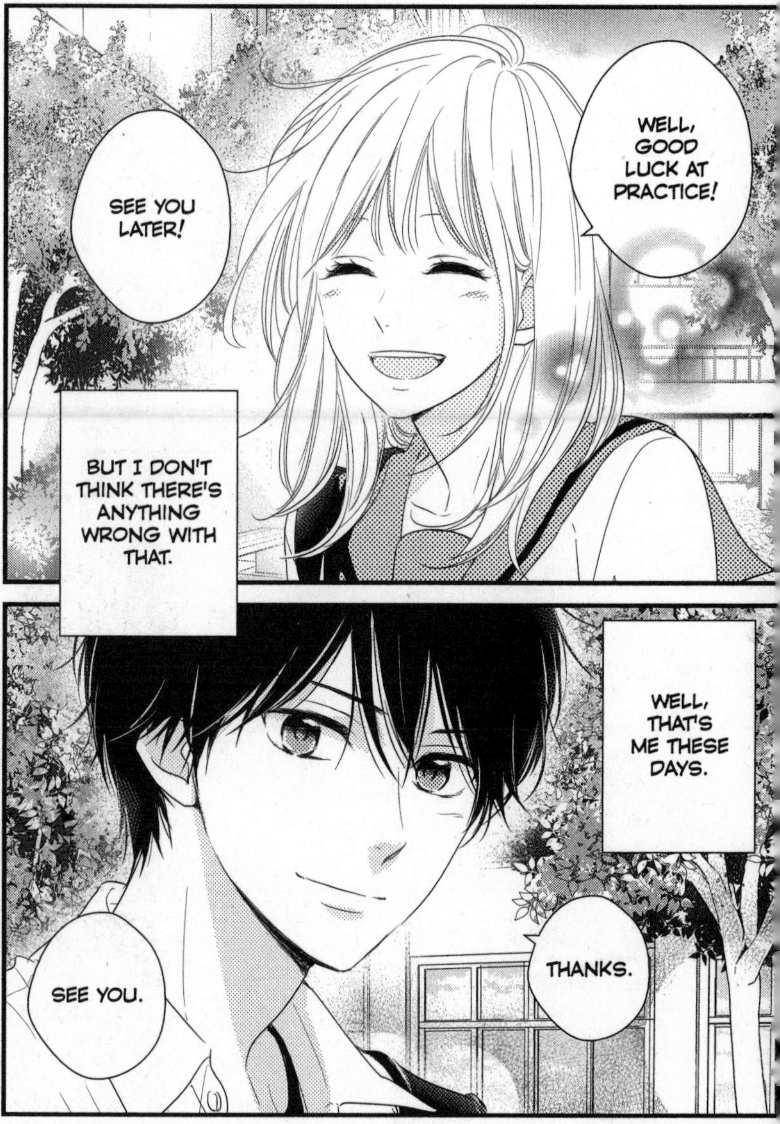
WELL, GOOD LUCK AT PRACTICE!
SEE YOU LATER!
BUT I DON'T THINK THERE'S ANYTHING WRONG WITH THAT.
WELL, THAT'S ME THESE DAYS.
THANKS.
SEE YOU.

Well! Thanks for reading Volume 6!!

Please check out Volume 7, too.

Let's meet again!

Anashin

A NEW MANGA SERIES FROM YURI!!! ON ICE CO-CREATOR MITSUROU KUBO!!

Again!!

アゲイン!!

KC KODANSHA COMICS

Kinichiro Imamura isn't a bad guy, really, but on the first day of high school his narrow eyes and bleached blonde hair made him look so shifty that his classmates assumed the worst. Three years later, without any friends or fond memories, he isn't exactly feeling bittersweet about graduation. But after an accidental fall down a flight of stairs, Kinichiro wakes up three years in the past… on the first day of high school!

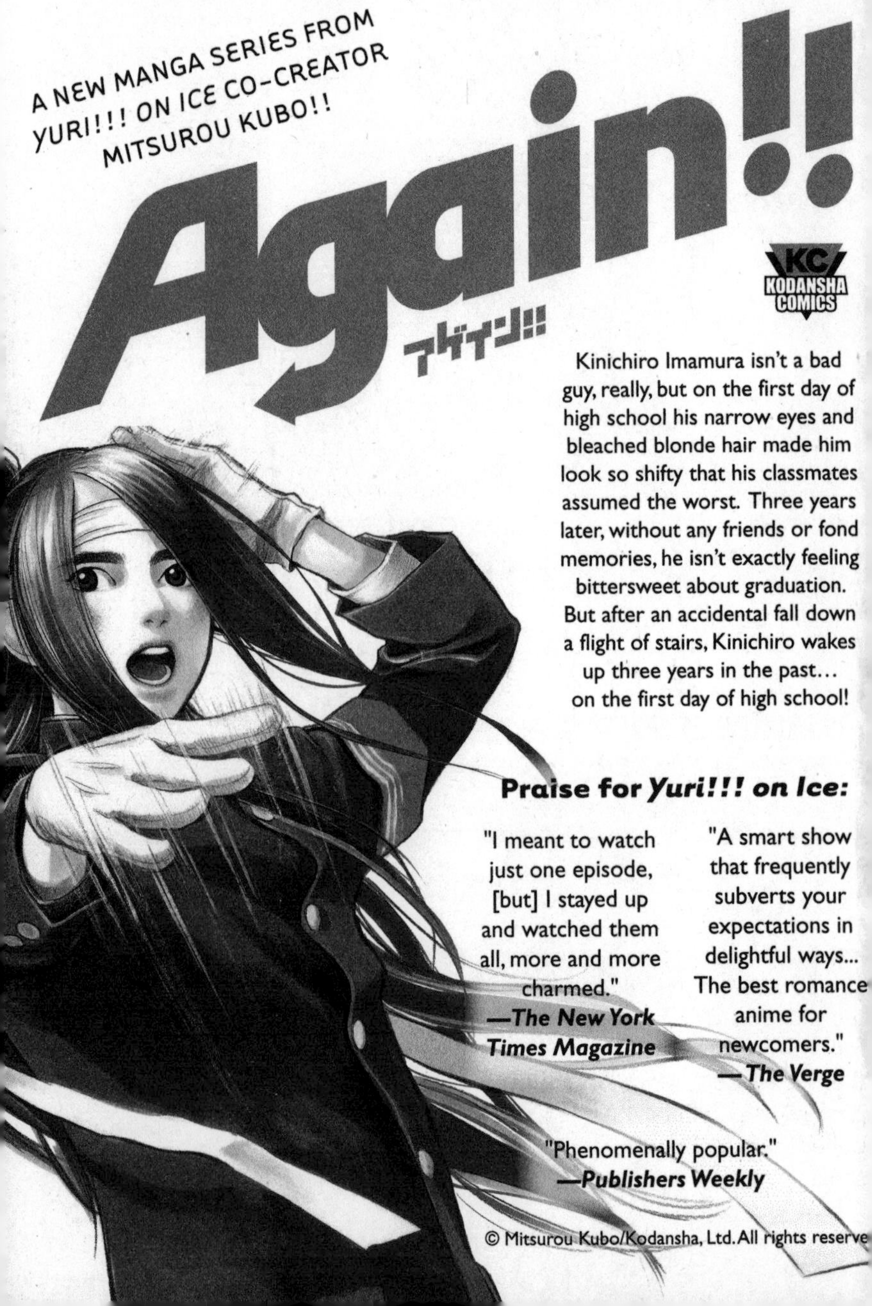

Praise for *Yuri!!! on Ice*:

"I meant to watch just one episode, [but] I stayed up and watched them all, more and more charmed."
—The New York Times Magazine

"A smart show that frequently subverts your expectations in delightful ways... The best romance anime for newcomers."
— The Verge

"Phenomenally popular."
—Publishers Weekly

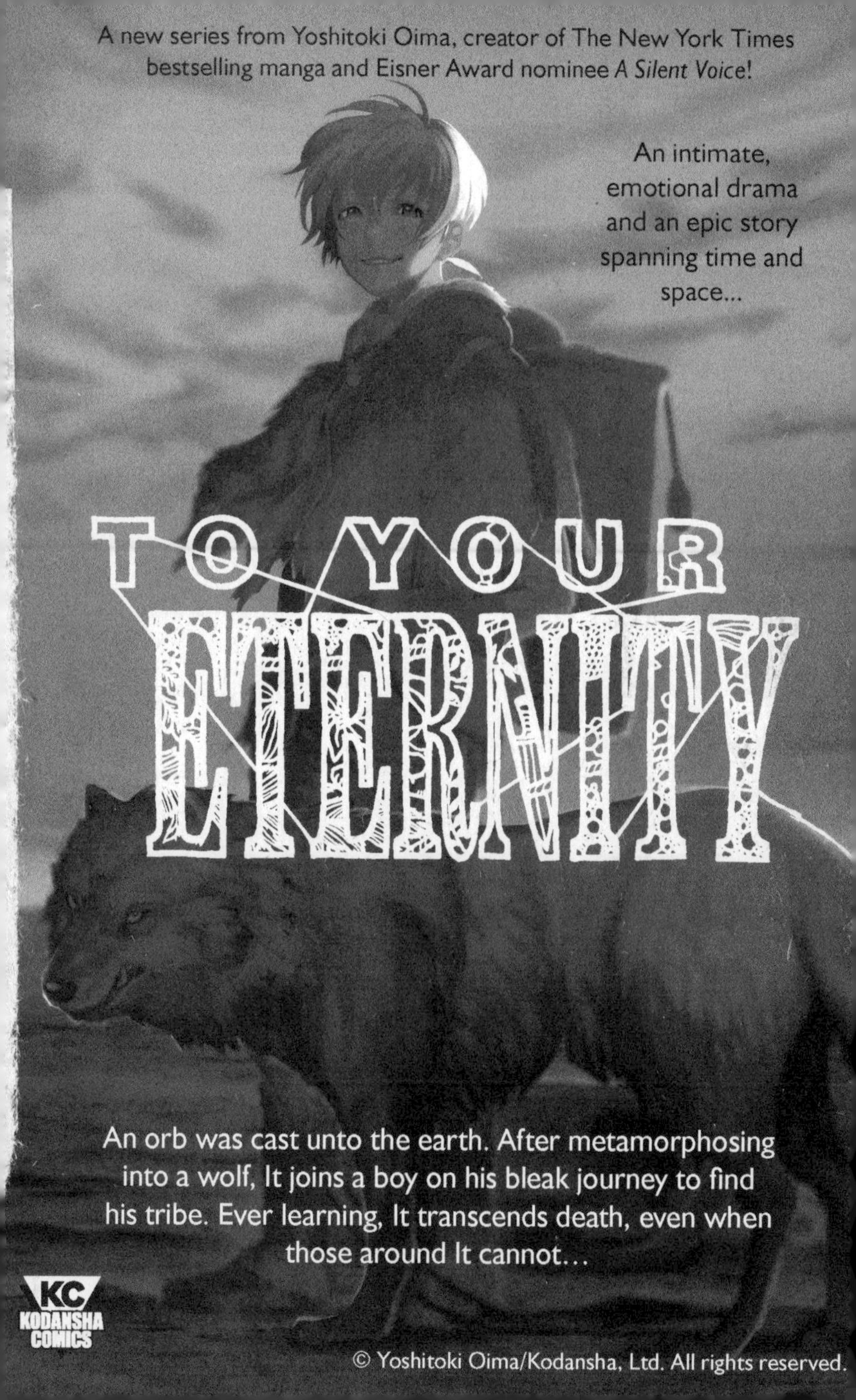
A new series from Yoshitoki Oima, creator of The New York Times bestselling manga and Eisner Award nominee A Silent Voice!
An intimate, emotional drama and an epic story spanning time and space...
TO YOUR ETERNITY
An orb was cast unto the earth. After metamorphosing into a wolf, It joins a boy on his bleak journey to find his tribe. Ever learning, It transcends death, even when those around It cannot...
KC KODANSHA COMICS
© Yoshitoki Oima/Kodansha, Ltd. All rights reserved.

Based on the critically acclaimed classic horror manga

The first new *Parasyte* manga in over 20 years!

NEO Parasyte f

BY ASUMIKO NAKAMURA, EMA TOYAMA, MIKI RINNO, LALAKO KOJIMA, KAORI YUKI, BANKO KUZE, YUUKI OBATA, KASHIO, YUI KUROE, ASIA WATANABE, MIKIMAKI, HIKARU SURUGA, HAJIME SHINJO, RENJURO KINDAICHI, AND YURI NARUSHIMA

A collection of chilling new *Parasyte* stories from Japan's top shojo artists

Parasites: shape-shifting aliens whose only purpose is to assimilate with and consume the human race... but do these monsters have a different side? A parasite becomes a prince to save his romance-obsessed female host from a dangerous stalker. Another hosts a cooking show, in which the real monsters are revealed. These and 13 more stories, from some of the greatest shojo manga artists alive today, together make up a chilling, funny, and entertaining tribute to one of manga's horror classics!

KC KODANSHA COMICS

Waiting for Spring volume 6 is a work of fiction. Names, characters, places, and incidents are the products of the author's imagination or are used fictitiously. Any resemblance to actual events, locales, or persons, living or dead, is entirely coincidental.

A Kodansha Comics Trade Paperback Original

Published in the United States by Kodansha Comics, an imprint of Kodansha USA Publishing, LLC, New York.

Publication rights for this English edition arranged through Kodansha Ltd, Tokyo.

ISBN 978-1-63236-587-3

Printed in the United States of America.

www.kodanshacomics.com

9 8 7 6 5 4 3 2 1
Translation: Alethea and Athena Nibley
Lettering: Sara Linsley
Editing: Haruko Hashimoto
Kodansha Comics edition cover design by Phil Balsman